Supplement

to

Music
Since
1900

SUPPLEMENT
──TO──
MUSIC SINCE 1900

Nicolas Slonimsky

CHARLES SCRIBNER'S SONS
New York

Library of Congress Cataloging-in-Publication Data

Slonimsky, Nicolas, 1894–
  Supplement to Music since 1900.

  Includes index.
  Contents: Music since 1970: descriptive chronology,
1970–1985—Music since 1900. Additions, amplifications,
corrections—Documents.
  1. Music—20th century—History and criticism.
2. Music—20th century—Chronology. I. Slonimsky,
Nicolas, 1894–   . Music since 1900. II. Title.
III. Title: Music since 1900.
ML197.S634 1971 Suppl.   780′.904   85-27627
ISBN 0–684–18438–9

Published simultaneously in Canada
by Collier Macmillan Canada, Inc.—Copyright under
the Berne Convention.

1 3 5 7 9 11 13 15 17 19   F/C   20 18 16 14 12 10 8 6 4 2

Printed in the United States of America.

Contents

Preface

The first edition of *Music Since 1900* appeared in 1937, under the imprint of W. W. Norton. A second printing was issued in 1938; it included but a few additions to the chronology. A substantial third edition was published in 1949 by Coleman-Ross Company. In addition to the three basic parts—Chronology, Explanation of Terms, and Letters and Documents—that edition introduced a Tabular View of Stylistic Trends in music: Increasing Grandiosity (1900–1914); Retrogressive Neo-Classicism (1915–1939); and Search for New Style (1939–1948). Each of these divisions had several subdivisions: Impressionism, Expressionism, Futurism, Neo-Primitivism, Neo-Romanticism, Neo-Nationalism, Neo-Utilitarianism, Sophisticated Folk Music, etc. Specific compositions were listed under each category, with additional descriptions of each, for example, "austere religionism," "exotic imagism," "impassionate megasymphonism," "operatic pathetism," etc. But this Tabular View proved so inflated in trying to extend it further in time that, with some pangs of regret, I had to drop it in the Fourth Edition published by Scribners in 1971. In that edition the basic part, Descriptive Chronology, was brought up to the year 1969. The section of Letters and Documents was greatly increased, adding Congressional Hearings on musicians accused of un-American activities, a statement "On the Use of Mao Tsetung's Thought" pertaining to the period of the Cultural Revolution in China, the text of the Charter of the Union of Soviet Composers, and personal letters from Charles Ives and Edgar Varèse. The Dictionary of Terms was enlarged to include a detailed analysis of modern techniques of composition.

The present Supplement comprises three sections: the continuation of Descriptive Chronology from 1970 to 1985; additional items as well as amplifications and rectifications of errors in the basic Chronology of 1900 to 1969; and several new documents. The Index covers names and subjects of the Supplement.

In an undertaking as Brobdingnagian and as quaquaversal as *Music Since 1900*, I had to rely on a number of helpers. The primary sources were composers whose works are listed in the Descriptive Chronology. Not all of them could supply precise dates of first performances of their major works, which were essential for chronological listing, and I had to search through local newspapers to pinpoint such dates. The bulletins issued by unions of composers in European countries were most useful for this purpose. The Russians were particularly cooperative, as were the Czechs, the Swedes, the Norwegians, the Dutch, the Rumanians, the Bulgarians, the Poles, the Yugoslavs. Often, welcome bits of information came from interested individuals who were not even professional musicians; the most helpful source for England, for instance, was David Cummings, a school teacher. For America, I relied on the fantastic omniscience of Dennis McIntire, a history professor. Quantitatively, the biggest chunk of material came from Michael Keyton, a mathematics instructor from Dallas, Texas; often he applied his unusual detective skill to check on dates. Profuse thanks are also due to my original helper in work on dictionaries, Steve Ellis of Glenview, Illinois, who displayed sheer magic in establishing correct dates of performances for works all over the expanding universe of music. Finally, two charming ladies, Laura Kuhn and Dina Klemm, excellent musicians in their own right, performed for me the most essential part in preparation of the final manuscript, one on her latest word processor, the other on an electric typewriter. But while so engaged, they did not limit themselves to faithfully transcribing my findings; both Laura and Dina added items and elucidated the analyses from their own practical knowledge of modern and exotic music and so enhanced the value of the present Supplement.

Nicolas Slonimsky
October 1985

Descriptive
Chronology
1.5.1900 - 6.13.1985

∽ 1970 ∾

5 JANUARY 1970

Roberto GERHARD, Catalan-born composer who exchanged his Iberian legacy for a tense serialism, dies at the age of seventy-three in his English home at Cambridge, where he took political refuge after the lamentable defeat of the Spanish loyalists.

8 JANUARY 1970

Jani CHRISTOU, Greek composer of great inventive powers, creator of a style of composition striving to embrace a totality of humanistic and metaphysical expression, for which he designed a surrealistic graphic notation (indicating a psychological metamusical state by the Greek letter *psi*, aleatory usages by a pair of dice, etc.), and extending the form and duration of an individual work into an infinity of temporal units, dies tragically with his wife, while driving at excessive speed, near Athens, on the eve of his forty-fourth birthday.

10 JANUARY 1970

Opsadno stanje (The State of Siege), opera by the 45-year-old Croatian composer Milko KELEMEN, after the surrealist tale *The Plague* by Camus, with the entire tonal fabric evolving out of a single motive and its derivatives, is produced in Hamburg under the German title *Der Belagerungszustand*.

14 JANUARY 1970

Improvisations on an Impromptu of Britten for orchestra by the 67-year-old British composer William WALTON is performed for the first time in San Francisco.

22 JANUARY 1970

Of Mice and Men, opera by the American composer Carlisle FLOYD, after Steinbeck's celebrated novel, is performed for the first time in Seattle.

28 JANUARY 1970

Intermission Piece by the 33-year-old American avant-garde composer Harold BUDD, designated to be played at random with the "amplitude spectrum barely audible" during intermission, with the audience "physically or conceptually absent," is realistically projected for the first time at Hartford, Connecticut, as the first of a long series of realizations all over the world wherever and whenever an intermission takes place, without the performers being aware of participating in a musical event.

3

30 JANUARY 1970

In Praise of Shahn, canticle for orchestra by the American composer William SCHUMAN, written in memory of the American painter Ben Shahn, is performed for the first time in New York.

1 FEBRUARY 1970

Conspiracy Eight, an indeterminate composition by Gordon MUMMA for a digital computer and eight manipulators, is premiered at the Massachusetts Institute of Technology in Cambridge.

5 FEBRUARY 1970

Concerto for Orchestra by the 61-year-old American composer Elliott CARTER, written in a structural style in which notes, harmonies, rhythms and timbres become figures and parameters of a metageometric complex, is performed for the first time by the New York Philharmonic.

6 FEBRUARY 1970

La visita meravigliosa, opera after H. G. Wells by the brilliant 58-year-old Italian composer Nino ROTA, is performed for the first time in Palermo.

14 FEBRUARY 1970

Love 200 for rock band and orchestra by the 40-year-old Australian composer Peter SCULTHORPE is performed for the first time in Sydney.

17 FEBRUARY 1970

Alfred NEWMAN, native American film composer, one of the few successful writers of cinematic music who was not born in Vienna, author of nearly 300 motion picture scores which transmogrified the most marketable elements found in the symphonies of Tchaikovsky, in the piano works of Rachmaninoff, and in the operas of Wagner, dies in Hollywood at the age of sixty-eight.

22 FEBRUARY 1970

Von A bis Z, abecedarian opera by the 50-year-old Italian composer and conductor Bruno MADERNA, is produced in Darmstadt.

25 FEBRUARY 1970

Agape, "a celebration for priests, musicians, actors and poets," by the 39-year-old American avant-garde composer Larry AUSTIN, expressive of spiritual love as opposed to carnal lust, is performed for the first time in Buffalo, New York.

2 MARCH 1970

Metahudba (Metamusic) for orchestra by the 49-year-old Czech composer Zbyněk VOSTŘÁK is performed for the first time in Prague.

18 MARCH 1970

Rhapsody for Orchestra by the greatly esteemed American composer Roger SESSIONS is performed for the first time in Baltimore.

21 MARCH 1970

Love and Conception by the totally emancipated radical American composer Daniel LENTZ, scored for a heterogeneous assortment of incongruous events, bodily exertions and physiological sound emissions, and reaching an aleatory climax when the male piano soloist and his female page turner cuddle up under the open lid of a grand piano and proceed to simulate a concrete copulation while a coordinated radio program continues to blare away the solo piano part, is performed for the first time under the composer's direction at the assembly hall of the University of California in Santa Barbara. (The composer, a faculty member, was peremptorily discharged from his post after the event.)

23 MARCH 1970

Carlos CHÁVEZ conducts in Houston, Texas, the first performance of his symphonic ode *Clio*, written in a firmly structured narrative technique symbolic of the Greek muse of history.

26 MARCH 1970

Count Down, an astronautical opera by the Italian composer Bruno BETTINELLI, is performed for the first time in Milan.

7 APRIL 1970

Polinteracões, a score of total music by the 33-year-old Brazilian pianist and composer Jocy DE OLIVEIRA, programmed as a synesthetic action involving sound, light and spatial effects such as inflatable floors and movable panels, comprising the impressions of the visual, aural, tactile, gustatory and olfactory senses, with an anatomic chart serving as a score for guidance of plural or singular participants, supplemented by a phonemic table indicating the proper verbalization of vocal parts, receives its first semiperformance on the occasion of the Catalytic Celebration of the Tenth Anniversary Festival of the New Music Circle in St. Louis. (It was interrupted in midcourse by the loud protest of the building superintendent as a noisy and noisome nuisance.)

8 APRIL 1970

The Martyred, opera by the American composer James WADE, longtime resident of Korea, to his own libretto dealing with the dramatic events of the Korean War in 1951, is produced in the Korean language in Seoul.

5

8 April 1970
Utrenja (Morning Prayer) by the foremost Polish avant-garde composer Krzysztof PENDERECKI, scored for two choruses, five soloists and percussion, to a text of an old Slavonic church service, is performed for the first time at the Cathedral of Altenburg, East Germany.

13 April 1970
Victory, opera by the 34-year-old British composer Richard Rodney BENNETT, after the novel by Joseph Conrad, is performed for the first time at the Royal Opera in Covent Garden, London.

13 April 1970
Second Symphony by the 37-year-old Norwegian composer Per NØRGAARD is performed for the first time in Aarhus.

14 April 1970
Kingdom Come, a spatial work by the American composer Henry BRANT, based on a wordless text and calling for stage orchestra, balcony orchestra, sirens, slide whistles, bells and buzzers, is performed for the first time in Oakland, California.

26 April 1970
The Mystic Trumpeter, after Walt Whitman, scored for narrator, chorus and orchestra by the 73-year-old American composer Howard HANSON, is performed for the first time in Kansas City, Missouri.

30 April 1970
Fourth Symphony, subtitled *Das Testament*, for orchestra and two pianos tuned a quarter-tone apart, by the 50-year-old German composer Giselher KLEBE, is performed for the first time in Wiesbaden in the form of a ballet.

4 May 1970
Voyages, by the 36-year-old American composer Charles FUSSELL, scored for soprano, tenor, female chorus, piano and wind instruments, plus a recorded speaker, to texts by Hart Crane, is performed for the first time at the University of Massachusetts in Amherst.

7 May 1970
The Fisherman and His Wife, children's opera after a grim Grimm fairy tale by the versatile American composer Gunther SCHULLER, is performed for the first time in Boston, with the composer conducting.

9 MAY 1970
Symphony by the Berlin-born English composer Alexander GOEHR is performed for the first time in London.

9 MAY 1970
Il coccodrillo (The Crocodile), opera by the 53-year-old Italian composer Valentino BUCCHI, is produced in Florence.

10 MAY 1970
Fourteenth Symphony and *Twenty-first Symphony* by the macrosymphonic English composer Havergal BRIAN are presented in London as world premieres.

22 MAY 1970
Zdravý nemocný (Le malade imaginaire), opera by the Czech composer Jiří PAUER to his own libretto based on the famous play of Molière, is produced in Prague.

24 MAY 1970
The Universal Prayer, for four soloists, chorus, three harps and organ by the Polish expatriate composer Andrzej PANUFNIK, to the poem by Alexander Pope, is performed twice in the same program to an audience of about 4,000 at its premiere at the Cathedral of St. John the Divine in New York, Leopold Stokowski conducting.

30 MAY 1970
Fibonacciana, concerto for flute and string orchestra by the 40-year-old Spanish composer Cristóbal HALFFTER, inspired by the cumulative accretion of numbers in the Fibonacci series (1, 2, 3, 5, 8, 13, 21, etc., each number being the sum of the preceding two), is performed for the first time in London.

31 MAY 1970
Violin Concerto by the 52-year-old Austrian composer Gottfried von EINEM is performed for the first time in Vienna.

4 JUNE 1970
Seventh Symphony by the British composer Benjamin FRANKEL, couched in an uncompromisingly dissonant vein, is performed for the first time in London.

8 JUNE 1970
Ombres, Hommage à Beethoven for string orchestra by the Bulgarian-born French music critic and composer André BOUCOURECHLIEV, is per-

7

formed for the first time in Toulouse on the occasion of Beethoven's bicentennial.

12 JUNE 1970
Triple Concerto for piano, double-bass, drums and orchestra by the 31-year-old American composer William McKINLEY is performed for the first time by the Chicago Symphony Orchestra.

19 JUNE 1970
The Forty-fourth Festival of the International Society for Contemporary Music opens in Basel with the stage performances of two short operas, *Der Traum des Liu-Tung* by the Korean composer Isang YUN (first produced in Berlin on 25 September 1965) and *Der magische Tänzer*, two scenes for two singers, two dancers, two actors, chorus, orchestra and tape by the 31-year-old Swiss composer and virtuoso oboist Heinz HOLLIGER.

20 JUNE 1970
At the second concert of the Forty-fourth Festival of the International Society for Contemporary Music in Basel, the following program of chamber orchestra music by Swiss composers is given:

Miroirs for winds, harp, piano, percussion and double-bass by Rudolf KELTERBORN. *Tempora* for violin and orchestra by Klaus HUBER. *Exécution ajournée* for thirteen musicians by Jürg WYTTENBACH. *In my end is my beginning*, cantata after T. S. Eliot for soprano, tenor and chamber orchestra by Jacques WILDBERGER. *Sonata per orchestra* by Robert SUTER.

21 JUNE 1970
At the third concert of the Forty-fourth Festival of the International Society for Contemporary Music in Basel, the following program for various instrumental and vocal groups is given in the morning:

Ikos by the Greek composer Dimitri TERZAKIS. *Ancora odono i colli* by the Italian composer Sylvano BUSSOTTI. *Hry* by Ilja ZELJENKA of Czechoslovakia. *Spectacles for Percussion and Tape* by Atli Heimir SVEINSSON of Iceland. *Alternance pour percussion* by Makoto SHINOHARA of Japan.

21 JUNE 1970
At the fourth concert of the Forty-fourth Festival of the International Society for Contemporary Music in Basel, the following program is presented in the evening:

Requiem profanum for soprano, alto, baritone, strings and piano by Erkki SALMENHAARA of Finland. *Continuum II. Trauerminuten für Dana Kosanova* for chamber orchestra by Bojidar DIMOV of Bulgaria. *Nocturne*, after Nietzsche, for two choruses, two cellos, two percussion groups and harp by Alfred JANSON of Norway. *The Approach to the Midden Man II* after H. Michaux, for mezzo-soprano, chamber orchestra and tape by Jacques GUYONNET of Switzerland. *XC*, after Ezra Pound, for soprano, chorus and chamber orchestra by Henrik-Otto DONNER of Finland.

23 JUNE 1970
At the fifth concert of the Forty-fourth Festival of the International Society for Contemporary Music in Basel, the following program of symphonic music is presented:

Altamira for chorus and orchestra by the Hungarian composer Zdolt DURKÓ. *Trajectoirs pour violon et orchestre* by the French composer Gilbert AMY. *Étude pour Folklora II* by the Yugoslav composer Vinko GLOBOKAR. *Variété* by the West German composer Peter Michael BRAUN.

24 JUNE 1970
Cello Concerto by the British composer Sir Arthur BLISS is performed for the first time at the Aldeburgh Festival with Mstislav Rostropovich as soloist.

24 JUNE 1970
At the sixth concert of the Forty-fourth Festival of the International Society for Contemporary Music in Basel, the following program of compositions for string quartet is given:

Steps of Silence by the Rumanian composer Anatol VIERU. *Aura* by the Spanish composer Tomás MARCO. *String Quartet* by the Australian composer Ross EDWARDS. *String Quartet* by the Polish composer Witold LUTOSLAWSKI.

25 JUNE 1970
At the seventh concert of the Forty-fourth Festival of the International Society for Contemporary Music in Basel, the following program of chamber music is given:

. . . sentire . . . for flute, cello and piano by Sven-Erik BÄCK of Sweden. *Spell Respell* for electric basset clarinet and piano by Anthony GILBERT of England. *Wind Quintet* by Rudolf ESCHER of Holland. *Soliloquium No. 1* for solo flute by Zoltán JENEY of Hungary. *La guerre* for soprano, piano, vibraphone, clarinet and two percussion groups by Ramon ZUPKO of the United States.

26 JUNE 1970
The Forty-fourth Festival of the International Society for Contemporary Music in Basel concludes with the following program of orchestral music:

Musik für Orchester by Andrzej DOBROWOLSKI of Poland. *Serenata II* by Antonio TAURIELLO of Argentina. *Rondo*, after H. Heissenbüttel, for voice and orchestra by Hans Ulrich LEHMANN of Switzerland. *Tricolore IV* by Pelle GUDMUNDSEN-HOLMGREEN of Denmark. *Plejaden II* by Günter KAHOWEZ of Austria.

27 JUNE 1970

Das kommt davon, oder Wenn Sardakai auf Reisen geht (That's What Happens, or When Sardakai Goes Traveling), opera by Ernst KRENEK, to his own libretto, is performed for the first time at the Hamburg State Opera.

5 JULY 1970

Thema for solo electrified oboe, four electric guitars, Hammond organ and eighteen wind instruments by the 35-year-old Dutch modernist Peter SCHAT is performed for the first time in Amsterdam.

14 JULY 1970

Waste Land Music, by the 26-year-old English avant-garde composer Tim SOUSTER, scored for saxophone, modulated piano, modulated organ and electronic synthesizer, is performed for the first time in London.

19 JULY 1970

The Rising of the Moon, opera by the 34-year-old British composer Nicholas MAW, is produced in Glyndebourne.

20 JULY 1970

Mme. Press Died Last Week at Ninety, an orchestral composition by the 44-year-old American ultramodernist Morton FELDMAN, commemorating his old Russian piano teacher, is performed for the first time in St. Paul de Vence, France.

25 JULY 1970

Tout un monde lointain for cello and orchestra by the 54-year-old French composer Henri DUTILLEUX is performed for the first time in Aix-en-Provence.

29 JULY 1970

John BARBIROLLI, British conductor of Italian and French parentage, whose impeccable taste won him numerous admirers, but whose lack of theatrical flamboyance became an obstacle to his success in the exteriorized musical societies of New York, and who was knighted in 1949 in appreciation for his devoted service to new and old English music, dies in London at the age of seventy.

30 JULY 1970

Georg SZELL, Hungarian-born conductor of a tremendous organizing capacity, who commanded the Cleveland Orchestra with imperious discipline and geometrically balanced sonorities, dies in Cleveland, a victim of a conglomerate of disabling diseases, at the age of seventy-three.

10 AUGUST 1970

Bernd Alois ZIMMERMANN, German composer of tense, expressionistic music, commits suicide in Königsdorf at the age of fifty-two, leaving behind a posthumous *Requiem* in which the desperate motto "Worauf hoffen?" ("What can we hope for?") is answered by a suicidally pessimistic conclusion, "There is nothing that awaits us except death."

12 AUGUST 1970

Opera, a spectacle for mixed media by the Italian composer Luciano BERIO, in which calculated chaos is integrated into an oxymoronic theatrical action, is performed for the first time in Santa Fe, New Mexico.

26 AUGUST 1970

Notturni ed Alba (Nocturnes and Dawn) for soprano and orchestra by the 31-year-old English composer John McCABE is performed for the first time in Birmingham, England.

27 AUGUST 1970

Septuria Lunaris, orchestral suite by the 28-year-old Swiss composer Matthias BAMERT, in seven movements, inspired by the seven "maria" on the face of the moon turned toward the earth, is performed for the first time at the Lucerne Festival.

27 AUGUST 1970

Marie Olénine D'ALHEIM, Russian soprano, who with her French husband Pierre d'Alheim perfervidly pursued the propaganda of Russian music in France, who joined the French Communist Party in 1949 and returned to Russia in 1959, dies in Moscow at the incredible, for sopranos, age of one hundred.

29 AUGUST 1970

Trobar clus for thirteen instruments by the 31-year-old American composer Barbara KOLB, wordlessly representing the ancient Provençal verse form of the rondeau, is performed for the first time in Tanglewood.

8 SEPTEMBER 1970

Essence of our Happiness, for tenor, chorus and orchestra by the British modernist composer Elisabeth LUTYENS, set in an atonally dodecaphonic idiom, is performed for the first time in London.

14 SEPTEMBER 1970

Hoe het is (What It's Like), for live electronic improvisers and fifty-two strings by the 31-year-old Dutch composer Louis ANDRIESSEN, is performed for the first time in Rotterdam.

18 SEPTEMBER 1970

Jimi HENDRIX, black American rock musician, dies in London at the age of twenty-seven, of asphyxiation induced by an overdose of barbiturates.

26 SEPTEMBER 1970

Dybuk, opera by the Czech-born Austrian composer Karl Heinz FÜSSL, is produced in Karlsruhe, West Germany.

29 SEPTEMBER 1970

Joe Hill, opera by the progressive British composer Alan BUSH, on the subject of the execution of the labor agitator Joe Hill in Salt Lake City on 19 November 1915, is performed for the first time in East Berlin.

1 OCTOBER 1970

Klangfarbenfunk I for orchestra, rock band and electronic sounds by the American composer Donald ERB is performed for the first time in Detroit.

1 OCTOBER 1970

Peter KONJOVIĆ, Serbian composer who succeeded in creating an indigenous type of national opera, making sensible use of the modalities of Serbian folk music couched safely within the tonal idiom of cosmopolitan romanticism, dies in Belgrade at the age of eighty-eight.

1 OCTOBER 1970

Catalogue des objets trouvés for chamber orchestra by the 44-year-old Austrian avant-gardist Friedrich CERHA is performed for the first time in West Berlin.

2 OCTOBER 1970

Daibutsu-Kaigen (The Great Image of Buddha), opera in three acts by the prime operatic composer of Japan, Osamu SHIMIZU, relating the dramatic events attendant upon the building of the great copper statue of Buddha in A.D. 747 in a Japanese village, is produced in Tokyo.

2 OCTOBER 1970

Norman DELLO JOIO conducts in Tampa, Florida, the first performance of his *Evocations* for chorus and orchestra.

6 OCTOBER 1970

Triplo Concerto a Tre, in three movements by Gian Carlo MENOTTI, is performed for the first time in New York.

10 OCTOBER 1970

Visions of Ishwara for orchestra by the 30-year-old black American composer Talib Rasul HAKIM, whose original name was Stephan A. Chambers before he converted to Sufism, is performed for the first time in New York.

14 OCTOBER 1970

Cello Concerto by the 57-year-old Polish composer of high intellectual attainments Witold LUTOSLAWSKI is performed for the first time in London, with Mstislav Rostropovich as soloist.

18 OCTOBER 1970

Five Fantasies of the Theater by Elie SIEGMEISTER, scored for multimedia participants, is performed for the first time at Hofstra University, Hempstead, New York.

18 OCTOBER 1970

Mantra für zwei Pianisten by Karlheinz STOCKHAUSEN, based on a triskaidecaphonic theme (with a perfunctory duplication of the central tone)— A, B, G-sharp, E, F, D, G, E-flat, D-flat, C, B-flat, G-flat, (A)—and *Heterogéneo* for two narrators, Hammond organ and orchestra by the 40-year-old Spanish composer Luis DE PABLO, are performed for the first time at Donaueschingen, West Germany, during the Days for Contemporary Music Festival.

20 OCTOBER 1970

At the third annual "Styrian Autumn" festival of contemporary music in Graz the following program is presented:

The world premiere of a partly aleatory *Formula* (*Edgar Varèse in memoriam*), op. 261, for orchestra by the fantastically productive Danish composer Niels Viggo BENTZON. *Ionisation*, seminal work for percussion ensemble and two sirens by Edgar VARÈSE. *Luna* for orchestra by the 38-year-old Danish composer Per NØRGAARD, dedicated to the moon, and commemorating the first lunar landing on 20 July 1969, in four phases (movements), using thirty-two notes employed in a horizontal serial arrangement in which certain notes fall in prescribed registers only. The world premiere of an "open end" orchestral work appropriately titled *Floating*, by the 39-year-old Norwegian composer Arne NORDHEIM, which lacks a beginning and has no appointed ending. (At this point the audience was invited to vote which work they would like to have repeated; Varèse and Nørgaard were the winners.)

23 OCTOBER 1970

Black Angels (Thirteen Images from the Dark Land) for electric string quartet by the 41-year-old American composer George CRUMB is performed for the first time in Ann Arbor, Michigan.

23 OCTOBER 1970

The third annual "Styrian Autumn" festival of contemporary music in Graz continues with the following program of orchestral music:

Déserts, symphonic poem with electronic sound, by Edgar VARÈSE. World premiere of *Irisation* by the 34-year-old Polish composer Marek STACHOWSKI, in three iridescent movements, each displaying an individual color effect. *Mouvement symphonique*, written in 1936, by the Serbian composer Slavko OSTERC (1895–1941). *Nasprotja* (*Contradictions*) for flute and orchestra by the 49-year-old Slovenian composer Primož RAMOVŠ, in three sections without pause, illustrating the motto *unus contra omnes*. *Étude pour Folklora II* by the 36-year-old French-born, Yugoslav-educated composer Vinko GLOBOKAR, making use of microtones.

24 OCTOBER 1970

The third annual "Styrian Autumn" festival of contemporary music in Graz continues with the following program:

The world premiere of *Triga einer chromatischen Leiter*, a collective, three-movement composition for eight players by Boris BLACHER and two of his pupils: the first movement, *West*, by Blacher, in five sections; the second movement, *Ost* (*East*), by the 31-year-old Japanese composer Sesshu KAI, a sparsely conceived piece representing the infinite simplicity of Zen thought; and the third movement, *Südost* (*Southeast*), by the 36-year-old Indonesian composer Paul Gutama SOEGIJO, representing a series of sonic oscillations. The world premiere of *Linien* for chamber ensemble by the 49-year-old Yugoslav-born composer living in Graz, Franz KORINGER, conceived as a progression of sonic "lines" that combine in sonic "surfaces." The world premiere of *Musique pour Graz* for chamber orchestra by Darius MILHAUD. *Octandre*, a modern classic for eight instruments by Edgar VARÈSE.

24 OCTOBER 1970

Kosmogonia, cosmopolitan work by Krzysztof PENDERECKI, is performed for the first time at the conference of the United Nations in New York. The work is scored for soprano, tenor, bass, chorus and orchestra, singing in Greek, Latin, Italian, Russian and English, in two parts—*Arche* (beginning), with a text from writings on the structure of the universe by Copernicus, Lucretius and the book of Genesis, and *Apeiron* (infinity), extolling the genius of man and exploration of the cosmos, drawing upon the poetic prognostications of Sophocles, Ovid, Leonardo da Vinci, and Giordano Bruno, and the pragmatic realization of the first Soviet cosmonaut Yuri Gagarin and the first American earth-orbiter John Glenn —all set in a fantastically diversified plasma of emancipated sounds.

26 OCTOBER 1970

The third annual "Styrian Autumn" festival of contemporary music in Graz continues with the following program:

Hyperprism, essay in sounding geometry, scored for wind instruments and percussion by Edgar VARÈSE. The world premiere of *Doppelt beflügeltes Band* (*Tape and Doubles*) for two pianos and tape by Ernst KRENEK, in five sections, the last of which uses elements of rock 'n' roll. The world premiere of *Zyklus* for cello, winds, harp and percussion by Wolfgang FORTNER, originally scored for cello and piano in 1964 and revised in the present amplified version in 1969. The world premiere of *Kammermusik 70* for wind quintet by the 30-year-old Vienna-born composer Martin BJELIK.

30 OCTOBER 1970
The third annual "Styrian Autumn" festival of contemporary music in Graz concludes with the following program:

Intégrales for wind instruments, double-bass and percussion by Edgar VARÈSE. *Chants et Prismes* for orchestra by the 51-year-old Polish-born, Austrian-domiciled composer Roman HAUBENSTOCK-RAMATI, written in 1957 and revised in 1967. The world premiere of *Peinture* for large orchestra by the 41-year-old Soviet composer Edison DENISOV, dedicated to the painter Boris Birger. *Pneuma* for thirty winds, organ, percussion and four transistor radios by the 31-year-old Swiss composer and master oboist, Heinz HOLLIGER (first performed at Donaueschingen on 18 October 1970). *Heterogéneo* for two narrators, Hammond organ and orchestra by the 40-year-old avant-garde Spanish composer Luis DE PABLO.

30 OCTOBER 1970
Faisceaux-Diffractions for twenty-eight instruments by the 32-year-old French composer Jean-Claude ELOY is performed for the first time at the Library of Congress in Washington, D.C.

31 OCTOBER 1970
Second Symphony, subtitled *Chance*, by the 35-year-old Soviet Georgian composer Giya KANCHELI, in a single movement subdivided into three sections, is performed for the first time in Tbilisi.

31 OCTOBER 1970
Three modern American works are performed for the first time at the Coolidge Festival in Washington, D.C.:

1. *Ancient Voices of Children* for soprano and boy soprano by the 41-year-old American composer George CRUMB, to the text by Federico García Lorca, with two instrumental interludes, *Dances of the Ancient Earth* and *Ghost Dance*. Instrumentation and performance include a plethora of percussion, including Tibetan prayer stones, a musical saw, a paper-threaded harp, a glass rod, a toy piano, glissando produced by a small chisel with a smooth cutting edge on piano strings to obtain high overtones, and vocal production diversifier by expelling breath violently like a sneeze, singing a glossolalia of vowels into the open piano, tongue clicking, shouting and whispering. 2. *Changes* for electronic tape

and digital computer by the 28-year-old American composer Charles DODGE. 3. *Mass* for soprano, clarinet and the electronic synthesizers Syn-Mill (an electric generator based on a design of Robert Moog and built by Edward Miller) and Syn-Ket (a portable electronic generator built by the Roman sound engineer Paul Ketoff), by the 35-year-old American composer John EATON.

9 NOVEMBER 1970
Cocktail Party for any number of uninvited guests playing any number of undetermined instruments by the 30-year-old Uruguayan composer Sergio CERVETTI is performed for the first time in Malmö, Sweden.

9 NOVEMBER 1970
Fifth Symphony by William Grant STILL, subtitled *Western Hemisphere*, in four movements reflecting respectively the vigor, the beauty, the nervous energy and the humanity of the continent, composed in 1945 and based on thematic materials from an earlier symphony, is performed for the first time by the Oberlin College Orchestra at Oberlin, Ohio.

10 NOVEMBER 1970
Nattstycken (Nocturnes) for alto, speaker and chamber ensemble by the 37-year-old American composer Alan STOUT is performed for the first time in Chicago.

11 NOVEMBER 1970
A Record of Our Time, "protest piece" for chorus, narrator, soloist and orchestra by the 56-year-old American composer Gail KUBIK, is performed for the first time in Manhattan, Kansas.

12 NOVEMBER 1970
Ecology of the Skin by the 23-year-old American avant-garde composer David ROSENBLOOM, scored for tape machines, computers and brain ("an electroencephalographic experience for performer/leader and group-dynamic brain waves"), is performed for the first time as part of the Electric Ear Series of the Electric Circus in New York.

14 NOVEMBER 1970
Cassandra by the 35-year-old Greek-American avant-gardist Theodore ANTONIOU, sound-action for dancers, actors, chorus, orchestra, tapes, lighting and projections, is performed for the first time in Barcelona.

17 NOVEMBER 1970
Sixth Symphony by the 48-year-old American composer Irwin BAZELON is performed for the first time in Kansas City, Missouri.

19 NOVEMBER 1970

Communication in a Noisy Environment, an event conceived by the 35-year-old American avant-gardist Gordon MUMMA, consisting of a number of artifacts (a racing Citroën car, with its horn blaring and neon-tubed windshield wipers swishing, a fire extinguisher emitting a foamlike spray, an amplified group of violins, clarinets, saxophones, police whistles and other music makers), takes place at the Automation House in New York.

24 NOVEMBER 1970

Third Symphony for soloists, double chorus, chamber chorus and orchestra by the 52-year-old American composer George ROCHBERG, containing quotations from Schütz, Bach, Mahler and Ives, is performed for the first time in New York.

29 NOVEMBER 1970

Frank ZAPPA's rock group The Mothers of Invention performs at the Lyceum Ballroom in London a phallic song, *Penis Dimension,* in which the tenor soloist broods over the insufficient length of his male organ while a chorus of young girls contradicts his pessimistic assessment.

29 NOVEMBER 1970

Croisées des couleurs croisées (Crosses of the Crossed Colors) for female voice, an undetermined number of grand pianos, tape recorders and two radio receivers dialed aleatorily, to texts from Indian and Negro political speeches by the 41-year-old surrealist Belgian composer Henri POUSSEUR, is performed for the first time in New York.

2 DECEMBER 1970

The Knot Garden, opera in three acts by the 65-year-old British composer Sir Michael TIPPETT (he was knighted by Queen Elizabeth in 1966), to his own libretto with seven people raveled in a psychophysical knot—a white musician homosexually involved with a black poet, a physically mangled female revolutionary, an aging psychoanalyst and a fluttering nubile girl lusted after by a married man who renounces his nuptial vows with his possibly lesbian wife—all this immersed in a shimmering sea of iridescent instrumental colors, is produced at Covent Garden in London.

3 DECEMBER 1970

Piano Concerto in Six Movements by the 47-year-old American composer Ned ROREM, diversified by emphatically allusive titles (*Strands, Fives, Whispers, Sighs, Lava, Sparks*), is performed for the first time by the American pianist Jerome Lowenthal with the Pittsburgh Symphony Orchestra, William Steinberg conducting.

4 DECEMBER 1970

Tragedy of Man, opera by the 63-year-old Hungarian composer György RÁNKI, is produced in Budapest.

9 DECEMBER 1970

Quadrodram for clarinet, trombone, piano, percussion, dancer and film by the 44-year-old American composer and clarinetist William O. SMITH, is performed for the first time in Seattle.

31 DECEMBER 1970

Oedipe-Roi, electronic ballet by the 50-year-old Italian composer and conductor Bruno MADERNA, is performed for the first time in Monte Carlo.

31 DECEMBER 1970

Cyril SCOTT, British composer who domesticated the harmonies and timbres of French Impressionism and created instrumental bagatelles of beguiling charm and exotic flavor, such as *Lotus Land*, pleasingly invoking the aura of Egypt, *Danse nègre* and *Jungle Book* after Kipling, but who strongly opposed any steps beyond his private Parnassus, and who described jazz as a work of the devil and embraced the astral beliefs of synthetic Hinduism, dies in Eastbourne, England, at the age of ninety-one.

⮒ *1971* ⮓

5 JANUARY 1971

Eighth Symphony by the prolific 69-year-old British composer Edmund RUBBRA is performed for the first time in Liverpool.

10 JANUARY 1971

Triple Concerto for woodwinds, brass, jazz quintet and orchestra by the 40-year-old American composer David AMRAM is performed for the first time in New York.

21 JANUARY 1971

Pulsations for electronic keyboard, jazz band and orchestra by 38-year-old Brazilian-born American composer Lalo SCHIFRIN is performed for the first time in Los Angeles.

25 JANUARY 1971

Invitation à l'Utopie for narrator, two female voices, four-voice chorus and instrumental ensemble by the 41-year-old Belgian modernist Henri POUSSEUR is heard for the first time on a broadcast over Brussels Radio.

28 JANUARY 1971

Thirty-second Symphony by the English megasymphonist Havergal BRIAN achieves its first performance in London three years after its completion.

30 JANUARY 1971

The Mountaineers, the first national opera of the Dagestan in the Caucasus, by the 35-year-old native composer Shirvani CHALAYEV, depicting in dramatic colors and stark asymmetrical rhythms the socialist passions in a remote Caucasian village during the civil war of 1920, is produced in Derbent, Dagestan, U.S.S.R.

3 FEBRUARY 1971

Frieze, third chamber symphony by the polysymphonic Danish composer Vagn HOLMBOE, is performed for the first time on the state radio of Denmark in Copenhagen.

5 FEBRUARY 1971

The Contemporary, opera by the 56-year-old Bashkir composer Hussain AKHMETOV, is performed for the first time in Ufa, the capital of the Bashkir Soviet Socialist Republic.

5 FEBRUARY 1971

Cello Concerto, composed in 1964 by the macrosymphonic English nonagenarian composer Havergal BRIAN, is performed for the first time in London.

11 FEBRUARY 1971

Ein Gespenst geht um in der Welt (A Specter Roams About in the World), cantata for voice and orchestra by the foremost Communist composer of Italy, Luigi NONO, to the words of the portentous preamble of the Communist Manifesto by Marx and Engels, issued in 1848, scored for a seemingly innocuous soprano, a pointedly hoarse chorus representing the bourgeoisie and a cunningly mistuned orchestra, is performed for the first time in Cologne.

11 FEBRUARY 1971

Compases para preguntas ensimismadas (Bars for Self-querying Questions) by Hans Werner HENZE, for viola solo and twenty-two players

(eleven strings, six winds, percussion, harp, harpsichord and celesta),
written with an introspective reticence concerned with subtle nuances
in a curiously impressionistic manner, is performed for the first time
by the Chamber Orchestra of Basel under the direction of its founder
and conductor Paul Sacher.

13 FEBRUARY 1971
Ostrov Afrodité (The Island of Aphrodite), opera in three acts by the
42-year-old Czech composer Jiří DVOŘÁČEK, to his own libretto after a
play by Alexis Parnis, is performed for the first time in a German version
in Dresden. Depicting the tense struggle in 1955 between the British
colonial authorities and the rebellious nationalistic Greek populace on
the island of Cyprus, the legendary birthplace of Aphrodite, the work is
musically organized along the lines of Socialist Realism, with the national
conflict characterized by tense trills and dramatic tremolos, ending in a
triumphant C major as the mother of a Greek patriot perfidiously executed
by the British magnanimously prevents the retaliatory execution of a
kidnapped British officer.

13 FEBRUARY 1971
Leviathan for double bassoon and chamber orchestra by the 50-year-old
English composer Ruth GIPPS is performed for the first time in London.

18 FEBRUARY 1971
Ninth Symphony by the extraordinary Swedish composer Allan PETTERS-
SON, set (as most of his symphonies) in a single gigantic movement, is
performed for the first time in Göteborg, conducted by Sergiu Comissiona to whom the work is dedicated.

20 FEBRUARY 1971
Second Symphony by the 51-year-old French composer André CASANOVA
is performed for the first time in Nice.

25 FEBRUARY 1971
Commemoration Symphony by Louis GESENSWAY is performed for the
first time by the Philadelphia Orchestra.

27 FEBRUARY 1971
La Fontana, one-act opera by the Italian composer Mario BUGAMELLI, is
performed for the first time in Trieste.

28 FEBRUARY 1971
Carmen, a collage from materials of Bizet's opera, by the 63-year-old
German composer Wolfgang FORTNER, is performed for the first time in
Stuttgart.

5 March 1971

Ninth Symphony, subtitled *Sinfonia: Janiculum,* by the American composer Vincent PERSICHETTI, is performed for the first time by the Philadelphia Orchestra.

5 March 1971

Tajemství elipsy (The Secret of Ellipsis) for orchestra by the 50-year-old Czech composer Zbyněk VOSTŘÁK is performed for the first time in Prague.

12 March 1971

Memory for electronic piano and electronic harpsichord by the Italian avant-garde composer Luciano BERIO is performed for the first time in New York, with the composer and Peter Serkin at the respective keyboards.

12 March 1971

The Most Important Man, opera in three acts with music and libretto by Gian Carlo MENOTTI, in which a black man in an unnamed segregated nation invents an ultimate formula to attain total dominion of the world and himself achieves a liaison with an unpigmented woman, strangles his laboratory assistant and then destroys himself and the formula in a luminous death dance, set to music with a liberal application of Africanesque percussion, is performed for the first time at the New York City Opera.

12 March 1971

The Capitoline Venus, opera by the American composer Ulysses KAY, is performed for the first time at the University of Illinois in Urbana.

19 March 1971

Stille und Umkehr (Stillness and Return) for orchestra by the German composer Bernd Alois ZIMMERMANN, written in a thanatological spirit of ultimate quietude dissolving at the end into shimmering quarter tones, is performed for the first time in Nuremberg, seven months and nine days after his inexplicable suicide.

21 March 1971

Octagon for piano and orchestra by the 45-year-old American composer William MAYER is performed for the first time by William Masselos as soloist with the American Symphony Orchestra under the direction of Leopold Stokowski in New York.

24 March 1971

Second Symphony by the South African-born English composer John JOUBERT is performed for the first time in London.

4 April 1971
The Scene-Machine, opera by the 36-year-old British composer Anthony GILBERT, is produced in Kassel, West Germany.

5 April 1971
Prayer, a sound event with magnetic tape by the Italian avant-garde composer Luciano BERIO, is performed for the first time in New York.

6 April 1971
Igor STRAVINSKY, musical demiurge of titanic powers, whose unique genius projected itself upon the world, transcending his Russian beginnings in achieving universality of technical means, and completing the cycle of creative expansion by adopting the serial method of composition during his last terrestrial years, dies in New York at the age of eighty-eight.

9 April 1971
Écran for orchestra by the 44-year-old Rumanian composer Anatol VIERU is performed for the first time at the Royan Festival in France.

15 April 1971
Fourth Symphony by the 38-year-old American composer Alan STOUT is performed for the first time by the Chicago Symphony Orchestra.

21 April 1971
Andrey Kostenya, opera by the 80-year-old Byelorussian composer Nikolai ALADOV, is performed for the first time in Minsk.

23 April 1971
First Symphony by the 43-year-old American composer Nicolas FLAGELLO is performed for the first time in New York.

23 April 1971
Hallelujah, "a joyous phenomenon with fanfares" by the 34-year-old American avant-garde composer Robert MORAN, scored for marching bands, drum and bugle corps, church choirs, organs, carillons, rock 'n' roll bands, television stations, automobile horns and other sounding implements, is staged in Bethlehem, Pennsylvania, hopefully with the participation of its entire population of 72,320 inhabitants.

25 April 1971
Staatstheater, "theatrical composition" for combined media by the Argentine-born German-domesticated avant-garde composer Mauricio KAGEL, is performed for the first time at the Hamburg State Opera.

26 April 1971

A Moment of History, oratorio in five movements by the 50-year-old Soviet Armenian composer Karen KHACHATURIAN, to documented texts of the Soviet Revolution, is performed for the first time in Moscow.

29 April 1971

Melusine, opera by the 35-year-old German composer Aribert REIMANN, to a libretto based on the medieval legend of a miscegenated Albanian princess who was doomed to change to a serpent from the waist down on Saturdays and who vanished forever after her husband surprised her during her weekly metamorphosis, is performed for the first time in Schwetzingen.

1 May 1971

The following program of modern pieces is performed for the first time at a special concert in Glasgow: *Bewegung* for orchestra by Luciano BERIO, *Horn Concerto* by Thea MUSGRAVE and *Alastor* by Iain HAMILTON.

2 May 1971

Forest Music for orchestra by the 32-year-old American-born Japanese composer Paul CHIHARA, forming a synthesis of his other instrumental pieces of sylvan inspiration (*Tree Music, Branches, Redwood, Willow, Rain Music, Driftwood, Logs*), and couched in a calligraphically impressionistic manner with pointillistic touches, is performed for the first time in Los Angeles.

4 May 1971

Busonism, an homage to the great romantic classicist Ferruccio Busoni for piano and orchestra by the Danish neoclassicist composer Niels Viggo BENTZON, is performed for the first time in Malmö, Sweden.

4 May 1971

Eppur si muove, orchestral piece by the 35-year-old Serbian composer Rajko MAKSIMOVIĆ, titled after Galileo's famous sotto voce asseveration, ". . . and yet it moves," after he was forced by the Inquisition in 1633 to recant his belief that the earth is an axially rotating and orbitally revolving celestial body, is performed for the first time in Belgrade.

5 May 1971

Flies, opera by the 50-year-old Egyptian composer Halim EL-DABH, to a libretto dealing with the tragic occurrence on the campus of Kent (Ohio) State University when four students were killed by National Guardsmen during an antiwar demonstration in 1970, the "flies" of the title referring to the victims, is performed for the first time in Washington, D.C.

9 MAY 1971

David VAN VACTOR conducts in Maryville, Tennessee, the first performance of his choral symphony *Walden*, to texts from Thoreau's celebrated
individualistic work. (Billed as the *Third Symphony*, *Walden* was
chronologically *No. 4*, his *Second Symphony* having actually been an
orchestral suite and his *Third Symphony* recorded as *No. 2*. Van Vactor
conducted a partial performance of *Walden* in Knoxville, Tennessee, on
1 March 1970.)

10 MAY 1971

Conflict for computerized sound by the 59-year-old Russian-born American composer Vladimir USSACHEVSKY, intended to represent the mystical
struggle between two ancient deities, is performed for the first time in
Salt Lake City.

16 MAY 1971

Owen Wingrave, television opera by Benjamin BRITTEN, based on a
short story by Henry James dealing with a pacifist youth who suffers
social reprehension for his convictions (as Britten himself had during
World War II), is broadcast for the first time by the BBC in London.

16 MAY 1971

Chant d'Automne for soprano and orchestra by the 42-year-old Soviet
composer Edison DENISOV (first-named in honor of Thomas A. Edison,
and whose name is also an anagram, minus the *v*, of his family name),
to poems by Charles Baudelaire, is performed for the first time in Zagreb.

17 MAY 1971

*Der langwierige Weg in die Wohnung der Natascha Ungeheuer (The
Tedious Journey to Natashca Monster's House)*, "show for seventeen" by
Hans Werner HENZE, is performed for the first time in Rome in an Italian
version.

18 MAY 1971

The Fifth Inter-American Music Festival opens in Washington, D.C.,
featuring the world premieres of *Reflections* for orchestra by the
Uruguayan composer Antonio MASTROGIOVANNI; *Piano Concerto* by
Morris KNIGHT of the United States; *Checan II* for orchestra by Edgar
VALCARCEL of Peru; and *Plexus* for orchestra in varied degrees of sonorous
density by the Uruguayan composer Sergio CERVETTI.

18 MAY 1971

Klíč (The Key) by the 50-year-old Czech composer Ivo JIRÁSEK is performed for the first time in Prague.

19 May 1971

L'Opéra des Oiseaux, opera by Antoine DUHAMEL after *The Birds* of Aristophanes, is produced in Lyon.

20 May 1971

The second concert of the Fifth Inter-American Music Festival is presented in Washington, D.C., featuring the world premieres of *Diagrams* for orchestra by Blas E. ATEHORTUA of Colombia; Concerto for Viola and Orchestra by Robert PARRIS of the United States; *The Windhover*, for bassoon and orchestra by Robert EVETT of the United States; and *Colores Mágicos* for harp and chamber orchestra by the Uruguayan-born American composer José SÉREBRIER.

20 May 1971

Huckleberry Finn, opera after Mark Twain by the American composer Hall OVERTON, is performed for the first time at the Juilliard American Opera Center in New York.

21 May 1971

Sinfonia in Do for chorus and orchestra by the 38-year-old Italian composer Niccolò CASTIGLIONI, to texts from works of Ben Jonson, Dante, Shakespeare and Keats, is performed for the first time in Rome.

23 May 1971

Der Besuch der alten Dame, opera in three acts by Gottfried VON EINEM, to the surrealist libretto of Friedrich Dürrenmatt, is produced at the Vienna Festival. The old lady *(alte Dame)* of the title returns to her native locality in Switzerland where she had been seduced at a tender age and abandoned by her amoral lover, becomes rich in the world as Madame Clair Zachanassian (a contraction of millionaire names Zacharoff, Onassis and Gulbenkian) and promises the villagers untold riches on condition that they kill her erstwhile seducer, an offer which is ultimately accepted by the impoverished citizens—a tale set to music in a suitably melodramatic fashion in a brilliantly heterogeneous score.

28 May 1971

The Resurrection of Christ, the second part of the grand mass *Utrenja* by Krzysztof PENDERECKI, is performed for the first time at the Münster Cathedral.

29 May 1971

Icarus, ballet by the 38-year-old Soviet composer Sergei SLONIMSKY, to a scenario by his otherwise unrelated namesake Yuri Slonimsky, in seven tableaux, depicting in neo-Grecian modalities and propulsively asymmetrical rhythms the immortal dream of human flight by heroic Icarus, imprisoned on the island of Crete by the tyrannous archons who sabotage the sturdy wings of his craft and so precipitate him to his death, is performed for the first time in Moscow.

1 JUNE 1971

The Forty-fifth Festival of the International Society for Contemporary Music opens in London with an afternoon concert of modern chamber music featuring the following program:

Second String Quartet by the 40-year-old Dutch composer Carel BRONS, consisting of thirteen sections of which four are quasi-aleatory in respect to dynamics, duration, tempo and articulation. *Confluencia sobre do sostenido (Confluence upon C-sharp)* by the 41-year-old Spanish composer Agustín BERTOMEU, the title indicating that the thematic phrases and sections recurrently return to the focal C-sharp. *Projection* for string quartet by the 41-year-old Japanese composer Joji YUASA, in which a single sound is regarded as an acoustical compound of many potential sounds in the overtone series which acquire either melodically or contrapuntally their own thematic values. *Abbreviaturen* by the 53-year-old German composer Jürg BAUER for thirteen solo string instruments, in four movements featuring microstructures, sound surfaces, tone clusters and aleatory passages.

1 JUNE 1971

At an evening concert of the opening day of the Forty-fifth Festival of the International Society for Contemporary Music in London, the following program of orchestral music is given:

J. D. E. by the 45-year-old Paris-born American composer Betsy JOLAS scored for fourteen instruments, the title suggesting an infinite meaninglessness. *Voyage into the Golden Screen* by the 38-year-old Danish composer Per NØRGAARD, the texture of the music based on the constant acoustical interference between closely adjacent notes. *Praxis* for eleven strings and piano by the foremost representative of the Greek musical avant-garde Jani CHRISTOU, who perished on the eve of his forty-fourth birthday on 8 January 1970 in an automobile accident near Athens; the titular word refers to purposeful action, contrasted to *metapraxis*, implying loss of emotional control, hysteric manifestations, such as six violinists striking the piano keyboard and the piano strings, at the same time furiously shouting the names of notes at random, the score being written out in associative notation with pictorial illustrations for metapractical actions. *Tetraeder* by the 43-year-old Austrian composer Irmfried RADAUER, with the musical events deriving from the number of apexes in a tetrahedron (hence the title), and scored for twelve instrumentalists seated in a manner suggesting the shape of an eponymous structure, the work concluding in an electronic coda generated by a computer. *Chamber Concerto* by the 44-year-old apostle of ultramodernism, the Hungarian-born György LIGETI, scored for thirteen players and consisting of four movements of metarhythmic complexity resulting from parallel progressions of solo parts moving at different tempi. (This latter work was first performed at the Berlin Music Festival, 1 October 1970.)

2 JUNE 1971

On the second day of the Forty-fifth Festival of the International Society for Contemporary Music in London, an afternoon concert of instrumental and vocal music is given with the following program:

Turba by the 27-year-old Hungarian composer Miklós MAROS, for a chorus and a singing conductor, with the phonetic text of disjected syllables and improvisatory episodes in which the chorus represents the crowd of the Latin title. *Requiem* by the 40-year-old Chilean-born Israeli composer Leon SCHIDLOWSKY, to a Latin text, with twelve solo voices periodically rising to a screaming pitch. *False Relationship and the Extended Ending* by the 45-year-old American avant-garde composer Morton FELDMAN, written for two nonsynchronous instrumental groups occasionally coming to a fortuitous confluence. . . . *Da un Divertimento* by the 24-year-old Sicilian avant-garde composer Salvatore SCIARRINO, for an instrumental ensemble, the title alluding to a planned divertimento which was never brought to completion.

2 JUNE 1971

The second day of the Forty-fifth Festival of the International Society for Contemporary Music in London continues in the evening with the following program:

An Imaginary Landscape for orchestra by the 37-year-old British avant-gardist Harrison BIRTWISTLE, with the musical design governed by a computer. *Second Piano Concerto* by Béla BARTÓK. *Siebengesang* by the 32-year-old Swiss master oboist and composer Heinz HOLLIGER, the seven parts alluded to in the title representing various orchestral groupings, with the oboe as a focal solo instrument played by the composer. *Variations for Orchestra*, op. 31, by Arnold SCHOENBERG.

3 JUNE 1971

On the third day of the Forty-fifth Festival of the International Society for Contemporary Music in London, the following program of orchestral music is presented:

Momentum, In Memoriam by the 54-year-old Hungarian composer Rudolf MAROS, father of Miklós Maros, whose work was played the day before, the memory evoked in the title being that of the fateful year 1945. *Enfiando per orchestra* by the 42-year-old Polish composer Augustyn BLOCH, composed for the Beethoven bicentennial and first performed in Beethoven's native city of Bonn on 12 October 1970 ("Enfiando" of the title meaning swelling out, for the music embodies a series of consecutive crescendos). *Haiku II* for voice and orchestra by the 44-year-old Dutch modernist Ton DE LEEUW, modeled after the Japanese miniature verse form, fragmented and pitched together so that syllables from different poems form a series of synchronized multivocables. *Tartinia MCMLXX* for violin and orchestra by the 29-year-old Brazilian composer Jorge ANTUNES, employing microtonal structures derived from differential tones, the discovery of which is traditionally credited to Tartini (hence the title), in nine continuous sections. *Per Bastiana Tai-Yang Cheng* by the 47-year-old Venetian avant-gardist Luigi Nono, the musical material derived from microtonal intervals contrapuntally surrounding the theme of the Communist Chinese anthem *Tai-Yang Cheng (The East Is Red)*.

4 JUNE 1971
In the course of the Forty-fifth Festival of the International Society for Contemporary Music in London the following program of chamber music is presented:

Zoom for clarinet and bongos by the 42-year-old Yugoslav composer Milan STIBILJ, the music marked by a prosodic rhythmic flow without a basic pulse. *Tételpár*, for oboe and piano by the 32-year-old Hungarian composer Attila BOZAY, in two movements (the title means a pair of movements) set in the cyclic form of Hungarian dances, in the dodecaphonic idiom. *Second String Quartet* by the 39-year-old English composer Hugh WOOD, constituting a continuous movement in thirty-nine sections, each shorter than the preceding one, except for a lyrical coda. *Quartet* for two pianos and two percussion players by the 36-year-old Polish composer Zbigniew RUDZINSKI, with the thematic material based on the principles of coexistence of opposition and a contrast between organized stable structures and nonorganized quasi-improvisatory materials.

4 JUNE 1971
A special concert of three stage works by the 39-year-old Berlin-born English composer Alexander GOEHR is presented in the evening at the Forty-fifth Festival of the International Society for Contemporary Music in London: *Naboth's Vineyard, Shadowplay–2* and *Sonata about Jerusalem*.

5 JUNE 1971
On the fifth day of the Forty-fifth Festival of the International Society for Contemporary Music in London the following program of chamber music is presented:

Variations for wind quintet, piano and recorded piano by the 36-year-old Australian composer Nigel BUTTERLEY, comprising fifteen variations on a dodecaphonic subject. *Tabuh Tabuhan* for wind quintet and two percussion players by the 42-year-old Australian composed Peter SCULTHORPE, making use of aboriginal rhythms. *Incredible Floridas* by the 39-year-old Australian composer Richard MEALE, in six movements inspired by poems of Arthur Rimbaud. *Revelation and Fall* by the 36-year-old English avant-garde composer Peter Maxwell DAVIES, for sixteen instruments and a soprano part ranging in expression from Sprechgesang to screaming through a megaphone, containing a large battery of primitivistic percussion, a railway guard's whistle, an oil drum, a knife grinder, dulcimer and handbells, to texts by the Austrian suicide poet Georg Trakl.

6 June 1971

Franz SCHUBERT's *Unfinished Symphony,* completed by Gerald ABRAHAM, is performed for the first time in this heterogeneous form in Liverpool.

7 June 1971

In the course of the Forty-fifth Festival of the International Society for Contemporary Music in London the following program of vocal and instrumental music by British composers is given:

Two Poems for voice and piano by 28-year-old Bill HOPKINS, to the words of James Joyce. *Second Piano Sonata* by 40-year-old Robert Sherlaw JOHNSON, in three movements making use of both the keyboard and the inside of the grand piano. *Poems of Wallace Stevens* by 38-year-old Justin CONNOLLY, for soprano and seven instrumentalists. *Islands* for soprano, tenor, narrator and instruments by 65-year-old Elisabeth LUTYENS, evoking four islands described by Sophocles, Shelley, Stevenson and Rabelais. *Leo* for chamber orchestra by the Catalan-born composer Roberto GERHARD (1897–1970), a work first performed at Dartmouth College in Hanover, New Hampshire, on 23 August 1969, the title bearing an astrological reference to the constellation of Leo.

8 June 1971

On the concluding day of the Forty-fifth Festival of the International Society for Contemporary Music in London the following program is given in an afternoon concert:

Invariant for bass clarinet, piano and tape by the 42-year-old Czech composer Václav KUČERA, based on the principle of invariance of some elements in a cybernetic system and set in a free variation form. *Epitase* by the 35-year-old Swiss composer Eric GAUDIBERT, the title being derived from epitasis, the point in Greek dramaturgy at which the action approaches the climax, scored for harpsichord, string trio and magnetic tape. *Dialogue* for cello and seven instruments by the 36-year-old Soviet composer Alfred SCHNITTKE, set in somber colors, beginning and ending with a cello cadenza. *Tetragon (Homage to Pablo Picasso)* by the 43-year-old Swedish modernist Bengt HAMBRAEUS, recorded on tape in four instrumental groupings with four separate loudspeakers placed in each of the four corners of the hall (whence the title, tetragon, a quadrangle), emulating Picasso's technique in multicolor painting visible on a big plate of glass.

8 June 1971

The Forty-fifth Festival of the International Society for Contemporary Music in London concludes with the following program at an evening concert:

In eius memoriam by the 45-year-old American composer Seymour SHIFRIN, written in memory of a friend, in three lyric sections with long solos. *From the Tibetan Book of the Dead* for soprano, chorus and prerecorded tape of elec-

tronic and concrete sounds, by the 37-year-old Canadian composer R. Murray
SCHAFER, to a text sung in the Tibetan language. *Versuch über Sprache*, by the
31-year-old German composer Nicolaus A. HUBER for quadrasonic tape, combining four unrelated linguistic fragments accompanied by instruments. *Chorali*
by the 35-year-old Finnish composer Aulis SALLINEN, written for thirty-two
wind instruments and percussion, in a hymnlike mode, with funereal allusions
(the work is dedicated to the memory of the composer's dead parents). *Présence*
for piano trio by the German composer Bernd Alois ZIMMERMANN (who committed suicide at the age of fifty-two on 10 August 1970), composed in 1961.
Atrées, an homage to Blaise Pascal, pioneer in the theory of probability, by the
foremost apostle of scientific electronic music, the Rumanian-born 49-year-old
Greek composer Iannis XENAKIS, for ten players, the music being the result of
a stochastic (probabilistic) calculation made on a computer, the title referring
to the Cretan dynasty of the Atrides whose fates were determined both by fate
and probability.

11 JUNE 1971
The Inspector General, opera by the Hungarian composer Eugene ZADOR
after the famous Gogol comedy of mutual deception and misrepresenta-
tion in Czarist Russia, composed in 1928 and radically revised and
orchestrated at a later date, with an English libretto by the composer, is
given its first stage performance in Los Angeles.

15 JUNE 1971
In the course of the Holland Festival, the world premiere is given in
Utrecht of *Spinoza*, opera in three acts by Ton DE KRUYF, dealing with
the expulsion of Baruch Spinoza from the Jewish community of Amsterdam for his heterodoxal views of Hebrew patriarchs as fallible men,
with Spinoza's leitmotif derived from the first and the last letter-note of
his name (S= Es= E-flat vs. A, forming the tritone, the "diabolus in
musica" of medieval theorists), and symbolizing the rabbi's curse upon
Spinoza, accompanied by an annihilating unison of C's, signifying the
rigid rectitude of millennial tradition.

19 JUNE 1971
Summer and Smoke, opera in two acts by the 45-year-old American composer Lee HOIBY after a play by Tennessee Williams dealing with the
unrequited love of a Mississippi girl who refuses to face reality and seeks
refuge in a fantasy world, set to music in an emotional Mahlerian idiom
with the application of expressionistic song-speech, is performed for the
first time in St. Paul, Minnesota.

20 JUNE 1971
Geisterliebe, opera by the Korean composer domesticated in Germany,
Isang YUN, is performed for the first time in Kiel.

25 JUNE 1971

Cornelius CARDEW, the British proponent of extreme modernism, presents in Newcastle-on-Tyne a performance of his Scratch Orchestra, featuring a piece by Greg BRIGHT instructing him to "behave as vulgarly as possible," while handing to children in the audience pieces of pink lavatory paper with copulative four-letter verbs written on them. (A second appearance by the orchestra was stopped by the municipal authorities.)

26 JUNE 1971

Guillermo URIBE-HOLGUÍN, prime composer of Colombia, author of symphonies written in the style of his teacher Vincent d'Indy, and of a remarkable set of piano pieces "en el sentimiento popular," reflecting the genuine modalities of Colombian songs and dances, dies in his native city of Bogotá at the age of ninety-one.

27 JUNE 1971

Oh, Mr. Fogg, comic chamber opera by the 49-year-old Czech composer Jan FISCHER, satirizing the hero of Jules Verne's novel *Around the World in Eighty Days*, is produced in Saarbrücken, West Germany.

6 JULY 1971

Louis ARMSTRONG, the great "Satchmo" (satchel-mouth) of American jazz, trumpeter extraordinary, dies in New York at the age of seventy.

23 JULY 1971

Béatris, opera by the 38-year-old French composer Jacques CHARPENTIER, based on a true story of a fourteenth-century French matron brought to trial on a charge of consorting with demons and of having carnal relations with a priest, and whose eloquent defense saved her from execution, is performed for the first time at Aix-en-Provence.

12 AUGUST 1971

Yerma, posthumous opera by Heitor VILLA-LOBOS, to a symbolic drama by Federico García Lorca, depicting the inner torment of a woman remaining barren (*yerma*) because of her husband's inexplicable refusal to have marital relations with her, and her equally inexplicable refusal to find another man, culminating in her superhuman and successful effort to strangle her inactive mate to death, is produced with the original Spanish libretto in Santa Fe, New Mexico.

18 AUGUST 1971

Second Symphony for soprano and orchestra by the precocious 19-year-old English composer Oliver KNUSSEN, using texts from poems by Georg

Trakl and Sylvia Plath, is performed for the first time by the Boston Symphony Orchestra under the direction of Gunther Schuller, in Tanglewood, Massachusetts.

28 AUGUST 1971

Two musical legends concerning the tragedy of Judas Iscariot by the 89-year-old Italian master Gian Francesco MALIPIERO, *L'iscariota* and *Uno dei dieci (One of the Twelve)*, both to his own libretti in which Judas is pictured as a true disciple of Christ, who by his betrayal intended to carry out the prophecy of resurrection, are produced in Siena.

8 SEPTEMBER 1971

Mass, a theater piece for singers, players and dancers, by the protean American composer, conductor, poet, conceptual actor, pianist and charismatically communicative lecturer Leonard BERNSTEIN, is performed for the first time at the opening of the John F. Kennedy Center for the Performing Arts in Washington, D.C. The work is set to texts from the Roman liturgy, in seventeen well-demarcated sections: (1) *Devotions Before Mass*, (2) *First Introit*, (3) *Second Introit*, (4) *Confession*, wherein the first subdivision, *Confiteor*, is based on mutually exclusive augmented, major, minor and diminished triads, (5) *Meditation #1*, (6) *Gloria*, (7) *Meditation #2*, (8) *Epistle: "The World of the Lord,"* (9) *Gospel-Sermon: "God Said,"* (10) *Credo*, (11) *Meditation #3: De Profundis, Part 1*, (12) *Offertory: De Profundis, Part 2*, (13) *The Lord's Prayer*, (14) *Sanctus*, (15) *Agnus Dei*, (16) *Fraction: "Things Get Broken"* and (17) *Pax: Communion*.

10 SEPTEMBER 1971

Fadograph from a Yestern Scene for orchestra by Samuel BARBER, after James Joyce's *Finnegans Wake*, is performed for the first time by the Pittsburgh Symphony Orchestra.

10 SEPTEMBER 1971

Beatrix Cenci, opera by Alberto GINASTERA dealing with a parricidal Italian matron who, in a complot with her mother and two brothers, exterminates her vicious Roman father, and who was beheaded on 11 September 1599 by papal order despite her defense in claiming that her father attempted incest upon her, is produced at the Kennedy Center in Washington, D.C.

18 SEPTEMBER 1971

The Stone Wall, a multimedia action for orchestra, chorus and a participant audience by the Australian avant-garde composer Malcolm WILLIAMSON, is performed for the first time by the BBC in London.

22 SEPTEMBER 1971

The Lovers for baritone, mixed chorus and orchestra by the American composer Samuel BARBER, to the text of the radical Chilean poet Pablo Neruda, is performed for the first time in Philadelphia.

2 OCTOBER 1971

Hystera—Paradies, Schwarz, opera by the German avant-garde composer Dieter SCHNEBEL, is produced at Cologne.

7 OCTOBER 1971

Sixth Symphony by the 64-year-old Berlin-born American composer Gene GUTCHË is performed for the first time in Detroit.

9 OCTOBER 1971

Sonora for orchestra by the 39-year-old Serbian composer Vladan RADOVANOVIĆ, set in a surrealistically micropolyphonic technique of "sonoriferous sculpturing," is performed for the first time in Belgrade.

12 OCTOBER 1971

Jesus Christ Superstar, rock opera with music by the 23-year-old British composer Andrew LLOYD WEBBER and lyrics by the 26-year-old British writer Tim RICE, with Jesus appearing as a fanatically suicidal martyr and Judas as an earnest believer in Christ's immortality, originally presented as a record album, receives its first stage performance on Broadway in New York. (A choral version was produced in Kansas City, Kansas, on 15 May 1971.)

17 OCTOBER 1971

Planto por las victimas de la violencia (Plaint for the Victims of Violence) for chamber ensemble and tape by the 41-year-old Spanish composer Cristóbal HALFFTER is performed for the first time in Donaueschingen, West Germany.

23 OCTOBER 1971

Kâmakalâ, a "triangle of energies" for three orchestral groups and five choral ensembles by the 33-year-old French composer Jean-Claude ELOY, is performed for the first time in Paris, directed by three synchronized conductors.

24 OCTOBER 1971

Carl RUGGLES, grand old man of American music whose few instrumental works such as *The Sun Treader* and *Men and Mountains* are imbued with a sui generis American expressionism, dies at the age of ninety-five in Bennington, Vermont, where he had retired from the world to devote himself mainly to painting abstract canvases.

3 NOVEMBER 1971

The Sacrifice, ballet by the 40-year-old Hungarian composer Sándor SZOKOLAY, is performed for the first time in Budapest.

9 NOVEMBER 1971

Ashmedai, opera by the Israeli composer Josef TAL, is produced in Hamburg. The story deals with a minor devil known in Christian demonology as Asmodeus, who persuades an adventurous king to let him rule his domain for a year as a test of the people's loyalty to the throne, with an unexpected outcome when the population, enjoying the newly proclaimed freedom of sin, unanimously votes for Ashmedai's continuance in office for life (i.e., forever, demons being immortal). Thematic tritones (the "diabolus in musica" of the pietistic musicasters of the Dark Ages) are rampant in a score which is further diabolized by a variety of gliding licks, electronic clicks, percussive kicks and dodecaphonic ticks.

18 NOVEMBER 1971

Sixth Symphony, subtitled *Labyrinth*, by Humphrey SEARLE is performed for the first time in Birmingham, England.

20 NOVEMBER 1971

Ninth Symphony, subtitled *Sinfonia semplice*, by the 66-year-old Estonian-born Swedish composer Eduard TUBIN, is performed for the first time in Stockholm.

26 NOVEMBER 1971

The British Prime Minister and amateur musician Edward Heath conducts the London Symphony Orchestra in a competent performance of Edward ELGAR's *Cockaigne Overture*.

3 DECEMBER 1971

De Natura Sonoris No. 2 for strings, wind and percussion by the foremost Polish modernist Krzysztof PENDERECKI is performed for the first time at the Juilliard School of Music in New York.

3 DECEMBER 1971

Rhythmicana for rhythmicon and orchestra by Henry COWELL, written in 1931, with the solo instrument being an electrostatic tonal-rhythmic device constructed by Leon Theremin according to Cowell's specifications, receives a belated first performance at Stanford University, in Palo Alto, California, with an electronic apparatus replacing the original instrument.

7 DECEMBER 1971

Eighth Symphony by the prolific British composer Benjamin FRANKEL is performed for the first time in Liverpool.

8 DECEMBER 1971

Memories of Morning: Night, monodrama for soprano and orchestra by the 34-year-old British composer Gordon CROSSE, is performed for the first time in London.

12 DECEMBER 1971

Mantrajana, a Buddhist symphonic poem by the 29-year-old Swiss composer Matthias BAMERT, based on the belief in redemption through the repetition of sacred formulas (mantras) and scored for four Oriental gongs, to be struck at six different points each, and a non-Oriental orchestra, is performed for the first time by the American Symphony Orchestra under the direction of the 89-year-old maestro Leopold Stokowski.

28 DECEMBER 1971

Max STEINER, Viennese-born master of cinematic melodramatic music that became a model of many emulators in the art, dies in Hollywood at the age of eighty-three.

31 DECEMBER 1971

Colonel Jonathan the Saint, opera in four acts by Dominick ARGENTO, is produced in Denver, Colorado.

ᘓ *1972* ᘔ

1 JANUARY 1972

Maurice CHEVALIER, gallant French chansonnier whose beguilingly debonair delivery belied the torrid eroticism of his songs, dies in his native Paris at the age of eighty-three.

8 JANUARY 1972

Fifteenth Symphony by Dmitri SHOSTAKOVICH, op. 141, in four classically designed movements in the benign key of C major, containing some innovations, such as a theme of twelve nonrepeated notes in a trumpet fanfare, an almost precise quotation from Rossini's *William Tell Overture* in the first movement, and the insertion of the Fate motive from Wagner's *Walküre* in the Finale, is performed for the first time by the Symphony Orchestra of the All-Union Radio and Television in Moscow, under the direction of Shostakovich's son, Maxim.

11 JANUARY 1972

From the Dead Sea Scrolls for chorus, children's chorus, two organs, tape and orchestra by the 51-year-old Czech-born Israeli composer Jacob GILBOA is performed for the first time in Hamburg.

16 JANUARY 1972

Lux Aeterna for Five Masked Players for soprano, bass flute (interchangeable with soprano recorder), sitar and two percussionists by the 42-year-old American composer George CRUMB is performed for the first time in Richmond, Virginia.

18 JANUARY 1972

L'Effacement du Prince Igor, symphonic essay by the Belgian innovator Henri POUSSEUR, is performed for the first time by the Belgian National Orchestra on its visit in New York.

21 JANUARY 1972

Fourth Symphony by the 68-year-old Russian-born American composer Nicolai LOPATNIKOFF is performed for the first time by the Pittsburgh Symphony.

21 JANUARY 1972

Concerto for baritone, cello and orchestra by the 35-year-old German composer Aribert REIMANN is performed for the first time in West Berlin.

25 JANUARY 1972

A Lincoln Address for narrator and orchestra by the American composer Vincent PERSICHETTI, to the text of Lincoln's second inaugural address of 4 March 1865, with the thematic materials adapted from his *Seventh Symphony* which was in turn derived from his work *Hymns and Responses*, receives its first performance by the St. Louis Symphony Orchestra conducted by Walter Susskind. The work was commissioned for the inaugural concert for President Richard Nixon's second term of office, but taken off the program on account of Lincoln's truculent invocation of the wrath of the Lord upon the rebellious South should they persist in their unrighteous struggle, a sentiment embarrassing to the Nixon Administration in the throes of liquidating the Vietnam War.

27 JANUARY 1972

Tenth Symphony by the 62-year-old Danish composer Vagn HOLMBOE is performed for the first time anywhere in Detroit, Sixten Ehrling conducting.

27 JANUARY 1972

The Labyrinth by the 55-year-old Italian composer Guido TURCHI is performed for the first time by the Chicago Symphony Orchestra.

30 January 1972

Karel Boleslav Jirák, prolific Czech composer of six symphonies and many other works, dies at the age of eighty in Chicago, where, as an emigrant from Czechoslovakia, he spent the last twenty-five years of his life.

3 February 1972

The Natural Sound Workshop, founded by Kirk Nurock and dedicated to the artistic exploration of bodily sounds, presents its first public performance in Greenwich Village in New York, with a group of naturally sounding men and women belching, burping, farting, hard breathing, regurgitating, sneezing, talking with mouths full, moaning, groaning, yowling, whistling, erupting in polyglot glossolalia, babbling, gabbling, blowing, singing while inhaling air, audibly stretching limbs and pandiculating, shaking, vibrating, lip-fluttering, tongue-clicking, snapping fingers, clapping hands, slapping exposed flesh, cracking bones, murmuring, mumbling, imitating animal sounds, rolling thighs, profusely salivating in chromatic tremolos, gargling, gurgling, gnashing teeth, making dental glissandos, sibilating, sighing, grunting, coughing, choking, gagging, cackling, giggling, cooing, tittering, yawning, cachinnating, whimpering, whining, shouting, screaming, chanting, bouncing, humping and somersaulting.

4 February 1972

Drumming by the American avant-gardist Steve Reich, in four long sections scored respectively for drums and a male voice, marimbas and female voices, glockenspiels, piccolos and whistles, suggesting in its intransigently concentrated drive the sound of the Indonesian gamelan accompanied by African drumming and rudimentary American ragtime, Indian raga, Japanese gagaku, Australian boomerang and Afro-Cuban heterorhythmics, is performed in its entire length by the Steve Reich Ensemble in London.

4 February 1972

Splash, a space composition for double-bass and percussion by the 33-year-old German composer Hans-Joachim Hespos, is performed for the first time on the German television network.

8 February 1972

Tikhon Khrennikov, foremost proponent of Soviet Socialist Realism in music, plays the solo part in the first performance in Moscow of his *Second Piano Concerto* in C major, in three sections, *Introduction, Sonata* and *Rondo*.

11 February 1972

Partita for harpsichord, electric guitars, harp, double-bass and orchestra by Poland's prime musical modernist Krzysztof Penderecki is performed for the first time at the Eastman School of Music in Rochester, New York.

14 FEBRUARY 1972

The Trial of Mary Lincoln, opera by the 26-year-old American composer Thomas PASATIERI, based on the true story of the trial of Lincoln's widow, on the suspicion of Confederate sympathies, is performed for the first time on the National Educational Television network in the United States.

17 FEBRUARY 1972

Sixth Symphony by the Czech-American composer Karel Boleslav JIRÁK is performed for the first time in Prague, eighteen days after his death in Chicago.

23 FEBRUARY 1972

Eighth Symphony by the individualistic Swedish composer Allan PETTERSSON, in two movements, set in an exalted empyrean idiom "to exorcise the fiendishness of existence and transfigure the repressed possibilities of happiness," alternating meditative episodes with contrasting martial passages, is performed for the first time by the Stockholm Philharmonic, Antal Dorati conducting.

25 FEBRUARY 1972

Den stora teatern (The Big Theater), opera by the 38-year-old Swedish composer Ulf BJÖRLIN, is produced in Göteborg.

1 MARCH 1972

Time Off? Not a Ghost of a Chance, "a charade in four acts and three interruptions" by the 65-year-old British composer Elisabeth LUTYENS, is produced in London.

2 MARCH 1972

Black Widow, opera by the American composer Thomas PASATIERI, is performed for the first time in Seattle, Washington.

3 MARCH 1972

Palast Hotel Thanatos by the 36-year-old German composer Dieter EINFELDT, a modernistic opera in one act dealing with the ghastly subject of multiple death, is performed for the first time in Hannover, Germany.

8 MARCH 1972

Cello Concerto by Krzysztof PENDERECKI is performed for the first time in Baltimore.

8 MARCH 1972

Seven Dodecaphonic Fragments for strings, the last work by the 71-year-old Slovenian composer Lucijan Marija Škerjanc, is performed for the first time in Ljubljana, not quite a year before his death.

16 March 1972
The 1972 Pulitzer Prize-winning *Windows* for orchestra and large percussion section by the 43-year-old American composer Jacob Druckman, with the titular windows described as memories of memories and shadows of shadows, is performed for the first time by the Chicago Symphony Orchestra, Bruno Maderna conducting.

17 March 1972
Vox Balaenae (Voice of the Whale) by George Crumb, scored for three masked players performing on electric flute, electric cello and altered electric piano, with the musical material derived from the recordings made of the actual sounds produced by a humpback whale, is performed for the first time at the Library of Congress in Washington, D.C.

22 March 1972
Non nova, orchestral piece by the 57-year-old Croatian composer Natko Devčić, set in an oscillating probabilistic technique within a controlled aleatory system, tantalizingly belying its negativistic title, and concluding with a cadenza for four percussion instruments, is performed for the first time in Zagreb.

23 March 1972
Aura, symphonic poem by the Italian avant-garde composer and conductor Bruno Maderna, is performed for the first time by the Chicago Symphony under the direction of the composer.

26 March 1972
Spaces for orchestra by the 65-year-old American composer Ross Lee Finney is performed for the first time in Fargo, North Dakota.

28 March 1972
Messe des voleurs, Les voleurs de Messe (Thieves' Mass, Mass Thieves) by the 35-year-old Basra-born French composer Paul Méfano, scored for electronics, organ, voices and instruments, is performed for the first time in Royan, France.

31 March 1972
Symphony Between Piano and Orchestra by the 51-year-old Slovenian composer Primož Ramovš, fashioned as a dialogue between the soloist

and the orchestra, in three connected movements, is performed for the first time in Ljubljana.

3 APRIL 1972

Ferde GROFÉ, American composer whose picturesque orchestral *Grand Canyon Suite* became one of the most beguiling pieces in American semi-classical repertory and who served the cause of symphonic jazz by expertly orchestrating Gershwin's *Rhapsody in Blue*, dies in Santa Monica, California, at the age of eighty.

3 APRIL 1972

Nigeria commemorates the seventy-fifth anniversary of the death of Johannes BRAHMS by issuing a 100-franc airmail stamp, adorned with his bearded portrait and a quotation from his *Lullaby*.

4 APRIL 1972

Stefan WOLPE, Berlin-born composer of Russian-Jewish extraction, who developed a highly personal—albeit unattractive to hoi polloi—style of writing, in which melodic angularity, intransigent atonality and intractable polytonality were combined with ancient Hebrew modalities and fertilized by polyrhythmic jazzicles, and who fled the Nazi monster to find peace in hospitable America where he became an admired teacher of an exclusive group of loyal local disciples, dies in New York a few months before reaching the biblical age of threescore and ten.

4 APRIL 1972

Seventh Symphony by the 59-year-old Welsh composer Daniel JONES is performed for the first time in London.

4 APRIL 1972

Fritz SPIEGEL, appearing at a "Tuesday Irritation Concert" at the Queen Elizabeth Hall in London, performs (not for the first time) his *Onanisms* for the solitary left hand on the phallomorphous piccolo and *Tactiles III* for two consenting male altos and prerecorded tape.

6 APRIL 1972

Lux, ballet by the 30-year-old Swedish composer Ulf GRAHN, is performed for the first time in Stockholm.

7 APRIL 1972

Towards Time's Receding by the American composer Robert WYKES, in three sections in a pyramidal profile, dynamically rising toward the middle and receding at the end, making use of attentuated impressionistic sonorities and asymmetrical rhythms, is performed for the first time in St. Louis.

8 APRIL 1972
Reflux, concerto for double-bass and wind ensemble by the 40-year-old American composer M. William KARLINS, is performed for the first time in Chicago.

13 APRIL 1972
Lord Byron, opera in three acts by Virgil THOMSON, to a libretto by Jack Larson, focused on the controversy regarding the erection of a monument to Lord Byron at Westminster Abbey, set to a characteristically Thomsonian, disarmingly bland melody, with candid allusions to such popular songs as *Auld Lang Syne, Ach du lieber Augustin* and *Three Blind Mice,* and ending in an apotheosis of disarmingly sharpless and alarmingly flatless C major, is performed for the first time at the Juilliard School of Music in New York.

14 APRIL 1972
Grass, concerto for double-bass and orchestra by the 33-year-old American composer Paul CHIHARA, is performed for the first time in Oberlin, Ohio.

14 APRIL 1972
Concertino for Chamber Orchestra by Roger SESSIONS, commissioned by the Fromm Music Foundation, in three movements with contrasting episodes spinning a fine web of astute variations, is performed for the first time (and immediately repeated) by the Contemporary Chamber Players of the University of Chicago, Ralph Shapey conducting.

14 APRIL 1972
Saint Louis, Roi de France, opera-oratorio in two parts by Darius MILHAUD to the poem by Paul Claudel, dramatically evolving as an operatic panorama of eleven scenes tracing the regal course of the canonized French King, is performed in a world premiere in Rio de Janeiro.

15 APRIL 1972
Julian by the 34-year-old American composer Charles FUSSELL, drama for orchestra and chorus after Gustave Flaubert's story of the apostate Roman emperor, is performed for the first time in Winston-Salem, North Carolina.

16 APRIL 1972
Anna Karenina, opera after Tolstoy by the Czech composer Emil HLOBIL, is produced in Ceské Budejovice.

24 APRIL 1972
Fourth Symphony by the 66-year-old English composer William ALWYN is performed for the first time in London.

27 APRIL 1972
Experimenta for a pianist and orchestra by the 42-year-old Polish modernist Boguslaw SCHAEFFER is performed for the first time in Poznań.

27 APRIL 1972
Second Symphony, subtitled *Isola Bella*, by the 41-year-old Danish composer Ib NØRHOLM is performed for the first time in Copenhagen.

3 MAY 1972
Allo, ici la terre (Hello, Earth Here), light and time show by the 43-year-old French composer Luc FERRARI with visual projections, of an indeterminate duration of a minimum of twenty minutes and a maximum of two hours, portraying the mortification of the beautiful Planet Earth, is presented for the first time in Bonn.

5 MAY 1972
Seventh Symphony by the 70-year-old Swedish composer Sten BROMAN, which includes electronic sound, is performed for the first time in Stockholm.

5 MAY 1972
Time Machine by the Dutch avant-garde composer Otto KETTING, inspired by the futuristic novel of H. G. Wells, scored for wind instruments and percussion in a highly dissonant counterpoint with major sevenths as anchor intervals and eruptive asymmetrical rhythms conveying the sense of acute temporal shifts into futurity, then reversing the time arrow toward the prehistoric past, with ecclesiastical chants coalescing into pandiatonic formations in a purifyingly white C major, is performed for the first time in Rotterdam.

11 MAY 1972
The Four-Note Opera by the 32-year-old American composer Tom JOHNSON, to his original libretto for five voices and piano in which the characters commit mass self-immolation at the end, the entire score based on four notes, A, B, D and E, in ostentatiously tetraphonic monotony fertilized by rhythmic diversification, is performed for the first time at the ultramodern emporium the Cubiculo in New York, with a prelude for a rebellious tape recording which demands individualistic deprogramming.

12 May 1972

Intrata for orchestra by the Cuban-born American avant-garde composer Aurelio DE LA VEGA, written in an ingeniously impressionistic manner, with a concertino for string instruments in elaborately polyrhythmic patterns, is performed for the first time by the Los Angeles Philharmonic Orchestra, Zubin Mehta conducting.

13 May 1972

The Trumpet of the Swan for narrator and orchestra, to the text of E. B. White, with music by Benjamin LEES, is performed for the first time in Philadelphia.

14 May 1972

Piano Concerto by the Berlin-born British composer Alexander GOEHR is performed for the first time in Brighton, England, with Daniel Barenboim as piano soloist.

16 May 1972

Flower and Hawk, monodrama by the 45-year-old American composer Carlisle FLOYD, is performed for the first time in Jacksonville, Florida.

17 May 1972

Solstices (ou Les Jours et las saisons tournent) for flute, clarinet, horn, double-bass and two percussionists by the 39-year-old Canadian composer Gilles TREMBLAY is performed for the first time in Montreal.

23 May 1972

Auto da fé, opera in eight episodes with prologue and epilogue by the 57-year-old Casablanca-born French composer Maurice OHANA, to his own libretto, scored for orchestra, triple chorus and electronics, "pour le plaisir de brûler les monstres," with a fiery crackling finale to portray the ritual burning of heretics, is performed for the first time in Lyon.

24 May 1972

Fourth Symphony by the inventive Yugoslav composer Aleksandar OBRADOVIĆ, in two movements, *Torches*, evolving from a generating dodecaphonic subject, and *Echoes*, dubbed "variations with a theme," the last variation being a canon for sixty voices, is performed for the first time in Belgrade.

26 May 1972

Eurydice, lyric drama by Jean-Michel DAMASE, to a play by Jean Anouilh, is produced in Bordeaux: A young man disenchanted with the unvirginal condition of a girl with whom he fell in love, lets her go after a quarrelsome night in a hotel; she is killed by an automobile and he spends the rest of his life in fantasies of her being a chaste nymph.

26 MAY 1972
Cantus arcticus, concerto for the voices of polar birds (on tape) and orchestra by the Finnish composer Einojuhani RAUTAVAARA, is performed for the first time in Oulu, Finland.

29 MAY 1972
Margaret Ruthven LANG, daughter of the Boston conductor and pianist Benjamin Johnson Lang, herself the composer of several symphonic overtures, piano pieces and songs, dies in her native Boston at the incredible age of one hundred and four.

1 JUNE 1972
The Triumph of Time for orchestra by the 37-year-old English composer Harrison BIRTWISTLE, based on an allegorical painting of Pieter Bruegel, embodying a huge funeral march of Mahlerian proportions, is performed for the first time by the Royal Philharmonic of London.

5 JUNE 1972
Wheel of the World, "entertainment" based on Chaucer's *Canterbury Tales* for actors, children's chorus, mixed chorus and orchestra by the 34-year-old British composer Gordon CROSSE, is performed for the first time at the Aldeburgh Festival.

7 JUNE 1972
Three Latin American Sketches, an orchestral set by Aaron COPLAND, astute stylizations of Mexican and Cuban melorhythms, is performed for the first time by the New York Philharmonic, André Kostelanetz conducting.

20 JUNE 1972
Cheap Imitation by John CAGE, a frankly titled orchestral piece, consisting of remembered fragments from Erik SATIE's *Parade*, is performed for the first time in Amsterdam.

20 JUNE 1972
Kitharaulos by Ernst KRENEK for harp (i.e., kithara), oboe (i.e., aulos), and string orchestra is performed for the first time in the course of the Holland Festival at The Hague.

20 JUNE 1972

To You for solo voice, six guitars, three bass guitars, four pianos, two Hammond organs, six humming tops and electronics by the 37-year-old Dutch composer Peter SCHAT is performed for the first time in Amsterdam.

22 JUNE 1972

Third Symphony by Sir Michael TIPPETT, in two movements, with a vocal part singing the blues, is performed for the first time by the London Symphony Orchestra, Colin Davis conducting.

22 JUNE 1972

The Wrestler, sacred opera by the 44-year-old German-born American composer Samuel ADLER, is produced for the first time in Dallas, Texas.

12 JULY 1972

Taverner, opera by the English modernist Peter Maxwell DAVIES, is performed for the first time at the Royal Opera House in Covent Garden, London. It is based on the life of John Taverner, English composer and organist who was incarcerated for a while for Protestant persuasions in the still Popish England in the early sixteenth century, but who subsequently became an energetic suppressor of Catholic monasteries, and is set to a modernistically polyphonic score applying hemidemisemidodecaphonic techniques, with a dramatic climax achieved when the soldiers of Henry VIII irrupt at the Mass service while the monks sing Taverner's own *Benedictus.*

17 JULY 1972

Den Fremmede (The Stranger), opera by the 49-year-old Danish composer Poul Rovsing OLSEN, is produced in Copenhagen.

18 JULY 1972

Goeran GENTELE, Swedish opera manager who was appointed general manager of the Metropolitan Opera House in New York as successor to Rudolf Bing, dies tragically in an automobile accident near Olbia, Sardinia, while on vacation with his family.

18 JULY 1972

Violin Concerto by Andrzej PANUFNIK, Polish-born composer of maternal English lineage, is performed for the first time by Yehudi Menuhin in London.

1 AUGUST 1972

Sim Tjong, opera by the 54-year-old Korean composer Isang YUN, is performed for the first time in Munich.

2 AUGUST 1972

Rudolph GANZ, Swiss-born musician who played the cello in his nonage, piano as an adolescent, began to compose romantically inspired music at an early maturity, went to America, became a highly respected piano teacher, and finally a competent symphonic conductor, who equally pleased untutored youth, skeptical professional players and financially endowed dowagers, dies in Chicago five years before reaching the centenary mark.

4 AUGUST 1972

Concerto for electronically amplified violin and orchestra by the uncompromising American avant-gardist Charles WUORINEN, written in an aggressively atonal style, is performed for the first time at Tanglewood, Massachusetts, by the avant-garde virtuoso Paul ZUKOFSKY and the Boston Symphony Orchestra under the direction of modern-minded Michael Tilson Thomas.

5 AUGUST 1972

David DEL TREDICI conducts in Saratoga, California, the first performance of his *Vintage Alice* for soprano, folk group and chamber orchestra, based on the text of the immortal tale by Lewis Carroll.

14 AUGUST 1972

Oscar LEVANT, American pianist whose neurasthenic self-deprecation made him a celebrity along the ephemeral pathways of Hollywood and New York, dies in Beverly Hills, California, at the age of sixty-five.

14 AUGUST 1972

Tiger Balm, ballet by the fearless New Zealander Anna LOCKWOOD, scored for a montage of concrete music on tape, is presented by ICES (International Carnival of Experimental Sound) in London.

15 AUGUST 1972

Cornelia Faroli, opera by the 58-year-old Czech composer Rafael KUBELIK, is performed for the first time in Augsburg, West Germany, under the direction of the composer.

17 AUGUST 1972

Ronald STEVENSON, 44-year-old Brythonic composer, plays in London, with the New York Philharmonic Orchestra, Norman del Mar conducting, the piano part in the first performance of his *Second Piano Concerto*, subtitled *The Continents*, acoustically reflecting the primal elements of native music in each of the five continents: Africa, hypnotically percussive; Australia and Asia, in pentatonic drone; Europe, West and East, concluding with a sonorific Russian march; North America, in an ebullient exposition of ragtime; and South America, an exotic apotheosis of the spirit of dance, with an epilogue in which the piano hammers out a reiterated chord "to assert human rights of many nations but only one race—the human race."

24 AUGUST 1972

Great Learning, Paragraph One, by the uncompromising British avant-gardist Cornelius CARDEW, wherein violence exercised by the revolutionary masses against the ruling class is justified by dialectical materialism of history, set for screechingly agonizing voices, deafening organ, loudly tapped stones, whistling solos and delirious drumming, and illustrated visually by sixteen ideograms of the Chinese text of the revolutionary slogan "Apply Marxism–Leninism–Mao Tse-tung thought in a living way to the problems of the present," is performed for the first time at the radio broadcast of the Promenade Concerts Series in London, by the Scratch Orchestra, with the composer conducting.

27 AUGUST 1972

Prometheus Bound for chorus, solo voices and orchestra, by the foremost Mexican composer Carlos CHÁVEZ, is performed for the first time at the Cabrillo Festival in Aptos, California, under the direction of the composer.

27 AUGUST 1972

Four centuries have passed since Claude GOUDIMEL, the French Huguenot who published the earliest editions of French Protestant chorales and composed music anticipatory of the homophonic style of Palestrina, died in the flames of the murderous St. Bartholomew Night in Lyon.

28 AUGUST 1972

René LEIBOWITZ, Polish-born composer and theorist, an astute explicator of dodecaphonic techniques, dies at his home in Paris at the age of fifty-nine.

2 SEPTEMBER 1972

Ich wandte mich und sah an alles unrecht, dass geschah unter der Sonne (I turned about and observed all the unjustices that occured under the sun), ecclesiastical action for two speakers, solo bass and orchestra, commissioned by the town of Kiel in connection with the Olympic Games of 1972, the last work of the suicidal pessimist Bernd Alois ZIMMERMANN, is performed for the first time in Kiel, West Germany.

5 SEPTEMBER 1972

Sixth Piano Concerto by Alexander TCHEREPNIN is performed for the first time in Lucerne.

7 SEPTEMBER 1972

A postage stamp of the denomination of 1.30 francs is issued by the Republic of Liechtenstein in honor of the American piano manufacturer Theodore STEINWAY (1883–1957), who was himself an impassioned philatelist.

7 SEPTEMBER 1972

Lorenzaccio, opera by the 41-year-old Florentine composer Sylvano BUSSOTTI, is performed at the opening of the Thirty-fifth International Festival of Contemporary Music in Venice.

16 SEPTEMBER 1972

Concerto for flute, oboe and orchestra by the foremost Hungarian modernist György LIGETI is performed for the first time in Berlin.

21 SEPTEMBER 1972

Flute Concerto by Walter PISTON, in a single movement comprised of three sections, *Aliquanto lento, Lento espressivo, Allegro assai*, with the thematic material pullulating in major sevenths and minor seconds in compact dissonant harmonies, is performed for the first time by the Boston Symphony Orchestra, with its first flutist Doriot Anthony Dwyer as soloist and Michael Tilson Thomas conducting.

3 OCTOBER 1972

Audiospectrum for orchestra by the 39-year-old Slovenian composer Darjan Božić, purporting to draw a parallel between optic and sonic waves and colors, with the entire spectrum extending from stillness (white) to deafening sonorous masses (black), is performed for the first time in Ljubljana.

5 OCTOBER 1972

A Ring of Time by the 44-year-old American composer Dominick ARGENTO, a cyclic orchestral suite of preludes and interludes, each being a variation on a fundamental tone row, revealed in its manifest form in a postlude entitled *Homage to Gustav Mahler*, the music traversing the seasonal—vernal, estival, autumnal and hibernal—moods, is performed for the first time by the Minnesota Orchestra to celebrate its seventieth anniversary, under the direction of Stanislaw Skrowaczewski.

7 OCTOBER 1972

Mother Svea, radio opera by the Swedish composer Hans EKLUND, is performed for the first time in Stockholm.

9 OCTOBER 1972

The Forty-sixth Festival of the International Society for Contemporary Music opens in Graz, Austria, with the first performance of the complete cycle of the theater work, *Spiegel I–VII*, by the 46-year-old bellwether of the Austrian avant-garde Friedrich CERHA, under his own direction, the title denoting seven mutually reflecting musical mirrors.

10 OCTOBER 1972

Wilderness Journal, symphony for bass-baritone, contralto, organ, orchestra, rubber-razzer, vibra-slap, mechanical cricket and sounds of nature (on tape) by John LA MONTAINE, based on texts from the *Essays and Journals* of Henry David Thoreau, in fifteen movements, based on a twelve-tone theme and its retrograde to portray the simplicity of Thoreau's contemplation, is performed for the first time in Washington, D.C., by the National Symphony Orchestra, Antal Dorati conducting.

10 OCTOBER 1972

On the second day of the Forty-sixth Festival of the International Society for Contemporary Music in Graz, the following program of instrumental music is presented:

Mouvements circulatoires for two chamber orchestras by the 65-year-old Japanese composer Yoritsuné MATSUDAIRA, modeled after the gagaku type of old Japanese court music, with the constituent orchestral groups intertwined in a circulatory movement. *To Earle*, by the 45-year-old Italian composer Franco DONATONI, for chamber orchestra, dedicated to the American ultramodernist Earle BROWN. *Theme* for oboe solo, two guitars, organ and wind ensemble by the 37-year-old Dutch member of the extreme avant-garde Peter SCHAT. *Chemins II B* for orchestra by the intransigent Italian innovator, 47-year-old Luciano BERIO, representing a radical metamorphosis of an earlier *Chemins II*.

10 OCTOBER 1972

Addio Garibaldi by Girolamo ARRIGO, "épopée musicale" in which the heroic Italian irredentist is betrayed by his patriotic followers to the accompaniment of a miscegenated orchestra, is produced at the Opéra-Comique in Paris.

11 OCTOBER 1972

On the third day of the Forty-sixth Festival of the International Society for Contemporary Music in Graz the following program is presented at an afternoon concert:

Lamentatio Jeremiae Prophetae, composed in 1941 by the astute Austrian modernist Ernst KRENEK, long domiciled in America, with thematic material derived from the fundamental tetrachord of the lamentation of the prophet Jeremiah according to the Catholic ritual and expanded into a dodecaphonic series by a process of melodic multiplication, modulation, rotation and permutation, scored for chorus a cappella. *Cromofonética* by the 30-year-old Brazilian composer Jorge ANTUNES, for vocal quartet, each voice being given three determined pitches, aggregating to the sonorous matrix of twelve different tones. *Nuits* by the Rumanian-born Greek apostle of stochastically calculated musical gospel Iannis XENAKIS, for twelve voices, dedicated to four political prisoners in Greece, making use of a variety of vocal techniques, including Japanese nasal sounds and neomedieval onomatopoeia. *Landschaften* by the 38-year-old Indonesian composer Paul Gutama SOEGIJO for chorus, lamenting the barbarity of the American war in Southeast Asia, making use of indeterminate melodic and rhythmic structures.

11 OCTOBER 1972

The third day of the Forty-sixth Festival of the International Society for Contemporary Music in Graz continues at an evening concert with the following program of theatrical music:

Glossolalia by the 42-year-old German composer Dieter SCHNEBEL, in which Pentecostal Babel becomes music. *Repertoire* by the 42-year-old Argentine-born apostle of the cosmopolitan avant-garde, now radicated in Germany, Mauricio KAGEL, conceived as a piece of "instrumental theater," in which actors who are also musicians perform according to a strict metronomical sequence but are free as to the use of materials of their musicodramatic action. *Ping* by the 38-year-old American avant-garde composer Roger REYNOLDS, scored for a variety of electronically amplified instruments, with the participation of visual elements.

12 OCTOBER 1972

On the fourth day of the Forty-sixth Festival of the International Society for Contemporary Music in Graz, the following program is given at an afternoon concert:

Musica per ventiquattro (24) by the 36-year-old Italian avant-garde composer Umberto ROTONDI, starting with monophonic synchrony of the twenty-four instruments and eventually achieving a totally independent instrumental confabulation leading to a creative disintegration. *Musica polymetrica* by the 40-year-old Czech composer Ilja ZELJENKA, based on the principle of metric modulation with asymmetrical displacements of structural fragments in multi-temporal instrumental combinations. *Al naar gelang* by the 49-year-old Belgian modernist Karel GOEYVAERTS, in five instrumental groups, programmed by players and audience by mutual consent. *Preludes and Fugue* by the 59-year-old Polish master composer Witold LUTOSLAWSKI, with the application of aleatory techniques in the sixth subject of the fugue.

12 OCTOBER 1972
On the fourth day of the Forty-sixth Festival of the International Society for Contemporary Music in Graz the following program is performed at an evening concert:

What's Next by the 41-year-old Japanese modernist Yori-Aki MATSUDAIRA, an aleatory quodlibet for toy instruments, motorcycles, bottles and a soprano. *Six Likes for Solo Tuba*, by the 37-year-old Greek modernist Theodore ANTONIOU, consisting of six comparatives (like a march, like a song, etc.), with the tuba used in extreme high and low ranges. *Karma-Dharma Drama* by the 51-year-old Rumanian-born Greek composer Anestis LOGOTHETIS, an audio-visual piece combining the spiritual elements of Indian karma, Buddhistic dharma and Greek drama.

13 OCTOBER 1972
Third Symphony by the English composer Ian PARROTT is performed for the first time at Aberystwyth.

13 OCTOBER 1972
On the fifth day of the Forty-sixth Festival of the International Society for Contemporary Music in Graz, the following program is given:

Cummings Is the Poet, an instrumental composition by the formidable apostle of the French avant-garde Pierre BOULEZ, inspired by the poetry of the American surrealist e.e. cummings. *Costellazioni* by the 27-year-old German modernist Robert WITTINGER, in four connected instrumental movements designed to create coordinated constellations of sonorities. *Melancolia* for violin and orchestra by the 41-year-old Hungarian modernist Josef Maria HORVATH, inspired by an etching of Dürer, wherein a magic square of coordinate numbers serves as the matrix. . . . *inwendig voller Figur . . .* by the 48-year-old Swiss composer Klaus HUBER, scored for several choruses and various instruments to texts in Greek, Latin, German and English from the Apocalypse.

14 OCTOBER 1972
On the sixth day of the Forty-sixth Festival of the International Society for Contemporary Music in Graz, the following program is presented:

Stop by the German apostle of scientific modern music Karlheinz STOCKHAUSEN, scored for six instrumental groups enriched by aleatory noises, to be stopped as soon as any sensible degree of coordination is accidentally attained. *Disturbances* by the 30-year-old Swedish composer Sven-David SANDSTRÖM, for six brass instruments, three of which are tuned a quarter tone lower than the rest. *Stanza* for harp and magnetic tape by the 42-year-old Japanese modernist Toru TAKEMITSU. *Omnipotence* by the 31-year-old Argentine composer Carlos Roqué ALSINA, for two soloists and chamber orchestra, the title connoting desire to communicate omnipotentially with art, people, nature and time. *Circle for*

Twelve Players by the 33-year-old Swiss oboe virtuoso and composer Heinz
HOLLIGER, in which the players are assigned instruments at random whether
they can play them or not. *Die Glocken sind auf falscher Spur* by the 46-year-old
German-born composer Michael GIELEN, constructed according to an intricate
system of basic intervals and inspired by surrealist poetry. *Linaia* by the master
of electronic and stochastic construction Iannis XENAKIS. *Concerto Grosso* by
the 38-year-old French born composer of Yugolsav extraction Vinko GLOBOKAR,
in five sections in which the instrumentalists are instructed to vacillate in their
behavior toward each other and their colleagues in the orchestra, with a chorus
offering encouraging advice.

14 OCTOBER 1972

The mortal remains of Alexander GLAZUNOV, who died in Paris on 21
March 1936, are transferred from their burial site in the cemetery at
Neuilly and interred at the laura of Alexander Nevsky in Leningrad, in
proximity to the graves of Glinka, Tchaikovsky and Rimsky-Korsakov.

15 OCTOBER 1972

Polytope, audiovisual spectacle by the panjandrum of scientific music
Iannis XENAKIS, is performed for the first time in its completely auto-
matized stochastic version, accompanied by laser projections, in Cluny,
France.

15 OCTOBER 1972

On the seventh day of the Forty-sixth Festival of the International Society
for Contemporary Music in Graz, the following program is presented at
an afternoon concert:

Galaxias for organ by the 75-year-old Argentine modernist Juan Carlos PAZ,
written in the manner of an aleatory passacaglia. *Traces de . . .* for organ by the
35-year-old German composer Hans Joachim HESPOS, inspired by the great
Baroque master of instrumental polyphony Girolamo Frescobaldi. *Non pulsando*
for organ by the 46-year-old Italian composer Giuseppe ENGLERT. *Mein blaues
Klavier* by the 45-year-old Chilean composer Juan ALLENDE-BLIN, for organ,
barrel organ and Jew's harp, inspired by a melancholic entry in Kafka's diary.
Variations III, a specimen of indeterminate music by the intransigent American
innovator John CAGE.

15 OCTOBER 1972

On the seventh day of the Forty-sixth Festival of the International Society
for Contemporary Music in Graz, the following program is given at an
evening concert:

Signals, a constructivist piece for voices by the Argentine modernist Eduardo
BERTOLA. *Commiato* by the 68-year-old Italian modernist Luigi DALLAPICCOLA,
for instruments and voices, being a dirge and farewell for a departed friend.
Erinnerung an eine Winterabenddämmerung by the 46-year-old Rumanian-born

Hungarian György Kurtág, an instrumental impression of a winter evening. *Musi-ken* by the 29-year-old Silesian-born American composer Rolf Gehlhaar, written with the application of concrete sounds, including scratching, scraping and grinding. *Engramas* for nine musicians and thirteen instruments by the 38-year-old Argentine composer Rufo Herrera, purporting to represent a subconscious excursion into the engrams of the embryonic and fetal past. *Contraction*, computer music for thirteen instruments, by the 45-year-old Austrian composer Irmfried Radauer.

16 October 1972
On the eighth day of the Forty-sixth Festival of the International Society for Contemporary Music in Graz, the following program is presented:

Seak by the 35-year-old Korean composer Junsang Bahk, for chamber ensemble (*seak* means delicate music), dedicated in memory of the Austrian modernist Hanns Jelinek based on an alternation of momentarily homogeneous groups of sounds. *The Straits of Magellan*, a geographical fantasy by the 47-year-old American modernist Morton Feldman, for seven instruments treated as purveyors of either extremely attentuated or imposingly massive sounds. *Melodies* by the 49-year-old Hungarian apostle of ultramodern impressionism György Ligeti, a condominium of melodic figures which grow gradually into rhythmically pulsating polyphonic conglomerates. *Opus Ghimel* by the 27-year-old Venetian conductor and composer Giuseppe Sinopoli, the melodic, rhythmic and contrapuntal texture being determined by digital computers. Three pieces named for Danish girls, *Nina Larker, Tina Norlov, Susanne Rudkjobing*, by the 31-year-old American composer active in Denmark, Maurice Weddington.

17 October 1972
The Forty-sixth Festival of the International Society for Contemporary Music in Graz concludes with the following program:

Unisonos by the 45-year-old Rumanian composer Stefan Niculescu, in which the thematic unisons expand into a temporary polyphony only to be retracted into the original monophony. *Chant d'automne* by the 44-year-old mathematically trained Russian composer Edison Denisov, for instrumental ensemble, inspired by a poem of Charles Baudelaire. *Concerto* for cello and orchestra by the masterly Polish modernist Witold Lutoslawski. *Nicina* for orchestra by the 38-year-old Slovenian composer Lojze Lebić, a piece connoting the fear of a mysterious menace, written in an idiom marked by polyphonic mobility.

20 October 1972
Eighth Symphony by the Welsh composer Daniel Jones is performed for the first time at the Swansea Festival in Wales.

21 October 1972
Décollage for two speaking choruses, electric guitar, electrically amplified cello, electric organ and magnetic tape by York Höller, descriptive of

the disintegration of palimpsestic collage, is performed for the first time at the Donaueschingen Festival.

22 OCTOBER 1972
Arbor, cantata to texts of Goethe, Dante, Shakespeare, Hitler, Mussolini, Martin Luther King and Ché Guevara by the 41-year-old Catalonian composer Xavier BENGUEREL, scored for soloists, four speakers, chorus and orchestra, is performed for the first time in Barcelona.

23 OCTOBER 1972
Elisabeth Tudor, operatic scenes by the 65-year-old German composer Wolfgang FORTNER, dealing with the lives of Queen Elizabeth I of England and Mary Stuart, "Queen of Scotland, former Queen of France, pretender to the English throne, murderess of her husband the King, and perjurer, executed in 1587," is produced in Berlin.

27 OCTOBER 1972
Soundings for eleven instruments and electronic tape by the 33-year-old American composer Barbara KOLB is performed for the first time at Lincoln Center in New York. (A revised version for full orchestra was premiered by the New York Philharmonic, Pierre Boulez conducting, on 11 December 1975.)

2 NOVEMBER 1972
Second Violin Concerto by the German composer Hans Werner HENZE, concluding with a prerecorded vocal homage by Hans Magnus ENZENS-BERGER to the German mathematical logician Kurt Gödel who enunciated his mind-boggling "Gödel's theorem," according to which in any sufficiently rich axiomatic system there is always an undecidable theorem, is performed for the first time in Basel.

8 NOVEMBER 1972
Seventh Symphony, subtitled *Israel*, by the French pianist-composer Robert CASADESUS, written in 1970 "in admiration for the people of Israel," but not specifically derived from Jewish motives, scored for a large orchestra with a textless chorus of men, women and children intoning the vowel "A," in three movements, *Maestoso, Andante dolce* and *Presto con fuoco*, is performed in a posthumous world premiere (Casadesus died in Paris on 19 September 1972 at the age of seventy-three) by the Musica Aeterna Orchestra and Chorus in New York, Frederic Waldman conducting.

9 NOVEMBER 1972
Prayer of the Emperor of China on the Altar of Heaven on 21 December 1539 by the American composer Ron NELSON, scored for a variety of

Sinoid percussion, a Chinese bell-tree, electric piano, piccolo playing in quarter tones, organ and chorus, and containing some aleatory passages, with the Emperor's prayer gradually submerged in the flood of tinkling and jangling sounds, is performed for the first time at Lawrence University in Appleton, Wisconsin, as a work commissioned for its 125th anniversary.

12 NOVEMBER 1972

Rudolf FRIML, Prague-born American composer of successful operettas, among them *The Firefly, Rose Marie* and *The Vagabond King,* as well as songs such as *Donkey Serenade* and *Indian Love Call,* dies in Hollywood twenty days before his ninety-third birthday.

15 NOVEMBER 1972

Chronoplastic for orchestra by the 43-year-old Japanese composer Joji YUASA is performed for the first time in Tokyo.

16 NOVEMBER 1972

Heliogabalus Imperator, a musical allegory by Hans Werner HENZE, is performed for the first time by the Chicago Symphony Orchestra as a commissioned work on the occasion of the orchestra's eightieth anniversary. A highly dissonant and flamboyantly sonorous orchestration quite realistically represents the advent to the Roman Empire of the adolescent Syrian Varius Avitus, who elevated the Assyrian god Baal to the pantheon of the Roman deities and who reigned under the name Heliogabalus to render homage to Helios, the sun, to which Baal was sacred, who erected a statue of Baal with a giant phallus of black stone imported from Syria, who ostentatiously deflowered a vestal virgin in front of a Christian church, and who was finally murdered with his equally paganized mother by outraged Roman soldiers in A.D. 220.

22 NOVEMBER 1972

Ninth Symphony by the scholarly Viennese octogenarian Egon WELLESZ, composed in seventeen days in 1971, set in three cyclic movements of a Baroque triptych in an expressionistic quasi-dodecaphonic idiom bristling with acoustically acute thematic major sevenths and minor ninths, maintained in somber tones and concluding in a hymnal mood, is performed for the first time in Vienna.

24 NOVEMBER 1972

Anti-Concerto for clarinet and orchestra by Paul Walter FÜRST is performed for the first time in Vienna, by the Austrian Radio Orchestra, with the soloist playing abnormal music on a normal clarinet.

55

27 November 1972

Symphony in F-sharp by the erstwhile wunderkind Erich Wolfgang KORNGOLD, cast in luscious modalities of late German romanticism, reaches a belated first performance, many years after the composer's death, by the Munich Philharmonic.

28 November 1972

Havergal BRIAN, Nestor of British music, who through the long years of nonrecognition obdurately persisted in composing large orchestral works until he exceeded Miaskovsky's record of symphonic proliferation by writing thirty-two symphonies, dies at last in his rural home at Shoreham-by-the-Sea, Sussex, England, at the age of ninety-six.

10 December 1972

Leo SMIT conducts the Buffalo Philharmonic in the first performance of his symphonic poem *Caedmon*.

16 December 1972

Winter Solstice for soprano, baritone, chorus and instruments by the 58-year-old Polish composer Andrzej PANUFNIK is performed for the first time in London.

27 December 1972

Anna LOCKWOOD, the eccentric composer from New Zealand, sinks an upright piano in Little Matthew Lake on the Toad Hall Ranch in Amarillo, Texas, to a depth of three feet, leaving it there to continue sinking in the muddy bottom, while her husband, Harvey Matusow, brandishes a bottle of gin and blows a cadenza on his clarinet.

27 December 1972

Fourth Symphony by the 49-year-old Serbian composer Vasilije MOKRANJAC, set in a single movement in which all ideas are derived from the opening twelve-tone row, is performed for the first time in Belgrade.

ᘛ 1973 ᘚ

5 January 1973

Pierre BOULEZ conducts in New York the first performance of his innovative score . . . *explosante/fixe* . . . for vibraphone, harp, violin, viola, cello, flute, clarinet, trumpet and Halaphone—a computerized electronic instrument named after its inventor Peter Haller and capable of projecting individual sounds metamorphosed as to pitch and timbre according to programmed instructions, thus acting as a superior stochastic transponder —projecting the modified sounds vectorially around the hall via flexibly positioned loudspeakers in fixed explosions (hence the title, derived from an essay by the grand prophet of Surrealism André Breton).

12 JANUARY 1973
Moira, "music in C for large orchestra," a tribute to the Greek goddess of Fate, by Werner EGK is performed for the first time in Nuremberg.

12 JANUARY 1973
Steel Symphony by the 39-year-old Spanish-born composer Leonardo BALADA is performed for the first time by the Pittsburgh Symphony Orchestra.

14 JANUARY 1973
Speculum Speculi (Mirror of a Mirror) for flute, oboe, bass clarinet, double-bass, piano, vibraphone, four drums and three gongs by the 34-year-old American composer Charles WUORINEN, representing "a sectional set of variations," with a dodecaphonic matrix serialized to correspond proportionately to the duration of each thematic note, so that intervallic leaps are from a shorter note to a longer one, is performed for the first time in Grand Forks, North Dakota, by an ensemble called Speculum Musicae.

18 JANUARY 1973
Tintomara, opera by the romantically conservative 46-year-old Swedish composer Lars Johan WERLE, dealing with a mystical creature named Tintomara and bearing reference to the regicide in Sweden in 1792 (which was also the subject of Verdi's opera *Un ballo in maschera*), is produced in Stockholm.

18 JANUARY 1973
Raumzeit Y (Space-time Y) by the German modernist Dieter SCHNEBEL is performed for the first time in Düsseldorf.

23 JANUARY 1973
Third String Quartet by Elliott CARTER, conceived as an interplay and a contest of two duos, one of a violin plus cello and one of a violin and viola, in the characteristically Carterian system of metrical modulation here megametrically expanded to a simultaneity of noncoincident sections (one dual group plays four sections against the other's six), and tempo marks as divergent as Maestoso pitched against a simultaneous

Furioso, all these tremendous complexities somehow resulting in the creation of a serene concordance of uncompromising dissonances, is performed for the first time by the Juilliard String Quartet in New York.

28 JANUARY 1973
Treemonisha, opera by the black ragtime pianist Scott JOPLIN (who died of tertiary syphilis in an insane asylum in New York on 4 April 1917), to his own libretto portraying in a series of set pieces and arias permeated with the spirit of Afro-American songs and rhythms, the story of a black baby girl found under a tree near Texarkana by the compassionate woman Monisha (who, naturally, names her Treemonisha), involving Negro plantation scenes and weird voodoo rituals, enlivened by Joplin's infectious ragtime rhythms, receives its first full stage production threescore and ten years after its composition, by an all-black cast as the final event of the Afro-American Musical Workshop Festival at Morehouse College in Atlanta, Georgia, orchestrated by T. J. Anderson and conducted by Robert Shaw. (An early production in concert form was given by Joplin in New York in 1915.)

6 FEBRUARY 1973
As a demonstration of the perishability of music, an upright piano is dropped to its utter destruction from a chartered helicopter from an altitude of 300 feet near the Detroit airport under the auspices of radio station WDET.

7 FEBRUARY 1973
Chamber Concerto for double-bass by the 31-year-old Swedish composer Ulf GRAHN is performed for the first time in Santa Barbara, California.

7 FEBRUARY 1973
Love's Labour's Lost, opera by the 69-year-old Russian-born American composer Nicolas NABOKOV, in three acts, to a libretto by W. H. Auden and Chester Kallman after Shakespeare, is performed for the first time in its original English version by the West-Berlin Deutsche Oper at its visiting appearance in Brussels.

8 FEBRUARY 1973
Makrokosmos, Volume I (*Twelve Fantasy-Pieces after the Zodiac for Amplified Piano*) by the American composer George CRUMB is performed for the first time in Colorado Springs. (Volume II is first performed in New York on 12 November 1974.)

9 FEBRUARY 1973
Kyldex I (abbreviation of Kybernetischluminodynamische Experimente) by the prime apostle of concrete music Pierre HENRY, set for five electronically activated erotic sculptures, human dancers, fifteen programmed

audiovisual sequences of variable durations determined by audience reaction, nine light-effect complexes, stroboscopic projections and a striptease (da capo ad lib.), extracurricularly accompanied by recorded dog barks and various assorted animal and human eructations, is produced in Hamburg.

19 FEBRUARY 1973

Roger SMALLEY conducts in London his *Strata* for strings, a macédoine of traduced quotations from works of Beethoven, Wagner, Mahler, Debussy, Schoenberg, Stravinsky, Anton von Webern, Ligeti, Stockhausen and Boulez.

28 FEBRUARY 1973

Violin Concerto by the 67-year-old French composer André JOLIVET is performed for the first time in Paris.

28 FEBRUARY 1973

The United States Postal Service puts out an eight-cent commemorative stamp for George GERSHWIN on the thirty-fifth anniversary of his death, in Beverly Hills, California, portraying a profile of Gershwin and a montage of characters from his opera *Porgy and Bess*.

3 MARCH 1973

Yaroslav the Wise, opera by the 70-year-old Ukrainian composer Yuli MEITUS, glorifying an early Russian prince, is produced in Donetsk.

9 MARCH 1973

Karlheinz STOCKHAUSEN conducts in London the first production of his multimedia pantomime *Ylem*, purporting to represent the formation of the primordial first substance (Hyle in Greek) which expands to a full-size universe and contracts to its initial atom every 80 billion years, with players instructed to wander and roam probabilistically with eyes closed carrying their instruments around and playing on them at will, finally congregating around the center of the contracted universe represented by a grand piano, electronium, three synthesizers and a closed television circuit.

16 MARCH 1973

Satyrikon, opera after Petronius by the 53-year-old Italian composer and conductor Bruno MADERNA, is produced in Scheveningen, Holland. (The first American performance was in Tanglewood, Massachusetts, on 6 August 1973.)

16 MARCH 1973

Universe, symphonic poem by the 37-year-old Soviet composer Alexander NEMTIN, reconstructed, recreated and synthesized from SCRIABIN's fragmentary sketches of his *Acte Préalable*, a preliminary to his projected cosmic *Mysterium*, and drawing more or less literally on Scriabin's piano pieces, the eighth sonata, *Guirlandes* and preludes from opus 74, and including a "color keyboard" paralleling Scriabin's own associations (C = red, G = orange, D = yellow, F-sharp = violet, etc.), with wordless chorus entering toward the end as it did in Scriabin's "Poem of Fire," *Prométhée*, is performed for the first time in Moscow under the direction of Kirill Kondrashin.

22 MARCH 1973
Second Piano Concerto by the foremost Argentine modernistic composer Alberto GINASTERA, completed by him only the day before, is performed for the first time by the prestidigital pianist Hilde Somer to whom it is dedicated, with the Indianapolis Symphony Orchestra under the direction of Izler Solomon. The work is in four movements, the first being a set of thirty-two variations on the seven notes D, F, A, C-sharp, E, G, B-flat of the abrasively dissonant initial chord of the second choral exposition of the Finale of Beethoven's *Ninth Symphony*, dodecaphonically developed by the complementary five notes; the second, a progressively polymetric *Scherzo* for the left hand alone; the third, a pensively homophonic *Quasi una fantasia*; and the last, *Cadenza e Finale*, a display of maximal pianofortitude with 1,860 eighth notes at ten per second and containing passages of sonic pandemonium with the application of tone clusters and aleatory interludes.

27 MARCH 1973
Levins Mühle (Levin's Mill), opera by the 29-year-old German composer Udo ZIMMERMANN, is produced in Dresden.

31 MARCH 1973
Fourth Symphony by the 66-year-old American composer Ross Lee FINNEY is performed for the first time in Baltimore.

8 APRIL 1973
Pantagleize, opera in three acts by the Viennese-born American composer Robert STARER, to an ironic political drama by the Belgian playwright Michel de Ghelderode in which a bumbling colonial general precipitates a revolution in an unnamed Belgian colony in West Africa by unwittingly uttering a secret signal "Oh, what a lovely day!" and scored in a highly dynamic atonal expressionistic idiom, with some mandatory injection of tetraphonic African motives, is produced at Brooklyn College.

14 APRIL 1973
Espace dernier, aleatory music for chorus, six instrumental groups and tape, completed by the 30-year-old Rumanian composer Costin MIEREANU in 1965, is performed for the first time in Royan, France.

16 APRIL 1973
Milena, cantata for soprano and orchestra by the brilliant Argentine composer Alberto GINASTERA, to texts from Kafka's letters, is performed for the first time in Denver, Colorado.

17 APRIL 1973
Infidelio, chamber opera by the 66-year-old British composer Elisabeth LUTYENS, completed in 1956, is given a belated first performance in London.

19 APRIL 1973
Violin Concerto, subtitled *Les Mécanismes de la mémoire,* by the 30-year-old Spanish composer Tomás MARCO, is performed for the first time at the Royan Festival in France.

20 APRIL 1973
The Picture of Dorian Gray, ballet after Oscar Wilde by the 67-year-old Russian composer Boris ARAPOV, is performed for the first time in Leningrad.

21 APRIL 1973
Violin Concerto by the American composer Ben WEBER is performed for the first time in Atlanta, Georgia.

21 APRIL 1973
Metamorphic Variations for orchestra by the 81-year-old British composer Sir Arthur BLISS is performed for the first time in London under the direction of Leopold Stokowski.

23 APRIL 1973
Myshkin, opera by the 38-year-old American composer John EATON, after *The Idiot* by Dostoyevsky is produced in Bloomington, Indiana.

23 APRIL 1973
Trumpet Concerto by the American composer Fisher TULL is performed for the first time in Houston with James Austin as soloist and Lawrence Foster conducting the Houston Symphony Orchestra.

23 APRIL 1973
Genesis, opera by the 41-year-old Australian composer Malcolm WIL-LIAMSON, is performed for the first time in London.

28 APRIL 1973
Musica Sacra for string orchestra by Alexander TCHEREPNIN is performed for the first time during the Easter Festival in Lourdes, as lame and halt

worshippers gather from all parts of the world in hope of a supernatural cure.

4 MAY 1973
Requiem by the prolific Swiss composer Frank MARTIN is performed for the first time in Lausanne.

4 MAY 1973
Gilgamesh, opera by the 40-year-old Danish composer Per NØRGAARD, is produced in Aarhus.

5 MAY 1973
Transformations, opera by the 38-year-old American composer Conrad SUSA, inspired by a poem by Anne Sexton, with symbolic themes illustrating the characters and events of children's fairy tales transmuted into surrealistic images, is performed for the first time by the Minnesota Opera in Minneapolis.

8 MAY 1973
Collage for string quartet, woodwind quartet and percussion by the 49-year-old Manchurian-born Russian-reared American composer Benjamin LEES (his natal family name was Lysniansky), the title referring to the collating of two independent musical groups and to thematic contents of their parts while wood blocks and snare drums punctuate the rhythms, is performed for the first time as a commissioned work at the University of Wisconsin in Milwaukee.

10 MAY 1973
Unter dem Milchwald, opera by the 38-year-old German composer Walter STEFFENS, to a libretto fashioned from the poem *Under Milkwood* by Dylan Thomas, is produced in Hamburg.

15 MAY 1973
Notturno by the 42-year-old American composer Donald MARTINO, scored for a chamber ensemble and resonant percussion, set in three distinguishable movements and nineteen perceivable subsections making use of preliminary noises, key-clicks of the flute and clarinet, blossoming into tones of definite pitch, is performed for the first time in New York, and later awarded the Pultizer Prize.

19 MAY 1973
Second Symphony by the English composer Havergal BRIAN, completed in 1931, is performed posthumously for the first time in Brighton.

25 MAY 1973

Piano Concerto by the Hungarian-American composer George BARATI is performed for the first time under the composer's direction in Santa Cruz, California.

31 MAY 1973

The trilogy *Lustro* by the 39-year-old Canadian composer R. Murray SCHAFER, consisting of three separately composed works—*Divan i Shams i Tabriz* for seven singers, tape and orchestra; *Music for the Morning of the World* for voice and tape; and *Beyond the Great Gate of Light* for seven singers, tape and orchestra—is performed for the first time in its entirety in Toronto.

5 JUNE 1973

Canticum Canticorum Salomonis (Solomon's Song of Songs) for chorus and orchestra by Krzysztof PENDERECKI is performed for the first time in Lisbon, under the composer's direction.

14 JUNE 1973

Seventh Symphony by the 64-year-old Serbian composer Milan RISTIĆ is performed for the first time in Belgrade.

16 JUNE 1973

Death in Venice, opera by Benjamin BRITTEN, after the novella of that name by Thomas Mann, is produced at the Aldeburgh Festival in England. It centers upon the fateful trip to Venice of an aging famous German writer Gustav Aschenbach (the name means a brook of ashes), where he platonically observes an Apollonian Polish adolescent boy disporting himself with Grecian grace on the beach, leading to his dismaying realization of forbidden love, and ultimately succumbing to the raging cholera epidemic, and is written in an austere, yet dramatic manner: Aschenbach's part is almost entirely in recitative; the Polish youth is represented choreographically, without words. (Thomas Mann himself visited Venice in 1911 and saw there the prototype of the Polish boy portrayed in his novella. As an old man, living in Sweden, the hero of *Death in Venice* recalled seeing Thomas Mann in Venice sixty years earlier. A motion picture based on *Death in Venice* changed Gustav Aschenbach to a composer, strongly suggesting Gustav MAHLER, and making use of Mahler's music on the soundtrack. This act of artistic travesty was denounced by Mahler's family and surviving friends. Mann had incurred the anger of Arnold SCHOENBERG for appropriating his musical genius in the novel *Doctor Faustus*; see Part Two, 13 November 1948, below.)

17 JUNE 1973
Masada 967, opera in fifteen scenes by the 62-year-old Polish-born Israeli composer Josef TAL, is performed for the first time in Jerusalem.

18 JUNE 1973
The Forty-seventh Festival of the International Society for Contemporary Music opens in Reykjavik with the following program of works by Icelandic composers:

Quartet for flute, clarinet, bass clarinet and horn by 27-year-old Jónas TÓMASson. *Five Pieces* for piano in a neoromantic vein by 32-year-old Halflidi HALLGRÍMSSON. *Requiem* by the prime composer of Iceland, Jón LEIFS (1899–1968).

19 JUNE 1973
On the second day of the Forty-seventh Festival of the International Society for Contemporary Music in Reykjavik, the following program is chamber music by Scandinavian composers is presented at an afternoon concert:

OHM by the 42-year-old Norwegian Arne NORDHEIM. *Pieces* for solo flute by the 51-year-old Norwegian composer Finn MORTENSEN. *Sonatina* for woodwind quintet by the 51-year-old Trieste-born Norwegian resident composer Antonio BIBALO. *Yan Guan* by the 44-year-old Norwegian composer Siguard BERGE. *Quintet* for woodwinds by the 22-year-old Finnish composer Erkki SALMENHAARA. *Etwas für . . .* for woodwind quintet by the 39-year-old Swedish composer Karl-Erik WELIN.

19 JUNE 1973
On the second day of the Forty-seventh Festival of the International Society for Contemporary Music in Reykjavik, the following program is given at an evening concert:

The Girl with an Umbrella for actor, guitar and tuba by the 37-year-old Greek composer Vasilis TENIDIS. *Musique piquante* for violin and piano by the 41-year-old Czech composer Marek KOPELENT, written in a candidly hedonistic manner. *Fourteen Epigrams for Oscar Wilde* by the 53-year-old Czech-born Israeli composer Jacob GILBOA, for speaker, piano and prerecorded piano played at double speed. *Suggestion* for clarinet solo by the 26-year-old Dutch composer Bart SCHURINK. *Meta-Phrases* by the American composer Homer LAMBRECHT, for saxophone and bass clarinet. *Lo tirtsakh* by the 37-year-old French composer Maurice BENHAMOU, for soprano, representing a vocal panorama of world terror from Hiroshima to the assassination of Martin Luther King (*Lo tirtsakh* means "Thou shalt not kill" in Hebrew). *Three Flutes and Percussion* by the 39-year-old Korean composer Chung Gil KIM, synchronizing Oriental and Occidental traits, with liberal application of dodecaphony. *Eidos* by the 47-year-old Japanese composer Hidenori TOKUNAGA, scored for saxophone and magnetic tape and representing the Socratic "idea" (eidos) of the universality of the human mind. *Chamber Concerto* for twelve performers by the 26-year-old Norwegian composer Olav Anton THOMMESSEN.

20 JUNE 1973
On the third day of the Forty-seventh Festival of the International Society for Contemporary Music in Reykjavik, the following program is presented:

An Old Song of the Sun and the Moon and the Fear of Loneliness for soprano, flute, piano and electronic sounds by Paul PEDERSEN of Canada. *Toccata* for soprano and flute by Harry FREEDMAN of Canada. *Synchronisms VI* for piano and magnetic tape by the Argentine-born American composer Mario DAVIDOVSKY. *Récit de Deux pour Trois Exécutants* for soprano, flute and piano by Bengt HAMBRAEUS of Sweden. *Trialogue* for soprano, flute and piano by the Canadian composer John WEINZWEIG. *Madrigal IV* for soprano, flute, piano and magnetic tape by Bruce MATHER of Canada. *Goathemala* for soprano and flute by the Belgian composer Karel GOEYVAERTS. *Voice* for flute and electronics by the Japanese composer Toru TAKEMITSU. *Bizzarreries* for flute, piano and magnetic tape by Atli Heimir SVEINSSON of Iceland.

21 JUNE 1973
On the fourth day of the Forty-seventh Festival of the International Society for Contemporary Music in Reykjavik, *A Tea Symphony or The Perils of Clara*, "a kitsch opera in nine drinks" for soprano, flute and piano by Gabriel CHARPENTIER, with a libretto by the composer, is presented at a noon concert.

21 JUNE 1973
On the fourth day of the Forty-seventh Festival of the International Society for Contemporary Music in Reykjavik, the following program is presented at an afternoon concert:

Tautologos, a flexible piece for instruments by Luc FERRARI of France. *Thanks to St. George* for cello solo by the Swedish composer Olov FRANZÉN. *Mimicry*, an onomatopoeic piece imitating sounds of nature by Bengt-Emil JOHNSON of Sweden. *Albumblätter* for piano by Luca LOMBARDY of Italy. *Stamp Music* by Ingvar LIDHOLM of Sweden. *Extrasensory Conception IV* by Sten HANSON of Sweden. *Quo vadis?* by Anders ELIASSON of Sweden.

21 JUNE 1973
On the fourth day of the Forty-seventh Festival of the International Society for Contemporary Music in Reykjavik, the following program is presented at an evening concert:

Dream about a House, a pantomime with orchestral accompaniment by the 39-year-old Icelandic composer Leifur THÓRARINSSON. *Quasi niente*, a piece for relaxation, a soft chair, a dark room, closed eyes and open ears by the 40-year-old Swedish composer Arne MELLNÄS. *Etymon* for voice and instruments by the English composer James STEVENS. *Bagatelles* for instruments by the 40-year-old Austrian composer Franz ENDRES. *Three Bagatelles* for instruments by the 34-year-old Italian composer Armando GENTILUCCI. *Notturno* for orchestra by the 38-year-old German composer Helmut LACHENMANN. *Folk Music* for nonsynchronized orchestral groups by the 35-year-old Polish composer Zygmunt KRAUZE.

22 JUNE 1973
Second Symphony, subtitled *Copernican Symphony,* for soprano, baritone, chorus and orchestra by the 39-year-old Polish composer Henryk Mikolaj GÓRECKI, is performed for the first time in Warsaw.

22 JUNE 1973
On the fifth day of the Forty-seventh Festival of the International Society for Contemporary Music in Reykjavik, the following program of chamber music, mostly by German composers, is presented:

Music for piano and four speakers by Paul-Heinz DITTRICH. *La-Sen No. 2* for solo cello by Maki ISHII of Japan. *Sotto voce* for flute, violoncello and piano by Friedhelm DOHL. *Trigolium* for flute, violoncello and piano by Hans ZENDER. *Four Short Studies* for solo cello by Bernd Alois ZIMMERMANN. *mit/gegen sich selbst I* for flute and magnetic tape by Erhard KARKOSCHKA. *Multiple Five* for flute and cello by Roman HAUBENSTOCK-RAMATI of Austria. *Rondo* for piano by Niels Frederic HOFFMAN.

23 JUNE 1973
The Forty-seventh Festival of the International Society for Contemporary Music in Reykjavik concludes with a program of string quartets by the Dutch composers Ton DE LEEUW and Enrique RAXACH, and by the Polish master of modern music Witold LUTOSLAWSKI.

6 JULY 1973
Third Oboe Concerto by the 53-year-old Italian composer and conductor Bruno MADERNA is performed for the first time in Amsterdam.

6 JULY 1973
Otto KLEMPERER, grand master of the German art of imperious orchestral playing whose renditions of symphonies of Beethoven and Mahler bore the stamp of authentic greatness, but who as a non-Aryan was exiled by the racially besotted National Socialist clique that had held Germany in obscurantist thrall, dies in Zürich at the age of eighty-eight.

7 JULY 1973
La reine morte (The Dead Queen), lyric drama by the 65-year-old Italian composer Renzo ROSSELLINI, with a libretto after Henri de Montherlant

dealing with political and emotional upheavals at a Renaissance court, is performed for the first time in Monte Carlo.

18 JULY 1973
Krzysztof PENDERECKI conducts the London Symphony Orchestra in Peterborough Cathedral in the first performance of his *First Symphony*.

19 JULY 1973
Faciebat Anno 1973 for twenty-four violins and orchestra by the 48-year-old Rumania-born French composer Marius CONSTANT is performed for the first time in Paris.

27 JULY 1973
Cacega Ayuwipi, written for thirty-five percussion instruments (the title means "The Decorative Drums") by the American Indian composer Louis BALLARD, is performed for the first time in Washington, D.C.

1 AUGUST 1973
Gian Francesco MALIPIERO, grand master of Italian music, fertile composer of operas, symphonies, concertos and chamber works, dies in Treviso, at the venerable age of ninety-one.

7 AUGUST 1973
The Hidden Landscape for orchestra by the 26-year-old British composer Nicola LeFANU is performed for the first time in London.

13 AUGUST 1973
Thea MUSGRAVE, 45-year-old Scottish composer, conducts at a Promenade concert in London the first performance of her *Viola Concerto*, worked out on finely textured neo-Baroque lines, with her husband Peter Mark as soloist.

20 AUGUST 1973
De Temporum Fine Comoedia (A Play of the End of Time) by Carl ORFF, in three scenes, *The Sybils, The Anchorites* and *Dies Illa*, is produced in Salzburg.

22 AUGUST 1973
Lennox BERKELEY conducts in Birmingham, England, the first performance of his orchestral work *Voices of the Night*.

5 SEPTEMBER 1973
Tamu-Tamu (meaning "guests" in Indonesian), chamber opera in two acts by the most successful opera composer in the United States, Gian

Carlo MENOTTI, commissioned by the Ninth International Congress of Anthropological and Ethnological Sciences, with the libretto by Menotti himself, sung and partly spoken in English and Indonesian, the plot dealing with victims of American air attacks in Southeast Asia, is produced in Chicago.

9 SEPTEMBER 1973
Polyptyque, six images of the Passion of Christ, for violin and two string orchestras by the 83-year-old Swiss composer Frank MARTIN, is performed for the first time in Lausanne.

14 SEPTEMBER 1973
The Philadelphia Orchestra under the direction of Eugene Ormandy, the first American orchestra ever to visit China, presents a concert in Peking with a program including the *Third Symphony* by Roy HARRIS, MOZART's *Haffner Symphony* and the *First Symphony of* BRAHMS.

15 SEPTEMBER 1973
Yvonne, Prinzessin von Burgund, opera by Boris BLACHER, in which a sadomasochistic prince weds the ugliest bride he can find, with a score designed to express "the agony of suffering in the language of Euclid," and written in a characteristically Blacherian dissonantly rhythmic idiom, is produced in Wuppertal, West Germany.

22 SEPTEMBER 1973
Stone Litany—Runes from a House of the Dead by the British composer Peter Maxwell DAVIES, scored for mezzo-soprano and orchestra, is performed for the first time in Glasgow.

25 SEPTEMBER 1973
Cello Concerto by the Soviet composer Edison DENISOV is performed for the first time in Leipzig.

27 SEPTEMBER 1973
Jot, oder Wann kommt der Herr zurück?, a mock-mystical opera by the 50-year-old Swiss composer Klaus HUBER, in three parts entitled *Sandstone Figures, How to Heal Wounds* and *Concrete Theater*, with the action of theologically metaphysical content (the mysterious word Jot in the title may be the Berlin dialect for Gott, God), is produced in Berlin.

9 OCTOBER 1973
Initium, an orchestral work by Carlos CHÁVEZ, is performed for the first time by the Akron Symphony Orchestra.

9 OCTOBER 1973

Third Symphony, subtitled *Day's Nightmare*, by the 42-year-old Danish composer Ib Nørholm, is performed for the first time in Copenhagen.

11 OCTOBER 1973

Third Symphony by the 38-year-old Soviet Georgian composer Giya Kancheli is performed for the first time in Tbilisi.

14 OCTOBER 1973

The Truth About Windmills, chamber opera by the 66-year-old American composer Alec Wilder, is produced in Rochester, New York.

19 OCTOBER 1973

The City, suite for orchestra and narrator in five movements by the 40-year-old American troubadour Rod McKuen, professionally arranged from his semi-improvised tunes and rhythms by Paul Ruhland, in five sections, with the untutored "poet-composer" himself narrating his own lines, depicting in pseudo-Whitmanesque verbal images the various aspects of an American city, is performed for the first time by the Louisville Orchestra under the direction of Jorge Mester.

20 OCTOBER 1973

Autumnmusic for orchestra and electronic sound by the 46-year-old American composer Donald Erb is performed for the first time in New Haven, Connecticut.

20 OCTOBER 1973

Queen Elizabeth II of England officially opens the giant opera house of Sydney, Australia, designed in the form of a ship under full sail by the Danish architect Jørn Utzon at a cost of about $150 million and fourteen years in construction, the ceremony being followed by a performance of Beethoven's *Ninth Symphony* by the Sydney Symphony Orchestra conducted by Willem Van Otterloo. (Actually, the initial public performance at one of the four different auditoriums of the Sydney Opera House was given on 28 September 1973, when Prokofiev's opera *War and Peace* was performed.)

22 OCTOBER 1973

Pablo Casals, the greatest master of the cello of the twentieth century and a noble spokesman for universal peace, who left his native Spain after it was captured by the fascistic General Franco, and who eventually settled in Puerto Rico, the native island of his mother, dies at the patriarchal age of ninety-six in San Juan.

25 October 1973

First Violin Concerto by Bohuslav MARTINŮ, composed in 1932, in three movements, which lay dormant for forty years, is brought to a belated performance by the Chicago Symphony Orchestra, fourteen years after Martinů's death, with soloist Josef Suk, grandson of the composer Josef Suk and great-grandson of Dvořák, Georg Solti conducting.

26 October 1973

Mutazioni for orchestra by the 30-year-old East German composer Udo ZIMMERMANN is performed for the first time in Dresden.

28 October 1973

Soundscapes I for flute, bass clarinet, English horn and percussion by the 31-year-old Swedish composer Ulf GRAHN is performed for the first time in Washington, D.C.

30 October 1973

Masada, oratorio by the 41-year-old American composer Marvin David LEVY, depicting in dramatic diction the heroic defense of a group of Jewish patriots who chose death rather than surrender in the last struggle of Judea against Roman soldiery at the ancient Jewish fortification of Masada, composed as a montage of tonal blocks superimposed on a collage of melodic patterns including synagogal cantillation, is performed for the first time in Washington, D.C.

2 November 1973

Son of Heldenleben by the Canadian composer R. Murray SCHAFER, based on the themes of the quasi-autobiographical symphonic poem of Richard Strauss, is performed for the first time by the Pittsburgh Symphony Orchestra.

3 November 1973

Matrix Symphony (Sinfonia da requiem) for narrator and orchestra by the 55-year-old Croatian composer Branimir SAKAČ, in three movements, *Ylem*, *Caspar Casparius* and *Gentle Fire*, constructed upon a matrix with serial submatrices, is performed for the first time in Opatija, Yugoslavia.

3 November 1973

Noon I! Kwak, a neo-Mayan exclamation by a San Franciscan teen-ager, Jim NOLLMAN, for seventeen performers consisting of thirty-three respirations accompanied by a continuous "duration chorus" reciting in equal time pulses "kwak, kwak, kwak . . . ," is performed for the first time in a tunnel in Golden Gate Park in San Francisco.

4 NOVEMBER 1973
Concerto for violin, cello and string orchestra by Halsey STEVENS, written in an alternately lyric and compactly modern style, is performed for the first time by the University of Southern California Symphony Orchestra, with soloists Eudice Shapiro and Gabor Rejto, Daniel Lewis conducting.

11 NOVEMBER 1973
First Symphony by the prolific Canadian composer Violet ARCHER, is performed for the first time in Vancouver.

13 NOVEMBER 1973
Ani Maamir, oratorio by Darius MILHAUD (the title means "I believe" in Hebrew), composed in the manner of a Biblical confabulation of the three patriarchs Abraham, Isaac and Jacob, demanding justice for the Jewish people from God, who eventually comes down and weeps with them, is performed for the first time in New York.

13 NOVEMBER 1973
Bruno MADERNA, modernistic Italian conductor and composer, a man of tremendous hulk (estimated avoirdupois, 100 kilos) the result of unrestrained bulimia, a bon vivant having an insatiable appetite for young female flesh (he acquired a 15-year-old girlfriend when he was 31), dies of inoperable cancer in Darmstadt, West Germany, where he lived, conducted and taught, at the age of 53.

14 NOVEMBER 1973
Enivrez-vous (Get Drunk!), "new electroacoustical experiment," by the pioneer of musique concrète Pierre HENRY, an agglomeration of sonorous structures generated by six tape recorders, two triple systems of perpetual aleatory music and a complex modulator of impulses and beats, plus Tibetan trumpets, ornithological trills, Hindu prayers, quotations from Monteverdi, and a waltz by Johann Strauss, is produced in Bordeaux, under the composer's direction.

18 NOVEMBER 1973
Alois HÁBA, Czech pioneer of music in quarter tones, third tones and sixth tones, who codified microtones and developed a special notation for them, dies in Prague at the age of eighty. (His younger brother, Karel Hába, also a valiant investigator of mini-intervals, predeceased Alois almost exactly by one year, dying in Prague on 21 November 1972.)

20 NOVEMBER 1973
Interval, a scoreless aleatory piece by Karlheinz STOCKHAUSEN for piano four hands, to be performed by two blindfolded pianists, who had to

be friends, is realized in New York by two female pianists, one of whom had to be brought from Washington, D.C., because the first pianist did not have a close piano-playing friend in New York.

21 November 1973

Piano Concerto by William KRAFT, timpanist of the Los Angeles Philharmonic, written in a modernistically romantic genre with a plethora of percussion, is performed for the first time by the Los Angeles Philharmonic, Zubin Mehta conducting, Mona Golabek soloist.

21 November 1973

Piano Concerto by the 49-year-old British composer Gerard SCHURMANN is performed for the first time in Portsmouth with John Ogdon as soloist.

4 December 1973

Centering, explicitly "closed-form" notated work for violin and ten instruments by the American musical innovator Earle BROWN, containing a mobile inner structure as the only reference to the "open-form" method of composition proselytized by him in most of his works wherein constituent sections and fragments can be freely reordered, is performed for the first time in Manchester, England.

5 December 1973

Gli Spaziali (The Space People), opera by Wladimir VOGEL, in three interlingual parts, *Leonardo da Vinci* (in Italian and German), *Roman de la Lune*, after Jules Verne (in French and German), and *Present Exploration of the Universe* (in German, English and Russian), set in a dodecaphonized neo-Renaissance polyphonic manner, is produced in Zürich.

6 December 1973

Fourth Symphony by Elie SIEGMEISTER, in four classically symmetric movements, scored for a very large orchestra, including a whole arsenal of Western and exotic percussion instruments, and written in a sharply aggressive dissonant idiom relieved by unapologetically melodious passages, is performed for the first time by the Cleveland Orchestra under the direction of Lorin Maazel.

9 December 1973

Candomblé, song cycle for soprano, piano and percussion by the 64-year-old Croatian composer Bruno BJELINSKI, based on sacred texts of Afro-Brazilians and incorporating stylistic elements of Latin American folklore, is performed for the first time in Zagreb.

14 December 1973

Variations and Epilogue for cello and orchestra by the 70-year-old Russian-born American composer Nicolai LOPATNIKOFF is performed for the first time by the Pittsburgh Symphony Orchestra, William Steinberg conducting.

30 December 1973

Henri Paul BUSSER, French composer and conductor, author of numerous operas, ballets, concert overtures and organ pieces, who served as conductor at the Paris Opéra for nearly half a century, dies in Paris in the fullness of his years at the patriarchal age of one hundred and one.

30 December 1973

Istrianic Frescoes, cantata by the 67-year-old Croatian composer Boris PAPANDOPULO, inspired by frescoes found in the churches in Beram, Istria, in three movements, *The Three Kings, Dance of Death* and *The Angels Sing*, is performed for the first time in Zagreb.

1974

4 January 1974

Hans Werner HENZE conducts in London the first performance of his *Stimmen (Voices)*, an album of twenty-two songs for mezzo-soprano, tenor and fifteen players manipulating some eighty different instruments, to texts of Italian, German, Cuban and American ballads, reflecting Henze's radical politics.

4 January 1974

Two musical stamps are issued in Czechoslovakia by the Federal Ministry of Post and Communications: one commemorating the centennial of the birth of the Bohemian composer Josef SUK, and one for the sesquicentennial of the birth of Bedřich SMETANA, each in the denomination of sixty hellers.

14 January 1974

Tenth Symphony by the turbulently romantic Swedish composer Allan PETTERSSON, set (as most of his symphonies) in one throbbing movement, and the only one to end in fortissimo, receives its first public performance in Stockholm (a recorded performance was broadcast over Swedish Television on 16 December 1973). The composer himself was in absentia, confined to a hospital bed tormented by chronic rheumatoid arthritis.

15 JANUARY 1974
Piano Personnage for piano and chamber ensemble by the 48-year-old Rumanian-born French composer Marius CONSTANT is performed for the first time in Paris.

23 JANUARY 1974
Colori ed improvvisazioni for orchestra by the 62-year-old Finnish composer Erik BERGMAN is performed for the first time anywhere in Zeeland, Holland.

24 JANUARY 1974
Introduction and Masque by the erstwhile prodigy of British music 23-year-old Oliver KNUSSEN, is performed for the first time by the Boston Symphony Orchestra.

28 JANUARY 1974
Valiant Deed, symphonic poem by the 94-year-old Galician-Ukrainian composer Stanislaus LUDKEWYCZ, glorifying the brave exploit of a revolutionary fighter, is performed for the first time in Kiev.

1 FEBRUARY 1974
Through and Through for orchestra by the 31-year-old Swedish composer Sven-David SANDSTRÖM is performed for the first time in Stockholm.

2 FEBRUARY 1974
Jean ABSIL, prolific Belgian composer whose variegated piano pieces and other works represent the golden mean of performable and listenable modernistic music, dies in Brussels at the age of eighty.

3 FEBRUARY 1974
On the occasion of the centennial of Gertrude Stein, a piece by Charles AMIRKHANIAN, entitled *she she and she*, for three male voices, is broadcast from Berkeley, California.

5 FEBRUARY 1974
Sganarelle, one-act comic opera by the Canadian composer Violet ARCHER, to her own libretto based on the first of the several plays of Molière wherein Sganarelle appears as an old duped fool, is produced in Edmonton, Canada.

5 FEBRUARY 1974
Five separate works by the 31-year-old Rumanian composer Costin MIEREANU, *Amnar, Rod, Amurg, Zbor* and *Apo*, collectively described as "reécriture spatio-temporelle," scored for chamber groups, film and tape, are performed for the first time in Paris.

9 February 1974

Concerto for orchestra, three electric guitars, piano, saxophone and percussion by the 41-year-old Soviet composer Sergei SLONIMSKY, in three sections, dramatic, lyric and festive, concluding with a simulacrum of a jam session, is performed for the first time in Leningrad.

15 February 1974

Kurt ATTERBERG, dean of Swedish music, composer of a number of sonorous symphonies and several impressively dramatic operas regularly performed by the Royal Opera of Sweden, guardian of eternal musical values solidly rooted in four-part harmony, dies in Stockholm at the age of eighty-six.

16 February 1974

Einstein, opera by the 79-year-old German composer Paul DESSAU, in which Einstein laments dodecaphonically that his discoveries resulted in the atomic murder of Hiroshima and Nagasaki and who is actually manhandled by an American military policeman when he resists the attempt by authorities to force him to cooperate in further atomic research, and whose two colleagues reflect the Manichean polarity of good (Communist) and bad (Imperialist) states of soul, is produced in East Berlin.

19 February 1974

Elevamini (First Symphony) by the 42-year-old Australian composer Malcolm WILLIAMSON, in three movements, written in 1957 in a style of sustained triads, rhythmic exertion and serial melos, is performed for the first time in Liverpool.

22 February 1974

Kosmochromie I for four loudspeakers and orchestra by the 63-year-old Dutch composer Berend GILTAY is performed for the first time in Utrecht.

23 February 1974

Breakfast Rhythms for clarinet and five instruments by the 35-year-old American composer Joan TOWER is performed for the first time in New York.

25 February 1974

Concerto for Orchestra by the British composer Richard Rodney BENNETT is performed for the first time in Denver.

1 March 1974

Das Orchester by the 39-year-old cosmopolitan Slovenian composer Vinko GLOBOKAR, in five suggestive sections (*Independence, Dependence, Promenade, Machine* and *Metamorphosis*) representing a free "happening" analyzing the historically important instrumental ensemble, is performed for the first time in Bonn, sans a baton-wielding, constricting conductor.

4 MARCH 1974
The first performance of *La cubana, oder ein Leben für die Kunst*, vaudeville by Hans Werner HENZE, is broadcast by NET Opera Theater in New York. (The stage premiere took place the following year, in Munich on 28 May 1975.)

5 MARCH 1974
The Seagull, opera by Thomas PASATIERI with a libretto based on a play by Chekhov, centered on the character of a young woman who is unloved and has to feed herself emotionally on psychological debris like a seagull in the wake of a brilliantly lighted ship, is produced for the first time in Houston, Texas.

10 MARCH 1974
Antoine et Cléopâtre, opera by Emmanuel DE BONDEVILLE, after Shakespeare's play, thematically based on two leading motives, one for Anthony and one for Cleopatra, immersed in fluid impressionistic harmonies, is produced in Rouen, France.

13 MARCH 1974
The Story of Vasco, opera by the 35-year-old British composer Gordon CROSSE, dealing with an Italian barber caught in a European war in the middle of the nineteenth century who, unwittingly recruited as a spy for the losing side, is unexpectedly proclaimed as a hero and dies in dodecaphonic glory, is produced by the Sadler's Wells Company in London.

15 MARCH 1974
L'Héritière, opera by Jean-Michel DAMASE, in which a rich father who cannot forget that in childbirth his daughter was the unwitting cause of death of her mother and who breaks her engagement to the man she loves by cutting off her inheritance, set to music in a mildly modernistic idiom, is produced in Nancy, France.

16 MARCH 1974
The Catiline Conspiracy, opera by the Scottish composer Iain HAMILTON, to a libretto by the composer based on Ben Jonson's play and centered on Cicero's famous apostrophe (Quousque tandem Catilina abutere patientia nostra?—How long then, Catilina, will you abuse our patience?) is performed for the first time in Stirling, Scotland.

17 MARCH 1974

Mockery, a scherzo for piano and dancer written in 1933 by the American composer John J. BECKER, is given its belated premiere in a posthumous performance in New York.

21 MARCH 1974

Second Symphony by the 47-year-old Rumanian composer Anatol VIERU is performed for the first time in West Berlin.

23 MARCH 1974

Music for Prague for band by the 47-year-old Prague-born Americanized composer Karel HUSA, in four diversified movements, with the third movement, *Interlude*, scored for percussion instruments only, and with the last section including a series of improvisations, the total effect being an integral representation of the historic, social and cultural aspects of the great city, is performed for the first time in Washington, D.C. (A revised version of the score, for full orchestra, was performed for the first time in Munich on 31 January 1970.)

26 MARCH 1974

The Beach of Falesá, first opera by the Welsh composer Alun HODDINOTT, based on a short story by Robert Louis Stevenson, is produced by the Welsh National Opera Company in Cardiff, Wales.

30 MARCH 1974

Dorian Gray, opera by the Dutch composer Hans KOCH, after the novel by Oscar Wilde in which the portrait of the beauteous English lad painted by one of his admiring friends grows old, while Dorian himself engages in "love that dares not speak its name," is produced in The Hague.

30 MARCH 1974

Music for a Summer Evening by George CRUMB for two amplified pianos and two percussionists busily blowing penny whistles and shaking thunder sheets, subtitled *Makrokosmos III*, in five romantically inspired movements suggesting a Kantian categorical imperative in a system of practical reason, *Nocturnal Sounds, Wanderer-Fantasy, The Advent, Myth* and *Music of the Starry Night*, with epigraphs from Quasimodo, Pascal and Rilke, is performed for the first time in Swarthmore, Pennsylvania.

16 APRIL 1974

Incident at Wounded Knee by the American Indian composer Louis BALLARD, scored for chamber orchestra and evoking the tragic massacre of the Oglala Sioux Indians in the Dakotas in the nineteenth century, in four sections, *Procession, Prayer, Blood and War* and *Ritual*, is performed for the first time in St. Paul, Minnesota.

17 April 1974

Aum (Om) for harp and orchestra by the 40-year-old English-born American composer Bernard RANDS, the title being a mantric word of three sounds representing the hypostatic union of Brahma, Vishnu and Siva, is performed for the first time in London.

27 April 1974

Two works by the 30-year-old Finnish composer Leif SEGERSTAM, *Patria* for orchestra and *Six Songs of Experience*, after Blake and Auden, for soprano and stereophonically placed conductorless orchestra, are performed for the first time in Stockholm.

1 May 1974

The Image of Man for chorus and orchestra by the 42-year-old American composer Michael COLGRASS is performed in Spokane, Washington, in a world premiere.

3 May 1974

This Music Seems Very Familiar, comic skit based on materials from Mozart's operas by the 39-year-old Danish composer Bent LORENTZEN, scored for four singers and tape, is performed for the first time in Kiel, West Germany.

5 May 1974

Seventh Symphony by the 52-year-old British composer Malcolm ARNOLD is performed for the first time in London.

5 May 1974

The Winter of the World for cello and chamber ensemble by the 67-year-old British composer Elisabeth LUTYENS is performed for the first time in London.

8 May 1974

The Gates of the Dream for soloists, chorus and orchestra by the 60-year-old British musicologist and composer Wilfrid MELLERS is performed for the first time in York, England.

16 May 1974

Dybbuk by Leonard BERNSTEIN, a ballet based on the Yiddish mystical play by Shlomo Ansky in which the errant spirit of a dead young man enters the body of his bereaved bride who then has to be torturously exorcised by knowledgeable rabbis to save her body and soul, is choreographed for the first time in New York by Jerome Robbins and his ballet troupe.

17 MAY 1974

New England's Prospect for choruses, narrator and orchestra by the 47-year-old American composer Donald ERB, commissioned for the one hundredth anniversary of the Cincinnati May Festival, is performed there for the first time.

20 MAY 1974

Sinfonia Concertante for flute, harp and strings in two movements by the Polish composer Andrzej PANUFNIK, now dwelling in England, numerically his *Fourth Symphony*, gravitating to the tonal center of C, expressing his devotion to his wife whose name was Camilla, but avoiding the use of explicit major or minor C triads, is performed for the first time in London.

23 MAY 1974

Dali for large orchestra by the 22-year-old American avant-garde composer Richard HAYMAN, composed at the command of Salvador Dali and microscopically notated on a toothpick with instructions to "ascend chromatically in slow pulse," is performed for the first time in New York.

24 MAY 1974

Edward Kennedy ELLINGTON, known to the world of popular music as Duke Ellington, who created a Harlem "jungle style" of big band playing characterized by piercing trumpets and intensely syncopated jazz rhythms, and who himself composed orchestral and choral music in the elevated concert manner of the blues, dies in New York at the age of seventy-five.

28 MAY 1974

Eighth Symphony by the 65-year-old Serbian composer Milan RISTIĆ, in three movements, the elegiac middle one being a eulogy for Ristić's teacher, Alois Hába, is performed for the first time in Belgrade.

5 JUNE 1974

Arnold SCHOENBERG's mortal remains are brought back from Los Angeles, where he died on 13 July, 1951, to his native Vienna during the centennial year of his birth.

8 JUNE 1974

An American Requiem by the 60-year-old avant-garde American composer Henry BRANT, a memorial observance of the Watergate scandal, to a text from the Old Testament, with seventeen instrumentalists sitting on the stage and five others spatially scattered in the concert hall, is performed for the first time in Mt. Lebanon, Pennsylvania.

11 JUNE 1974

Thea MUSGRAVE conducts the first performance, in Aldeburgh, England, of her opera *The Voice of Ariadne*, after a novella by Henry James, *The Last of the Valerii* with the action, taking place in Rome in 1870, concerned with Marco Valeri, who digs up an ancient statue of the goddess Juno in his Roman estate and becomes so infatuated with his find that his American wife decides to rebury it, the "voice of Ariadne" symbolizing Valeri's neglected wife.

14 JUNE 1974

It Is Not Here, light-and-sound piece by the 22-year-old American avant-gardist Richard HAYMAN, is realized in Morse code at the Museum of Modern Art in New York.

18 JUNE 1974

Cendrées for chorus and orchestra by Iannis XENAKIS, creator of a mathematically logical stochastic style of composition, is performed for the first time in Lisbon.

22 JUNE 1974

Darius MILHAUD, noble French composer who began his career as a member of the modernistic group Les Six and who by the strength of his inventive talent organized the modern techniques of polytonality and polyrhythmics into a distinctive universal style of composition, whose catalogue embraces works of every genre, and who continued to compose music despite his long, crippling illness, dies in Geneva at the age of eighty-one.

23 JUNE 1974

The Strumpet, opera by the 47-year-old Czech composer Ivan JIRKO, is produced in Olomouć.

30 JUNE 1974

Chlopi (Townspeople), opera by the 61-year-old Polish composer Witold RUDZIŃSKI, depicting in passionate Polonian tones the heroic futility of the national Polish insurrection of 1863 against the Russians, is performed for the first time in Warsaw.

11 JULY 1974

Libertas, cantata in three movements for brass, chorus and orchestra by the 68-year-old Croatian composer Boris PAPANDOPULO, an homage to the free and artistic city of Dubrovnik during the fifteenth through eighteenth centuries of its existence, with the motto, "Non bene pro toto libertas venditur auro" (Liberty cannot be sold for gold), is performed for the first time in Dubrovnik.

25 July 1974

Symparanekromenoi for orchestra by the 30-year-old Hungarian-born Canadian composer John FODI, the title being a Greek polynome translatable as *Those who are living lives that are spiritually entombed*, is performed for the first time in Toronto.

8 August 1974

The original version of *Chords* for orchestra by the 31-year-old American composer Fred LERDAHL, designed as a mosaic of alternatively consonant and dissonant chords, is performed for the first time at the Berkshire Music Center in Tanglewood. (A revised version was performed for the first time by the New York Philharmonic under the direction of Arthur Weisberg on 3 June 1983.)

17 August 1974

This Worlde's Joie, oratorio to words from early English texts by the Welsh composer William MATHIAS, in four sections designed to reflect the seasons of the year and the span of human life, is performed for the first time at the Fishguard Music Festival, Wales.

3 September 1974

Harry PARTCH, American "transcontinental hobo," as he liked to style himself, who during his wanderings fashioned a whole band of home-made instruments to which he attached folksy names, such as blow-boys (a hybrid of bellows and an automobile horn), dies in San Diego, California, at the age of seventy-three.

3 September 1974

Shenandoah, ingratiatingly tuneful musical play by Gary GELD, a nostalgic recollection of the terrible battle in the Shenandoah Valley in 1862 during the American Civil War, is produced in East Haddam, Connecticut, preliminary to its New York opening 23 December 1974.

6 September 1974

Le Jeu de Sainte Agnes, "ecclesiastical action" to texts from a fourteenth-century manuscript by the 49-year-old Rumanian-born French composer Marius CONSTANT, scored for six singers, five actors, one dancer, Hammond organ, electric guitar, trombone and percussion, is performed for the first time in Besançon.

19 September 1974

Ghost and Dream Dancing for orchestra by the 40-year-old British composer Anthony GILBERT is performed for the first time in Birmingham.

6 OCTOBER 1974

Mack and Mabel, a musical comedy by Jerry HERMAN relating in sentimental semifictional tones the unmarried amours of the American silent
movie producer Mack Sennett and his beloved Mabel Normand, is produced in New York.

11 OCTOBER 1974

Violin Concerto by the Ukrainian-born Canadian composer George
FIALA is performed for the first time in Winnipeg.

12 OCTOBER 1974

Fête galante et pastorale, space music for a castle by the 36-year-old
Polish composer and pianist Zygmunt KRAUZE, utilizing thirteen tapes and
six instrumental groups, is performed for the first time in Graz, Austria.

18 OCTOBER 1974

Third Symphony by the English composer Havergal BRIAN, completed
in 1932, is given its first performance posthumously, broadcast by the
BBC in London.

20 OCTOBER 1974

Tristan, richly allusive score by Hans Werner HENZE for piano, orchestra
and recorded tapes, in six movements, containing quotations from a
medieval troubadour song, *Lamento di Tristan,* as well as references to
Wagner's *Tristan und Isolde,* with a climatic discordant uproar epit-
omizing the social turmoil of the modern world, is performed for the
first time in London by the London Symphony Orchestra, Colin Davis
conducting.

20 OCTOBER 1974

Brass Quintet by the 65-year-old American composer Elliott CARTER,
arranged in a neo-Baroque manner with instrumental groups forming
transitory concertinos, and with each instrument specializing in an
individually apportioned interval, is performed for the first time in
London, broadcast by the BBC.

20 OCTOBER 1974

O-ke-wa by the fearlessly dissident American composer Daniel LENTZ,
a ritual chant to onomatopeic words of the Seneca Indian tribe, scored
for twelve voices, two drummers and four bone raspers shuffling around
the audience from dusk to dawn shaking small bells with piercing
sounds, is performed for the first time, under the direction of the
indomitable composer himself, in Rotterdam, Holland, by the group
called San Andreas Fault, so named after the major fracture of the
earth's crust running northwestward through southern California.

22 OCTOBER 1974

The Forty-eighth Festival of the International Society for Contemporary Music, held in Holland, opens in Rotterdam with the following program:

Gieter (*Watering Can*) for orchestra by the 23-year-old Dutch composer Guus JANSSEN, in five movements arranged in a steadily decelerating progression, with one instrument after another committing a musical hara-kiri, figuratively disemboweling itself until only a whiff of rarefied air remains at the end. *Parodia ad Perotinum* by the 40-year-old German composer Georg KRÖLL, based on an organum of the great master of the Ars Antiqua (*parodia* here means emulation, not parody). *Heaventree* by the 26-year-old British composer Nigel OSBORNE, a poem of poems, represented by the polymorphic world of European verse, with the matrix assembled from Latin, French, German, Italian, Russian and Polish vocables, in four movements, based on fricative, vocal, plosive and nasal sounds. *Chronoplastic* for orchestra by the 45-year-old Japanese composer Joji YUASA, a member of the transsonic group of Tokyo, the work being a combination of static and kinetic fields with transitional mutations of both the temporal (chrono) and spatial (plastic) elements fused in the cosmic environment and leading to terrestrial catharsis.

23 OCTOBER 1974

Karlheinz STOCKHAUSEN conducts the South West German Radio Symphony in London in the first performance of his work *Inori*, employing a mime as a tacit soloist with an electronic ensemble.

23 OCTOBER 1974

On the second day of the Forty-eighth Festival of the International Society for Contemporary Music the following program of electronic music is presented at an afternoon concert in Utrecht:

Les ailes by the 49-year-old Polish composer Wlodzimierz KOTOŃSKI, in which the wings in the title indicate the eternal desire of humankind to fly into cosmic spaces. *Basic Barrier*, a computerization by the Hungarian composer Támás UNGVARY, representing an inexorable separation of finite human entities. *Keiserens nye slips* (*The King's New Necktie*) generated by a computer and ending in a sonic vacuum symbolic of the nonexistent cravat. *Alphas und andere Rhythmen* by the 31-year-old German physicist Ulricke TRÜSTEDT, and her husband, 35-year-old Dieter TRÜSTEDT, a synthetic piece generated by statistic impulses, various sequencers and square wave beats.

23 OCTOBER 1974

On the second day of the Forty-eighth Festival of the International Society for Contemporary Music, the following program of orchestral music is given in an evening concert in Utrecht:

A Song of Degrees by the 33-year-old American composer Curtis SMITH, in which piano strings are bowed under the lid. *Innervation II* by the 28-year-old Japanese composer Masaru TANAKA, in which the floating rhythms are supposed

83

to affect the nervous system. *Parodie* by the 36-year-old Korean composer Junsang BAHK, scored for flute, cello, percussion and electroacoustic equipment. *Bien* by Tona SCHERCHEN, modernist daughter of the conductor Hermann Scherchen, representing constant mutations of sonic ingredients without altering the indivisible entity of the goodness implied in the title. *Rotation* by the 27-year-old Persian composer Doriansch DOWLATSHAHI, derived from classical Iranian modes. *Aerophonie* by the 35-year-old German composer Wilfried MICHEL, structured along sonorific lines.

24 OCTOBER 1974
Eleventh Symphony by the prolific Swedish composer Allan PETTERSSON is performed for the first time in Bergen, Norway.

24 OCTOBER 1974
On the third day of the Forty-eighth Festival of the International Society for Contemporary Music in Holland, the following program of chamber music is presented in Rotterdam:

Limine for string trio by the 36-year-old Italian composer Davide ANZAGHI, based on an interplay of long sustained notes and florid atonal counterpoint. *Tre Studi per Quattro* for four recorders by the 56-year-old German composer Jürg BAUR, a compendious work of rotating thematic fragments, overblown harmonic tones and aleatory episodes. *Annäherung* for brass by the 23-year-old German composer Christian DETHLEFFSEN, expressing erotic approximations. *Trio* for harp, viola and oboe by the 31-year-old German composer Hans DARMSTADT. *String Quartet* by the 27-year-old Japanese composer Katsuhiro TSUBONOH.

25 OCTOBER 1974
On the fourth day of the Forty-eighth Festival of the International Society for Contemporary Music the following program is presented in Rotterdam:

Arabeschi by the 42-year-old Italian composer Niccolò CASTIGLIONI. *Cello Concerto* by the 48-year-old American original Morton FELDMAN. *Abschied,* symphonic poem by the 36-year-old Dutch composer Reinbert DE LEEUW, reflecting the paroxysm and expiration of nineteenth-century romanticism.

26 OCTOBER 1974
On the fifth day of the Forty-eighth Festival of the International Society for Contemporary Music the following afternoon program of orchestral music is presented in Rotterdam:

Tre Pezzi by Rob DU BOIS. *The Magic of Music* for chorus by Ton DE LEEUW. *Sound of Silence* for brass band by Tera de Marez OYENS. *Sound Poem in Shikara Tala* for chorus by David PORCELIJN. *Sage de Vénise* for percussion by John HELSDINGEN. *Milaraspa* for two choruses, eight instrumental groups and narrator by Bernard VAN BEURDEN.

26 October 1974
On the fifth day of the Forty-eighth Festival of the International Society
for Contemporary Music in Holland, the following program is presented
at an evening concert in The Hague:

Lied per tredici (13) strumenti by the 47-year-old Italian composer Franco
DONATONI, based on thirteen sounds subordinated to fifteen variants in thirty-
two beats. *Wind Quintet* by the 29-year-old English composer Stephan Peter
LAWSON. *Fond Youth Is a Bubble* by the 21-year-old English composer Bene-
dict MASON. *A Pair of Wings* for three sopranos by the 24-year-old English
composer Nicholas SACKMAN to text by the fifteenth-century English poet
Stephen Hawes. *Quanta* for violin and wind ensemble by the 33-year-old
Brazilian composer Fernando CERQUEIRA. *Elements of Logic* by Jan VRIEND,
36-year-old Dutch composer, and Jos KUNST, 38-year-old Dutch composer,
working in collaboration, scored for an impressive ensemble of five flutes, seven
clarinets, six bassoons, nine saxophones and brass, the logic in the title being
the syllogism leading from given premises to the total reorganization of the
world and the philosophy of humankind.

27 October 1974
On the sixth day of the Forty-eighth Festival of the International Society
for Contemporary Music in Holland the following program of orchestral
music is presented at an afternoon concert in Amsterdam:

The Machine by the 39-year-old Dutch composer Otto KETTING, based on a
single ten-tone chord, with the anachronistic C major scale intruding into the
orderly progression of thematic elements. *Aura* by the generally admired and
deeply mourned Italian composer and conductor Bruno MADERNA (1920–
1973), inspired by the contrapuntal art of the Italian masters of the Renaissance.
Through and Through by the 32-year-old Swedish composer Sven-David
SANDSTRÖM, the title alluding to the lengthy melodic line symbolic of the
indestructibility and interminability of true art. *Prelude, Interlude et Aprèslude*
by the 67-year-old Japanese composer Yoritsuné MATSUDAIRA, written in a free
form of old Japanese dances in which the tempi of participating instruments are
not compatible.

27 October 1974
On the sixth day of the Forty-eighth Festival of the International Society
for Contemporary Music in Holland the following program of orchestral
music is presented at an evening concert in Amsterdam:

Fan It by the 29-year-old Dutch composer Jacques BANK, suggesting that the
music is an ever-expanding and contracting fan. *Querimonia* for cello and orchestra by the 29-year-old French composer Jacques LENOT, based on a twelve-
tone series that gradually annexes alien twelve-tone themes until it expands to
sixty tones, with the cello querimoniously sticking to the primordial dodecaphonic series. *Sette Canzoni alla tristezza* by the 26-year-old Italian modernist
Claudio BILUCAGLIA, the seven songs of sadness of the title referring to the

seven recent deaths of Stravinsky, G.M. Gatti, Casals, Picasso, Neruda, Malipiero and Maderna.

28 OCTOBER 1974
The Forty-eighth Festival of the International Society for Contemporary Music in Holland concludes in Hilversum with the following afternoon program:

Opus 6 by the 21-year-old German composer Wolfgang VON SCHWEINITZ, with several flutes playing in monodic conjunction against heterophonic strings. *Lunar Possession Manual 1973* for soprano and various instruments by the 29-year-old American-born composer of Dutch extraction Burr VAN NORSTRAND, with subliminal selenological allusions to calendarical lunacy of Endymionlike youths. *Rondo* by the 27-year-old Italian composer Salvatore SCIARRINO for flute solo accompanied by a shimmering ensemble of violins. *Aus aller Welt stammende* by the 36-year-old Polish composer Zygmunt KRAUZE, based on a folk melody of central Poland. *Second Concerto* for piano and nineteen instruments by the 36-year-old German composer Aribert REIMANN.

1 NOVEMBER 1974
Double-bass Concerto by the 62-year-old French composer Jean FRANÇAIX is performed for the first time in Frankfurt.

9 NOVEMBER 1974
Egon WELLESZ, greatly cultured composer of the Viennese school, an early associate of Schoenberg, who was also an eminent music historian and lucid analyst and codifier of the modalities of Byzantine music, dies in his ninetieth year, in Oxford, England, where he held a professorship at the University after being forced by the Nazis to leave his native Vienna.

10 NOVEMBER 1974
Six Grand Pianos Bash Plus Friends by the 61-year-old American composer Henry BRANT, scored for six grand pianos, three piccolos, trumpet, trombone and percussion, is performed for the first time in Riverdale, New York City.

12 NOVEMBER 1974
Makrokosmos, Volume II *(Twelve Fantasy-Pieces after the Zodiac for Amplified Piano)* by the American composer George CRUMB is performed for the first time in New York. (Volume I was first performed in Colorado Springs on 8 February 1973.)

15 NOVEMBER 1974
A Bayou Legend, opera by the dean of American black composers William Grant STILL, to a libretto by his wife, Verna Arvey, reflecting an old

legend of the region of Biloxi within a stone's throw of Still's own birthplace in Woodville, Mississippi, in which a young Cajun falls in love with an astral creature, is hanged for consorting with spirits, but unites with her in the beyond, written in a melodious operatic style fertilized by sensitively authentic Southern melorhythms, is produced for the first time, thirty-three years after its composition, by the all-black troupe of Opera/South in Jackson, Mississippi.

17 NOVEMBER 1974

Fifth Symphony by the Yugoslav composer Aleksandar OBRADOVIĆ, in a symmetrically subdivided single movement, is performed for the first time in Opatija.

20 NOVEMBER 1974

Des Canyons aux étoiles, grandiose musicorama for piano and orchestra by the 65-year-old French composer Olivier MESSIAEN, inspired mainly by the topography and ornithology of Bryce Canyon in Utah, replete with Messiaenic songbird calls against an instrumental accompaniment including the specially designed Eolophone (wind machine) and Geophone (earth machine, a tray of sand shaken harmoniously), in twelve tableaux depicting the ascent from the deep canyons to stars in the sky, is performed for the first time in New York by Musica Aeterna, which commissioned the work, with Messiaen's wife Yvonne Loriod, wearing a star-studded gown, as piano soloist and Frederic Waldman conducting.

21 NOVEMBER 1974

Frank MARTIN, eminently cultured Swiss composer, whose operas, symphonic, choral and chamber music are marked with spiritual distinction and technical fluency embracing the entire spectrum of modern devices including modified dodecaphony, dies in his adoptive home in Naarden, Holland (he was married to a Dutch woman), at the age of eighty-four.

21 NOVEMBER 1974

Eighth Symphony by Peter MENNIN, cast in four movements, each with Biblical overtones, *In the Beginning, Day of Wrath, Out of the Depths* and *Praise Ye the Lord*, written in a straightforward neoclassical style with the tonal foundation clearly in evidence through a complex and often dissonant network of well-placed notes, is performed for the first time by the New York Philharmonic, Daniel Barenboim conducting.

1 DECEMBER 1974

The Ministry of Post and Communications of Czechoslovakia issues a postage stamp in honor of the Czech violinist František ONDŘÍČEK (1857–1922), with an impressive photographic image of him holding a violin under his right arm.

6 DECEMBER 1974

Charles WUORINEN, the intransigent American composer, plays with the New York Philharmonic, Erich Leinsdorf conducting, the solo part in the world premiere of his one-movement *Second Piano Concerto*, for an electronically amplified piano exercising a sonic hegemony, with the orchestra functioning as a duplicator, fragmentor and integrator of the discordant musical materials.

9 DECEMBER 1974

Holly from the Bongs, opera by the 37-year-old British composer Gordon CROSSE, is produced in Manchester.

11 DECEMBER 1974

Sixth Symphony in four neoclassically ordained movements by the 76-year-old Italian-American composer Vittorio RIETI is performed for the first time in New York.

13 DECEMBER 1974

Hod po mukah Ambroza Matije Gupca zvanog Beg (The Torturous Journey of Ambrose Matija Gubec, Named Beg), scenic oratorio by the 67-year-old Croatian composer Ivan BRKANOVIĆ, an epic portrayal of the bloody peasant uprising in Croatia of 1573, led by Gubec, is produced in Zagreb.

20 DECEMBER 1974

André JOLIVET, brilliant composer of instrumental and vocal music in a modernistic vein, with elements of classicism, romanticism and impressionism, integrated into a distinct personal idiom which included occasional dodecaphony and electronic sound, who traveled far and wide to conduct concerts of his works, organized in Paris a progressive performing group Spirale and in his leisure moments wrote poetry, dies in Paris at the age of sixty-nine.

26 DECEMBER 1974

Knudåge RIISAGER, prolific symphonic composer of modern Denmark, author of numerous pragmatically effective instrumental works and imaginatively constructed ballets, dies in Copenhagen at the age of seventy-seven.

∽ 1975 ∾

8 JANUARY 1975
San Francisco Polyphony by György LIGETI, spiraling forth from a melorhythmic pulse in the eye of the sonorific hurricane to extreme turbulence as a transcendental image of the grand city of St. Francis with its heterogeneous topography and eclectic Occidental-Oriental population, its imposing modern edifices, and its ancient Spanish missions over the bay, is performed for the first time by the San Francisco Symphony under the direction of Seiji Ozawa.

8 JANUARY 1975
Richard TUCKER, the son of Jewish immigrant parents in New York, whose real name was Reuben Ticker, who reached the summit of singing artistry as a leading tenor at the Metropolitan Opera House, dies suddenly of a heart attack in Kalamazoo, Michigan, on the day of an announced concert there, at the still vigorous age of sixty-one.

9 JANUARY 1975
The Chagall Windows for orchestra by the 35-year-old English composer John McCABE, inspired by the phantasmagorically colorful stained-glass windows by the Russian-Jewish-French-American painter Marc Chagall, is performed for the first time by the Hallé Orchestra in Manchester England.

13 JANUARY 1975
Fourth Symphony by the 39-year-old Soviet Georgian composer Giya KANCHELI, commemorating the semimillennium of the death of Michelangelo, in a single movement, is performed for the first time in Tbilisi. (The U.S. premiere was given by the Philadelphia Orchestra on 13 January 1978.)

18 JANUARY 1975
Ein wahrer Held (A Real Hero), opera by the 49-year-old German composer Giselher KLEBE, after Synge's play *The Playboy of the Western World*, is performed for the first time in Zürich.

6 FEBRUARY 1975
A new version of Samuel BARBER's opera *Anthony and Cleopatra*, radically rewritten and reorchestrated, with the libretto restructured by Gian Carlo MENOTTI, and the musical fustian and tinsel removed from the original

score of the abortive production at the Metropolitan Opera House in New York on 16 September 1966, is performed anew under the direction of Menotti at the Juilliard School of Music in New York.

13 FEBRUARY 1975
Prismen for flute, oboe, clarinet, harp, percussion and orchestra by the 67-year-old German composer Wolfgang FORTNER is performed for the first time in Basel.

14 FEBRUARY 1975
Das Geheimnis des entwendeten Briefes, opera by the German composer Boris BLACHER, after *The Purloined Letter* by Edgar Allan Poe, is produced in Berlin.

19 FEBRUARY 1975
Luigi DALLAPICCOLA, the Italian composer whose cosmopolitan ideals and modern expertise in dodecaphonic techniques did not affect the profoundly Italian essence of his music, dies in Florence at the age of seventy-one.

21 FEBRUARY 1975
Still and Moving Lines of Silence in Families and Hyperbolas, a fantastical aleatory divertissement by the fearlessly nonconformist 43-year-old radical American composer Alvin LUCIER, is performed for the first time in New York.

14 MARCH 1975
Quintet Concerto for two trumpets, French horn, trombone, tuba, and orchestra by the 58-year-old American composer Ulysses KAY is performed for the first time in New York.

15 MARCH 1975
Galileo Galilei for vocal soloists, chorus and orchestra by the 49-year-old American composer Lee HOIBY, glorifying the Italian astronomer who set the earth in motion in defiance of the clerical edict legislating that it should stand still, is performed for the first time in Huntsville, Texas.

20 MARCH 1975
Turbae ad passionem Gregorianam, sacred work in a Gregorian manner by the 58-year-old Argentine composer Alberto GINASTERA, scored for three singers, choir of treble voices, mixed chorus and orchestra, is performed for the first time as a commissioned work by the Mendelssohn Club of Philadelphia on the occasion of its centennial.

27 March 1975
Sir Arthur BLISS, the English composer who began his career as a radical modernist early in the century, moderated his musical language to a point of total tonal respectability, was knighted in 1950 and appointed Master of the Queen's Musick in 1953, dies in London at the age of eighty-three.

2 April 1975
Pierre BOULEZ conducts the first performance of his orchestral work *Rituel in memoriam Bruno Maderna* in London.

4 April 1975
Violin Concerto by the 56-year-old American composer George ROCHBERG, in five movements, titled Introduction, Intermezzo, Fantasia, Intermezzo, Epilogue, wherein the odd-numbered sections are related in thematic and structural materials, whereas the two Intermezzi differ in mood, the first scherzoid, the second, lulling, the total being cast in an outspoken historical sequence of thematic and stylistic structures, ranging from the classically Mozartian to the post-Romantic modernistic techniques, illustrating Rochberg's return to the musical traditions, is performed for the first time by Isaac Stern and the Pittsburgh Symphony Orchestra conducted by Donald Johanos.

4 April 1975
Al Gran Sole Carico d'amore (the title, "In the great sun laden with love," is a line from a poem by Rimbaud), a panoramic socialistic opera by Luigi NONO, in several historic tableaux portraying the French Commune of 1871, Czarist Russia shaken by bloody revolt, social upheavals in Cuba and Chile, and culminating in the American debacle in Vietnam, with a female quartet commenting on the passing events as stages in class struggle, making use of dodecaphonic progressions as promulgated by Nono's father-in-law, Arnold Schoenberg, is produced in Milan.

11 April 1975
Ensembles for Seventeen by the 28-year-old Israeli pianist and composer Shulamit RAN, set for high female voice and sixteen instrumentalists, to a text from the concluding lines of *Othello.* is performed for the first time, and immediately repeated, by the Contemporary Chamber Players of the University of Chicago, Ralph Shapey conducting.

11 April 1975
The Dawns Are Quiet Here, opera by the 52-year-old Soviet composer Kirill MOLCHANOV, describing in a series of lachrymogenic scenes the horrors of the Nazi invasion of Russia, contrasted with the heroic

patriotic repulse, replete with folklike tunes and rousing military marches in the finest tradition of Socialist Realism, is produced at the Bolshoi Theater in Moscow.

16 APRIL 1975
Noise and Silence for harpsichord, celesta and percussion by the 43-year-old Soviet composer Sofia GUBAIDULINA is performed for the first time in Moscow.

19 APRIL 1975
Abaris ou Les Boréades, last opera by Jean-Philippe RAMEAU, completed by him shortly before his death in 1764, the plot dealing with a priest of Apollo in love with the Queen of Bactria, who cannot marry her because she is a Boréade, a descendant of the wind god Boréas, and must marry a windy relative, with a happy dénouement secured as Abaris opportunely discovers that he, too, is a boreal through his nymph mother, is performed 211 years after its composition for the first time anywhere by the Monteverdi Choir and Orchestra in London.

29 APRIL 1975
Two; onwards: inwards, outwards, (upwards, downwards) . . . around-wards . . . towards . . . for two pianos and orchestra by the 31-year-old Finnish composer and conductor Leif SEGERSTAM is performed for the first time in Helsinki.

1 MAY 1975
The government of Nicaragua issues a set of fifteen stamps depicting the world's greatest opera singers in their most famous roles alongside a musical excerpt from each particular opera, starting with the denomination of one centavo and featuring not only dead persons, according to philatelic convention (among them Melba, Chaliapin and Caruso), but also living singers (among them Callas, Nilsson and Gobbi).

2 MAY 1975
A Concord Cantata by the 76-year-old American composer Randall THOMPSON, written for the bicentennial of Concord, Massachusetts, is performed there for the first time.

8 MAY 1975
Roqué CORDERO conducts in Normal, Illinois, the first performance of his *Six Mobiles for Orchestra*.

10 MAY 1975
Karel HUSA conducts in Boulder, Colorado, the first performance of his piece for narrator and orchestra, *The Steadfast Tin Soldier*.

13 MAY 1975
Der lange Weg zur grossen Mauer (The Long Road to the Great Wall), opera by the Austrian composer Kurt SCHWERTSIK, is produced in Ulm.

14 MAY 1975
Fourth Symphony by the 31-year-old Polish composer Krzysztof MEYER is performed for the first time in Zagreb.

19 MAY 1975
Celebration for tape and orchestra by the 44-year-old American composer Roger HANNAY is performed for the first time in New York.

20 MAY 1975
i.330, opera by the 37-year-old French composer Jacques BONDON, to a libretto after the socio-futural novel *We* by the Russian expatriate author Eugene Zamiatin written in 1920, wherein humans of a remote future are forbidden to make love or to think, and are identified only by number and code letter under the rule of a "benefactor," set to music in an appropriately mechanistic idiom, is produced at Nantes.

27 MAY 1975
Ave Maris Stella by the 40-year-old British composer Peter Maxwell DAVIES, scored for flute, clarinet, marimba, piano, viola and cello, derived from medieval plainchant and consisting of nine contrasting sections forming a self-generative sonata principle, is performed for the first time at the Bath Festival by the music-theater group called The Fires of London.

3 JUNE 1975
Heaven Music by the 44-year-old avant-garde composer Larry AUSTIN, scored for a congregation of exulting flutes, is performed for the first time in Tampa, Florida.

18 JUNE 1975
Partizanka Ana (Freedom Fighter Anna), opera in one act by the 61-year-old Yugoslav composer Rado SIMONITI, depicting the Yugoslav people's fight against the Nazi forces, is produced in Ljubljana.

20 JUNE 1975
Simfonija Faronika for chorus and orchestra by the 78-year-old Slovenian composer Matija BRAVNIČAR is performed for the first time in Ljubljana.

24 JUNE 1975
Cello Concerto by the 45-year-old Spanish composer Cristóbal HALFFTER is performed for the first time in Granada, Spain.

24 JUNE 1975

Eighth Symphony, with chorus, subtitled *In candidum*, by the 82-year-old Swedish composer Hilding ROSENBERG is performed for the first time in Malmö.

8 JULY 1975

The Philosopher in the Kitchen, "gastronomic meditation" for contralto and orchestra by the 43-year-old German-born Canadian composer Lothar KLEIN, is performed for the first time in Toronto.

13 JULY 1975

Still Life, with Moonbeams for orchestra by the 30-year-old South African composer Peter KLATZOW is performed for the first time in Johannesburg.

17 JULY 1975

Ratsumies (The Horseman), opera by the 40-year-old Finnish composer Aulis SALLINEN, is produced at the Savonlinna Opera Festival.

9 AUGUST 1975

Dmitri SHOSTAKOVICH, supreme Soviet composer whose symphonies, concertos and chamber music created a powerfully dramatic and poignantly lyrical style that combined classically melodious and romantically harmonious manners of composition with a proclamatory modern idiom, dies of lung cancer in Moscow, at the age of sixty-eight.

2 SEPTEMBER 1975

Viimeiset Kiusaukset (The Last Temptations), opera by the 53-year-old Finnish composer Joonas KOKKONEN, to a libretto dealing with the Finnish evangelist Paavo Ruotsalainen, who revived the purity of the Finnish Lutheran church in the first half of the nineteenth century, set to music in a passionate hymnal style in sonorous Mussorgskian harmonies, is performed for the first time in Helsinki. (The first American performance took place at the Metropolitan Opera in New York on 26 April 1983.)

20 SEPTEMBER 1975

Captain Jinks of the Horse Marines, musical comedy by the 54-year-old American composer Jack BEESON, is performed for the first time in Kansas City, Missouri.

21 SEPTEMBER 1975

The Young Penis Symphony (a.k.a. First Symphonie) by the Korean composer Nam June PAIK is performed for the first time in San Francisco by a cast of ten young (and not so young) penises protruded through a Japanese rice paper curtain, followed by a female sequel, *La Mamelle (The Young Breast Symphony)*, composed by Ken FRIEDMAN, and featuring a pair of protruding mammary glands.

24 SEPTEMBER 1975
Lowell CROSS presents in Iowa City the total realization of SCRIABIN's symphonic poem *Prometheus*, including the mystic part for color organ *(luce)* on a specially designed electronic keyboard which coordinates color projections to accompany changes of pitch in the score, with James Dixon conducting the University of Iowa Symphony Orchestra.

11 OCTOBER 1975
Assembly and Fall, symphonic poem by Ned ROREM, is performed for the first time by the North Carolina Symphony Orchestra conducted by John Gosling.

20 OCTOBER 1975
Unseen Leaves for soprano, oboe, tapes, slides and lights by the 47-year-old American composer Lawrence Moss is performed for the first time in Washington, D.C.

21 OCTOBER 1975
Symphony 1972, Phoenix for orchestra by the 30-year-old South African composer Peter KLATZOW is performed for the first time in Cape Town (Kaapstad).

22 OCTOBER 1975
Third Symphony by the celebrated British novelist Anthony BURGESS (who began his career as a composer), in four movements, classically formal, romantically expansive and typically English in its tonal impact, with a literary coda for tenor and baritone from Shakespeare's *Love's Labour's Lost*, to the lines of the pedant Holofernes who sings a snatch of a Venetian ballad, accompanied by a mandolin, with ornithological allusions to the hooting of an owl, the spring song of the cuckoo and the trilling of the nightingale, ending in a formidable explosion of C major, is performed as a commissioned work by the University of Iowa Symphony Orchestra, conducted by James Dixon.

24 OCTOBER 1975
Twenty-sixth Symphony by the fantastically fertile American composer of Armenian stock Alan HOVHANESS, is performed for the first time in San Jose, California.

24 OCTOBER 1975

An die Nachgeborenen (To Posterity) for soloists, chorus and orchestra by the 57-year-old Austrian composer Gottfried VON EINEM is performed for the first time in New York.

25 OCTOBER 1975

The Forty-ninth Festival of the International Society for Contemporary Music opens in Paris with the following program:

Phases for orchestra by the 41-year-old Dutch composer Ton BRUYNEL. Le Départ pour la lune for electroacoustical tape by the 31-year-old French composer Georges BOEUF. Música para sintetizador for electroacoustical tape by the 44-year-old Argentine composer Francisco KRÖPFL. Thunders of Spring Over Distant Mountains for tape by the 32-year-old American composer Robert MORRIS. Pace for tape by the 44-year-old Norwegian composer Arne NORDHEIM. Aum for orchestra, thematically representing the mystical triad of sounds symbolizing Brahma, Vishnu and Siva by the English-born American composer Bernard RANDS (first performed in London on 17 April 1974). Sillages for orchestra by the 33-year-old Swiss composed Michel TABACHNIK. Stratus for orchestra by the 37-year-old Japanese composer Yoshihisa TAÏRA.

26 OCTOBER 1975

On the second day of the Forty-ninth Festival of the International Society for Contemporary Music in Paris the following works are presented:

Naissances for oboe and string trio by the 44-year-old French composer Claude LEFEBVRE. Ensaio for mezzo-soprano, double-bass and cymbals by the 38-year-old Brazilian composer Mario FICARELLI. Simulation for tuba solo by the 44-year-old Japanese composer Yori-Aki MATSUDAIRA. Two conjunct pieces by the 30-year-old Italian composer Fernando GRILLO: Paperoles for double-bass solo and Étoile for cello solo. Point/Lines for clarinet, tape and projections by the 28-year-old Polish composer Krzysztof KNITTEL. Disappearances for piano and band by the 38-year-old Swedish composer Bengt-Emil JOHNSON. Wild Flowers for two pianos by the 29-year-old British composer Michael FINNISSY. Segni for piano by the 38-year-old Italian composer David ANZAGHI. Frieze for four pianos by the 33-year-old American composer John McGUIRE. In memoriam Johannes Ockeghem for electronic tape by the 39-year-old Slovenian composer Ivan PARIK. Waga Kokora, Imada . . . for electronic tape by the 25-year-old Japanese composer Kazutaka TAZAKI. Mobile by the 44-year-old Polish composer Eugeniusz RUDNIK.

27 OCTOBER 1975

On the third day of the Forty-ninth Festival of the International Society for Contemporary Music in Paris the following program is presented:

Soria Moria for string orchestra by the 43-year-old Argentine composer Gerardo GANDINI. Ka for saxophone, double-bass and orchestra by the 37-year-old German composer Hans Joachim HESPOS. *D* for orchestra by the 28-year-old British composer Barry GUY. *Duel,* a ludibund piece for two orchestras and two conductors, by the mathematical Greek composer Iannis XENAKIS. The world premiere of *Prelude, Interlude and Postlude* for orchestra by the 68-year-old Japanese composer Yoritsune MATSUDAIRA.

27 OCTOBER 1975
The third day of the Forty-ninth Festival of the International Society for Contemporary Music in Paris continues at a night concert featuring the following program of electronic-acoustic works:

Epicentrum by the 25-year-old American composer Carter THOMAS. *La Panaderia* by the 36-year-old Argentine composer Eduardo KUSNIR. *Titre perdu* by the 24-year-old French composer Michel REDOLFI. *Slopes* by the 29-year-old British composer Denis SMALLEY. *Tokyo 1969* by the 42-year-old Japanese composer Toshi ICHIYANAGI.

28 OCTOBER 1975
On the fourth day of the Forty-ninth Festival of the International Society for Contemporary Music in Paris the following symphonic works are presented:

Me-Ti by the 27-year-old Italian composer Sandro GORLI. *Passage* by the 47-year-old Japanese composer Ryo ENDO. *Vagues, Chemins, le Soufflé* by the 29-year-old French composer Gérard GRISEY.

At a later concert on the same day, the following electronic works are presented:

Midnight by the 33-year-old Finnish composer Antero HONKANEN. *Bestiary* by the 30-year-old American composer Barry SCHRADER. *Panoramic sonore* by the 38-year-old Japanese composer Akimichi TAKEDA. *Aion* by the 36-year-old German composer Nicolaus HUBER.

30 OCTOBER 1975
The Forty-ninth Festival of the International Society for Contemporary Music in Paris concludes with the following program of symphonic works:

Befragung by the 27-year-old German composer Peter RUZICKA. *Portraitspiel* by the 35-year-old German composer Wilfried MICHEL. *Fumon 2* by the 45-year-old Japanese composer Hifumi SHIMOYAMA.

10 NOVEMBER 1975
Fifth Symphony, subtitled *We Are the Echoes,* by the German-born American composer Samuel ADLER, scored for mezzo-soprano and orchestra, is performed for the first time in Fort Worth, Texas.

10 November 1975

Utmost for wind quintet, trumpet, trombone, tuba and percussion by the 33-year-old Swedish composer Sven-David SANDSTRÖM is performed for the first time in London, Pierre Boulez conducting.

20 November 1975

Regnbueslangen (The Rainbow Snake) for orchestra by the 39-year-old Danish composer Erik NORBY, after an American Indian fable, is performed for the first time in Copenhagen.

21 November 1975

Aurora for orchestra by the 53-year-old Scottish composer Iain HAMILTON is performed for the first time in New York.

22 November 1975

Piano and Orchestra for piano and orchestra by the innovative American avant-gardist Morton FELDMAN is performed for the first time in Metz, France.

22 November 1975

Friedrich BLUME, grand master of German musicology, founder of the voluminous historical and biographical encyclopedia *Die Musik in Geschichte und Gegenwart*, dies in his native town of Schlüchtern, West Germany, at the age of eighty-two.

5 December 1975

Air Music, ten variations for orchestra by the 52-year-old American composer Ned ROREM, which was to win the 1976 Pulitzer Prize, marked by gay urbanity with a harmonious whiff of Parisian *je ne sais quoi*, is performed for the first time by the Cincinnati Symphony Orchestra, Thomas Schippers conducting.

8 December 1975

Mass in Honor of the Blessed Virgin Mary by the 62-year-old American composer Norman DELLO JOIO is performed for the first time in Washington, D.C.

16 December 1975

Der Kaiser von Atlantis, opera by the Austrian composer Viktor ULLMANN, written in 1944 at the Theresienstadt concentration camp in Czechoslovakia shortly before his transfer to Auschwitz where he was put to death, the score turning up in 1972 in the hands of the British conductor Kerry Woodward who restored the barely legible manuscript, is produced for the first time in Amsterdam.

98

⁓ 1976 ⁓

4 JANUARY 1976
A *Wisconsin Symphony* by the American composer Otto LUENING, reflecting the multifarious ethnic origins of the people of Wisconsin in some recognizable strains of regional folksongs and some unrecognizable modifications thereof (such as a retrograde version of the state song, "Oh, Wisconsin"), in four movements, scored for a lush orchestra magnified by electronic sonorities, is performed for the first time in Milwaukee, the composer's birthplace, Kenneth Schermerhorn conducting the Milwaukee Symphony Orchestra.

5 JANUARY 1976
Georges MIGOT, significant French composer whose music, though rarely played outside of France, has the appealing virtue of modern euphonism, dies in Levallois near Paris at the age of eighty-four.

6 JANUARY 1976
Oscar ESPLÁ, Spanish composer of fine Iberian-flavored instrumental and vocal pieces, dies in Madrid at the age of eighty-nine.

8 JANUARY 1976
Bi-Centurion for orchestra by the 68-year-old German-born American composer Gene GUTCHË, commemorating the United States bicentennial, is performed for the first time in Rochester, New York.

11 JANUARY 1976
Music for a Festive Occasion by the American composer Donald ERB, scored for orchestra, electronic sounds and forty water goblets, is performed for the first time by the Cleveland Orchestra, Lorin Maazel conducting.

13 JANUARY 1976
Concertino Pastorale, subtitled *A Forest Rhapsodie*, for two flutes and orchestra, by the American composer John BECKER (1886–1961), completed in 1933, containing a "Rustic Dance" that imitates the song of the meadowlark, written in a highly dissonant idiom, with the flutes tuned a quarter tone apart, is performed posthumously for the first time at the Cincinnati Conservatory of Music.

16 JANUARY 1976

Concerto for Piano Trio and Orchestra by the 61-year-old Italian composer Riccardo MALIPIERO, nephew of Gian Francesco Malipiero, is performed for the first time in Milan.

23 JANUARY 1976

Paul ROBESON, great black American bass whose performing genius extended to Shakespearean plays and whose singing was of extraordinary sonorous and yet profoundly lyric quality, but whose radical political beliefs aroused barbarian wrath among reactionary groups of the American populace, dies in Philadelphia at the age of seventy-seven.

24 JANUARY 1976

The Beth Alpha Mosaic for female voice, chamber ensemble and tape by the 55-year-old Czech-born Israeli composer Jacob GILBOA is performed for the first time in Chicago.

28 JANUARY 1976

Phlegra for eleven instruments by the 53-year-old Greek composer Iannis XENAKIS is performed for the first time in London.

29 JANUARY 1976

Concertmasters, a concerto for three violins and orchestra by the American composer Michael COLGRASS, a vividly Vivaldian triple concerto with proleptic leaps into dodecaphony and other modern devices, is performed for the first time by the violinists Gordon Staples, Bogos Mortchikian and Joseph Goldman with the Detroit Symphony Orchestra, Aldo Ceccato conducting.

4 FEBRUARY 1976

Portugalin nainen (The Woman of Portugal), opera by the 35-year-old Finnish composer Erkki SALMENHAARA, is produced in Helsinki.

5 FEBRUARY 1976

The Adequate Earth for two male narrators, baritone, three choruses and orchestra by the 49-year-old American composer Robert WYKES, set to Donald Finkel's poems about Antarctica, is performed for the first time in St. Louis.

10 FEBRUARY 1976

Thirteenth Symphony for speaker, chorus and orchestra by the prime American symphonist Roy HARRIS is performed for the first time by the National Symphony Orchestra in Washington, D.C., Antal Dorati conducting.

10 FEBRUARY 1976

Southern Harmony for orchestra by the 59-year-old American composer Ulysses KAY is performed for the first time in Raleigh, North Carolina.

13 FEBRUARY 1976

Lily PONS, glamorous French coloratura soprano whose slender beauty and thrush-like trills fascinated audiences in opera and solo recitals all over the world and whose fame reached such universality that a locality in Maryland was named Lilypons in her honor dies in Dallas, Texas, at the age of seventy-seven.

20 FEBRUARY 1976

Colloquy for orchestra, tape and various chairs by the Russian-born American composer Vladimir USSACHEVSKY is performed for the first time in Salt Lake City by the Utah Symphony Orchestra, Maurice Abravanel conducting.

20 FEBRUARY 1976

Dreamsound by the 24-year-old American avant-gardist Richard HAYMAN, a sleep event in which the composer makes various sounds for the benefit of slumbering participants, is snored for the first time in Berkeley, California.

24 FEBRUARY 1976

A Mirror on Which to Dwell for soprano and nine players by the 67-year-old American composer Elliott CARTER, to a cycle of six poems by Elizabeth Bishop, is performed for the first time in New York.

27 FEBRUARY 1976

Echoes from an Invisible World by Leslie BASSETT, a romantically impressionistic orchestral piece, with the title taken from a phrase by the Italian patriot Giuseppe Mazzini and suggesting reality reflected in the world of fantasy, is performed for the first time, as part of the American bicentennial celebration, by the Philadelphia Orchestra, conducted by Eugene Ormandy.

29 FEBRUARY 1976

Bilby's Doll, opera composed for the United States bicentennial by the 49-year-old American composer Carlisle FLOYD, wherein Doll, a young French girl brought to America by a sea captain named Bilby, is accused of witchcraft by Bilby's wife (who contends that Doll had caused to wither the fetus in her womb), eventually becomes herself convinced that she is a witch and prays for Satan to come to her rescue, is produced in Houston.

1 MARCH 1976
Jean MARTINON, French composer of modernistically programmatic symphonies and other works, who also had a fine career as a conductor in France and America, dies in Paris at the age of sixty-six.

3 MARCH 1976
Mary, Queen of Scots, ballet by the 36-year-old British pianist and composer John McCABE, is produced in Glasgow.

8 MARCH 1976
Piano Concerto by the American pianist and composer William BOLCOLM is performed for the first time by Bolcolm as soloist with the Seattle Symphony Orchestra, Milton Katims conducting.

11 MARCH 1976
Trombone Concerto by Donald ERB is performed for the first time by Stuart Dempster on the trombone with the St. Louis Symphony Orchestra under the direction of Leonard Slatkin.

11 MARCH 1976
Fifth Symphony by the 69-year-old American composer David VAN VACTOR is performed for the first time in Knoxville, Tennessee.

13 MARCH 1976
Concerto for violin, small orchestra and synthesized tape by Milton BABBITT, mathematically minded serial composer, is performed for the first time in New York.

19 MARCH 1976
Second Piano Concerto, subtitled *Landscapes of the Mind I* by the 49-year-old American composer Marga RICHTER, is performed for the first time in Tucson, Arizona, with William Masselos as soloist.

19 MARCH 1976
Vox Humana, song cycle by the melancholically existential Swedish composer Allan PETTERSSON, scored for organ, strings and voices, in three parts to words by Latin American proletarian poets and American Indian songsters, concluding with the poem *The Great Joy* by the communist Chilean Nobel Laureate Pablo Neruda, is performed for the first time on the Swedish Radio.

25 MARCH 1976
Cello Concerto by the Korean-born German-resident composer Isang YUN is performed for the first time in Royan, France.

30 MARCH 1976

Zodiac for orchestra by the English composer Richard Rodney BENNETT, a United States bicentennial commission, is performed for the first time by the National Symphony Orchestra under the direction of Antal Dorati in Washington, D.C.

31 MARCH 1976

Second Violin Concerto by the American composer Ross Lee FINNEY is performed for the first time by Robert Gerle on the violin with the Dallas Symphony Orchestra conducted by Louis Lane, to celebrate the one hundredth convention of the Music Teachers National Association.

1 APRIL 1976

Ines de Castro, opera by the 30-year-old American composer Thomas PASATIERI, based on an apparently true historical episode involving the mistress of Pedro I of Portugal who was assassinated by a court clique in 1355, whose corpse was exhumed by her imperial lover who forced her assassins to kiss her skeletal remains during her postmortem coronation, is produced in Baltimore.

1 APRIL 1976

Symphony of Spirituals by the American composer Morton GOULD is performed for the first time by the Detroit Symphony Orchestra under the direction of Aldo Ceccato.

1 APRIL 1976

Third Violin Concerto by David DIAMOND is performed for the first time by Piotor Janowski on the violin with the New York Philharmonic conducted by Leonard Bernstein.

2 APRIL 1976

Nicolaus Copernicus, oratorio by the 79-year-old Polish organist and composer Boleslaw SZABELSKI, composed to glorify the semimillennium of the birth of the great Polish astronomer who put the earth in axial and circumsolar motion, is performed for the first time in Poznań (actually with a calendarical delay of three years: Copernicus was born in 1473).

6 APRIL 1976

Tenth Symphony by William SCHUMAN, subtitled *American Muse*, in three symmetric movements—a slow movement flanked by two fast ones —is performed for the first time by the National Symphony Orchestra of Washington, D.C., Antal Dorati conducting, on the same program with two other world premieres of works by Schuman: *The Dead Young Soldiers*, for soprano, French horn, woodwinds and strings, a lamentation to words by Archibald MacLeish, and a new concert version of Schuman's baseball cantata, *Casey at the Bat*, for baritone-reciter, soprano, chorus and orchestra.

13 APRIL 1976

Sinfonia di Sfere (Symphony of the Spheres), the fifth symphony by the 62-year-old Polish-born British composer Andrzej PANUFNIK, in three palindromic movements, each of which evolves from a focal monomelodic cell, with the central section of the middle movement mirroring itself in an orgiastic dance, is performed for the first time in London.

14 APRIL 1976

Vaque-T'ao for orchestra by the 38-year-old Swiss-born French composer Tona SCHERCHEN-HSIAO, daughter of the famous conductor Hermann Scherchen, is performed for the first time in Paris.

15 APRIL 1976

Passion for solo voices, chorus and orchestra by the 43-year-old American composer Alan STOUT, with Christ portrayed by a male trio symbolizing the Trinity, employing occasional serial devices, aleatory passages and microtonal harmonies, is performed for the first time as a commissioned work by the Chicago Symphony Orchestra, Margaret Hillis is conducting.

23 APRIL 1976

Meeting for Equal Rights: 1866, cantata by the 62-year-old American composer Vivian FINE, is performed for the first time in New York.

24 APRIL 1976

Music for Eighteen Musicians for violin, cello, two clarinets, four pianos, four female voices, three marimbas, two xylophones and a metallaphone by the 39-year-old American composer Steve REICH, who unintentionally became the guru of modern minimalism by extracting a maximum effect from a minimum of musical material, is performed for the first time in New York.

24 APRIL 1976

Morton GOULD conducts the first performance of his *American Ballads* for orchestra, in Queens, New York.

24 APRIL 1976

The Voyage of Edgar Allan Poe, opera by the fertile American composer Dominick ARGENTO, depicting a hallucinatory voyage into Poe's past shortly before his death, recalling his marriage to a child bride, her early death, his recovery of her from the region of death, and her second final death, with copious quotations from Poe's poem *Annabel Lee*, is performed for the first time in St. Paul, Minnesota.

25 APRIL 1976
Magic, Magic, Magic for chorus and chamber orchestra by the 61-year-old American composer Gail KUBIK is performed for the first time in San Antonio, Texas.

25 APRIL 1976
Statement 1976 for soprano, chorus brass, strings and percussion by the 72-year-old American composer Irwin FISCHER, commemorating the United States bicentennial, is performed for the first time in New Haven, Connecticut.

28 APRIL 1976
Animus-Anima for orchestra by the 27-year-old Canadian composer Steven GELLMAN is performed for the first time in Paris.

2 MAY 1976
New Land, New Covenant for soloists, children's chorus, mixed chorus and orchestra by the 79-year-old American composer Howard HANSON, to words by Isaac Watts, T. S. Eliot, John Newton, the Bible and the Declaration of Independence, is performed for the first time in Bryn Mawr, Pennsylvania.

4 MAY 1976
Varii Capricci, a symphonic suite by the prime British composer Sir William WALTON, is performed for the first time in London. (A choreographed version was produced by the Royal Ballet in London on 19 April 1983.)

6 MAY 1976
America, 1976, choral symphony written for the American bicentennial by the 62-year-old Polish-American composer Jacques BERLINSKI, is performed for the first time in San Diego.

6 MAY 1976
Concerto for Bassoon and Low Strings in five movements by the remarkable 44-year-old Soviet composer Sofia GUBAIDULINA, of ethnic Tatar origin, in which the bassoon indulges in audacious acrobatic feats of atonal saltation with tricky trills, transcendental tremolos, labial glissandos and shrieks and laughter through the tube, accompanied by

four cellos and three double-basses in a visuviation of euphonious discords deployed over their entire diapason, is presented for the first time in the Hall of the Union of Soviet Composers in Moscow, with Valery Popov as soloist in a prescribed series of salto mortale virtuosity.

11 MAY 1976
Second Symphony with chorus by the 55-year-old American composer William BERGSMA, subtitled *Voyages*, is performed for the first time in Great Falls, Montana.

14 MAY 1976
Landscapes and Remembrances for soloists, chorus and orchestra by Gian Carlo MENOTTI is performed for the first time in Milwaukee.

20 MAY 1976
Third Symphony, subtitled *Rustica*, by the 51-year-old Macedonian composer Vlastimir NIKOLOVSKI, incorporating folk instruments such as the zurla, tapan and kaval, is performed for the first time in Skopje.

22 MAY 1976
Flute Concerto by the 47-year-old Soviet composer Edison DENISOV is performed for the first time in Dresden.

27 MAY 1976
Colonial Variants for orchestra by the American composer Norman DELLO JOIO is performed for the first time by the Philadelphia Orchestra under the direction of Eugene Ormandy.

12 JUNE 1976
The Last of the Mohicans, opera by the 36-year-old American composer Alva HENDERSON, is produced in Wilmington, Delaware.

19 JUNE 1976
Das Mädchen aus Domremy, opera by the 51-year-old German composer Giselher KLEBE, based on Schiller's play dealing with Joan of Arc, is performed for the first time in Stuttgart.

23 JUNE 1976
Kinkakuja (The Temple of the Golden Pavilion), opera by the 41-year-old Japanese composer Toshirō MAYUZUMI, is performed for the first time in Berlin.

3 JULY 1976

Violin Concerto by the fruitful American composer Alan HOVHANESS is performed for the first time by the National Symphony Orchestra in Wolf Trap Farm Park near Washington, D.C., with Yehudi Menuhin as soloist and André Kostelanetz conducting.

12 JULY 1976

We Come to the River, "action for music," by the radical German composer Hans Werner HENZE, centered on a murderous army general, attacked by demented pacifists who gouge his eyeballs, set to a score ranging from insanely inappropriate bel canto to planned pandemonium as the musicians invade the stage to the deafening sounds of a marching band, with celestial diaphony superimposed on an infernal cacophony, is produced for the first time at Covent Garden in London.

13 JULY 1976

Max BUTTING, prolific German composer who adopted varied techniques from academic euphony to sophisticated dodecaphony, dies in Berlin at the age of eighty-eight.

19 JULY 1976

Visions of Terror and Wonder for mezzo-soprano and orchestra by the 42-year-old American composer Richard WERNICK, to texts from the Bible and the Koran in Hebrew, Arabic and Greek, is performed for the first time at the Aspen Music Festival in Colorado.

25 JULY 1976

Einstein on the Beach, phantasmagorical spectacle by the surrealistically minimalistic American composer Philip GLASS, to the scenario of a dadaistically propended dramatist Robert Wilson, in which hypnopompic events are oxymoronically juxtaposed in a deliberately antisyllogistical sequence, is produced at the Festival of Avignon, France. (The first American performance was given at the Metropolitan Opera in New York on 21 November 1976.)

26 JULY 1976

Die Versuchung (The Temptation), opera in two acts by the 65-year-old Polish-born Israeli composer Josef TAL, is produced at the Munich Festival.

4 AUGUST 1976

First Symphony, subtitled *The Halcyon*, by Gian Carlo MENOTTI, is performed for the first time in Saratoga Springs, New York, by the Philadelphia Orchestra conducted by Eugene Ormandy.

6 AUGUST 1976

Gregor PIATIGORSKY, famed Russian violoncellist whose romantic talent was served by a total virtuosity and who was the favorite soloist of Richard Strauss (he called him "mein Don Quixote," for Piatigorsky played the cello solo in that work many, many times under the composer's direction), and who eventually settled in America, dies in Los Angeles of lung cancer at the age of seventy-three.

8 AUGUST 1976

David DEL TREDICI conducts in San Francisco the first performance of his orchestral work *An Alice Symphony*, subtitled *Illustrated Alice*, inspired by the works of Lewis Carroll. (An operatic *Alice* by Del Tredici was performed on 7 October 1976.)

28 AUGUST 1976

My Kinsman, Major Molineux, one-act opera, after Nathaniel Hawthorne, by the 30-year-old American composer Bruce SAYLOR, is produced in Pittsburgh.

2 SEPTEMBER 1976

Third Symphony for chorus, organ and orchestra by the 44-year-old Norwegian composer Per NØRGAARD is performed for the first time in Copenhagen.

5 SEPTEMBER 1976

Something to Do, cantata-musical by the 62-year-old American composer Morton GOULD, is performed for the first time in Washington, D.C.

24 SEPTEMBER 1976

Missa elettronica by the foremost Polish master of experimental modern music Boguslaw SCHAEFFER, consisting of five liturgical choral sections (*Kyrie, Gloria, Credo, Sanctus* and *Agnus Dei*) separated by electronic interludes, the tonal armamentarium including heterophony and polytonality, is performed for the first time at the Evangelical Church of Warsaw as part of the Warsaw Autumn Festival.

29 SEPTEMBER 1976

Two synchronized scores by John CAGE, *Renga* (a Japanese poetic structure, in graphic notation comprising 361 drawings by Thoreau), and *Apartment House 1776* for four vocal soloists, representing four ethnic groups of America in 1776, featuring a pseudo-Indian chief rhythmically slapping his belly, are performed as a pluralistic bicentennial tribute by the Boston Symphony Orchestra, conducted by Seiji Ozawa.

7 October 1976

Final Alice, "an opera, written in concert form" by the 39-year-old American composer David DEL TREDICI, spoken and sung by an amplified soprano to a text from Lewis Carroll's *Alice's Adventures in Wonderland* and *Through the Looking Glass,* scored for a large orchestra that includes a theremin, a banjo, an accordion and a mandolin, set in a beguilingly euphonious, harmonious and melodious idiom, and ending with the soloists signing off by counting to thirteen in Italian, in sly allusion to the composer's name (tredici = 13), is performed for the first time by the Chicago Symphony Orchestra, with Barbara Hendricks as narrator-soloist and Sir Georg Solti conducting.

8 October 1976

Slovenica for orchestra by the 45-year-old Slovenian composer Alojz Srebotnjak, in three movements (*Antiphone, Dance* and *Mourning Chant*), based on modernistically treated archaic Slovenian folk modalities, is performed for the first time in Ljubljana.

13 October 1976

Charles WUORINEN conducts in Cleveland the first performance of his *Tashi Concerto* for four instruments and orchestra, with the Tashi Chamber Music Ensemble as soloists.

22 October 1976

Mi-parti for orchestra by the masterly Polish composer Witold LUTOSLAWSKI is performed for the first time in Rotterdam.

24 October 1976

The Fiftieth Festival of the International Society for Contemporary Music opens in Boston with the following program of music by Canadian composers, presented at an afternoon concert:

Offrandes III by the 47-year-old Quebec composer Serge GARANT, scored for three cellos, two harps, piano and percussion, the third of a series of his works inspired by Bach's *Musical Offering. Madrigal III* by the 37-year-old Toronto-born composer Bruce MATHER, scored for contralto, marimba, harp and piano. *Lalita: Shadows II* by the 37-year-old Nova Scotian composer Robert AITKEN, derived from a matutinal Hindu imploration and scored for flute solo and ensemble. . . . *le sifflement des vents porteurs de l'amour* . . . (a quotation from a Renaissance canticle), by the 46-year-old Quebec composer Gilles TREMBLAY, scored for flute and percussion, evoking the whistling of winds bringing streams of love. *Arcana* by the Ontario-born 43-year-old avant-garde composer and theorist R. Murray SCHAFER, the title referring to a mysterious text in Egyptian hieroglyphs discovered in the ninth century, scored for several singers intoning symbolic phonemes with the accompaniment of an instrumental ensemble.

24 October 1976

The second concert of the Fiftieth Festival of the International Society for Contemporary Music in Boston is given in the evening with the following program:

Chanson for soprano and instruments by the 48-year-old Italian composer Vittoria FELLEGARA, written in an antifunctional harmonic system to a text from *Matines* by Paul Éluard. *Second Symphony* by the 24-year-old Glasgow-born composer Oliver KNUSSEN, scored for soprano and chamber orchestra, illustrating the hypnopompic state of a dreamy sleeper. *Origo* for orchestra by the 45-year-old Hungarian-born Austrian composer Josef Maria HORVATH, purporting to represent the origin of a species as part of a genus, in which the various aspects of the music trace the evolutionary lines of all art. *Meridian* by the 42-year-old British composer Harrison BIRTWISTLE for voices and instruments in convoluted interplay.

25 October 1976

On the second day of the Fiftieth Festival of the International Society for Contemporary Music in Boston the following afternoon program is given:

Strömung for orchestra by the 54-year-old Japanese composer Yoshirō IRINO (first performed in Teheran on 17 September 1973), the title suggesting a saying of Confucius that all things pass away as in a stream, scored for a shimmering continuum of subdued harmonies. *Études for Two Pianos* by the 32-year-old Montreal-born composer John HAWKINS, in three movements of which the finale is polymetric. *Nightflies* by the 33-year-old Swedish composer Daniel BÖRTZ, scored for voice, clarinet, trombone, percussion, piano, electric organ and cello, set to a symbolistic Swedish text. *Argia Ezta Ikusten* by the 47-year-old Basque composer Carmelo A. BERNAOLA, scored for clarinet, vibraphone, assorted percussion and piano, to text by the Basque poet Gabriel Aresti. *Solentiname* for instrumental group by the 38-year-old Venezuelan composer Alfredo DEL MONACO, the title being a solemn homage to the commune of Solentiname in Nicaragua. *Music for Winds, Percussion, Cello and Voices* by the 50-year-old American composer Rolv YTTREHUS, in a serial system of composition.

25 October 1976

On the second day of the Fiftieth Festival of the International Society of Contemporary Music in Boston, the following program of chamber music is given in an evening concert:

Portrait of Lili Boulanger by the 33-year-old Brazilian composer Almeida PRADO, scored for string quartet, flute and piano, written as an homage to the early blooming and untimely withered French composer Lili Boulanger, using fragments of her melodies. *Meditación en Fa* for oboe solo by the 39-year-old Uruguayan composer Juan José ITURRIBERRY, structured on the persistent note F, with occasional microtonal oscillations around it. *Mosaico* by the 37-year-old Dutch composer Ton DE KRUYF, for oboe and string trio, and consisting of seven short movements separated by graded pauses. *Sonata* for flute and piano by the 46-year-old Hungarian composer Jozsef SOPRONI, written in a free sonata form.

Chamber Music No. 2 by the 52-year-old American composer Leonard ROSEN-MAN, scored for chamber orchestra, singer and electronic tape to the text of the martyred Spanish poet Federico García Lorca.

26 OCTOBER 1976
On the third day of the Fiftieth Festival of the International Society for Contemporary Music in Boston, the following program is presented in an afternoon concert:

Drei Bilder von Li Tai-bo by the 53-year-old Korean composer In-Chan CHOI, scored for singer, flute, harp, cello and percussion to the text of three poems by the ancient Chinese poet Li Tai-bo. *Indian Summer* for chamber ensemble by the 47-year-old Slovenian composer Milan STIBILJ, glorifying the colorful forests of early autumn in America. *Disegno per Sestetto d'Ottoni* for brass sextet, by the 29-year-old Swedish composer Anders ELIASSON. *Else (Hommage)* by the 66-year-old Israeli composer Josef TAL, intended to describe a colloquy with people of Jerusalem, scored for vocalist, narrator and chamber group, and inspired by the poems of Else Lasker-Schüler. *Two Pieces for Four Clarinets* by the 49-year-old Israeli composer Tzvi AVNI. *Pequeño Triptico* for two pianos and percussion by the 36-year-old Argentine composer José MARANZANO. *Piece for Trumpet and Seven Instruments* by the Berlin-born American composer Stefan WOLPE (1902–1972).

26 OCTOBER 1976
On the third day of the Fiftieth Festival of the International Society for Contemporary Music in Boston, an evening concert is given with the following program of orchestral music performed by the University of Iowa Symphony Orchestra conducted by James Dixon:

The Rainbow Snake by the 40-year-old Danish composer Erik NORBY, inspired by the Indian legend of the serpentine origin of the rainbow (first performed in Copenhagen on 20 November 1975). *Entropies* by the 38-year-old Swiss composer Jim GRIMM, descriptive of the dialectical contradiction between order and disorder. *Concerto for Orchestra* by the 40-year-old British composer Anthony PAYNE, built on a process of gradual intervallic convolution. *Catena* by the 42-year-old Korean composer Sukhi KANG, representing a concatenation of sixty fragments.

26 OCTOBER 1976
Concerto for string quartet, winds, brass and percussion by Walter PISTON is performed for the first time in Portland, Oregon.

27 OCTOBER 1976
On the fourth day of the Fiftieth Festival of the International Society for Contemporary Music in Boston, the following program of chamber music is given in an afternoon concert:

String Quartet III/b by the 39-year-old Czech composer Tadeáš SALVA. *Piano Sonata* by the 36-year-old French composer René KOERING. *Geometrics* for string quartet by the 30-year-old American composer Robert POLLOCK, based on the geometric progressions of rhythms, intervals and tempi. *Piano Control* by the 39-year-old Swiss composer Thomas KESSLER, in which the solo piano part is regulated by a synthesizer generating different pitches, timbres, rhythms and dynamics. *String Quartet* by the 44-year-old Australian composer Richard MEALE, based on a chaconne forming variations in a complex chordal progression.

27 OCTOBER 1976
On the fourth day of the Fiftieth Festival of the International Society for Contemporary Music in Boston, the following program is presented in an evening concert by the Boston Symphony Orchestra under the direction of Seiji Ozawa:

Renga with *Apartment House 1776* by the formidable 64-year-old American iconoclast John CAGE, originally performed by the Boston Symphony Orchestra on 29 September 1976, embodying two collated scores played with aleatory freedom under the supervision of the conductor and making use of any instruments to form a desired balance. *Anarchia* for percussion and orchestra by the 47-year-old Cretan composer Nikos MAMANGAKIS in which the serial principle is evolved to the point of total anarchy. *Chronicles* by the 50-year-old American composer Seymour SHIFRIN, to Hebrew texts from the Old Testament.

28 OCTOBER 1976
Con tutta forza for forty-one wind instruments and six percussionists by the 34-year-old Swedish composer Sven-David SANDSTRÖM is performed for the first time in Stockholm.

28 OCTOBER 1976
On the fifth day of the Fiftieth Festival of the International Society for Contemporary Music in Boston, a concert of chamber music is given with the following program:

Alborada for viola and piano by the 23-year-old Venezuelan composer Emilio MENDOZA. *String Quartet No. 6* by the 43-year-old British-born Australian composer John EXTON. *Fourth Piano Sonata* by the 46-year-old Finnish composer Usko MERILÄINEN. *Air* for soprano, percussion and piano by the 33-year-old Norwegian composer Magne HEGDAL. *Concerto a Quattro* for string quartet by the 32-year-old Canadian composer John FODI.

29 OCTOBER 1976
On the sixth day of the Fiftieth Festival of the International Society for Contemporary Music in Boston, the following program of works by American composers is given in an afternoon concert:

Crossworks for chamber ensemble by the 32-year-old composer Paul LANSKY. *Six Études* for piano by the 61-year-old learned composer/theorist George PERLE. *Bittere Nüsse*, songs romanticizing acrid nuts by the 48-year-old John

HUGGLER. *Songs of Nature* by the 38-year-old New York composer John HEISS. *Block Songs* for soprano and children's toys by the 46-year-old T. J. ANDERSON. *Six Dumb-shows* by the 38-year-old John HARBISON, scored for flute, clarinet, violin, cello and electric piano, with material taken from his opera, *Winter's Tale*, after Shakespeare.

29 OCTOBER 1976
On the sixth day of the Fiftieth Festival of the International Society for Contemporary Music an evening concert of electronic music is presented at the Massachusetts Institute of Technology in Cambridge, featuring the following works:

Resa for computer by the 49-year-old Norwegian-born, German-educated Swedish composer Knut WIGGEN (*resa* is the Swedish word for travel). *Chimaera* for bass clarinet and tape by the 46-year-old Spanish-born Dutch composer Enrique RAXACH. *Ars recte computandi* (*Art of Correct Calculation*) by the group BBK, organized in 1973 and consisting of Pierre BARBAUD, Frank BROWN and Genevieve KLEIN. *Electra* for tape by the 44-year-old Yugoslav composer Vladan RADOVANOVIĆ. *Harry's Wonderland* for bass clarinet and tape by the 45-year-old Belgian composer André LAPORTE. *Group Variations II* by the 42-year-old American composer Benjamin BORETZ.

30 OCTOBER 1976
On the seventh day of the Fiftieth Festival of the International Society for Contemporary Music in Boston, the following program is presented in an afternoon concert:

Catena, a chain of episodes for chamber ensemble by the 41-year-old Hawaiian composer Donald SUR. *Cantus Contra Cantum II* for violin and cello by the 49-year-old French composer Jacques-Louis MONOD. *Valentine* for solo double-bass by the 48-year-old American composer Jacob DRUCKMAN, with the player sadistically assaulting the instrument with bow and timpani stick while singing sustained tones with loudly punctuating accents. *String Quartet* by the 37-year-old Florida-born composer Ellen Taaffe ZWILICH, in four movements involving some clever contrapuntal convolutions while keeping the melody in a pleasingly fluid state. *Echoes and Anticipation* by the 53-year-old American composer Ezra LADERMAN, scored for oboe and seven instruments in three movements, *Nuances*, *Strata* and *Changing Textures*.

30 OCTOBER 1976
The Fiftieth Festival of the International Society for Contemporary Music in Boston concludes with an evening concert with the New England Conservatory Symphony Orchestra, under the direction of Gunther Schuller, performing the following program:

Fassade by the 40-year-old German composer Helmut LACHENMANN, projecting a rectilinear marching meter in contrapuntal internal articulations. *Inner Space* by the 37-year-old American composer David Stock, gravid with clusters of sonic matter mutually interacting in several different tempi. *Voix* by the 36-year-old Portuguese composer Jorge Peixinho, scored for mezzo-soprano and chamber orchestra, leading to a gradual disintegration of the material into autonomous elements, with all participants, including the audience, becoming distraught but still attempting to follow the guiding thread of the music. *Sinfonia* by the 30-year-old Dutch composer Tristan Keuris, in four parts connected by a fragmentary tissue. *Jazz Concerto* by the 47-year-old master of Polish modern music Boguslaw Schaeffer, in which jazz elements are organized in an arresting classical form.

31 October 1976
Jonah, opera after the tragedy by Marin Sorescu, by the 50-year-old Rumanian composer Anatol Vieru is produced in Bucharest.

4 November 1976
Cello Concerto by the American composer Donald Erb is performed for the first time by Lynn Harrell and the Rochester (New York) Philharmonic Orchestra, conducted by David Zinman.

5 November 1976
In Wilderness is the Preservation of the World, orchestral fantasy after Thoreau by the 39-year-old American composer Brian Fennelly, is performed for the first time in Davenport, Iowa.

9 November 1976
Rosina Lhévinne, grande dame of Russian piano pedagogy who taught a plethora of wunderkinder of all ages in Europe and America and who gave brilliant duo-piano recitals with her virtuoso pianist husband Josef Lhévinne whom she survived by 31 years, dies at the matriarchal age of ninety-six in Glendale, California.

12 November 1976
Walter Piston, enlightened master of music whose works embody the best cultural achievement of American music and who as a Harvard University professor educated a number of talented composers, dies in his home at Belmont, Massachusetts, at the age of eighty-two.

14 November 1976
Night of the Moonspell, three-act opera by Elie Siegmeister, based on Shakespeare's *Midsummer Night's Dream*, with the action transferred to a festive mardi gras in Louisiana circa 1900, set to music full of euphonious dissonance and rhythmic asymmetries in depicting Cajun

voodoo rites, is produced in Shreveport, Louisiana, as a commissioned United States bicentennial piece.

14 November 1976

The Secret History of the Birth of the Nation for narrator, chorus and orchestra by the 64-year-old American composer Don Gillis is performed for the first time in York, Pennsylvania.

15 November 1976

Fourth Symphony by the American composer George Rochberg is performed for the first time by the Seattle Youth Symphony.

20 November 1976

Jubilee, opera by Ulysses Kay, with the action taking place on an antebellum plantation in Georgia, in which both the slave owner and his slaves unite in an optimistic jubilee when all men are really equal, is performed for the first time in Jackson, Mississippi.

26 November 1976

Isis and Osiris, lyric drama by the enlightened British composer Elisabeth Lutyens, is performed for the first time at Morley College in London.

1 December 1976

Letter from Mozart by Michael Colgrass, a pseudoepistolary musical collage of Mozartomorphic tunes culled from genuine bits of Mozartiana, and mulcified in a plasma of polyrhythmic, polymetric, polytonal and sometimes aleatory ingredients, requiring two conductors to beat non-coincident meters, is performed for the first time in New York.

4 December 1976

Benjamin Britten, greatly endowed British composer whose many operas and church parables established a harmonious link with the Elizabethan era of English music and who succeeded in creating a modern idiom along national lines, as exemplified in his operas *Peter Grimes*, *The Turn of the Screw* and *Gloriana*, composed for the coronation of Queen Elizabeth II, as well as in his educational music for the young, such as *Let's Make an Opera*, and who was elevated to the peerage of Great Britain in 1976 and became a Lord, dies in Aldeburgh at the age of sixty-three.

10 December 1976

Triptih dalmatinskih gradova (Triptych of Dalmatian Cities) for orchestra by the 70-year-old Croatian composer Milo Cipra is performed for the first time in Zagreb.

17 DECEMBER 1976

Kabale und Liebe, opera by the 58-year-old Austrian composer Gottfried VON EINEM, after Schiller's play, is produced in Vienna.

20 DECEMBER 1976

Windungen for twelve cellos by the 54-year-old Greek mathematician-musician-philosopher Iannis XENAKIS is performed for the first time in Bonn.

24 DECEMBER 1976

Symphonic Movement by the reclusive, hermetically individualistic Swedish composer Allan PETTERSSON is performed for the first time on Swedish Radio.

29 DECEMBER 1976

On the occasion of the centennial of the birth of Pablo CASALS, three years, nine weeks and five days after his death in exile from fascistic Spain, the royal government of new democratic Spain issues a postage stamp in his honor, and the municipal assembly of Barcelona attaches the name of Calle Casals to a city street.

✑ *1977* ✑

1 JANUARY 1977

Roland HAYES, inspired black singer whose parents were former slaves, dies in Boston at the age of eighty-nine.

5 JANUARY 1977

Der Schuhu und die fliegende Prinzessin, opera by the 33-year-old German composer Udo ZIMMERMANN, the Schuhu being a wise birdman who captured the flying princess of Tripoli in midair, set to music with electroacoustical ornithomorphic effects, is produced in Dresden.

17 JANUARY 1977

Chamber Concerto for viola d'amore and eleven instruments by the 35-year-old Swedish composer Ulf GRAHN is performed for the first time in Washington, D.C.

19 JANUARY 1977

Ninth Symphony by the 68-year-old Serbian composer Milan RISTIĆ, written in a neoclassical manner, is performed for the first time in Belgrade.

2 FEBRUARY 1977

The Royal Hunt of the Sun, opera by Iain HAMILTON, composed in 1966–1968 to a libretto arranged from Peter Shaffer's play dealing with the fall of the Inca Empire and the death of the Inca sun king Atahualpa, with a score full of ominous pentatonic invocations, is produced for the first time by the English National Opera in London.

6 FEBRUARY 1977

Malooley and the Fear Monster, a "family opera" in one act by the American composer John POZDRO, is performed for the first time in Lawrence, Kansas.

7 FEBRUARY 1977

Palinode for orchestra and computer synthesis by the 34-year-old American composer Charles DODGE is performed for the first time in New York.

17 FEBRUARY 1977

Symphony of Three Orchestras by the foremost modern American composer Elliott CARTER, derived from the concept of the Baroque concerto grosso, with each of the component orchestras representing a concertino of soloists set against the entire ensemble, in twelve movements preceded by a spacious exordium and concluded by a grandiloquent peroration, is performed for the first time by the New York Philharmonic Orchestra, Pierre Boulez conducting.

22 FEBRUARY 1977

Culminations for orchestra by the 34-year-old Swedish composer Sven-David SANDSTRÖM is performed for the first time on Swedish Radio.

23 FEBRUARY 1977

The Prophet, oratorio by the American composer Gardner READ, based on text by the Lebanese mystic Kahlil Gibran, is performed for the first time by the Boston University Orchestra and Chorus.

14 MARCH 1977

Tamburlaine, lyric drama for radio, in twenty-four scenes, lasting about eighty-five minutes without a break, by the Scottish composer Iain HAMILTON, based on Marlowe's play dealing with the legendary Mongol warrior, is performed for the first time in London.

22 MARCH 1977

ČSV for orchestra by the 35-year-old Norwegian composer John PERSEN, the ambiguous acronym of the title meaning "dare to admit you are a Lapp," is performed for the first time in Oslo.

26 MARCH 1977

The 150th anniversary of BEETHOVEN's death is marked in Peking by a televised performance of his *Fifth Symphony*, revoking the ban on Beethoven, heretofore denounced by the cultural Chinese authorities as an imperialistic revisionist bourgeois composer.

1 APRIL 1977

Symphony in D Major, in the style of Mozart by the 33-year-old Polish composer Krzysztof MEYER, written in such an authentic Mozartean idiom as to confuse and seduce even the most suspicious of the Mozartologists, is performed for the first time in Poznań, on April Fool's Day.

4 APRIL 1977

Eugene ZADOR, Hungarian-American composer of operas and symphonic works, many of them steeped in Magyar folklore, dies of cancer of the prostate gland in Hollywood at the age of eighty-two.

14 APRIL 1977

Lily, opera by the 58-year-old, hemidemisemimodernistic American composer Leon KIRCHNER, based on the novel *Henderson the Rain King* by Saul Bellow (Lily is Henderson's lissom wife), scored with a variety of quaquaversal expressionistic techniques, including a chorus singing in a made-up African language, is performed for the first time by the New York City Opera.

21 APRIL 1977

Symphony in nine movements for large orchestra and six solo instruments by the innovative Polish modernist Boguslaw SCHAEFFER is performed for the first time in Wroclaw, with the composer at the piano as one of the soloists.

24 APRIL 1977

Damals, by the 69-year-old German composer Wolfgang FORTNER, after text by Samuel Beckett, scored for mime, narrator, mezzo-soprano, baritone, harpsichord, guitar, piano and live electronics, is performed for the first time in Baden-Baden.

27 APRIL 1977

Violin Concerto by the 43-year-old Polish modernist Krzysztof PENDERECKI is performed for the first time in Basel.

29 APRIL 1977

Quartet Plus for narrator and double string quartet by the 54-year-old American composer Lukas Foss is performed for the first time in New York.

2 MAY 1977

Fifth Symphony, subtitled *Visions of Time*, by the American composer Elie SIEGMEISTER is performed for the first time by the Baltimore Symphony Orchestra conducted by Sergiu Comissiona.

3 MAY 1977

Fleuves (Rivers) for orchestra by the 44-year-old Canadian composer Gilles TREMBLAY is performed for the first time in Montreal.

4 MAY 1977

Forty Piano Études in Modus Lascivus by the 75-year-old Hungarian-American violist and composer Tibor SERLY is performed for the first time in its entirety by the composer's wife, Miriam Molin, in New York.

5 MAY 1977

Star-Child by George CRUMB, subtitled *A Parable for Soprano, Antiphonal Children's Voices, Male Speaking Chorus and Large Orchestra*, supplemented by a peal of twenty handbells and carillons of bell ringers, with the text in Latin from the Vulgate, is performed for the first time by the New York Philharmonic led by Pierre Boulez, aided and abetted by three simultaneous conductors.

5 MAY 1977

Fluctuante-Immuable for large orchestra by the 38-year-old French composer Jean-Claude ELOY, suggesting in its title the immutability of fluctuation, is performed for the first time in Paris under the direction of Jean-Claude Casadesus.

13 MAY 1977

Neither by the American modernist Morton FELDMAN, a monodrama after an original text by Samuel Beckett, scored for soprano and orchestra, is performed for the first time in Rome. (The American premiere took place in New York on 21 November 1978.)

14 MAY 1977

On the opening day of the Fifty-first Festival of the International Society for Contemporary Music in Bonn, the following program is presented at an afternoon concert:

Quemadmodum for string quartet by the 34-year-old Hungarian composer Zoltán JENEY, the relative pronoun of the title indicating a reference to traditional structures. *Seul opus 38* for bass clarinet solo by the 36-year-old Chicago-born Danish-resident composer Maurice WEDDINGTON. *A Wind/Tornado Piece/*

Cyclone by the 29-year-old American composer Joan LA BARBARA, with the audience placed in the static eye of the hurricane.

14 MAY 1977

At an evening concert on the first day of the Fifty-first Festival of the International Society for Contemporary Music in Bonn, the following program of choral music under the slogan "Spaces with Voices—Voices of the Innerspace" is presented:

Integrale Musik with tape by the 30-year-old German composer Peter Michael HAMEL. *Ritual for the Thirsty Earth* for seven voices and instruments by the 46-year-old Rumanian composer Myriam MARBE, derived from Rumanian folk tunes. *Sanctus* for ten solo voices, ten metronomes, bells and chorus by the 33-year-old Brazilian composer Jamary OLIVEIRA. *The Gentleness of Rain Was in the Wind* for three female and three males voices by the 47-year-old Austrian composer Gerhard RÜHM. *Les Sources Transfigurées* for vibraphone, tam-tam and vocal ensemble by the 34-year-old Belgian composer André VAN BELLE. *Requiem Hashshirim* for choir by the 31-year-old Venetian conductor-composer Giuseppe SINOPOLI.

15 MAY 1977

On the second day of the Fifty-first Festival of the International Society for Contemporary Music in Bonn the following program of "Music of a Special Sound" is presented at an afternoon concert:

Genklang for five pianists by the 30-year-old Danish composer Karl Aage RASMUSSEN. *Jackson* for bass-baritone by the Australian composer Helen STANDRING, to a text of letters by the black inmate of Soledad Prison George Jackson. *Influx* for string quartet by the 44-year-old Japanese composer Hidenao ITO. *Cluster* for an optional number of pianists, and *Piano Trio*, by the 34-year-old Mexican composer Mario LAVISTA. *Appels* for seven wind instruments, two percussionists, piano and double-bass by the 28-year-old French composer Michael LEVINAS.

15 MAY 1977

At an evening concert on the second day of the Fifty-first Festival of the International Society for Contemporary Music in Bonn, the following program announced as "Music for Children with Children: I" is given:

Kommunikationsspiele, a demonstration with a youth group by the 40-year-old Swiss composer Hans WÜTHRICH. *Pieces* for instruments constructed by school children, program supervised by the British instructor Hugh DAVIES. *Jeux avec le Scriptoson* (games with a scientifically scripted phonograph disc) by the 30-year-old French composer Jean Ives BOSSEUR.

15 MAY 1977

Moses, opera by the 43-year-old Hungarian composer Zsolt DURKÓ, is performed for the first time in Budapest.

16 May 1977

On the third day of the Fifty-first Festival of the International Society for Contemporary Music in Bonn, the following program of "Music with Exotic Sounds" is presented:

Cabotaje IIIc for flute and tape by the 37-year-old Uruguayan composer Ariel MARTINEZ. *Chanson* for wind instruments by the 45-year-old Italian composer Mario BERTONCINI. *Kontrasignatur* for double-bass and tape by the 37-year-old German composer Wilfried MICHEL. *Transpositio ad infinitum* for solo cello by the 53-year-old Swiss composer Klaus HUBER. *Ach Golgatha!* for harp, organ and percussion by the 54-year-old Belgian composer Karel GOEYVAERTS, based on a passage from Bach's *St. Matthew Passion.*

18 May 1977

On the fourth day of the Fifty-first Festival of the International Society for Contemporary Music in Bonn an orchestral concert is given with the following program:

Morphogenesis by the 24-year-old German composer Hans-Jürgen VON BOSE. *Gespenster (Ghosts)* for singer/narrator, tape and orchestra, to a text by Bertolt Brecht, by the 38-year-old German composer Nicolaus A. HUBER. *Houdini Symphony* by the 42-year-old avant-garde Dutch composer Peter SCHAT, scored for four soloists, chorus and orchestra, in four movements drawn from his circus opera on the life of the famous magician Houdini. (The entire opera was produced in Amsterdam on 29 September 1977.)

19 May 1977

A Water Bird Talk, a protracted monologue to the music of Dominick ARGENTO, adapted from Chekhov's parodistic lecture on the harm on tobacco smoking, is performed for the first time at the Brooklyn Academy of Music in New York.

19 May 1977

On the fifth day of the Fifty-first Festival of the International Society for Contemporary Music in Bonn, two programs featuring "Music for Children with Children" are presented, including *Fountains of My Sky* by the 35-year-old Rumanian composer Horatio RADULESCU; *Yobikake (The Call)* by the 26-year-old Japanese composer and educator Chisako SHIMIZU; and *Polyagogie* by the Greek master of pedagogical stochastics Iannis XENAKIS.

19 May 1977

The fifth day of the Fifty-first Festival of the International Society for Contemporary Music in Bonn continues at an evening concert of "All Sound-Space Music" with the following program:

Orange Air, collaborative work by the American composers Richard FEIT and Richard SCHAER. *Peripathetisches zur Lage* by the 42-year-old Austrian composer Otto M. ZYKLAN. *Dentist Music* by the 39-year-old Polish-born composer Piotr LACHERT, conceived as a kind of orthodontic laboratory of the musical future. *The Sinking of the Titanic* for instruments and projections by the 34-year-old British composer Gavin BRYARS, based on hymns played by the ship band before the unsinkable *Titanic* went down at 2:20 A.M. on 15 April 1912.

20 MAY 1977
On the sixth day of the Fifty-first Festival of the International Society for Contemporary Music in Bonn, an afternoon concert featuring the following program of "Narrative Music" is presented:

Piano Concerto by the 43-year-old Italian composer Danilo LORENZINI. *Kouklokosmos (Puppet World)*, an electronic fairy tale by the 44-year-old Greek composer Stephanos WASSILIADIS. *Solo* for piano and live electronics by the 29-year-old Finnish composer Jukka TIENSUU. *Hörfilm (Audio Film)*, audiovisual environment for tape, multivision and headphones by the 29-year-old Chilean-born Hungarian composer János DARVAS.

20 MAY 1977
The sixth day of the Fifty-first Festival of the International Society for Contemporary Music in Bonn continues with the following program at an evening concert of orchestral music, presented under the general rubric "Reflections":

Variations on a Theme by Mozart by the 24-year-old German composer Wolfgang VON SCHWEINITZ. *Reflections of Narciss and Goldmund* for two chamber orchestras, harp, piano and celesta by the 24-year-old British composer Robert SAXTON, inspired by the novel by Hermann Hesse. *Ding (Thing)* by the 34-year-old Swiss composer Roland MOSER. *Accanto* for clarinet and orchestra by the 42-year-old German composer Helmut LACHENMANN.

21 MAY 1977
The Fifty-first Festival of the International Society for Contemporary Music in Bonn concludes with a program of orchestral works by four international grand masters of modern music: *Punkte* by Karlheinz STOCKHAUSEN; *Don* by Pierre BOULEZ; *Piano Concerto* by John CAGE; and *Il Canto sospeso* by the innovative Italian composer Luigi NONO.

18 JUNE 1977
The Martyrdom of Saint Magnus, chamber opera in one act and nine scenes by the British composer Peter Maxwell DAVIES, is performed for the first time at the twelfth-century Orkney Cathedral, in Kirkwell, where Saint Magnus was buried, recounting the saga of the unnatural murder of the pious Earl Magnus by his own cousin in 1117, to the composer's

libretto drawn from George Mackay Brown's novel *Magnus*, the thematic material derived from medieval plainchant.

22 JUNE 1977

Napoli milionaria, comic opera by the 65-year-old Italian composer Nino ROTA, making sport of the American occupation of Naples in 1945 that produced black-market Neapolitan millionaires, is produced in Spoleto.

26 JUNE 1977

Karadjordje (Black George) or *Seme zla (The Seed of the Wicked)*, television opera by the 66-year-old Serbian composer Stanojlo RAJIČIĆ to the text by Ivan Studen, depicting the psychological aspect of the conflicts between Karadjordje and Miloš Obrenović, the leaders of the first and second Serbian revolts against Ottoman rule in the early nineteenth century, ending in Karadjordje's defeat, is produced on Belgrade Television.

6 JULY 1977

The Ice Break, opera by Sir Michael TIPPETT dealing with the reunion of a political prisoner with his family after a great many years, involving the estrangement of his son who questions his father's courage and his daughter who offers herself to a black athlete in a gesture of atonement for racial guilt, all this heavily embroiled in a network of semiotics, symbols and psychedelic signals implanted in a complex contrapuntal web, is produced at the Royal Opera House, Covent Garden, in London.

29 JULY 1977

Fourth Symphony by the 71-year-old Russian composer Boris ARAPOV, scored for mezzo-soprano, baritone, narrator, two choirs and orchestra, is performed for the first time in Leningrad.

7 AUGUST 1977

Seventh Symphony, subtitled *A Sea Symphony*, for orchestra and chorus by the 80-year-old American composer Howard HANSON, to text from Walt Whitman, is performed for the first time for the fiftieth anniversary of the National Music Camp at Interlochen, Michigan.

16 AUGUST 1977

Elvis PRESLEY, superduper star of American rock 'n' roll, popularly described as "Elvis the Pelvis" because of his habit of rotating the lower part of his torso, whose fantastically successful career ended in a bottomless pit of erotic perversity and conspicuous drug consumption, expires at his lavishly accoutered home at Memphis, Tennessee, at the age of forty-four.

17 AUGUST 1977

Petro PETRIDIS, Greek composer of great cultural attainments (he could recite Homer in extenso from memory), dies in Athens at the age of eighty-five.

20 AUGUST 1977

Voyager I, American spacecraft, is shot off on a mission to reconnoiter Jupiter, Saturn and Uranus, containing a two-hour recorded message for any extraterrestrial beings owning a phonograph who may intercept it, including musical bits by the three B's and a rock piece by a fourth B, Chuck Berry.

6 SEPTEMBER 1977

Mary, Queen of Scots, opera by the 49-year-old Scottish composer Thea MUSGRAVE, is produced at the Edinburgh Festival.

13 SEPTEMBER 1977

Leopold STOKOWSKI, symphonic conductor of unequaled histrionic gifts whose patrician appearance suggested his paternal Polish origin, and who as music director of the Philadelphia Orchestra for many years created a unique Stokowski sound, dies still in full possession of his artistic powers at Nether Wallop, Hampshire, England, at the fulfilled age of ninety-five.

16 SEPTEMBER 1977

Maria CALLAS, prima donna assoluta, born in New York of Greek parents, whose career was in itself a series of operatically melodramatic peripeteias and whose temperamental antics on and off stage were the favorite pabulum of sensational newspaper stories, dies suddenly of a heart seizure in her Paris apartment at the age of fifty-three.

22 SEPTEMBER 1977

Dawnpath, chamber opera by the 30-year-old British composer Nicola LEFANU, is produced in London.

29 SEPTEMBER 1977

Houdini, a circus opera by the Dutch composer Peter SCHAT, scored for seven soloists, chorus, orchestra, dancers, escapologists and acrobats, is produced in Amsterdam. (An orchestral version, titled *Houdini Symphony,* was first performed in Bonn on 18 May 1977.)

29 SEPTEMBER 1977

Alexander TCHEREPNIN, prolific Russian composer, son of the romantically nationalist composer Nicolas Tcherepnin, who departed from ancestral legacy, lived in China and Paris, eventually becoming an American citizen, joined the modern movement by among other things adopting a scale of nine degrees and practicing a rhythmic polyphony which he called interpunctus, dies suddenly at the age of seventy-eight while returning from a walk with his Chinese wife, Lee Hsien-ming, at the entrance of his Paris apartment.

29 SEPTEMBER 1977
On the occasion of the semimillennial anniversary of Uppsala University, *Twelfth Symphony* by the romantic Swedish composer Allan PETTERSSON, entitled *De Döda på Torget (The Dead in the Marketplace)*, inspired by the poetry of the Chilean Nobel Laureate Pablo Neruda and throbbing with irreconcilable discords in a turbulent polyphonic setting voicing a heart-rending protest against the unspeakable cruelty of the military Chilean regime, is performed for the first time by the Stockholm Philharmonic.

6 OCTOBER 1977
Fourth Symphony in one movement by Sir Michael TIPPETT, set in a dissonant idiom, restrained by a disciplined classical form, completed on 18 April 1977, is performed for the first time as a commissioned work by the Chicago Symphony Orchestra, Sir Georg Solti conducting.

8 OCTOBER 1977
Requiem for chorus, organ, piano, electric bass, electric guitar, brass, percussion and celesta by the 42-year-old Soviet modernist Alfred SCHNITTKE is performed for the first time in Budapest.

11 OCTOBER 1977
Songfest, a suite of twelve pieces for six singers and orchestra by Leonard BERNSTEIN, is performed for the first time in Washington, D.C.

14 OCTOBER 1977
Bing CROSBY, immensely popular American crooner and a talented cinematic comedian, dies suddenly during a game of golf at La Moraleja Golf Course outside of Madrid, at the age of seventy-four.

15 OCTOBER 1977
Westerlings, "four songs and a prayer with seascapes" for unaccompanied chorus by the 43-year-old British composer Peter Maxwell DAVIES, to a text by George Mackay Brown utilizing traditional Orkney Norn (a language native to the residents of the Island of Orkney, out of common use for over two hundred years), receives its first performance by the BBC Singers at the Concert Hall, Broadcasting House in London, John

Aldis conducting. (The American premiere by the Berkeley Contemporary Chamber Players, Christopher Fulkerson conducting, took place on 26 March 1984.)

5 NOVEMBER 1977
Guy LOMBARDO, Canadian-born American bandleader, wizard of the golden sound, publicized as the purveyor of "the sweetest music this side of Heaven," whose New Year's radio and television broadcasts became the quintessence of American life, dies in Houston, Texas, at the age of seventy-five.

13 NOVEMBER 1977
Strange Tenderness of Naked Leaping for orchestra by the 46-year-old American composer of Polish descent Lucia DLUGOSZEWSKI is performed for the first time in Santa Fe, New Mexico.

17 NOVEMBER 1977
English Horn Concerto by the 61-year-old American composer Vincent PERSICHETTI is performed for the first time in New York.

30 NOVEMBER 1977
A *Flock Descends Upon the Pentagonal Garden* for orchestra by the 47-year-old Japanese composer Toru TAKEMITSU is performed for the first time in San Francisco.

1 DECEMBER 1977
American Cantata for tenor, soprano, two speakers, chorus and orchestra by the 55-year-old American composer Lukas Foss is performed for the first time in New York.

6 DECEMBER 1977
Clarinet Concerto by the 39-year-old American composer John CORIGLIANO is performed for the first time in New York.

21 DECEMBER 1977
Johann Nepomuk DAVID, Austrian composer of a number of compactly wrought symphonies and pieces of chamber music, dies in Stuttgart at the age of eighty-two.

⟨ 1978 ⟩

10 JANUARY 1978

Timbres, Espace, Mouvement for orchestra by the French composer Henri DUTILLEUX is performed for the first time by the National Symphony Orchestra, conducted by Mstislav Rostropovich, in Washington, D.C.

16 JANUARY 1978

Aeneas on the Saxophone for voices, clarinet, French horn, trombone, viola and double-bass by the American composer Ezra SIMS, based on a sui generis eighteen-tone scale, is performed for the first time on the composer's fiftieth birthday at the Dinosaur Annex in Boston.

17 JANUARY 1978

Sixth Symphony, subtitled *Sinfonia Mistica*, by the eminent Polish-born naturalized British) composer Andrzej PANUFNIK, based heavily on hexalogical numerology (six sections, six recurring melodic patterns, six triads at the root of the harmonies, six rhythmic units in every bar), is performed for the first time by the Northern Sinfonia under the direction of Christopher Seaman, in Middlesborough, England.

18 JANUARY 1978

Ivan DZERZHINSKY, Soviet composer who wrote music fitting to perfection into the scheme of Socialist Realism and who received an exceptional verbal accolade from Stalin himself after the production of his dialectically patriotic opera *And Quiet Flows the Don* to a libretto fashioned from the Bolshevistically orthodox eponymous novel by Sholokhov, dies in Leningrad, largely unsung and unhailed, at the age of sixty-eight.

19 JANUARY 1978

L'invitation au voyage for chamber orchestra and speaker by the 39-year-old Swiss-born French composer Tona SCHERCHEN-HSIAO, daughter of the famous conductor Hermann Scherchen, is performed for the first time in Paris, under the direction of Pierre Boulez.

2 FEBRUARY 1978

First Symphony by the English composer Peter Maxwell DAVIES is performed for the first time in London.

12 FEBRUARY 1978

The Women in the Garden, chamber opera for five singers and nine instruments by the 64-year-old American composer Vivian FINE, to her own feminist libretto portraying Emily Dickinson, Isadora Duncan, Gertrude Stein and Virginia Woolf, is produced in San Francisco.

13 FEBRUARY 1978
Fiery Winds for orchestra by the radical 43-year-old American modernist Roger REYNOLDS is performed for the first time in New York.

20 FEBRUARY 1978
Arietten for piano and orchestra by the 60-year-old Austrian composer Gottfried VON EINEM, is performed for the first time in Berlin.

22 FEBRUARY 1978
Introitus for piano and chamber orchestra by the 46-year-old Soviet composer Sofia GUBAIDULINA, of Tatar paternity and Russian maternity, is performed for the first time in Moscow.

27 FEBRUARY 1978
Fifth Symphony by the 42-year-old Soviet Georgian composer Giya KANCHELI, dedicated to the memory of his parents, is performed for the first time in Tbilisi.

2 MARCH 1978
Janus for trombone and jazz orchestra by the 51-year-old American composer and jazz clarinetist William O. SMITH is performed for the first time in Seattle.

8 MARCH 1978
A *Gentle Spirit*, chamber opera after a story by Dostoyevsky by the 34-year-old British composer John TAVENER, is produced in London.

12 MARCH 1978
Witold LUTOSLAWSKI conducts the Berlin Philharmonic in the first performance of his *Les Espaces du sommeil* for baritone and orchestra, with Dietrich Fischer-Dieskau as soloist.

14 MARCH 1978
Adieu Robert Schumann for contralto and orchestra by the Canadian composer R. Murray SCHAFER, to text from Clara Schumann's diaries chronicling Schumann's madness, is performed for the first time in Ottawa.

17 March 1978

Deaï for three orchestras by the 50-year-old American composer, conductor and educator Gunther SCHULLER is performed for the first time in Tokyo. (The first American performance was in Tanglewood, Massachusetts, on 4 August 1979.)

6 April 1978

Nicolas NABOKOV, Russian composer, first cousin of the novelist Vladimir Nabokov, who lived in Paris and in America and wrote a number of fine ballets and symphonic music in a modernistic but quite pleasurable vein, dies in New York at the age of seventy-four.

6 April 1978

Triptychon by the 70-year-old German composer Wolfgang FORTNER, in three parts, *Hymnus I* for six brasses, *Improvisation* for large orchestra and *Hymnus II* for eighteen-voice string orchestra, is performed for the first time in Düsseldorf.

12 April 1978

Le Grand Macabre, eschatological anti-opera by the musical thaumaturgist Györgi LIGETI, dealing with the apocalyptic ultima hora and written in a gloriously antimusical idiom of beguiling allure, with singers shouting and whispering inarticulate vocables, to the altered text adapted from dramas by the Belgian surrealist Michel de Ghelderode, the action being set in a chimeric town of Breugelland, and centered on the thanatopherous necro-czar who sexually mutilates a local hausfrau before ordering the world's end, but shrinks himself into a death mask when the forces of life refuse to stop functioning, is produced for the first time in Stockholm.

14 April 1978

Claudia Legare, fourth opera by the 60-year-old American composer Robert WARD, to a libretto dealing with an American counterpart of Ibsen's independent woman Hedda Gabler, with the action taking place in Charleston, South Carolina, shortly after the Civil War, is produced by the Minnesota Opera in St. Paul.

18 April 1978

Stark såsom Döden (Strong Like Death), church opera by the 35-year-old Swedish composer Sven-David SANDSTRÖM, is produced in Stockholm.

20 April 1978

Fireballs for orchestra by the 34-year-old Polish composer Krzysztof MEYER is performed for the first time in Warsaw.

21 April 1978

Danton and Robespierre, opera by the 43-year-old American composer John EATON, is performed for the first time in Bloomington, Indiana.

1 May 1978

Aram KHACHATURIAN, brilliant Soviet composer born in Tiflis, Georgia, of Armenian parents, whose quasi-Oriental ballet music throbs with animal energy and whose harmonies richly resonate with euphonious bitonalities, dies in Moscow of lung cancer at the age of seventy-four.

6 May 1978

The Fifty-second Festival of the International Society for Contemporary Music opens in Stockholm with a city event of Fireworks and Water Music, coordinated by Lars-Gunnar Bodin, Sten Hanson, Bengt Emil Johnson, Arne Mellnäs, Jan W. Morthenson and Leo Nilson.

7 May 1978

On the second day of the Fifty-second Festival of the International Society for Contemporary Music, the following program of chamber music is presented at an afternoon concert in Stockholm:

Miroirs for harpsichord and tape by the 40-year-old Canadian composer Micheline Coulombe SAINT-MARCOUX, consisting of six "moments" representing six "jeux de miroirs" (plain mirror, magic mirror, concave mirror, parabolic mirror, extension mirror and superimposed mirror), all polyphonically mirrored. *Discantus III* for solo saxophone by the 40-year-old Finnish composer Paavo HEININEN, treating the saxophone as a lyric instrument as well as a playful jazz medium. *Inundations: Willow* for soprano, piano and tape by the British composer Stephen MONTAGUE, to a text limited to four words of various amorous implications. *The Lost Jugglery* for mezzo-soprano, cello, piano and percussion by the 28-year-old Swedish composer Mikael EDLUND, portraying the territorial struggle of several players seeking dominance. *Toujours plus . . .* for harpsichord and organ by the 33-year-old French composer Graciane FINZI, a study in cumulative dodecaphony.

7 May 1978

The second day of the Fifty-second Festival of the International Society for Contemporary Music in Stockholm continues at an evening concert with the following program of orchestral works:

Partiels by the 32-year-old French composer Gérard FRISEY, an analytic essay on the overtone series. *Consort Music* by the 31-year-old Austrian-born Finnish composer Herman RECHBERGER, constructed of a series of ten subsidiary consorts, each formed by a Morse code rhythm. *Love-Charm Songs* for voice and orchestra by the 39-year-old Finnish composer Jarmo SERMILÄ, to texts from South American Tupi-Indian magic incantations. *Inner Light III* by the 39-

year-old British composer Jonathan HARVEY, being an invocation of the solipsistic notions of the philosopher Rudolf Steiner.

8 MAY 1978
On the third day of the Fifty-second Festival of the International Society for Contemporary Music, the following program of chamber music and multimedia works is presented at an afternoon concert in Stockholm:

Row Music for solo piano by the 39-year-old American composer William HELLERMANN, reflecting an Oriental mantra in a twelve-tone row derived from Alban Berg's *Mutterakkord*. *Il y a mille et mille soleils* for flute, harp and percussion by the French composer Nicole LACHARTRE, inspired by the notion of thousands of dying and resurrecting suns. *The Poem*, a video composition by the American composers Barbara SYKES, Tom DEFANTI, Drew BROWNING and Bob SNYDER. *Mobile* for solo cello by the Polish composer Anna MACIEJASZ-KAMINSKA, containing eighteen segments of which six are subdivided into sixty structural articulations. *Inharmonique* for computer sounds and voice by the French composer Jean-Claude RISSET.

9 MAY 1978
Twelve weeks before his death, Carlos CHÁVEZ conducts at the Inter-American Music Festival in Washington, D.C., the first performance of his *Trombone Concerto*.

9 MAY 1978
On the fourth day of the Fifty-second Festival of the International Society for Contemporary Music, an afternoon concert of chamber music with the following program is given in Helsinki:

Hirmos for soprano, alto, tenor, bass and chamber orchestra by the 49-year-old Greek composer Michael ADAMIS, to texts from medieval Byzantine hymnology. *Breath* for soprano, tape and chamber ensemble by the 48-year-old Japanese composer Hifumi SHIMOYAMA, to words from the Japanese traditional Noh drama. *Images* for electric piano, electric bass and two percussionists by the 33-year-old Canadian composer Donald STEVEN, consisting of seven miniatures designed to explore the musical dimensions of time and space. *Three Pieces for Piano* by the 55-year-old Uruguayan composer Hector TOSAR, based on thematic groups of three, four and twelve notes. *Bedu* for baritone and chamber ensemble by the 58-year-old Israeli composer Jacob GILBOA, in eight sections of metamorphoses of a Bedouin call. *Elixir*, a miniconcerto for flute and chamber ensemble by the 35-year-old American composer Joseph SCHWANTNER. *Routine Investigations* by the 52-year-old American composer Morton FELDMAN, an esoteric inquiry into the nature of sound.

9 MAY 1978
On the fourth day of the Fifty-second Festival of the International Society for Contemporary Music taking place in Helsinki, the following program of orchestral music is given at an evening concert:

Topo Ostinato by the 42-year-old Iranian-born Austrian composer Iraj SCHIMI, a musical essay on the correlation of the composer's proclivities and a listener's propensities. *Concerto Seven,* "for Daniel in the lion's den," for violin and orchestra by the 37-year-old Austrian composer Dieter KAUFMANN, being fragments from *Concertomobil,* a symbol of constant inner struggle between the composer and performer. *Atembogen* by the 39-year-old Swiss oboe virtuoso and composer Heinz HOLLIGER, an idyll reigning between silence and sound. *Tide* by the 43-year-old Danish composer Bent LORENTZEN, progressing from a single tenuous tone to a sonoriferous finale. *Piano Concerto* in one movement by the 40-year-old Polish composer Zygmunt KRAUZE. *The Turning Point* by the 34-year-old Finnish composer Pehr Henrik NORDGREN, inspired by a sojourn in a small Japanese village.

10 MAY 1978

On the fifth day of the Fifty-second Festival of the International Society for Contemporary Music, the following program of chamber music is presented at an afternoon concert in Helsinki:

Music for Upright Piano and Amplified Cello by the 51-year-old Finnish composer Einojuhani RAUTAVAARA. *Triptych* for three French horns by the 34-year-old Greek composer Agapitos AGAPITOS, a serially organized piece freely extending into an entire domain of available tones. *Solfatára* for saxophone and percussion by the 67-year-old Finnish composer Erik BERGMAN, inspired by the sulfuric fumes of an extinct volcano near Naples. *Divertimento* for violin and chamber orchestra by the 41-year-old Italian composer Umberto ROTONDI, based on a psychic automatism along surrealist lines. *Sinistro* for guitar and accordion by the 30-year-old Finnish composer Jukka TIENSUU, being a darksome synthesis of intuitive and stochastic formations. *Nosotros (We)* for violin, clarinet, vibraphone and piano by the 38-year-old Spanish composer Jesús VILLA-ROJO, an individualistically collective invocation of experimental laboratory work.

10 MAY 1978

On the fifth day of the Fifty-second Festival of the International Society for Contemporary Music, the following program of chamber music is given at an evening concert in Helsinki:

Octet by the 43-year-old French composer François-Bernard MÂCHE, set in the traditional classical form with novel excrescences. *Sirató (Lament)* by the 61-year-old Hungarian composer Rudolf MAROS, derived from a Hungarian folk song expressing sorrow. *Akāša* for six trombones by the 30-year-old Finnish composer Mikko HEINIÖ, the title meaning the sound-carrying medium, with aleatory rhythms. *Relations* for flute and piano by the 47-year-old Japanese composer Makoto SHINOHARA, symbolizing a relationship between two persons in alternating cordiality and discord. *Music for Chambers* by the 37-year-old Italian-born American composer Marc-Antonio CONSOLI, an amalgam of three separate compositions. *Six Turkish Folk Poems* by the 48-year-old Dutch composer Theo LOEVENDIE.

11 May 1978

On the sixth day of the Fifty-second Festival of the International Society for Contemporary Music, the following program of electroacoustic music is presented at an afternoon concert in Helsinki:

Traum des Einsamen (*Dream of the Lonely One*) by the 42-year-old Swedish composer Támás UNGVARY. *Music for the Morning of the World* for soprano with four-channel tape by the 45-year-old Canadian composer R. Murray SCHAFER, inspired by medieval Persian poetry, both erotic and religious. *Microhabitat* by the 39-year-old Yugoslav composer Paul PIGNON, a musical reverberation of artificial intelligence. . . . *From Behind the Unreasoning Mask* for trombone, percussion and four-channel tape by the 44-year-old American composer Roger REYNOLDS, framed by six simultaneous transient events with some improvisatory intercalations. *Rothko* by the 28-year-old Belgian composer Peter BEYLS, a musical reflection of the abstract expressionistic work of the suicidal painter Mark Rothko.

11 May 1978

The sixth day of the Fifty-second Festival of the International Society for Contemporary Music continues with the following program of orchestral music given at an evening concert at Helsinki:

In Memoriam by the 39-year-old Brazilian composer Marlos NOBRE, dedicated to the composer's father who was an amateur guitar player. *Spur* for accordion and orchestra by the 47-year-old Norwegian composer Arne NORDHEIM, the title suggesting an impulse generated in the subconscious. *Cantata Y* by the 43-year-old Hungarian composer Sandor BALASSA, composed for the 700th anniversary of the town of Györ. *Time of Orchestral Time* by the 49-year-old Japanese composer Joji YUASA, in three parts, each designated to represent a single macrocosm lasting twenty minutes.

12 May 1978

On the seventh day of the Fifty-second Festival of the International Society for Contemporary Music, the following program of intermedia and music theater is presented in Helsinki:

Penetrations VI by the 49-year-old Argentine-Canadian composer Alcides LANZA. *Oedipe Sphinx/Crimes sans initiales* by the French composer Gherasim Luca-Gilles EHRMANN. *Synchrone Klänge aus dem Rauschen* by the 35-year-old German composer Ulrike TRÜSTEDT, comprising elements of environmental noises and semiotics.

12 May 1978

Sixth Symphony by the Yugoslav composer Alekcandar OBRADOVIĆ, subtitled *Explicatio duplex, expressio triplex*, in three movements, *Allegro* for wind instruments, *Largo* for strings and *Finale* for full orchestra, repeating the musical contents of both previous movements (hence the Latin subtitle), is performed for the first time in Belgrade.

13 MAY 1978
On the eighth day of the Fifty-second Festival of the International Society for Contemporary Music, the following program of chamber music is presented in Helsinki:

Voice of the Shades for soprano, violin and clarinet by the 39-year-old Australian composer Jennifer FOWLER. *Music for Violin Solo* by the 32-year-old American composer Daria SEMEGEN, in which the violin makes use of tone clusters and other unviolinistic sonorities. *Q for Five* for soprano saxophone and chamber ensemble by the 26-year-old British composer Jonty HARRISON, with Q assigned five different functions, including a cue and a queue. *Ritos* for harp by the 39-year-old Brazilian composer Ricardo TACUCHIAN, in which primitive Indian rituals are organized in a sophisticated modern technique. *I Am Goya*, to the text of Andrey Voznesensky, for bass baritone and chamber ensemble by the 30-year-old British composer Nigel OSBORNE, reminiscing of the hideous Russian war winter of 1941. *Biálogo* for French horn, guitar and tape by the 28-year-old Portuguese composer Paulo BRANDÃO, a dialectic interchange between the guitar and the French horn resulting in a biological synthesis.

14 MAY 1978
On the ninth day of the Fifty-second Festival of the International Society for Contemporary Music, the following program of chamber music is presented at an afternoon concert in Helsinki:

Metaboles IV by the 32-year-old Austrian composer Klaus AGER, illustrating the musical metabolism through a seventy-two-tone system, including overtones and combination tones. *String Quartet No. 2* by the 37-year-old Finnish composer Erkki JOKINEN. *Cordes Plus* for viola and tape by the 42-year-old French composer Maurice BENHAMOU, in which the viola is given four extra strings (which explains the title). *Vēdomí souvislosti (Imaginable Connections)* by the 49-year-old Czech composer Václav KUČERA, in which a stream of dissonance leads to a final fugue. *Mutationen XII* for double-bass, tape and chamber ensemble by the 59-year-old Brazilian composer Claudio SANTORO, representing the process of democratization of electronic music by giving the performers equal rights to decide what to play.

14 MAY 1978
The Fifty-second Festival of the International Society for Contemporary Music concludes in Helsinki with the following program of percussion music presented at an evening concert:

Redskap by the 27-year-old Swedish composer Klas TORSTENSSON, the title meaning a tool for solving the problems of musical structure. *Campanella* by the 43-year-old Polish composer Zbigniew RUDZIŃSKI, in which a variety of bells and other metal percussion instruments results in a sonoriferous tintinnabulation (hence the title). *Sound First!* by the 51-year-old Japanese composer Michiharu MATSUNAGA, being an exclamatory celebration of sound as a primary element of all music. *A-Hun* by the 50-year-old Japanese composer Minoru KOBASHI, the title being a Sanskrit word beginning with the opening of the mouth and ending with the closing of it. *Siderals,* an audiovisual composition by the 35-year-old Polish composer Marta PTASZYŃSKA, the title suggesting constellations that are in constant motion, requiring 117 percussion instruments to account for it.

22 MAY 1978
The National Afro-American Philharmonic Orchestra, with an all-black personnel, presents its first concert at the Academy of Music in Philadelphia under the direction of James Frazier.

30 MAY 1978
Fourth Symphony by the 75-year-old English composer Sir Lennox BERKELEY is performed for the first time by the Royal Philharmonic Orchestra under the direction of Sir Charles Groves in London.

2 JUNE 1978
A World Within, tape composition for ballet consisting of multitrack recordings of a horn by the 31-year-old British composer Giles SWAYNE, based on the life of the Brontë sisters, is performed for the first time in Stoke-on-Trent.

7 JUNE 1978
Thirteenth Symphony by the solipsistic Swedish composer Allan PETTERSSON is performed for the first time in Bergen, Norway.

9 JUNE 1978
Thirty-fifth Symphony by the interminably fruitful 67-year-old American composer Alan HOVHANESS, scored for Korean instruments and orchestra, is performed for the first time in Seoul, Korea.

16 JUNE 1978
The Two Fiddlers, opera for young people by the 43-year-old British composer Peter Maxwell DAVIES, is performed for the first time in Orkney.

21 JUNE 1978
Evita, a show by the 30-year-old British wonderboy of the musical theater, Andrew LLOYD WEBBER, based on the fantastic career of the cabaret singer who married the Argentine populist dictator Juan Perón, and who became an object of well-nigh goddesslike worship among the Argentine populace after her untimely death of cancer ("Don't cry for me, Argentina," she sings), is produced in London.

11 July 1978

Fourth Symphony by the 39-year-old English composer John McCABE is performed for the first time by the Royal Philharmonic Orchestra of London under the direction of Charles Dutoit.

13 July 1978

Second Symphony for vocal soloists, chorus and orchestra by the 53-year-old English composer Anthony MILNER is performed for the first time in Liverpool.

18 July 1978

Violin Concerto by the 49-year-old Soviet composer Edison DENISOV is performed for the first time in Milan.

2 August 1978

Carlos CHÁVEZ, thaumaturgical Mexican composer, conductor and educator whose works conveyed the essence of Latin American lore within the contrapuntal set of cosmopolitan musical science and who for years guided the destinies of new music of his land, dies in Mexico City at the age of seventy-nine.

5 August 1978

At a meeting of citizens of Parowan, Utah, it is resolved to name a local mountain Mt. Messiaen, in honor of the French composer Olivier MESSIAEN, who spent a month in Utah in 1973 and wrote a symphonic work, *Des Canyons aux étoiles*, to glorify the natural beauty of the state.

18 August 1978

The Duchess of Malfi, opera by the 35-year-old American composer Stephen Douglas BURTON, is produced at Wolf Trap Farm Park near Washington, D.C.

25 August 1978

Sunday Morning, eight-part symphonic suite by the American composer Ned ROREM, inspired by the eponymous poem by Wallace Stevens, is performed for the first time by the Philadelphia Orchestra in Saratoga Springs, New York, conducted by Eugene Ormandy.

5 September 1978

Piano Concerto by the Soviet composer Edison DENISOV is performed for the first time in Leipzig.

8 September 1978

Pantcho VLADIGEROV, prime Bulgarian composer whose ballets, symphonic music and chamber music are permeated with asymmetrical native melorhythms, dies in Sofia at the age of seventy-nine.

14 September 1978

Essay No. 3 for orchestra by Samuel BARBER is performed for the first time by the New York Philharmonic, conducted by Zubin Mehta on his debut as the orchestra's newly appointed musical director.

28 September 1978

Eighth Concerto for orchestra by the 74-year-old Italian composer Goffredo PETRASSI is performed for the first time in Chicago.

26 October 1978

First Symphony by the intransigent Dutch modern composer Peter SCHAT, commissioned by the city of Amsterdam to commemorate the ninetieth anniversary of the Concertgebouw Orchestra, is performed for the first time by that orchestra in Amsterdam, Colin Davis conducting.

2 November 1978

Viola Concerto by the 50-year-old American composer Jacob DRUCKMAN is performed for the first time by Sol Greitzer as soloist with the New York Philharmonic conducted by James Levine.

3 November 1978

Exotic Suite for two violins, two electric guitars, saxophone and percussion by the 46-year-old Soviet composer Sergei SLONIMSKY, in three parts, *Configurations, Love's Tears* and *Dance with a Tambourin,* is performed for the first time in Leningrad.

16 November 1978

Spatial Concerto, subtitled *Questions from "Genesis,"* for piano, sixteen women's voices and orchestra by the adventurous American composer Henry BRANT, in one continuous movement consisting of ten nonrecurring sections, with the pianist instructed to play on the strings under the lid, is performed for the first time by the Tucson Symphony, conducted by George Trautwein, with Hilde Somer as a courageous piano soloist.

17 November 1978

Dr. Heidegger's Fountain of Youth, opera by the 57-year-old American composer Jack BEESON, based on the story by Nathaniel Hawthorne, is produced for the first time in New York.

22 November 1978

Fourth Symphony by the American composer Easley BLACKWOOD is performed for the first time by the Chicago Symphony Orchestra conducted by Sir Georg Solti.

25 November 1978

Frankenstein!!, a "pandemonium" by the 35-year-old Austrian composer Heinz Karl GRUBER, for a baritone chansonnier who recites children's verses in a mock-scary manner, and orchestra, is performed for the first time in London. (A version for a vocalist and a twelve-member ensemble was performed for the first time at the Berlin Festival of New Music on 30 September 1979.)

29 November 1978

Paradise Lost, "sacra rappresentazione" by the prime Polish modernist composer Krzysztof PENDERECKI, originally planned for a production during the 1976 American bicentennial, comes to a belated performance by the Lyric Opera of Chicago.

30 November 1978

Punainen viiva (The Red Line), opera by the 43-year-old Finnish composer Aulis SALLINEN, to the composer's own libretto based on a Finnish novel by Ilmari Kianto (1874–1970) dealing with an unexpected victory of women's suffrage in Finland in 1907 (the red line of the title was the mark of support on the new social order to be put on the ballot), set to music in a highly dramatic manner with a strong injection of Finnish folk modalities and an ample infusion of unambiguous dissonance, is performed for the first time in Helsinki. (The first American performance took place at the Metropolitan Opera in New York on 27 April 1983.)

2 December 1978

Jazavac pred sudom (The Badger Before the Jury), the first nationalist opera of Bosnia by the 77-year-old composer Vlado MILOSEVIĆ, inspired by a folk legend wherein Austro-Hungarian rule in Bosnia is wittily satirized, is produced in Sarajevo (the historic locality where a Bosnian youth assassinated the heir to the Austrian throne in the summer of 1914, precipitating the First World War).

3 December 1978

William Grant STILL, whose popularity earned for him the appellation "Dean of Afro-American Composers," and whose many works were profoundly infused with the pride of his race as expressed in his use of folk-like thematic sources, dies in Los Angeles at the age of eighty-three.

10 December 1978

Syringa, cantata by the American composer Elliott CARTER, scored for soprano and chamber ensemble, is performed for the first time in New York.

18 DECEMBER 1978

Triple Concerto for clarinet, bass clarinet, contrabass clarinet and chamber orchestra by the 47-year-old American composer Donald MARTINO is performed for the first time by the Group for Contemporary Music, at the Manhattan School of Music in New York.

∽ *1979* ∽

9 JANUARY 1979

Un enfant appelle for soprano, cello and orchestra by the 63-year-old French composer Marcel LANDOWSKI, to poems of Marie-Noël, is performed for the first time in Washington, D.C., with Galina Vishnevskaya and Mstislav Rostropovich as spousal soloists.

11 JANUARY 1979

Gaku-no-Michi (Voices of Music) by the 40-year-old French composer Jean-Claude ELOY, set for four tapes, originally recorded at the Nippon Studio of electronic music in Tokyo in 1978 with an admixture of concrete music, is performed publicly for the first time in its totality lasting four hours at the Autumn Festival in Paris.

16 JANUARY 1979

Thirty-sixth Symphony for solo flute and orchestra by the indefatigable Alan HOVHANESS is performed for the first time by Jean-Pierre Rampal and the National Symphony Orchestra in Washington, D.C., under the direction of Mstislav Rostropovich. On the same concert the *Contrabassoon Concerto*, the first concerto ever written for this instrument, plying the depths of the sound spectrum, by the learned American composer Gunther SCHULLER, receives its premiere with Lewis Lipnick as soloist.

18 JANUARY 1979

Reflections of Emily for treble voices, piano, harp and percussion by the 55-year-old American composer Peter MENNIN, to texts from poems of Emily Dickinson, is performed for the first time in New York.

25 JANUARY 1979

The intransigent Italian avant-gardist Luciano BERIO conducts in Los Angeles the first performance of his *Ritorno degli Snovidenia (Return of Dreams; snovidenia* is a Russian word for dream visions) for cello and orchestra.

29 JANUARY 1979
Aftertones of Infinity, symphonic poem by the American composer Joseph SCHWANTNER, which won the 1979 Pulitzer Prize, is performed for the first time by the New York Philharmonic, Lukas Foss conducting.

29 JANUARY 1979
Third Violin Concerto by the 44-year-old Soviet composer Alfred SCHNITTKE is performed for the first time in Moscow.

3 FEBRUARY 1979
Galileo Galilei, opera by the American composer Ezra LADERMAN, originally written as an oratorio for television, to the libretto by Joe Darion, is performed for the first time in Binghamton, New York.

3 FEBRUARY 1979
Musique pour un Vernissage by the 40-year-old American composer Barbara KOLB, scored for flute, violin, viola and guitar, originally intended to be played as "furniture music" or "music to walk by" à la Satie, is premiered as a concert piece at the Kennedy Center in Washington, D.C., Leon Fleischer conducting.

10 FEBRUARY 1979
A *Solo Requiem* for soprano and two pianos by the 62-year-old American composer of mathematical bent Milton BABBITT is performed for the first time in New York.

24 FEBRUARY 1979
Lulu, opera by Alban BERG with the unfinished third act completed by Friedrich CERHA, is performed for the first time in its enhanced version in Paris with Pierre Boulez conducting.

1 MARCH 1979
Palintropos for piano and orchestra by the 35-year-old British composer John TAVENER is performed for the first time in Birmingham, England.

7 MARCH 1979
Klaus EGGE, romantically inclined, intellectually inventive Norwegian composer, who signed his scores with the autobiographical notes E-g-g-e, dies in Oslo at the age of seventy-two.

17 MARCH 1979
Orpheus, a story in six scenes by the 52-year-old German composer Hans Werner HENZE, is given its world premiere by the Württemberg State Opera in Stuttgart.

24 March 1979

Concerto for flute, oboe and orchestra by the 49-year-old Soviet composer Edison Denisov is performed for the first time by Aurele Nicolet and Heniz Holliger as soloists with the orchestra of the West German Republic in Cologne.

10 April 1979

Nino Rota, Italian composer of operas, oratorios, and symphonic works in a pleasingly modernized settecento manner, dies in Rome at the age of sixty-seven.

11 April 1979

Teuta, ballet in three acts by the 73-year-old Croatian composer Boris Papandopulo, glorifying in martial sonorities the imperious Queen Teuta of the once powerful ancient kingdom of Illyria on the eastern shores of the Adriatic, who daringly defied Rome until she was finally subdued by the Roman navy in 228 B.C., is produced in Novi Sad, Yugoslavia.

12 April 1979

Fifteenth Symphony, with chorus, subtitled "I have faith in this earth," by the 59-year-old Soviet composer Moisei Vainberg, is performed for the first time in Moscow.

20 April 1979

Sial for Baroque instruments and chamber ensemble by the 60-year-old Croatian composer Branimir Sakač, representing in musical terms the two principal elements of the earth's crust, silicon (Si) and aluminum (Al), is performed for the first time in Zagreb.

22 April 1979

Miracles for boys' choir and orchestra by Gian Carlo Menotti, to words from verses written by children, is performed for the first time in Fort Worth, Texas.

28 April 1979

Concerto piccolo for a saxophone player performing alternatively on four saxophones (bass, tenor, alto, soprano) and for six percussionists by the 50-year-old Soviet composer Edison Denisov is performed for the first time in Bordeaux.

28 April 1979

Mangrove for orchestra by the Australian composer Peter Sculthorpe is performed for the first time in Sydney, on the eve of his fiftieth birthday.

30 April 1979

Full Moon in March, opera by the 40-year-old American composer John Harbison, to a text by Yeats, is performed for the first time in Cambridge, Massachusetts.

1 May 1979

Cheers for orchestra by the brilliant American composer Morton Gould is performed for the first time in Boston.

2 May 1979

Quintets for orchestra by the 57-year-old American composer Lukas Foss is performed for the first time in Cleveland.

3 May 1979

Medea, opera by the 52-year-old American composer Ray Luke, is produced in Boston.

4 May 1979

Eighth Symphony by the 57-year-old English composer Malcolm Arnold is performed for the first time by the Albany (New York) Symphony.

16 May 1979

Double Concerto for violin, cello and orchestra by the American composer Ned Rorem is performed for the first time in Cincinnati.

18 May 1979

As of a Dream by the 66-year-old American composer Norman Dello Joio, scored for narrator, chorus and orchestra to a text by Walt Whitman, is performed for the first time in Midland, Michigan.

19 May 1979

Animalen (The Animals), opera by the 53-year-old Swedish composer Lars Johan Werle, to a libretto treating the fateful antagonism between America and Russia in which representatives of both nations hurl their slogans at each other, but whose enmity is unexpectedly challenged by the animals of the world who force both sides to reconcile their differences, is produced in Göteborg.

3 June 1979

La Loca, opera by the 67-year-old Italian-born composer Gian Carlo Menotti, commissioned by the San Diego Opera to honor the quinquegenarian opera mistress Beverly Sills, based on the true story of fifteenth-century Juana of Castile who goes mad after her husband, father and son try to usurp her throne and contrive to have her incarcerated for nearly fifty years, is produced in San Diego, with Sills herself in the leading role.

5 JUNE 1979
Kentervilski duh (The Ghost of Canterville), comic opera by the 73-year-old Croatian composer Boris PAPANDOPULO, after the satirically fantastic tale by Oscar Wilde, is produced in Osijek.

6 JUNE 1979
Aureole for orchestra by the American composer Jacob DRUCKMAN, commissioned by and dedicated to Leonard Bernstein, is performed for the first time by the New York Philharmonic Orchestra, Bernstein conducting.

17 JUNE 1979
Concerto Festivo by the 64-year-old Polish composer Andrzej PANUFNIK, in three movements, *Pomposo* for brass only, *Lirico* for strings and woodwinds and *Giocoso* for full orchestra, is performed for the first time by the London Symphonic Orchestra, without a conductor.

21 JUNE 1979
Octet by the 42-year-old American composer Steve REICH, scored for string quartet, two pianos and two clarinets (doubling on flute and piccolo), is performed for the first time by members of the Netherlands Wind Ensemble under the direction of Reinbert de Leeuw, at Radio Frankfurt.

23 JUNE 1979
Symphonie en l'honneur du Soleil by the 82-year-old French composer Jean RIVIER is performed for the first time on the "Day of the Sun" in Paris, as a commission of the French Ministry of Culture.

27 JUNE 1979
Paul DESSAU, German composer, one of the most fervent and intelligent practitioners of socialist music in a fitting amalgam with *Gebrauchsmusik*, who however refused to abandon his endemic experimentalism, dies in East Berlin at the age of eighty-four.

10 JULY 1979
Arthur FIEDLER, Boston-born and -bred scion of a German-Jewish family of musicians, who from a humble beginning as a viola player in the Boston Symphony rose to the heights of pop fame as conductor of the celebrated Boston Pops Orchestra, ministered to a relaxed summer audience undisturbed by the clinking of beer mugs and clanking of salad dishes, dies in Brookline, Massachusetts, of a recurrent heart

attack at the age of eighty-four, just short of completing half a century of presiding over the Pops, and deeply mourned by the people of Boston.

12 JULY 1979
Hymn for chorus and orchestra by the 40-year-old British composer Jonathan HARVEY, written for the 900th anniversary of the Winchester Cathedral, is performed there for the first time.

9 AUGUST 1979
Nymph and Satyr, ballet by the 82-year-old American composer Howard HANSON, is performed for the first time in Chautauqua, Tennessee.

20 AUGUST 1979
The Winter's Tale, opera after Shakespeare by the 40-year-old American composer John HARBISON, is performed for the first time in San Francisco.

6 SEPTEMBER 1979
Third Symphony by the 27-year-old British composer Oliver KNUSSEN is performed for the first time by the BBC Symphony Orchestra in London.

10 SEPTEMBER 1979
Stanislaus LUDKEWYCZ, Polish composer and educator, who composed romantic tone poems and piano works inspired by Ukrainian lore, and who as a soldier in the Austrian army was taken prisoner by the Russians in the First World War, dies in Lwów (after 1945 spelled Lvov as part of the Ukrainian Socialist Republic) at the all but incredible age of one hundred, honored by the Soviet government with the Order of the Red Banner.

11 SEPTEMBER 1979
The Fifty-third Festival of the International Society for Contemporary Music opens in Athens with the following program:

Das Glashaus, operetta for seven musicalizing actors by the 42-year-old Swiss composer Hans WÜTHRICH-MATHEZ, conducted by the composer. *Minimal* for bass clarinet, electronic manipulations and automatic percussion by the 28-year-old German-born Dutch composer Michael FAHRES. *The Horn of Plenty*, a musical cornucopia for amplified horn, percussion and tape by the 43-year-old Belgian composer Claude A. COPPENS, with the rhythmic organization derived from all prime numbers up to 1,453 (the year when Constantinople fell to the Turks), in five acts symbolizing the senses of the eye, the ear, the brain, the tongue and the nose. *Kijo*, theater piece for baritone and five percussionists by the 51-year-old Japanese composer Minoru KOBASHI.

12 SEPTEMBER 1979
On the second day of the Fifty-third Festival of the International Society
for Contemporary Music in Athens, the following program of Swiss music
is presented at an afternoon concert:

Zeitraum for violin, alto flute, cello and bass clarinet by 36-year-old Urs Peter
SCHNEIDER. *Von Magischem Nr. 7* by 35-year-old Peter STREIFF, scored for
two horns, organ, two strings and piano, based on an automatic script in graphic
notation. *Schattenküsse* for solo piano by 36-year-old Rolland MOSER, written in
an ostentatiously comprehensible idiom.

12 SEPTEMBER 1979
On the second day of the Fifty-third Festival of the International Society
for Contemporary Music in Athens, the following program is given at an
early evening concert:

Piano Duo by the 33-year-old Italian composer Luca LOMBARDI. *Blick der Natur*
for soprano, mezzo-soprano, clarinet, horn and percussion by the 51-year-old
Slovenian composer Jakob JEŽ, with a text of pure acoustic quality without
imposition of a specific means. *Intervals* for chamber choir, flute, cello and harp
by the 45-year-old Dutch composer Joep STRAESSER. *Refractions* for two amplified pianos by the 36-year-old Swedish composer Mats PERSSON, symbolizing
an acoustic refraction of several different sounds. *Stabat Mater* for a cappella
choir by the 33-year-old Norwegian composer Olav Anton THOMMESSEN. *Beta*
by the 43-year-old Austrian composer Klaus AGER, originally intended for the
duration of twenty-four hours and requiring forty-eight vocalists, forty-eight
percussion players, and twelve tam-tams, ballet and lights, with performers
executing bilabial and dental vocables, striving to achieve an unending flow of
sound.

12 SEPTEMBER 1979
The second day of the Fifty-third Festival of the International Society
for Contemporary Music continues in Athens, with a late night concert
featuring the following program of electronic works:

Cellule 75 for piano, percussion and tape by the 33-year-old French composer
Luc FERRARI. *Homenaje a la flecha clavada en el pecho de Don Juan Deaz de
Solis* (*Homage to the arrow plunged into the breast of Don Juan Deaz de Solis*)
for tape by the 39-year-old Uruguayan composer Coriún AHARONIAN. *En Pyri*
(*In Fire*) by the 46-year-old Macedonian composer Stephanos VASSILIADIS,
scored for amplified double-bass, tape and projections, in memory of the great
Greek composer Jani CHRISTOU who perished in an automobile accident.

13 SEPTEMBER 1979
On the third day of the Fifty-third Festival of the International Society
for Contemporary Music in Athens the following program is given in an
afternoon concert:

Sol-Jay by the Australian composer Helen STANDRING, scored for two trombones and concerned with the psychology of freedom. *Stichomythia II* for solo guitar by the 44-year-old Greek composer Theodore ANTONIOU. *Colori* for solo piano by the 44-year-old Danish composer Bent LORENTZEN, in five movements symbolized by five perceived colors, red, white, gold, azure and black, with the last movement reflecting the Latin American music of black composers. *Intermezzo* for six flutes by the 39-year-old Slovak composer Juraj BENEŠ, the metrical foundation being represented by a minim divided into six to eleven semiquavers. *Piano Piece I* by the 45-year-old Berlin-born composer Erhard GROSSKOPF, conceived as a quasi sonata. *Cello Einsatz* for solo cello by the 48-year-old East German composer Paul-Heinz DITTRICH. *Syneirmoni (Associations)* for chamber ensemble by the 69-year-old Hellenist Yannis PAPAIOANNOU.

13 SEPTEMBER 1979
On the third day of the Fifty-third Festival of the International Society for Contemporary Music in Athens, the following program of modern Hungarian music is given at an evening concert:

Capricorn Concerto for chamber orchestra by the 46-year-old Miklós KOCSÁR. *Monologo* for violin by the 48-year-old László KALMÁR. *Quartet* by the 49-year-old László SÁRY, based on a serial set of tones, rhythms and dynamics. *Improvisation* for cimbalom by the 46-year-old István LÁNG. *Improvisations I* for zither solo by the 40-year-old Attila BOZAY. *Eight Duos* for violin and cimbalom and *In Memory of a Winter Sunset* for soprano, violin and cimbalom by the 53-year-old György KURTÁG. *Pro Somno Igoris Stravinsky Quieto*, a memorial piece for chamber ensemble by the 58-year-old András SZÖLLÖZY.

14 SEPTEMBER 1979
On the fourth day of the Fifty-third Festival of the International Society for Contemporary Music in Athens a special presentation is given at Delphi of *The Midnight Sun* by the 50-year-old Japanese composer Joji YUASA, a double homage to Apollo, Greek god of the Sun, and Amaterasu, the Japanese sun god.

15 SEPTEMBER 1979
On the fifth day of the Fifty-third Festival of the International Society for Contemporary Music in Athens, an afternoon concert is given with the following program:

Tromboffolón for horn, trumpet, trombone (interchangeable with tuba) and tape by the 49-year-old Uruguayan composer Ariel MARTÍNEZ. *Tayutai* for koto and baritone by the 47-year-old Japanese composer Makoto SHINCHARA, analyzing psychological dilemmas between hope and despair. *Korpus et Antikorpus* by the 36-year-old Brazilian composer Agnaldo RIBEIRO, scored for thirteen instruments and representing the sonic battle between life-asserting generators (corpus) and life-denying sound generators (anticorpus). *Encomium to Skalkottas* for solo clarinet by the 50-year-old Greek composer Nikos MAMANGAKIS, being an homage to the late Greek composer Nikos SKALKOTTAS.

Arsis for flute, two pianos, two percussionists and double-bass by the 26-year-old Venezuelan composer Emilio MENDOZA. *Il Fa-To-Re* for solo recorder by the 32-year-old Austrian-born Finnish composer Herman RECHBERGER, the tonal materials being derived from the three notes F, B-flat and G. *Stationen* for wind ensemble by the 30-year-old German composer Raimund JÜLICH.

15 SEPTEMBER 1979
The fifth day of the Fifty-third Festival of the International Society for Contemporary Music in Athens continues with an evening concert presenting the following program of Polish music:

Quartet for four actors consisting of twenty-five musical and nonmusical scenes by the 50-year-old foremost empiricist Boguslaw SCHAEFFER. *Spirale II* by 49-year-old Loencjusz SIUCIURA, scored for flute, cello, harpsichord, celesta and piano. *Dichromia* for flute and piano by 51-year-old Adam WALACIŃSKI, a study in contrasts of two colors. *Lamentation* by 54-year-old Andrzej NIKODEMOWICZ, scored for soprano, flute, cello and two pianos. *C'est-à-dire* by 33-year-old Józef RYCHLIK, scored for flute, cello, harpsichord, two pianos and tape, the title being an explicative French expression meaning "that is to say." *Bel canto* for soprano, cello, celesta and percussion by Krystyna MOSZUMARŃSKA-NAZAR. *Heraklitiana* by Boguslaw SCHAEFFER, a spectacle for four actors (speaking four different European languages), piano and tape, inspired by the maxim of Heraclitus that all life is motion.

16 SEPTEMBER 1979
The sixth day of the Fifty-third Festival of the International Society for Contemporary Music in Athens continues with an evening concert presenting the following program of Austrian music:

Scenes from the opera *Daidalia oder das Leben einer Theorie* by the 58-year-old Bulgarian-born ethnically Greek composer, resident of Austria, Anestis LOGOTHETIS. *Curriculum* for thirteen wind instruments by the 53-year-old Austrian modernist and scholar Friedrich CERHA. *Gegenstimme* for voice, cello and tape by 29-year-old Wilhelm Zobl. *Cacophony-Euphony* for actress, tape and live electronics by 38-year-old Dieter KAUFMANN, representing the dichotomous imbalance of dissonances and consonances. *Sonata* for solo cello by the 60-year-old Polish-born cosmopolitan composer Roman HAUBENSTOCK-RAMATI. *Frankenstein Suite*, a "pandemonium" for baritone, quintet and toy instruments by 36-year-old Karl Heinz GRUBER.

17 SEPTEMBER 1979
Fifth Symphony for string orchestra by the 36-year-old Polish composer Krzysztof MEYER is performed for the first time in Bialystok.

17 SEPTEMBER 1979
On the seventh day of the Fifty-third Festival of the International Society for Contemporary Music in Athens, an early evening concert is given featuring the following works:

Piano by the 53-year-old American ultramodernist Morton FELDMAN. *Quartet* for flute and strings by the 50-year-old Greek composer Michael ADAMIS. *Quilisma* for piano and string quartet by the 47-year-old Italian composer Niccolò CASTIGLIONI. *Strangeness, Charm and Color* for piano, two trumpets and trombone by the 36-year-old German composer Rolf GELHAAR, portraying the subatomic particles (quarks, whose characteristics are denoted by the titular terms), in their constant collisions, consisting of twenty-seven exponentially related structures. *Liturgia Profana* by the Greek composer Dimitris TERZAKIS, scored for choir, soloists, cellos and percussion.

17 SEPTEMBER 1979

The seventh day of the Fifty-third Festival of the International Society for Contemporary Music in Athens continues with a late evening concert of the following program of electronic music:

Terrortorium for tape by the 30-year-old Greek composer Vanghelis KATSOULIS, portraying the apocalyptic horrors of life and death. *Androgyny* for quadraphonic tape by the 32-year-old Canadian composer Barry TRUAX, inspired by the *I Ching*, implying the simultaneous presence of the male/female elements. *Antiphony I* for tape by the 50-year-old Greek composer Nikiphoros ROTAS. *Myr* for computer-controlled tape, electronic transformations and slide projections by the 28-year-old Swedish composer Rolf ENSTRÖM, representing the chaotic state of the world and the necessity of mankind to prove its right to exist.

18 SEPTEMBER 1979

On the eighth day of the Fifty-third Festival of the International Society for Contemporary Music in Athens, the following program of American music is presented at an afternoon concert:

Synchronisms No. 6 for piano and electronic sounds by the 45-year-old Argentine-born American composer Mario DAVIDOVSKY. *Granites* for piano by the 84-year-old composer/astrologer Dane RUDHYAR, written in 1929, representing a continuity of sonorities in its five connected sections. *Philomel* for soprano and tape by the 63-year-old musical mathematician Milton BABBITT, inspired by the myth of Philomel who acquired the voice of a nightingale after she was raped by the King of Thrace, with the various mutations arranged in serial tropes. *Two Stevens Songs* for soprano and tape by 38-year-old John MELBY to the text of two poems by Wallace Stevens. *Five Pieces for Piano* by the 82-year-old master of American music Roger SESSIONS, written in the modified twelve-tone system.

18 SEPTEMBER 1979

The eighth day of the Fifty-third Festival of the International Society for Contemporary Music continues in Athens with the Danish Radio Symphony Orchestra presenting the following program at an evening concert:

The Statue of III by the 33-year-old Japanese composer Katsuhiro TsUBONOH. *Music in Twilight* for piano and orchestra by the 40-year-old Polish composer Tomasz SIKORSKI, in a single movement. *Flute Concerto* by the 41-year-old Icelandic composer Atli Heimir SVEINSSON. *Twilight* by the 47-year-old Danish composer Per NØRGAARD.

18 SEPTEMBER 1979

At a special archaeological event at the Philopappos Hill facing the Acropolis in Athens in the context of the Fifty-third Festival of the International Society for Contemporary Music, a multimedia spectacle is presented at night with music by the 28-year-old French composer Patrick FLEURY under the title *Espace IX*.

19 SEPTEMBER 1979

On the ninth day of the Fifty-third Festival of the International Society for Contemporary Music in Athens two concerts of music by the greatly esteemed and deeply mourned Greek composer Nikos SKALKOTTAS (1904–1949) are presented, including thirty-six piano pieces, an overture, violin concerto and *Symphony* in one movement, subtitled *The Return of Ulysses*.

20 SEPTEMBER 1979

On the tenth day of the Fifty-third Festival of the International Society for Contemporary Music in Athens the following program of chamber music is presented at an afternoon concert:

Carols for solo trombone and percussion by the 25-year-old Rumanian composer Serban NICHIFOR. *Fast Dances, Slow Dances* for piano by the 33-year-old British composer Michael FINNISSY, performed by the composer. *La espiral eterna* for solo guitar by the 40-year-old Cuban composer Leo BROUWER. *Mono-status* for three clarinets by the 26-year-old British composer Avril ANDERSON. *Tremor* for violin and tape by the 39-year-old Swedish composer Jan W. MORTHENSON.

20 SEPTEMBER 1979

The Fifty-third Festival of the International Society for Contemporary Music in Athens concludes with the following program of chamber music at an evening concert:

Carmen Criaturalis for solo horn, strings, and percussion by the Argentine composer Alicia TERZIAN. *Ach, trauriger Mond* (*Oh, Sad Moon*) for percussion and chamber orchestra by the 31-year-old German composer Theo BRAND-MÜLLER, a lament for Federico García Lorca, murdered by the Falangists during the Spanish Civil War. *God's Duet* from *Les Enfants du Sable* for baritone, soprano and chamber ensemble by the 37-year-old Greek composer Georg COUPOUROS. *Dasselbe ist nicht dasselbe* (*The Same Is Not the Same*) for solo side drum by the 40-year-old German composer Nikolaus A. HUBER, expressing the self-contradiction of all music. *Sternengesang* for chamber orchestra by the 32-year-old Lithuanian-born Israeli composer Michael BAROLSKY, reflecting the tenets of Kabbalistic mysticism. *Canción desesperada* for soprano, two basses and chamber orchestra by the 38-year-old Spanish composer Francisco OTERO.

29 SEPTEMBER 1979
Ivan WYSCHNEGRADSKY, Russian composer who for years lived in France and wrote music in quarter tones and other microtonal intervals, and who enjoyed recognition within a circumscribed group of admirers of his fine character and of his distinguished talent, dies in Paris at the age of eighty-six.

30 SEPTEMBER 1979
Te Deum by the foremost Polish composer Krzysztof PENDERECKI, who combines ultramodernism with fervent Catholicism, is performed for the first time in Assisi, Italy.

1 OCTOBER 1979
Thérèse, opera by the 35-year-old British composer John TAVENER, is produced at Covent Garden in London.

1 OCTOBER 1979
Roy HARRIS, extraordinary American composer whose symphonies and chamber music reflect in their rough-hewed harmonies and modally inflected melodies the stark sound of essential America, who found symbolic significance in the circumstance of his birth in Lincoln County, Oklahoma, on Lincoln's birthday, dies in Santa Monica, California, at the age of eighty-one.

10 OCTOBER 1979
Apocalyptica, "scenic vision" by the 55-year-old Croatian composer Milko KELEMEN, a multimedia spectacle wherein biblical associations serve as allegorical symbols for the alienation of people of the totalitarian and atomic era, is produced in Graz, Austria.

20 OCTOBER 1979
Opus Cygne for flute and orchestra by the 48-year-old Italian composer Sylvano BUSSOTTI is performed for the first time in Baden-Baden, West Germany.

22 OCTOBER 1979
Nadia BOULANGER, the legendary nourrice of several generations of American composers, including Aaron Copland, Roy Harris, Walter Piston, Virgil Thomson, Elliott Carter and David Diamond, as well as of such moderns as Igor Markevich, Jean Françaix, Lennox Berkeley and

Dinu Lipati, whose own artistic credo was encompassed within the neoclassical traditions of Stravinsky and Ravel, dies in Paris, blind and nearly deaf, at the age of ninety-two.

25 OCTOBER 1979
Violin Concerto by the 59-year-old American composer Earl KIM is performed for the first time by Itzhak Perlman and the New York Philharmonic Orchestra under the direction of Zubin Mehta.

2 NOVEMBER 1979
Arctica for orchestra by the Finnish composer Erik BERGMAN is performed for the first time in Utrecht, Holland.

16 NOVEMBER 1979
The Donner Party, "dramatic opera in three acts" by the American composer Ronald McFARLAND, to the story of stranded travelers in the Rockies in the winter of 1846 who resorted to cannibalism of dead comrades to survive, is produced for the first time at Chico State University in California. (The second performance took place on 31 July 1982, at the Squaw Valley Theater in the historic town of Squaw Valley, near Donner Pass in Nevada.)

16 NOVEMBER 1979
Amorgos by the 44-year-old French composer François-Bernard MÂCHE, scored for twelve instruments and sea waves recorded at Amorgos Island of the Cyclades group of the Greek Aegean Islands, is performed for the first time in concert form at a festival in Metz, France.

18 NOVEMBER 1979
Celestial Mechanics, subtitled *Makrokosmos IV*, cosmic dances for amplified piano, four hands, by the 50-year-old American composer George CRUMB, is performed for the first time in New York.

24 NOVEMBER 1979
Second Symphony by the 47-year-old Soviet composer Sergei SLONIMSKY, in three movements: *Andante*, in which three basic themes intertwine creating a shimmering succession of alternatingly lyric, dramatic and elegiac moods; *Vivace ben ritmato*, permeated with urban refrains and plunging into the syncopated rhythms of Soviet jazz; and *Lento cantabile*, leading to the fugal finale in an ornamental *ricercar*, is performed for the first time in Leningrad, Gennady Rozhdestvensky conducting.

29 NOVEMBER 1979
Flores musicales for violin, oboe, cello and psaltery electronically manipulated by the 36-year-old composer Ivan TCHEREPNIN, son of Alexander

Tcherepnin, grandson of Nicholas Tcherepnin, is performed for the first time in Boston.

3 DECEMBER 1979
Eleven young rock fans die of asphyxiation, crushed by multitudes at the doors outside Riverfront Coliseum in Cincinnati trying to get seats to hear a concert by the pronominally named British group, THE WHO.

7 DECEMBER 1979
A *Christmas Carol*, opera by the remarkable Scottish composer Thea MUSGRAVE, is performed for the first time by the Virginia Opera Association in Norfolk.

9 DECEMBER 1979
Concerto for piano and string orchestra by the 45-year-old Soviet composer Alfred SCHNITTKE is performed for the first time in Leningrad.

16 DECEMBER 1979
Not by Might, oratorio based on the Books of the Maccabees by the 41-year-old American organist and composer Simon SARGON, is performed for the first time in Dallas, Texas.

30 DECEMBER 1979
Richard RODGERS, greatly endowed American composer of popular music whose *South Pacific* became a Broadway classic, dies in New York at the age of seventy-seven.

 1980

17 JANUARY 1980
Ninth Symphony by the highly significant, independently thinking American composer Roger SESSIONS, in three movements, incorporating for the first time in his music a full-fledged twelve-tone row, is given its world premiere by the Syracuse (New York) Symphony Orchestra, Christopher Keene conducting.

17 JANUARY 1980
Gradations for orchestra by the Soviet composer Vladimir ZAGORTSEV is performed for the first time, fourteen years after its completion, by the New York Philharmonic, Zubin Mehta conducting.

24 JANUARY 1980

Three Colloquies for French horn and orchestra by the 69-year-old American composer William SCHUMAN is performed for the first time by Philip Myers as virtuoso soloist with the New York Philharmonic Orchestra directed by Zubin Mehta.

25 JANUARY 1980

Second Violin Concerto by the recondite Swedish composer Allan PETTERSSON, employing some of his own ballad tunes, is performed for the first time on the Swedish Radio in Stockholm.

8 FEBRUARY 1980

Erschöpfung der Welt (Exhaustion of the World), opera by the Argentine-born German-radicated noumenally cosmopolitan composer Mauricio KAGEL, is produced in Stuttgart.

19 FEBRUARY 1980

Variations for winds, strings and keyboards by the 43-year-old soi-disant minimalist American composer Steve REICH is performed for the first time in New York. (A revised version for full orchestra was first performed by the San Francisco Symphony on 14 May 1980.)

23 FEBRUARY 1980

In Memory of a Summer Day for soprano and orchestra by the American composer David DEL TREDICI, Part I of his serial tone poems *Child Alice*, inspired by Lewis Carroll's children's classic, and which won for him the 1980 Pulitzer Prize, is performed for the first time with Phyllis Bryn-Julson, soprano, and the St. Louis Symphony Orchestra, Leonard Slatkin conducting. (Part II was first performed 13 September 1980, Part III 8 May 1981, Part IV 19 November 1981.)

1 MARCH 1980

The Cry of Clytaemnestra, opera by the 45-year-old American composer John EATON, is performed for the first time in Bloomington, Indiana.

5 MARCH 1980

Ringed by the Flat Horizon for orchestra by the 20-year-old British composer George BENJAMIN is performed for the first time in Cambridge.

23 MARCH 1980

Joan TOWER plays in New York for the first time her piano work *Petroushskates*, having a dual allegiance to Stravinsky's ballet and Olympic Games ice skaters.

28 March 1980

Farne for orchestra by the 32-year-old British composer Nicola LeFanu is performed for the first time in Bradford.

29 March 1980

Annunzio Paolo Mantovani, Italian conductor and composer of popular music, who became a British subject and achieved fame as the harmonious creator of the melodious "Mantovani sound" conducive to listening pleasure among worldwide multitudes, dies in Tunbridge Wells at the age of seventy-four.

1 April 1980

The Trumpet Major, opera after Thomas Hardy by the 50-year-old Welsh composer Alun Hoddinott, is produced in Manchester.

5 April 1980

Max Brand, Austrian composer, a pioneer of modern "machine music" of which his opera *Maschinist Hopkins*, to his own libretto, was an examplar, dies in undeserved oblivion at Langenzersdorf, near Vienna, at the age of eighty-three.

7 April 1980

Sixth Symphony by the 44-year-old Soviet Georgian composer Giya Kancheli is performed for the first time in Tbilisi. (A revised version was given in Leipzig on 22 October 1981, conducted by Kurt Masur.)

12 April 1980

Jubilum for orchestra by the remarkable Argentine composer Alberto Ginastera, commissioned for the 400th anniversary of the city of Buenos Aires, is performed for the first time there in the Teatro Colón.

23 April 1980

Cello Concerto by the 52-year-old Serbian composer Aleksandar Obradović is performed for the first time in Belgrade.

23 April 1980

Symphony St. Florian, subtitled *Missa invisibilia*, by the 45-year-old Soviet avant-garde composer Alfred Schnittke, is performed for the first time anywhere by the BBC Symphony Orchestra in London, Gennadi Rozhdestvensky conducting.

1 May 1980

Second Symphony, subtitled *Christmas Symphony*, by the 46-year-old Polish composer Krzysztof Penderecki, containing a musical quotation from the hymn *Silent Night*, is performed for the first time by the New York Philharmonic in Lucerne during its European trip, under the direction of Zubin Mehta, to whom the score is dedicated.

8 MAY 1980

Copernicus (Rituel de mort), chamber opera for soloists, instrumentalists and tape by the 32-year-old Canadian composer Claude VIVIER, is produced in Montreal.

10 MAY 1980

A *Lyric Symphony* by the 53-year-old American composer Robert WYKES is performed for the first time in St. Louis, Missouri.

12 MAY 1980

Piano Concerto by the 41-year-old American composer John HARBISON, written in an effective manner deliberately using the lyrical, dramatic and prestidigital techniques of yore, while retaining the thematic anchors of free atonality and euphonious dissonances, is performed for the first time by the American Composers Orchestra in New York, Gunther Schuller conducting, with Robert Miller as soloist. (It subsequently received the Kennedy Center Award for playable American instrumental music.)

14 MAY 1980

Folk Sinfonia by the 49-year-old Yugoslav composer Boris ULRICH, a collage of medieval and Renaissance elements combined with folkloric motives, culminating with a metamorphosed quotation from Monteverdi's *Incoronazione di Poppea*, is performed for the first time in Zagreb. (It was also produced as a ballet in Zagreb on 9 May 1981.)

18 MAY 1980

Jesu Hochzeit, opera by the 62-year-old Austrian composer Gottfried VON EINEM, in which Christ takes a wife, scandalizing the whole of Christendom, is produced in Vienna.

21 MAY 1980

Prism for orchestra by the American composer Jacob DRUCKMAN is performed for the first time by the Baltimore Symphony Orchestra under the direction of Sergiu Comissiona.

24 MAY 1980

Far calls, Coming far! for violin and orchestra by the 49-year-old Japanese modernist Toru TAKEMITSU, the title being taken from the final paragraph of James Joyce's *Finnegans Wake*, and based on a motive of six notes (E-flat, E, A, C-sharp, F and A-flat), is performed for the first time in Tokyo by Ida Kavafian with the Tokyo Metropolitan Orchestra.

2 JUNE 1980

The world premiere is presented at Bath, England, of Elliott CARTER's *Night Fantasies* for piano, commissioned by and dedicated to four pianists, Paul Jacobs, Gilbert Kalish, Ursula Oppens and Charles Rosen, each of whom subsequently played the work during the 1983 Elliott Carter Festival at the University of Southern California in Los Angeles.

18 JUNE 1980

Notations for orchestra by the cerebrally celebrated French composer Pierre BOULEZ is performed for the first time by the Orchestre de Paris, Daniel Barenboim conducting.

20 JUNE 1980

Allan PETTERSON, remarkable Swedish composer of symphonic and other music permeated with the spirit of radical melancholy, who said about himself, "I am not a composer, I am a voice crying out in the noise of the times," dies in Stockholm crippled by a plethora of degenerative diseases, at the age of seventy-nine.

21 JUNE 1980

Hermetic British composer Peter Maxwell DAVIES conducts in Kirkwall, Orkney, the first performance of his work *The Yellow Cake Revue* for singers and piano, to a text by the composer which inveighs against the ominous threat of covertly radioactive uranium mining in the Orkney Islands.

28 JUNE 1980

José ITURBI, brilliant Spanish pianist acclaimed for his genuine Iberian virtuosity, dies in Hollywood at the age of eighty-four.

28 JUNE 1980

Yoshiro IRINO, Japanese composer who was born in Vladivostok, Siberia, who wrote music in highly advanced techniques permeated with genuine Nipponese melorhythms, dies in Tokyo at the age of fifty-eight.

29 JUNE 1980

The Fifty-fourth Festival of the International Society for Contemporary Music in Israel opens with a concert of chamber music in Jerusalem presenting the following program:

Dialogo 3 for two pianos by the 37-year-old Swedish composer Daniel BÖRTZ. *Renascence* for clarinet solo and tape by the 38-year-old American composer Jonathan D. KRAMER. *The Sunflower* for string quartet by the 26-year-old Danish composer Erik HÖJSGAARD. *Aspro* for clarinet, trombone, cello and piano by the 32-year-old Finnish composer Jukka TEINSUU, the title suggesting singularly rough, austerely barren, acridly pungent and hermetically morose substances. *Arnold Schoenberg in Memoriam* for string quartet by the 39-year-old Polish composer Bronislaw Przybylski, based on a tone row composed on the musical letters in Schoenberg's name. *Epigono* for guitar solo by the 43-year-old Portuguese composer José António Lopes e Silva, the title signifying the living endurance of the immediate past. *Strides* for piano solo by the 51-year-old Dutch composer Theo Loevendie, based on Harlem "stride piano" jazz technique. *About an Old Tune* for piano quartet by the 51-year-old Russian-born Israeli composer Mark Kopytman, the music being an echo of Jewish tunes in a heterophonic setting.

30 June 1980

On the second day of the Fifty-fourth Festival of the International Society for Contemporary Music in Israel, a choral concert is presented in Jerusalem with the following program:

Yogi by the 36-year-old Japanese composer Mayako Kubo. *Requiem* for twelve solo voices by the 49-year-old Chilean composer Leon Schidlowsky. *Jarchas de dolor de ausencia* (*Solace in the Sadness of Absence*) by the 50-year-old Spanish composer Cristóbal Halffter. *Motetus paraburi* for mezzo-soprano, tenor and baritone by the 43-year-old Swiss composer Hans Ulrich Lehmann. *Chorbuch* for choir, piano and harmonium by the 49-year-old Argentine-born German empiricist Mauricio Kagel.

1 July 1980

On the third day of the Fifty-fourth Festival of the International Society for Contemporary Music in Israel, the following program of orchestral music is presented at an afternoon concert in Jerusalem:

Scintilla Prisca for cello and piano by the 43-year-old American composer Brian Fennelly, an homage to his late wife Priscilla (the title means pristine spark). *2+2+2+2* for two flutes, two clarinets, two violas and two cellos by the 33-year-old French composer Gérard Garcin. *String Quartet* by the 30-year-old Belgian composer Franklin Gyselynck. *Zalmen*, subtitled *Madness of God*, for violin by the 43-year-old American composer Norman Dinerstein, evoking the Yom Kippur celebration in Russia. *Koss* for brass quintet by the 42-year-old German composer Hans-Joachim Hespos.

1 July 1980

On the third day of the Fifty-fourth Festival of the International Society for Contemporary Music in Israel, the following program of chamber music is presented by the Jerusalem Symphony Orchestra at an evening concert:

Concerto by the 24-year-old Austrian composer Thomas Pernes, based on a harmonic progression of thirty-eight chords burgeoning into a series of 132 chords in thirty-eight rhythmic patterns. *Cello Concerto* by the Hungarian master of ingeniously interwoven musical patterns, György Ligeti, using a sui generis technique of micropolyphony. *Portrait* for harpsichord and orchestra by

157

the 53-year-old Italian composer Franco DONATONI. *Program Music 1980* by the 53-year-old German-born Israeli composer Tzvi AVNI, in four pictorial movements: *The Machine Game, The Dream of the Broken Mirror, Magritte—A Dilemma?*, a surrealistic superposition of incongruous visual and tonal elements producing a new reality, and *It's a Busy Day in the Beehive*, picturing the death of a male hornet after mating with the queen bee.

2 JULY 1980
On the fourth day of the Fifty-fourth Festival of the International Society for Contemporary Music in Israel, an afternoon concert of electroacoustic music is presented with the following program in Tel Aviv:

Clouds by the 45-year-old Swedish composer Lars-Gunnar BODIN. *Echoes* by the 43-year-old Argentine composer Beatriz FERREYRA. *Return to Clarity* by the 31-year-old Israeli composer Mike SHADOWSKY. *The Pulses of Time* by the 34-year-old New Zealand composer Denis SMALLEY. *Half-Synthetic Boxtrot* by the Finnish composer Marja VESTERINEN, the piece being a parody of a pop concert. *Mr. Frankenstein's Babies* by the 32-year-old German composer Klaus RÖDER, the title representing the microtonal divisions of the composer's own voice.

2 JULY 1980
On the fourth day of the Fifty-fourth Festival of the International Society for Contemporary Music in Israel, an early evening concert of chamber music is given in Tel Aviv with the following program:

Solstice for clarinet, violin, cello and electronics by the 34-year-old Rumanian-born Israeli composer Gabriel IRANYI. *Territoires de l'oubli (Territories of Oblivion)* for piano by the 33-year-old French composer Tristan MURAIL. *Metamorphoses* for flute and string quartet by the 46-year-old Korean composer Sukhi KANG. *Four Songs to Icelandic Poems* for contralto, piano, cello and flute by the 28-year-old Icelandic composer Hjalmar RAGNARSSON. *Iambe* for chamber ensemble by the 44-year-old French composer Michel DECOUST, written in iambic prosody, alternating short and long pulses. *String Quartet No. 2* by the 41-year-old Hungarian composer Attila BOZAY. *Homenaje a Marcel Duchamp* for guitar and flute, a tribute to the famous painter and masterful chess player, by the 35-year-old Spanish composer Francisco ESTÉVAZ. *Mesmerized* for mezzo-soprano, piano, three trumpets and three percussionists by the 37-year-old Dutch composer Jacques BANK, to text from the diary of the English poet Gerard Manley Hopkins.

2 JULY 1980
On the fourth day of the Fifty-fourth Festival of the International Society for Contemporary Music in Israel, a late evening concert, announced as "New Dimensions in Music," is given in Tel Aviv with the following program:

Minos' for harpsichord by the 29-year-old Finnish composer Anneli ARHO. *Fall* for cello, trombone and piano by the 25-year-old Swedish composer Lars

SANDBERG. *Wind Drumming* for woodwind quintet and four percussionists by the 31-year-old Danish composer Poul RUDERS. *Psalm 117* for double-bass by the 30-year-old Rumanian-born Israeli composer Dan LUSTGARTEN. *Oralleluiants* for soprano and chamber ensemble by the 48-year-old Canadian composer Gilles TREMBLAY, the title being a biverbal compact of "orants" (people praying) and "alleluia."

3 JULY 1980

On the fifth day of the Fifty-fourth Festival of the International Society for Contemporary Music in Israel, the following program of chamber music is presented in Beersheba:

Hael for violin, string orchestra and percussion by the 44-year-old Jewish-French composer Maurice BENHAMOU, a musical interpretation of the eighteenth Benediction of the Jewish liturgical calendar glorifying the Lord. *On a Delphic Reed* by the 32-year-old Italian composer Sandro GORLI, scored for oboe solo. *Cors et cordes* for basset horn, two English horns, two French horns, strings and harpsichord by the 37-year-old Dutch composer Geert VAN KEULEN. . . . *With Neither Boundary Nor Rim* . . . by the 56-year-old Swiss composer Klaus HUBER, scored for viola solo (the title is taken from the poem by Hui-k'o, founder of Chinese Zen Buddhism). *Violet Elegy for Monseigneur Romero* by the 38-year-old Brazilian composer Jorge ANTUNES, scored for children's chorus and piano, dedicated to the memory of the progressive Archbishop Oscar Arnulfo Romero of El Salvador, slain in the cathedral by right-wing death squads, with the violet color of the title represented by the thematic note E.

5 JULY 1980

The Fifty-fourth Festival of the International Society for Contemporary Music in Israel concludes with a concert of chamber music at the Kibbutz Shefayim with the following program:

Mensurale by the 41-year-old Italian composer Armando GENTILUCCI, scored for strings and set in the polyphonic idiom of the Flemish "canone mensurale." *Sextet* by the 27-year-old Venezuelan composer Emilio MENDOZA. *Expressions* for strings by the 52-year-old Hungarian composer Kamillo LENDVAY. *Heu de cordes*, an educational "game of strings" with some optional electroacoustical devices echoing the music, by the 34-year-old French composer Fernand VANDENBOGAERDE. *What Name Shall I Call*, a song cycle for soprano and chamber ensemble by the Polish-born 71-year-old composer Shlomo YOFFE, to texts by a member of the Kibbutz who fell in the Yom Kippur War. *Ison I* by the 53-year-old Rumanian composer Stefan NICULESCU, for fourteen wind instruments (the word *ison* is taken from a term of Byzantine monody, wherein a melody is accompanied by a specially assigned long-held tone).

5 JULY 1980

Branchings for orchestra by the 51-year-old American composer Donald KEATS is performed for the first time at the Colorado Music Festival in Boulder.

12 July 1980
Sopiana for flute, piano and magnetic tape by the 45-year-old French composer François-Bernard MÂCHE is performed for the first time in Pecs, Hungary.

20 July 1980
The Last Twilight for chorus, brass and percussion by the 52-year-old Scottish composer Thea MUSGRAVE is performed for the first time in Santa Fe, New Mexico.

23 July 1980
Cry for twenty-eight amplified solo voices, depicting the creation of the world, by the 34-year-old British composer Giles SWAYNE, is performed for the first time in London.

2 August 1980
Pollicino, or The New Adventures of Tom Thumb, "community opera" by the 54-year-old German modernist Hans Werner HENZE, is performed for the first time in Montepulciano, Italy.

15 August 1980
Summer Solstice, symphonic poem by Ezra LADERMAN, is performed for the first time by the Philadelphia Orchestra under the direction of Michael Tilson Thomas in Saratoga Springs, New York.

20 August 1980
Eleventh Symphony by the 79-year-old English composer Edmund RUBBRA is performed for the first time by the BBC Northern Symphony Orchestra in London.

22 August 1980
Triple Concerto for violin, viola, cello and orchestra by the 75-year-old British composer Sir Michael TIPPETT, in three integrated sections, with the concertino of three participating soloists figuratively curtseying before the ripieni, is performed for the first time in London, Sir Colin Davis conducting the London Symphony Orchestra.

22 August 1980
Piers Plowman, opera-cantata in two acts to the poem of William Langland by the 56-year-old British composer of Dutch and Hungarian descent Gerard SCHURMANN, is performed for the first time at the Three Choirs Festival held in the Gloucester Cathedral.

24 August 1980

Double Concerto for oboe, harp and chamber orchestra by Witold LUTOSLAWSKI is performed for the first time by the virtuoso oboist Heinz Holliger with his wife Ursula as harpist at the Ursula Collegium Musicum in Lucerne under the direction of Paul Sacher.

1 September 1980

The Post Office of Great Britain issues a set of commemorative postage stamps glorifying four English conductors: 12 pence for Sir Henry Wood; 13½ pence for Sir Thomas Beecham; 15 pence for Sir John Barbirolli; and 17½ pence for Sir Malcolm Sargent.

5 September 1980

Satyagraha, opera by the 43-year-old American composer Phillip GLASS, dedicated to the political theory of *Satya* and *agraha* (truth and resolution in the original Sanskrit) and adapted from the Indian epic Bhagavad-Gita, the libretto dealing with the life of Mahatma Gandhi in South Africa before his ascent to glory as a prophet of nonviolence, in six ritualistic tableaux with timeless, motionless, changeless music (at one point Gandhi walks at night singing a scale E to E thirty times; at another point a progression of second inversions of a triad is repeated 143 times), is produced in Rotterdam, Holland.

13 September 1980

Happy Voices by the 43-year-old American composer David DEL TREDICI, Part II of his symphonic series *Child Alice*, based on *Alice in Wonderland* and *Through the Looking Glass* by Lewis Carroll, is performed for the first time by the San Francisco Symphony Orchestra, Edo De Waart conducting. (Part I was first performer 23 February 1980, Part III 8 May 1981, and Part IV 19 November 1981.)

15 September 1980

The Servants, opera by the 46-year-old Welsh composer William MATHIAS, to a libretto by Iris Murdoch, is produced by the Welsh National Opera in Cardiff.

24 September 1980

Orchestra for orchestra by the 49-year-old American composer Richard FELICIANO is performed for the first time in San Francisco.

1 October 1980

Entrata for orchestra by Luciano BERIO is performed for the first time by the San Francisco Symphony.

10 October 1980

Maurice MARTENOT, French inventor of the Ondes Martenot for electronic keyboard, dies as a result of a vélocipede accident in Paris four days before his eighty-second birthday.

11 October 1980

A *Fanfare in Memory of André Kostelanetz* by Leonard BERNSTEIN is performed for the first time by the New York Philharmonic, Zubin Mehta conducting.

12 October 1980

Ludi Leopoldini (Leopoldian Games), variations on a theme of Leopold I, Holy Roman emperor 1640–1705, for orchestra by the 62-year-old Austrian composer Gottfried VON EINEM, is performed for the first time in Berlin.

30 October 1980

Requiem by the 51-year-old Soviet composer Edison DENISOV, set for soprano, tenor, chorus and orchestra to the trilingual (German, French, English) text by the modern German poet Francisco Tanzer, in five sections (*Anflug des Lächelns, Fundamental Variation, Danse permanente, Automatic Variation, La Croix*) and containing a quotation from Mozart's *Requiem*, is performed for the first time in Hamburg.

14 November 1980

Piano Concerto by György LIGETI is performed for the first time by Anthony di Bonaventura as soloist with the Cologne Radio Symphony Orchestra, his brother Mario di Bonaventura conducting.

28 November 1980

Two Minor Desperations for chamber orchestra by the 56-year-old German-born American conductor Gerhard SAMUEL is performed for the first time by the San Francisco Symphony Orchestra, the composer conducting.

28 November 1980

Where the Wild Things Are, fantasy opera by the 28-year-old Scottish composer Oliver KNUSSEN, the central character being a small boy confronted with monsters singing in "pidgin Yiddish," and the whole score a mosaic of some twenty-five interdependent microforms, is performed for the first time, in its first version, in Brussels. (The eventual definitive version was first performed on 9 January 1984 in London.)

28 November 1980

Apocalypsis for soloist, chorus and orchestra by the 47-year-old Canadian composer R. Murray SCHAFER, an allegorical spectacle about the destruction of the world according to St. John the Divine, is performed for the first time in London, Ontario.

29 NOVEMBER 1980

Violin Concerto by the 50-year-old Spanish composer Cristóbal HALFFTER is performed for the first time in Madrid.

4 DECEMBER 1980

Orpheus in Pecan Springs, ballad opera by the 63-year-old American composer William LATHAM, to a libretto by Thomas Holliday, is performed for the first time in Denton, Texas.

8 DECEMBER 1980

John LENNON, 40-year-old British singer and song writer, the social philosopher of the glorious Liverpudlian band The Beatles, is gunned down in front of his New York apartment by an assailant besotted by his adulation of Lennon to the point of identifying himself with him.

24 DECEMBER 1980

Alec WILDER, American composer of versatile talents equally amusing in operas, operettas, musical comedies and finely structured chamber music, who was also capable of writing popular songs in a hedonistic and ingratiating style, dies in Gainesville, Florida, at the age of seventy-three.

1981

18 JANUARY 1981

All Done from Memory for violin solo by the 53-year-old American composer Ezra SIMS, based on an eighteen-tone scale of his own device, is performed for the first time by Janet Packer at a Dinosaur Annex Concert in Boston.

23 JANUARY 1981

Samuel BARBER, American composer whose patrician style in composition was etched along fine romantic lines and yet stamped with an unmistakably modernistic imprint and whose poignant *Adagio for Strings* became one of the most affecting and most frequently played American instrumental works, dies of cancer in New York at the still creative age of seventy.

25 JANUARY 1981
Third Symphony, subtitled *Sevastopol,* by the 65-year-old Soviet composer Boris TCHAIKOVSKY, unrelated to the great Tchaikovsky, is performed for the first time in Moscow.

31 JANUARY 1981
Mary Stuart, opera-ballad by the 49-year-old Soviet composer Sergei SLONIMSKY, in three tableaux to a historically accurate libretto by Yakov Gordin, wherein the march of events related by folk narrators traces the fate of the tragic Queen of Scotland, with the sinister Protestant minister John Knox leading the resistance to the Catholic ruler, set to music with an astute application of genuine Scottish melorhythms, invested in darksome dissonant harmonies, is produced in Kuibishev, U.S.S.R. (A Leningrad performance followed on 18 April 1981, and on 26 May 1984 the opera was produced, in a German translation, in Leipzig.)

13 FEBRUARY 1981
Aïs for solo percussionists, amplified baritone and orchestra by the 58-year-old Greek composer and musical mathematician Iannis XENAKIS is performed for the first time in Munich.

19 FEBRUARY 1981
Abélard and Héloise, fifth opera by the 63-year-old American composer Robert WARD, based on the tragic story of the medieval theologian Abélard who was brutally castrated by the uncle of his secret bride Héloise, is performed for the first time in Charlotte, North Carolina.

26 FEBRUARY 1981
Second Symphony by the 46-year-old British composer Peter Maxwell DAVIES, in four classically designed movements, thematically derived from a variety of sources including the plainsong melody *Nativitas Tua, Dei Genetrix,* sacred to the birthday of the Virgin Mary (which happens also to be the composer's own birthday, about 1954 years later), is performed for the first time by the Boston Symphony Orchestra, Seiji Ozawa conducting.

26 FEBRUARY 1981
Howard HANSON, grand American composer and educator who proclaimed his faith in the eternal values of musical romanticism, whose symphonies expressed his deeply felt affinity to his Scandinavian ancestry, dies in Rochester at the age of eighty-four.

1 MARCH 1981
Canti Lunatici for soprano and nine instruments by the 47-year-old British-born American composer Bernard RANDS, based on lunar poems

in English, French, German, Italian and Spanish, is performed for the first time at the Contemporary Music Festival at California Institute of the Arts in Valencia.

10 MARCH 1981
Ninth Symphony, subtitled *Sinfonia Capricciosa*, by the 57-year-old American composer Peter MENNIN, is performed for the first time by the National Symphony Orchestra under the direction of Mstislav Rostropovich in Washington, D.C.

10 MARCH 1981
The Czechoslovak Federal Ministry of Telecommunications issues a set of postage stamps which includes three honoring the composers Mikuláš SCHNEIDER-TRNAVSKY, MOZART and SHOSTAKOVICH.

20 MARCH 1981
Million d'Oiseaux d'or for orchestra by the 56-year-old French composer Serge NIGG is performed for the first time in Boston by the Toulouse Orchestra on its United States tour.

23 MARCH 1981
Partita for violin and orchestra by the 51-year-old Soviet composer Edison DENSIOV is performed for the first time in Moscow by Leonid Kogan, soloist, with his son Pavel Kogan conducting the orchestra.

28 MARCH 1981
The Trojan Women, ballet for orchestra by the 59-year-old Czech-born American composer Karel HUSA, is performed for the first time by the Louisville Symphony Orchestra under the direction of the composer.

2 APRIL 1981
Orphikon, a symphony in three movements by the Czech conductor and composer Raphael KUBELIK, is performed for the first time by the New York Philharmonic Orchestra under the direction of the composer.

4 APRIL 1981
Dnevnik jednog ludaka (Diary of a Madman), television opera by the 70-year-old Serbian composer Stanojlo RAJIČIĆ, to the composer's own libretto after Gogol's tale, is produced on Belgrade Television.

8 APRIL 1981
Sixth Symphony by the British composer Robert SIMPSON is performed for the first time by the London Philharmonic Orchestra conducted by Sir Charles Groves.

10 APRIL 1981

Concerto for orchestra by the 49-year-old Swedish composer Ulf GRAHN is performed for the first time in Philadelphia.

12 APRIL 1981

La mujer y su sombra, opera by the 38-year-old Mexican composer Miguel ALCAZAR, to a libretto of Paul Claudel dealing with an Oriental woman who cannot move without her shadow, which possesses a different personality and a different voice, set to music in a sonorously somber atonal idiom with an ample assortment of drums and cymbals, is performed for the first time in Mexico City.

15 APRIL 1981

Clarinet Concerto by the Polish-born American composer Stanislaw SKROWACZEWSKI is performed for the first time by Joseph Longo as soloist with the Minnesota Orchestra, Skrowaczewski conducting.

15 APRIL 1981

Harmonium by the 34-year-old American composer John ADAMS, scored for chorus and orchestra, containing three sections—*Negative Love* to words by John Donne, *Because I Could Not Stop for Death* and *Wild Nights,* both to words by Emily Dickinson—is performed for the first time in San Francisco, Edo de Waart conducting.

18 APRIL 1981

Skorogovorka (Russian for "tongue twister") for wind orchestra and percussion by the 31-year-old Swedish composer Johnny GRADERT is performed for the first time on Swedish Radio in Stockholm.

23 APRIL 1981

Ravi SHANKAR, North Indian sitar virtuoso, performs his *Rāga-Mālā* (*Garland of Ragas*) with the New York Philharmonic Orchestra conducted by his Parsi compatriot Zubin Mehta.

23 APRIL 1981

Concerto for violin, cello and chamber orchestra by the 45-year-old Estonian composer Arvo PÄRT is performed for the first time in London.

24 APRIL 1981

Violin Concerto by the American composer Ellis B. KOHS is performed for the first time by Eudice Shapiro, with Daniel Lewis conducting the University of Southern California Orchestra in Los Angeles.

24 APRIL 1981

Willie Stark, opera by Carlisle Floyd, modeled after the career of Huey Long, with a marginal participation of other American demagogues such as Bilbo, Talmadge, Wallace and McCarthy, set with illustrative realism but occasionally drifting into a sentimental music, is produced for the first time in Houston, Texas.

29 APRIL 1981
Trumpet Concerto by the 54-year-old American composer Donald ERB is performed for the first time by Don Tison as soloist with the Baltimore Symphony Orchestra, Sergiu Comissiona conducting.

30 APRIL 1981
Descencio by the remarkably innovative Soviet composer of Tatar origin Sofia GUBAIDULINA, depicting the glossolalia descended upon the Apostles of Pentecost that enabled them to "speak in tongues" (the scoring, in three groups of threes—three trombones, three percussionists and three stringed instruments, harp, piano and celesta—is symbolic of three Trinities), is performed for the first time at the Centre Pompidou in Paris.

2 MAY 1981
Alan HOVHANESS, prodigiously prolific 70-year-old American composer of Armenian antecedents, conducts the first performance by the Vermont Symphony of his *Forty-sixth Symphony*, subtitled *To the Green Mountains*.

6 MAY 1981
Angel of Dusk, concerto for double-bass and orchestra by the 53-year-old Finnish composer Einojuhani RAUTAVAARA, dedicated to the memory of Olga Koussevitzky, the last widow of the fabled double-bass virtuoso and illustrious conductor Serge Koussevitzky, is performed for the first time on the Finnish Radio in Helsinki.

7 MAY 1981
Anna Karenina, opera by the Scottish composer Iain HAMILTON after Tolstoy's novel of adulterous passion, the penalty for which was death (the epigraph on the novel was from the Bible, "The Vengeance is Mine, I shall repay"), is performed for the first time by the English National Opera in London.

8 MAY 1981
All in the Golden Afternoon by the greatly gifted 44-year-old American composer David DEL TREDICI, Part III of the symphonic series *Child Alice*, based on *Alice in Wonderland* by Lewis Carroll, commissioned by ARCO Petroleum Products Co. in honor of Eugene Ormandy's eightieth birthday, is performed for the first time by Benita Valente, soprano, and the Philadelphia Orchestra, Ormandy conducting. (Parts I and II were

167

respectively premiered on 23 February and 13 September 1980, Part IV on 19 November 1981.)

9 MAY 1981
The Infernal Machine for orchestra by the 32-year-old American composer Christopher ROUSE, after a play by Jean Cocteau retelling the Oedipus myth, the infernality of the music being represented by an instrumental *perpetuum mobile* setting, is performed for the first time at the Evian Festival in France.

11 MAY 1981
Cats, an ailurolatrous musical by the unfailingly successful 33-year-old British tunesmith Andrew LLOYD WEBBER, inspired by *Old Possum's Book of Practical Cats* by the felinamorous poet T. S. Eliot, is produced in London. (The first Broadway production took place on 7 October 1982.)

17 MAY 1981
The world premiere is given at Castle Herrenchiemsee, near Munich, of *Symphony in F Major* for two oboes, two horns, strings, and harpsichord, in three movements, apparently composed by MOZART at the age of nine.

18 MAY 1981
Sequoia for orchestra including fifty-four percussion players by the 42-year-old American composer Joan TOWER is performed for the first time by the American Composers Orchestra in New York.

20 MAY 1981
Das Opfer der Kerze (The Sacrifice of the Candle) for instrumental and electronic ensemble by the 60-year-old Czech composer Zbyněk VOSTŘÁK is performed for the first time in Baden-Baden, West Germany.

1 JUNE 1981
De Tijd (Time) for winds, pianos, harps, guitars, percussion and women's voices by the 41-year-old Dutch composer Louis ANDRIESSEN, portraying the passage of time and its synthesis when, as Dante said, "tutti i tempi son presenti," is performed for the first time in Amsterdam.

18 JUNE 1981
The Gay Men's Chorus presents its first open-air concert on Capitol Hill in Washington, D.C., in a program of works by BRUCKNER, SCHUBERT, SIBELIUS, IVES, COPLAND, RIEGGER, Randall THOMPSON, Irving BERLIN and George GERSHWIN, singing from memory, marking perhaps the greatest exhibit of technical expertise and purity of intonation since the sublime castratosphere of the Italian Baroque.

6 July 1981

Aurora Natola, wife of Alberto GINASTERA, plays the solo part in his *Second Cello Concerto*, dedicated to her, at its first performance in Buenos Aires.

30 July 1981

Vociano, a theater work for soprano and piano by the 60-year-old American composer Pia GILBERT, based on imaginary languages suggesting Slavic, Central European, and Oriental phonemes, receives its first performance at the Aspen Music Festival.

10 August 1981

Akhmatova: Requiem for soprano, baritone and ensemble by the 37-year-old British composer John TAVENER to poems by Anna Akhmatova (1889–1966), the Russian poetess intermittently ostracized by the Soviet authorities for the suffused eroticism of her verse, is performed for the first time in Edinburgh.

17 August 1981

Robert Russell BENNETT, American composer and arranger of extraordinary dexterity whose own works were respectable presentations of American and cosmopolitan themes, dies in New York at the age of eighty-seven.

22 August 1981

Image, Reflection, Shadow for orchestra by the British composer Peter Maxwell DAVIES is performed for the first time at the Lucerne Festival.

26 September 1981

The Fifty-fifth Festival of the International Society for Contemporary Music in Belgium opens with the following program of electronic music and mixed media in an afternoon concert in Brussels:

Uitgebreid parametrisch nr. 3B for trombone and electronics, and *Parametrische modellen* for solo computer/synthesizer by the 34-year-old Belgian composer Joris DE LAET. *Animus* for trombone and tape by the 53-year-old American composer Jacob DRUCKMAN. *From a Pitch to a Voltage* for trombone and electronics by the Belgian composer Leo VERHEYEN. Four experimental pieces for various ensembles by the 43-year-old Polish composer Piotr LACHERT.

26 September 1981

At the first evening concert of the Fifty-fifth Festival of the International Society for Contemporary Music in Brussels, the following program of choral and organ music is presented:

Veni Sancte Spiritus—Veni Creator by the 42-year-old Australian composer Jennifer FOWLER. *Les Anges de l'Apocalypse* by the 49-year-old Belgian composer Paul UY (pseudonym for Uyttebroeck). *Lapponia* by the 70-year-old Finnish composer Erik BERGMAN, picturing sunless winter, midnight summer sun and polar storm in Lapland. *Ricercar* by the 53-year-old Swedish composer Bengt HAMBRAEUS. *Doe* by the 45-year-old Belgian composer Frans GEYSEN. *Musique de Jour* by the 55-year-old French composer Betsy JOLAS. *Choral Concerto No. 1* by the 39-year-old Spanish composer Tomás MARCO. *Organum III* by the 47-year-old French composer Xavier DARASSE.

27 SEPTEMBER 1981

On the second day of the Fifty-fifth Festival of the International Society for Contemporary Music in Belgium, the following program is presented in Brussels:

Swinging Music by the Polish composer Kazimierz SEROCKI (1922–1981). *Empirical Rag* by the 44-year-old American composer Brian FENNELLY. *Humpty Dumpty Sat on a Waltz* by the American-born Israeli composer Joan Franks WILLIAMS. *Danse des ministres chez M. Pompidou* by the 52-year-old French composer Luc FERRARI. *Fantastic Rondos* by the 43-year-old Icelandic composer Atli Heimir SVEINSSON. *A Flemish Round* by the 50-year-old Belgian composer André LAPORTE. *Warsaw Workshop Waltz* by the 41-year-old Portuguese composer Jorge Rosado PEIXINHO. *Dal-a* by the 47-year-old South Korean composer Sukhi KANG. *Dance Vision* by the 51-year-old Greek composer Iannis IOANNIDIS. *Sweet Sixteenths, a Cakewalk* by the 37-year-old American composer William ALBRIGHT.

28 SEPTEMBER 1981

On the third day of the Fifty-fifth Festival of the International Society for Contemporary Music in Belgium, the following program of chamber music is presented at an afternoon concert in Brussels:

Double for two prepared pianos by the 37-year-old Hungarian composer László VIDOWSZKY. *Episodes* for trombone solo by the 34-year-old Israeli composer Dan YUHAS. *Voix intérieure* for two cellos by the 51-year-old East German composer Paul-Heinz DITTRICH. *Dianima* for two cellos by the 27-year-old Norwegian composer Ole LÜTZOW-HOLM. *Time and Motion* for bass clarinet by the 38-year-old British composer Brian FERNEYHOUGH. *Regime II, Type A* for two pianos by the 42-year-old Canadian composer Bruce MATHER.

28 SEPTEMBER 1981

On the third day of the Fifty-fifth Festival of the International Society for Contemporary Music in Belgium, the following program is presented at an evening concert in Brussels:

Concerto for Percussion and Wind Ensemble by the 60-year-old Prague-born naturalized American composer Karel HUSA. *Frises* for wind orchestra by the Belgian composer Jacqueline FONTYN. *Essay* for horn and wind ensemble by the 52-year-old Belgian composer Jan SEGERS. *Rhapsodie* for wind orchestra by the 67-year-old Belgian composer Jean LOUEL.

29 SEPTEMBER 1981

On the fourth day of the Fifty-fifth Festival of the International Society for Contemporary Music in Belgium, an afternoon concert of electronic music and mixed media is presented in Ghent with the following program:

Yantra 8 for piano and tape by the 35-year-old Cuban-born Canadian composer Sergio BARROSO, based on an old Tibetan cosmogram generating intermitable melorhythms. *Kompositie 1979* for tape by the 59-year-old Dutch composer Jan BOERMAN. *Sonata* for double-bass and tape by the 50-year-old Belgian composer Lucien GOETHALS. *Das Unrecht in meinem Bad (Injustice in My Bath)* for tape and slides by the 26-year-old Austrian composer Martin SCHWARZEN-LÄNDER. *Estallido breve* for bass clarinet and tape by the 31-year-old Argentine composer Ricardo MANDOLINI. *Hanging* for tape by the 35-year-old Swedish composer Tommy ZWEDBERG. *Monologo II* for clarinet, piano and tape by the Chinese composer Man-Yee LAM.

29 SEPTEMBER 1981

On the fourth day of the Fifty-fifth Festival of the International Society for Contemporary Music in Belgium, the following program is presented at an evening concert of chamber music in Ghent:

Octet for flute, oboe, bass clarinet, tuba, violin, viola, double-bass and piano by the 33-year-old American composer David OLAN. *Rainbow Studies* for piano and wind quartet by the 35-year-old British composer Colin MATTHEWS. *Voci Siciliani (Sicilian Voices)* for mezzo-soprano, flute, clarinet, guitar and string quartet by the 40-year-old, Italian-born American composer Marc-Antonio CONSOLI. *Sonata* for cello, piano solo and chamber ensemble by the 38-year-old British composer Tim SOUSTER.

30 SEPTEMBER 1981

On the fifth day of the Fifty-fifth Festival of the International Society for Contemporary Music in Belgium, the following program is presented at an afternoon concert of theater music and mixed media in Brussels:

124 E. 107th St. for percussion, narrator-actor and tape by the 34-year-old Puerto Rican composer William ORTIZ-ALVARADO, depicting the Puerto Rican urban experience in the United States and deploying Afro-American rhythms. *Roundabouts* for four marimbas by the 47-year-old Dutch composer Joep STRAESSER. *Bouffe* for a person alone on stage by the 35-year-old British composer Michael FINNISSY. *Cardini,* spoken solfeggio for solo voice by the 51-year-old Italian composer Paolo CASTALDI, the text consisting exclusively of note names. *Music* for tape and bass clarinet by the 60-year-old Polish composer Andrzej DOBROWOLSKI. *The Temporary and Tentative Extended Piano,* sound-theater by the 32-year-old American composer Carson KIEVMAN.

30 September 1981

On the fifth day of the Fifty-fifth Festival of the International Society for Contemporary Music in Belgium, an early evening concert of electronic music is given in Brussels with the following program:

. . . la taupe by the 36-year-old French composer Christian Clozier. *Orchestrations I* by the American composer Joe Davidow. *Ascents* by the 27-year-old American composer Michael William Gilbert. *Llanto* by the 27-year-old Uruguayan composer Leo Masliah. *Chanta Khat* by the 39-year-old American composer Michael Ranta. *Cantico* by the 54-year-old Portuguese composer Affonso Souza.

30 September 1981

On the fifth day of the Fifty-fifth Festival of the International Society for Contemporary Music in Belgium, the following program of chamber music is given at an evening concert in Brussels:

Such a Nice Lady for clarinet, violin, viola, cello and piano by the 41-year-old American composer Alvin Singleton. *Linia* for chamber ensemble by the 28-year-old Australian composer Gerard Brophy. *Mythologies* for flute, clarinet, trumpet, violin, cello and harp by the 33-year-old British composer Nigel Osborne. *La Vita Nuova* for soprano and chamber ensemble by the 46-year-old British composer Nicholas Maw.

1 October 1981

Sadhana for cello and chamber orchestra by the American composer Paul Creston, inspired by the philosophy of the Indian poet Rabindranath Tagore, cast in the form of theme and variations, is performed for the first time, in honor of Creston's imminent seventy-fifth birthday, by the Los Angeles Chamber Orchestra under the direction of Gerard Schwarz, in El Cajon, California.

1 October 1981

On the sixth day of the Fifty-fifth Festival of the International Society for Contemporary Music in Belgium, the following program of chamber music is presented at an afternoon concert in Brussels:

Pasargada T.50 for recorder quartet by the 50-year-old Brazilian composer Brenno Blauth. *Capriccio* for trumpet solo by the 49-year-old Czech composer Marek Kopelent. *Eleven Echoes of Autumn* for violin, alto flute, clarinet and prepared piano by the 52-year-old American composer George Crumb. *The Eighth Ancestor* for baroque flute, alto recorder, cello and harpsichord by the 29-year-old American composer Beth Anderson, to a Zen text in which an eighth ancestor discusses the idea that logical argument is not the way to truth. *Signes en blanc* for piano by the 52-year-old Soviet composer Edison Denisov. *Landschappen III* for brass quintet by the 36-year-old Belgian composer Wilfried Westerlinck.

172

1 OCTOBER 1981

On the sixth day of the Fifty-fifth Festival of the International Society for Contemporary Music, an early evening concert for wind orchestra is given in Brussels with the following program:

Eroptosis by the 22-year-old Belgian composer Luc BREWAEYS. A fantastically dissonant but clearly identifiable *Variations on America*, based on *My Country 'tis of Thee*, by Charles IVES. *Meditation* by the 56-year-old American composer Gunther SCHULLER. *Tuten und Blasen* by the 40-year-old Austrian composer Dieter KAUFMANN. *La Tromba è mobile* by the French-born composer of Slovenian descent Vinko GLOBOKAR.

1 OCTOBER 1981

On the sixth day of the Fifty-fifth Festival of the International Society for Contemporary Music in Brussels, a special chamber music concert is presented in the evening in connection with the exhibit "Musicians, Painters, Poets, and Their Scores," featuring the following program:

Le Jardin des secrets by the 38-year-old Rumanian-born French composer Costin MIEREANU. *Glimpses* by the 40-year-old French composer André MOURET. *Autre Temps—Autres Moeurs* by the 39-year-old French composer François NOWAK. *Portrait de John Cage* by the Belgian composer Françoise VAN KESSEL. *Satie's Dream* by the 34-year-old French composer Jean-Yves BOSSEUR. *Erratum musical* by Marcel DUCHAMP. *Les Noces d'Icare et Mnémosyne* by the 52-year-old Belgian composer Henri POUSSEUR.

2 OCTOBER 1981

On the seventh day of the Fifty-fifth Festival of the International Society for Contemporary Music in Brussels, the following program of chamber music is presented at an afternoon concert:

Hymnos for piano by the 42-year-old Polish composer Tomasz SIKORSKI. *Un grand sommeil noir* for soprano, flute and harp to words by Paul Verlaine by the 38-year-old Polish composer Marta PTASZYŃSKA. *Rege (Tale)* for two identical and a third different kind of instrument by the 27-year-old Hungarian composer Zsolt SEREI. *Tetramegrate* for harp, celesta, harpsichord and piano by the 33-year-old Italian composer Adriano GUARNIERI. *Riverberi* for two pianos by the 51-year-old Belgian composer Raymond BAERVOETS. *Modèle réduit* for bass clarinet and piano by the 52-year-old Belgian composer Henri POUSSEUR.

2 OCTOBER 1981

On the seventh day of the Fifty-fifth Festival of the International Society for Contemporary Music in Brussels, the following program of orchestral music is given at an evening concert:

And the mountains rising nowhere . . . for wind orchestra, piano and percussion by the 38-year-old American composer Joseph SCHWANTNER. *Violin Concerto* by the 45-year-old Belgian composer Philippe BOESMANS. *Innanzi* for double-bass and orchestra by the 40-year-old Swiss composer Gérard ZINSSTAG. *Aquatilis* by the 33-year-old Belgian composer Jean-Louis ROBERT.

2 OCTOBER 1981
On the seventh day of the Fifty-fifth Festival of the International Society for Contemporary Music in Brussels, a solo clarinet recital is given by Florian Popa in a program of the following works:

Sonata by the 53-year-old Rumanian composer Tiberiuh OLAH. *Amour* by the 53-year-old German master of scientific music Karlheinz STOCKHAUSEN. *Consonnance IV* for clarinet and tape by the Rumanian composer Liana ALEXANDRA. *Claribior* by Eugen WENDUEL. *Chalumeau* by the 47-year-old Yugoslav composer Lojze LEBIĆ.

3 OCTOBER 1981
On the eighth day of the Fifty-fifth Festival of the International Society for Contemporary Music in Brussels a theater piece by the American film composer Richard LERMAN, *Incident at Three Mile Island,* subtitled *Perhaps an Elegy for Karen Silkwood,* dealing with the accident that befell the worker Karen Silkwood at a possibly radioactive laboratory, is performed at an afternoon concert.

3 OCTOBER 1981
On the eighth day of the Fifty-fifth Festival of the International Society for Contemporary Music in Brussels, the following program is presented at a late afternoon concert:

Symfonie for string orchestra by the 42-year-old Dutch composer Louis ANDRIESSEN. *Concerto* for piano, twenty-four instruments and carillons by the 56-year-old Italian composer Aldo CLEMENTI. *Double* for winds and double-basses by the 49-year-old Italian composer Guido BAGGIANI. *LO* for trombone and twelve strings by the Swiss-born French composer Tona SCHERCHEN-HSIAO.

3 OCTOBER 1981
On the eighth day of the Fifty-fifth Festival of the International Society for Contemporary Music in Brussels, the following program of orchestral music is given at an evening concert:

Hé, très doulz Roussignol joly, variations on old French ballads and virelais, by the 44-year-old German composer Rolf RIEHM. *Égalisation* for twenty-five musicians by the 50-year-old Japanese composer Makoto SHINOHARA. *Sori* by the 36-year-old South Korean composer Younghi PAGH-PAAN. *Variations* by the 29-year-old German composer Reinhard FEBEL.

4 OCTOBER 1981

On the ninth day of the Fifty-fifth Festival of the International Society for Contemporary Music in Brussels, the following program of chamber music is presented at a morning concert:

Winternacht for flute, clarinet, cornet, horn, violin, cello and piano by the 29-year-old Danish composer Hans ABRAHAMSEN. *Lokale Musik T2: Leichte Tänze* by the 32-year-old German composer Walter ZIMMERMANN. *Chlebnicov* for chamber orchestra by the 30-year-old German composer Robert PLATZ, an homage to the Russian dadaistic poet of the title.

4 OCTOBER 1981

The Fifty-fifth Festival of the International Society for Contemporary Music in Brussels concludes with an evening concert of the following program of orchestral music:

Liederen for wind instruments, two pianos and double-bass by the 35-year-old Dutch composer Diderik WAGENAAR. *Transit* for forty-eight strings by the 50-year-old Belgian composer André LAPORTE. *Litanie III* for orchestra by the 58-year-old Belgian composer Karel GOEYVAERTS. *Scenes from Basho* for orchestra by the 52-year-old Japanese composer Joji YUASA. *Morendo* for orchestra, mixed choir and tape by the 41-year-old Swedish composer Jan MORTHENSON.

15 OCTOBER 1981

Violin Concerto by the American composer Robert STARER is performed for the first time by Itzhak Perlman and the Boston Symphony Orchestra, Seiji Ozawa conducting.

18 OCTOBER 1981

Répons by Pierre BOULEZ, written for an ensemble of twenty-four instruments placed in the middle of the hall and six other players stationed against the walls, all these connected to a musical computer system capable of reacting to human gestures, is performed for the first time at the Donaueschingen Festival of Contemporary Music in West Germany.

22 OCTOBER 1981

Fourth Symphony for brass and orchestra by the 57-year-old American composer Ezra LADERMAN is performed for the first time by the Los Angeles Philharmonic under the direction of Carlo Maria Giulini, as a musical salutation on the occasion of the eightieth birthday of Dorothy Chandler, the munificent founder of the Los Angeles Music Center.

23 OCTOBER 1981

Concerto for orchestra by the supremely intellectual American composer Roger SESSIONS, in three connected sections, *Allegro, Largo* and *Allegro maestoso*, couched in a characteristically Sessionsesque manner, successively lyrical, earnestly calm and festive, united by a latent polyphony of tremendous acoustical force, is performed for the first time by the Boston Symphony Orchestra as a commissioned work for its centennial.

30 OCTOBER 1981
Fourth Symphony, subtitled *Indian Rose Garden and Chinese Witch Lake*, by the 49-year-old romantically intellectual Norwegian composer Per NØRGAARD is performed for the first time in Hamburg.

2 NOVEMBER 1981
Thea MUSGRAVE conducts the Royal Philharmonic Orchestra in London in the first performance of her orchestral work *Peripeteia*, written to celebrate the bicentenary of the birth of the London music publisher Vincent Novello.

5 NOVEMBER 1981
Third Symphony by the 45-year-old Soviet composer of German origin Alfred SCHNITTKE is performed for the first time in Leipzig.

5 NOVEMBER 1981
La Tragédie de Carmen, opera by the 66-year-old Rumanian-born French composer Marius CONSTANT, is produced in Paris.

19 NOVEMBER 1981
Quaint Events, fourth and last part of an orchestral series by the 44-year-old American composer David DEL TREDICI, inspired by Lewis Carroll's children's classic *Alice in Wonderland*, is performed for the first time by the Buffalo Philharmonic under the direction of Julius Rudel. (The previous three parts of Del Tredici's orchestral pieces descriptive of Alice's adventures were, respectively, the Pulitzer Prize–winning *In Memory of a Summer Day* for soprano and orchestra, first performed in St. Louis, 23 February 1980; *Happy Voices* for soprano and orchestra, first performed in San Francisco on 16 September 1980; *Child Alice* for soprano and orchestra, first performed in Philadelphia, 8 May 1981; other pieces by Del Tredici pertaining to Alice are *Vintage Alice*, *Adventures Underground* and *An Alice Symphony*.)

19 NOVEMBER 1981
Sixth Symphony by the 75-year-old American composer David VAN VACTOR is performed for the first time in Knoxville, Tennessee. (A version for band was premiered at Ball State University in Kentucky on 13 April 1983.)

21 NOVEMBER 1981
Tehillim (*Psalms* in Hebrew) for four sopranos, percussion, woodwinds, electric organs and string quartet by the 45-year-old American composer

Steve REICH, who, turning away from his primitivistically minimalistic and pervasively repetitive musical patterns, came to pursue the recessive traits of his ancestral Judaism, is performed for the first time in Houston, Texas. (A full orchestral version was performed on 16 September 1982 by the New York Philharmonic, Zubin Mehta conducting.)

24 NOVEMBER 1981
Forty-seventh Symphony, subtitled *Walla Walla, Land of Many Waters*, for soprano and orchestra by the interminably productive American composer Alan HOVHANESS is performed for the first time in Walla Walla, Washington.

26 NOVEMBER 1981
Fourteenth Symphony, completed by the passionately romantic Swedish composer Allan PETTERSSON in 1978, is performed posthumously, for the first time, in Stockholm.

13 DECEMBER 1981
Cornelius CARDEW, intransigent British avant-gardist who conducted a group called Scratch Orchestra and composed such works as *Three Winter Potatoes* scored for piano, triangles, balloons but no potatoes, and who toward the end of his career became a prophet of militant latitudinarianism and disestablishmentarianism, embraced the doctrine of Mao Dzedung, vehemently denounced his erstwhile idols Stockhausen and Cage and penitently renounced his own former ultramodernistic notions of art, dies at the age of forty-five in a preposterous street accident in London, run over by a truant automobile.

20 DECEMBER 1981
An Occurrence at Owl Creek Bridge, radio opera for baritone, three speakers, tape and orchestra by the 53-year-old Scottish composer Thea MUSGRAVE, is performed for the first time in London.

23 DECEMBER 1981
Magnifico, festive overture by the 65-year-old Serbian composer Vitomir TRIFUNOVIĆ, glorifying the patriotic Serbian resistance to the Nazi invaders during the Second World War, is performed for the first time in Belgrade.

27 DECEMBER 1981
Hoagy CARMICHAEL, American jazz pianist and composer of popular songs among which *Stardust* became a sentimental American classic, dies at his retreat at Rancho Mirage, California, at the age of eighty-one.

∽ 1982 ∾

14 JANUARY 1982

Cello Concerto by the 59-year-old American composer George WALKER is performed for the first time by Lorne Munroe as soloist with the New York Philharmonic, Zubin Mehta conducting.

22 JANUARY 1982

Three Hallucinations for orchestra by the 43-year-old American composer John CORIGLIANO, derived from his score to the film *Altered States*, is performed for the first time in Syracuse, New York.

25 JANUARY 1982

Undici colori (Eleven Colors) for solo bassoon, stamping right foot and slide projections by the 56-year-old Cuban-born American composer Aurelio DE LA VEGA is performed for the first time in Los Angeles.

28 JANUARY 1982

Eighth Symphony, subtitled *Sinfonia Votiva*, by the Polish composer Andrzej PANUFNIK, is performed for the first time by the Boston Symphony Orchestra under the direction of Seiji Ozawa.

2 FEBRUARY 1982

Cinque (5) sonetti del Michelangelo Buonarroti for voice and chamber orchestra by the fantastically individualistic British Parsi composer Kaikhosru Shapurji SORABJI is performed for the first time in Toronto, nearly sixty years after its composition.

9 FEBRUARY 1982

Der gelbe Klang, experimental stage composition by the Expressionist Russian painter Vasily KANDINSKY, published in a literary form in the compendium of modern aesthetics *Der Blaue Reiter* in 1912, a theater spectacle consisting of five intensely yellow images with a musical score chanted by a basso profondo, tenor and chorus, fashioned by the Russian composer Thomas VAN HARTMANN, comes to a belated realization at the Guggenheim Museum in New York.

18 FEBRUARY 1982

Phantasmagoria, a Fantasy, compacted from sketches of the projected *Universe Symphony* by Charles IVES, arranged by Larry AUSTIN for orchestra, narrator, tape and digital synthesizer, is performed for the first time at North Texas State University in Denton.

19 FEBRUARY 1982
Requiem: De ur alla minnen fallna (Requiem: Mutely the Bereaved Memories Speak) for four soloists, mixed chorus, children's chorus and tape by the 39-year-old Swedish composer Sven-David SANDSTRÖM is performed for the first time in Stockholm.

20 FEBRUARY 1982
John ADAMS, 35-year-old modernistic pluralistic minimalist American composer, conducts the San Francisco Symphony in the first performance of his *Grand Pianola Music*, scored for two winds, two brass, three percussionists, three female singers and two pianos.

20 FEBRUARY 1982
Prologo e Fantasia for orchestra by the 79-year-old British composer Sir William WALTON is performed for the first time in London.

21 FEBRUARY 1982
Margot la Rouge, opera by Frederick DELIUS written in 1902 but laid aside for eighty years before it was unearthed from the dusty heap of forgotten manuscripts, to a story dealing with an originally virtuous girl becoming a *fille de joie et de détresse* on Paris boulevards, and her pimp, killed by her fiancé, is performed for the first time by the BBC orchestra and chorus in London. (The first stage performance was given in St. Louis on 9 June 1983, conducted by the faithful Deliusian Eric Fenby.)

26 FEBRUARY 1982
Wonder's Edge by the 45-year-old American composer Harold BUDD, scored for piano, electric guitar and electronics, is performed for the first time in San Francisco.

5 MARCH 1982
Concerto de la fidélité for soprano and orchestra, written in 1981 by the still creatively functioning 89-year-old French composer Germaine TAILLEFERRE, is performed for the first time in Paris.

6 MARCH 1982
Food, a stylistically eclectic theater piece for soprano, baritone, trumpet, piano, and snare-drum by the 60-year-old American composer Pia GILBERT, to a culinary text taken from John Cage's "Where Are We Eat-

ing? And What Are We Eating?" incorporating a recipe for sweet nut rolls, receives its first performance at the Contemporary Music Festival at the California Institute of the Arts in Valencia.

6 MARCH 1982

Meteor Farm by the 68-year-old American composer Henry BRANT, scored for orchestra, jazz band, two percussion ensembles, two sopranos, Javanese gamelan orchestra, West African drummers and South Indian musicians, is performed for the first time at Wesleyan University in Middletown, Connecticut, directed by the composer.

7 MARCH 1982

Quiet Music for orchestra by the 49-year-old Soviet composer Sergei SLONIMSKY is performed for the first time in Leningrad.

9 MARCH 1982

La Vera Storia, veristic opera by the Italian avant-gardist Luciano BERIO, employing singers, actors, dancers and acrobats and featuring the Swingle Singers offstage and a wordless soprano, is performed for the first time at La Scala, in Milan, under the direction of the composer.

12 MARCH 1982

The Telltale Heart, chamber opera by the 35-year-old American composer Daniel KESSNER, after a scary tale by Edgar Allan Poe, is performed for the first time in Utrecht, Holland.

12 MARCH 1982

Eighth Symphony by the 76-year-old Austrian composer Marcel RUBIN is performed for the first time in Vienna.

18 MARCH 1982

Sonneries for orchestra by the 55-year-old American composer Donald ERB is performed for the first time in Rochester, New York.

20 MARCH 1982

Second Symphony, subtitled *Birds of Sorrow,* by the 43-year-old American composer Paul CHIHARA is performed for the first time in Los Angeles.

29 MARCH 1982

Carl ORFF, German composer and theorist whose scenic oratorio *Carmina Burana* to texts assembled from medieval student songs became a classic of modern music despite the general unfamiliarity of the idioms employed (Latin, old French, Catalan, etc.), and who initiated an attractive method of musical training by constructing a whole ensemble of sonoriferous instruments, dies in Munich at the age of eighty-six.

31 March 1982

The Orchestral Noises of October Nights for orchestra by the 31-year-old American composer James UNDERWOOD is performed for the first time in Bloomington, Indiana.

3 April 1982

The Shivaree, opera by the Canadian composer John BECKWITH, dealing with a successful if maddening shivaree (i.e., charivari, a wedding-night mock serenade) staged by the young lover of the third wife of a middle-aged merchant in rural Ontario ca. 1900, is produced in Toronto.

6 April 1982

Southern Voices for orchestra by the 40-year-old American avant-garde composer Doris HAYS, based on actual folk songs of the South, is performed for the first time in Chattanooga, Tennessee.

14 April 1982

A Bride from Pluto, opera by Gian Carlo MENOTTI, is produced at the Kennedy Center in Washington, D.C.

15 April 1982

Offertorium for violin and orchestra by the 50-year-old half-Tatar, half-Russian Soviet composer Sofia GUBAIDULINA, the title referring to the mercurially appearing, disappearing and reappearing "Royal Theme" given to Bach on his visit to Potsdam on 7 May 1747 by King Frederic the Great, herein surrounded by a flowering abundance of original thematic material forming atonal asymptotes to shifting central tones, and magniloquently fructified by sonorific orchestration, is performed for the first time by the Soviet violinist Oleg Kogan with the Culture Symphony Orchestra in Moscow, conducted by Gennadi Rozhdestvensky.

20 April 1982

Les Hommages by the 56-year-old American composer Ronald McFAR-LAND, a smorgasbord of twentieth-century pianistic styles in "twenty-four preludes in twenty-four keys," two each in the manner of Poulenc, Satie, Prokofiev, Stravinsky, Chopin, Berg, Joplin, Fauré, Bartók, Gershwin, Liszt and Ravel, is performed for the first time by Caesar Cancino in San Anselmo, California.

2 May 1982

Il tessuto d'Arabeschi for flute and string quartet by the 89-year-old British Parsi composer Kaikhosru Shapurji SORABJI is performed for the first time in Philadelphia.

5 MAY 1982

First Symphony, subtitled *Three Movements for Orchestra,* by the American composer Ellen Taaffe ZWILICH is performed for the first time by the American Composers Orchestra in New York under the direction of Gunther Schuller.

11 MAY 1982

Black Pentecost, cantata by the English composer Peter Maxwell DAVIES, decrying industrial air pollution, is performed for the first time in London by the varivocal soprano Jan DeGaetani and tenor Michael Rippon with the Philharmonia Orchestra under the direction of Simon Rattle.

23 MAY 1982

Count-Down for sixteen-part choir and two percussionists by the 35-year-old British composer Giles SWAYNE is performed for the first time at the Bath Festival.

30 MAY 1982

Tod ist ein langer Schlaf (Death Is a Long Sleep), variations on a theme by Haydn for cello and orchestra by the 53-year-old Soviet composer Edison DENISOV, is performed for the first time in Moscow.

4 JUNE 1982

Minutes Till Midnight, opera in two acts by the 64-year-old American composer Robert WARD, centered on an idealist atomic scientist who inadvertantly invents an annihilating doomsday bomb, is produced in Miami, Florida.

6 JUNE 1982

The Silken Drum, chamber opera by the 43-year-old Icelandic composer Atli Heimir SVEINSSON, is produced in Reykjavik.

7 JUNE 1982

Solo Observed for piano, winds and strings by the 59-year-old American composer Lukas FOSS is performed for the first time, in Miami.

19 JUNE 1982

The Postman Always Rings Twice, opera by Stephen PAULUS after the novel by James M. Cain, is produced in St. Louis.

21 JUNE 1982

Forty-eighth Symphony, subtitled *Vision of Andromeda,* by Alan HOVHANESS is performed for the first time in Miami, Florida.

25 JUNE 1982

Concerto for two pianos by the 50-year-old American composer Michael COLGRASS is performed for the first time in Miami, Florida.

28 JUNE 1982

Sixth Symphony for organ and orchestra by the 75-year-old American composer Paul CRESTON is performed for the first time in Washington, D.C.

4 JULY 1982

Sinfonietta della Notte for orchestra by the American composer Gloria COATES is performed for the first time in Lund, Sweden.

10 JULY 1982

Maria JERITZA, prima donna assoluta, of Czech parentage (her real name was Jedlitzka), whose career took her to the heights of fame in Europe and America, and to whom Richard Strauss dedicated in 1948 his last song *Malven* ["Der geliebten Maria diese letzte Rose," he inscribed on the manuscript—(For) Beloved Maria, this last rose], dies in Orange, New Jersey, at the age of ninety-four. (The song was first publicly performed on 10 January 1985.)

18 JULY 1982

Stern Grove Grand Ceremonial Overtures by the American composer Henry BRANT, scored for two chamber orchestras, jazz drummer and three martial karate artists, one of them being Brant's son Joaquin Ives Brant, is performed for the first time in San Francisco. (The title was subsequently changed to *Horizontals Extending.*)

31 JULY 1982

The Confidence Man, first opera by the American composer George ROCHBERG, based on Herman Melville's novel, is produced for the first time at the Santa Fe Opera in New Mexico.

16 SEPTEMBER 1982

Housewarming for orchestra by the multifariously gifted American composer Morton GOULD is performed for the first time in Baltimore.

17 SEPTEMBER 1982

Three Sisters Who Are Not Sisters, opera by the 55-year-old American composer David AHLSTROM to the words of Gertrude Stein, is performed for the first time in San Francisco.

21 September 1982

Concerto for two violins and orchestra by the 41-year-old Finnish composer Erkki SALMENHAARA is performed for the first time in Helsinki.

22 September 1982

Beyond Neon: Post-Commercial Sound Sculptures for French horn and orchestra by the imaginative 36-year-old Norwegian composer Olav Anton THOMMESSEN is performed for the first time in Minneapolis.

1 October 1982

Vermont Counterpoint for eleven flutes, ten of them recorded on tape, by the 46-year-old American composer Steve REICH, who inadvertently became the prophet of musical minimalism by virtue of primitivistic maximalism of repeated patterns in his works, is performed for the first time in New York.

2 October 1982

Avanti! (Forward!) for orchestra by the 50-year-old Latvian-American composer Gundaris PONÉ is performed for the first time in Washington, D.C.

4 October 1982

Glenn GOULD, Canadian-born pianist of extraordinary gifts who devoted endless hours to etch the technical ingredients to the point of crystal-clear lucidity in the works of Bach, and who became virtually an anchorite in self-imposed seclusion, dies suddenly in Toronto at the age of fifty.

4 October 1982

Koyaanisqatsi (a Hopi Indian word meaning "life out of balance"), film without words using the techniques of acceleration and lentification, with musical accompaniment featuring the deep voices of native American Indians, by the extraordinary American composer Philip GLASS—whose motto seems to be *e minimis multum,* or *festina lente* (oxymoronic maxim meaning "hurry slowly")—is premiered at Radio City Music Hall Film Festival in New York.

14 October 1982

Kinetic Poem for piano and orchestra by the 52-year-old Finnish composer Usko MERILÄINEN is performed for the first time in Helsinki.

15 October 1982

Third Symphony in one movement by the 62-year-old Soviet Armenian composer Karen KHACHATURIAN is performed for the first time in Moscow.

16 October 1982

Violin Concerto by the 33-year-old Danish composer Poul RUDERS is performed for the first time in Copenhagen.

19 October 1982

Sixteenth Symphony by the 62-year-old Soviet composer Moisei VAINBERG is performed for the first time in Moscow.

23 October 1982

Soldier Boy, Soldier, opera by the 54-year-old black American composer T. J. ANDERSON, to a libretto by Leon Forrest dealing with a black Vietnam veteran's return home, is performed for the first time at Indiana University in Bloomington.

29 October 1982

Doctor Faustus Lights the Lights, opera by the 55-year-old American composer David AHLSTROM to words of Gertrude Stein, is performed for the first time in San Francisco.

30 October 1982

The Fifty-sixth Festival of the International Society for Contemporary Music, in conjunction with the Styrian Autumn Festival, opens in Graz, Austria, with the following program of brass band music presented at a morning concert:

Entmilitarisierte Zonen (Demilitarized Zones), march paraphrases by the 39-year-old Austrian composer Heinz Karl GRUBER. *Ständchen für einen Potentaten (Serenade for a Potentate)* for cello and brass band by the 41-year-old Austrian composer Dieter KAUFMANN. *Altiplano* by the 47-year-old Swedish composer Folke RABE, depicting the life among the Inca descendants in the high plateau of the Andes. *Prinz Johannes Wanderung* by the 52-year-old Austrian composer Franz SCHÖGGL. *Ragtime and Habaneras* by the 56-year-old German composer Hans Werner HENZE, consisting of eleven miniatures.

30 October 1982

The first day of the Fifty-sixth Festival of the International Society for Contemporary Music continues in Graz with the following works presented throughout the evening:

Fireworks for orchestra by Igor STRAVINSKY. *Fürst Igor, Stravinsky* for bass and chamber ensemble by the 51-year-old Argentine-born German ultramodernist Mauricio KAGEL, with material drawn from Borodin's opera *Prince Igor* and his namesake Igor Stravinsky. *Atmospheres* for orchestra by the 59-year-old Hungarian master modernist György LIGETI, first performed at the Donaueschingen Festival on 22 October 1961. *Avant d'Être (Before Being)* for violin, cello and six wind players by the 28-year-old Greek composer Nicos CORNILIOS, depicting in macrorhythmic structures the fetal anticipation of imminent parturition. *Credo in US* for chamber ensemble by the prime American innovator John CAGE. *Improvisation sur Mallarmé* for soprano and orchestra by the greatly influential French composer of dialectically structured musical edifices Pierre BOULEZ. *Tem* for orchestra by the 44-year-old German composer Volker HEYN, in which a tone cluster stretched across the entire diapason of acoustical sounds is eventually compressed into a single tone, the Tem. *Tea for Two* for orchestra, the famous tune of Vincent YOUMANS variegated and orchestrated by Dmitri SHOSTAKOVICH and used in one of his early ballets.

31 OCTOBER 1982

On the second day of the Fifty-sixth Festival of the International Society for Contemporary Music in Graz, the following works are presented:

Kreuzspiel for orchestra by the 54-year-old legislator of elusive aleatory molecules of tonal monads Karlheinz STOCKHAUSEN. *Tristes* for chamber orchestra by the 36-year-old French composer Jean-Claude WOLFF, in which the wistful essence of the music, expressed in sequences of atonal Angst, is cast in aquatic green colors. *Configurations* for orchestra by the 25-year-old Austrian composer Gerhard PRÄSENT, depicting the inexorable machinery of modern life. *Quintette à la Memoire d'Anton Webern* for chamber orchestra by the 54-year-old Belgian composer Henri POUSSEUR, written in a strict canonic style typical of the Webernian web. *Sonata* for two pianos by the 59-year-old Belgian composer Karel GOEYVAERTS, forming an oxymoronic synthesis of Webern's dodecaphony with Messiaen's neo-Gregorianism. *Piano-Piano* for solo piano by the 32-year-old Uruguayan composer Carlos DE SILVEIRA, in which musical cellular motives alternate with pregnant silences. *Nocturnes* for piano and tape by the remarkable 47-year-old French linguist, philosopher and composer François-B. MÂCHE. *Piano Variations* by the inventive German modernist Hans Werner HENZE. *We Think for the Future* for piano by Cornelius CARDEW, the uncompromising English concocter of inexorably incongruous and overwhelmingly illogical repetitive sonic structures who lost his life when he was run over on 13 December 1981 by a mindless automobilist. *Necessity is a Mother . . .* for three actresses and amplified double-bass by the 42-year-old American composer Alvin SINGLETON, a wordless theater piece glorifying motherhood. *Piece for Small Orchestra, String Quartet*, and ten *Studies for Player Piano* by the 70-year-old American composer, living in Mexico, Conlon NANCARROW, the initiator of piano music composed directly on perforated player-piano rolls in hyper-pianistic counterpoint.

1 NOVEMBER 1982

On the third day of the Fifty-sixth Festival of the International Society for Contemporary Music in Graz, the following electronic works are presented:

Gioco di Velocità by the 29-year-old Italian composer Roberto DOATI. *La Folia* by the 28-year-old Polish composer Pawel SZYMANSKI. *Ode for Elestase* by the 29-year-old Japanese composer Akira NISHIMURA. *Opus 1* by the 24-year-old Austrian composer Martin SIEREK. *Pourquoi as-tu jeté ta pantoufle?* (*Why Did You Throw Your Slipper?*) by the 23-year-old French composer Xavier

GRACIA. *Wellenmusik II* by the 33-year-old Japanese composer Takehito SHIMAZU. *The Stones of Jerusalem* by the 42-year-old Israeli composer Joseph DORFMAN.

Continuing throughout the afternoon and evening, the Festival presents the following works:

Die sechs Vermessenen (*The Six Surveyors*) for piano by the supremely intellectual 82-year-old Austrian-born master composer Ernst KRENEK. *Two Pianos and Violin* by the 30-year-old American composer Bunita MARCUS, a modernistically contrapuntal *ménage à trois*. *Four North American Ballads* for piano by the 44-year-old American composer Frederic RZEWSKI, in which simple folk tunes are magnified through tonal augmentation and compressed through melodic diminution, incorporating improvisatory sections. *Gamelan Corn* by Philip CORNER. A set of violin solo works including *Soundings* by Malcolm GOLDSTEIN.

2 NOVEMBER 1982
On the fourth day of the Fifty-sixth Festival of the International Society for Contemporary Music in Graz, a morning concert of electronic music by Latin America composers presents the following program:

Creación de la tierra by the Belgian-born Colombian composer Jacquiline NOVA. *Suiana-Wanka* by the 27-year-old Uruguayan composer Fernando CONDON. *Imposible a la Equis* by the 45-year-old Guatemalan composer Joaquín ORELLANA. *Gran Tiempo* by the 42-year-old Uruguayan composer Coriún AHARONIÁN. *Tramos* (*Stretches*) by the 43-year-old Argentine composer Eduardo BÉRTOLA. . . . *después el silencio* . . . (. . . *After the Silence* . . .) by the 57-year-old Argentine composer Hilda DIANDA. *Huauqui* by the 42-year-old Argentine composer Graciela PARASKEVAIDIS.

2 NOVEMBER 1982
The fourth day of the Fifty-sixth Festival of the International Society for Contemporary Music in Graz continues throughout the evening, presenting the following works:

Somos nueve (*We Are Nine*) for nine instrumentalists by the 33-year-old American composer Alfredo RUGELES, written in the manner of a modernized concerto grosso. *Interiors* for chamber ensemble by the 28-year-old Australian composer Trevor PEARCE, in twelve sections with subterranean juxtapositions and subliminal interpolations rich in deliberately meaningless tonal dislocations and psychosomatic coagulations. *Missa Viva 1978* for orchestra by the 39-year-old Israeli composer Arie SHAPIRA, with a verbal allusion to Tel Aviv (which means the Hill of Spring in Hebrew) and to an anonymous girl's name Aviva so that Missa viva when coalesced into Missaviva pays court to Aviva and Tel Aviv, with the sonic climax serving as an anticlimatic peroration. *The River* for orchestra by the 27-year-old French composer Pascal DUSAPIN, in which the aquatic flux is figuratively split into microhydrographical monads. *Thanatos Eros*, symphonic improvisations for orchestra by the 52-year-old German composer Dieter SCHNEBEL, wherein love and death merge into an oxymoronic liebestod. *Katabiosis* for ensemble by the 27-year-old Scottish composer Stephen FERGUSON, descriptive of the breakdown of living cells in an atonal progeria. *Tres impressoẽs cancioneirigenas* for chamber ensemble by the Brazilian composer Jorge ANTUNES, the third word in the title being a combination of two Portuguese words, cancioneiro (chanson) and cancerigenas (carcinogenic), the "three impressions" pronouncing damnation on the dictatorial period of former Brazilian politics. *Die Atmer der Lydia* for orchestra by the 32-year-old Swiss composer Christoph DELZ, a "transcomposition" of pulmonary functions of an unidentified female named Lydia.

3 NOVEMBER 1982
On the fifth day of the Fifty-sixth Festival of the International Society for Contemporary Music in Graz, a concert of electronic music from Austria presents the following program:

Excerpts from "Faust" after Nikolaus Lenau by Werner RUTTINGER. *Suite on E* by 34-year-old Werner RADITSCHNIG. *ORC 17* by 36-year-old Klaus AGER. *Fantasmata* by the 61-year-old Bulgarian-born composer Anestis LOGOTHETIS. *Memento* by the 45-year-old Polish-born composer Ryszard KLISOWSKI. *Mugl entsteigt* (*Mugl Descends*) by 29-year-old Günther RABL. *Bach* by the Japanese composer resident in Germany Mayako KUBO. *Uraufführung* (*First Performance*) by 22-year-old Klaus KARLBAUER. *Spital* by the 30-year-old French-born composer Flora ST. LOUP. *Requiem* by 29-year-old Bruno LIBERDA.

3 NOVEMBER 1982
The fifth day of the Fifty-sixth Festival of the International Society for Contemporary Music in Graz continues throughout the evening with the following program:

Pezzo grazioso for wind quintet by the 46-year-old Polish composer Marek STACHOWSKI. *Once Upon a Time* for wind quintet by the 31-year-old Finnish composer Anneli ARHO, a musical remembrance of a pleasant day. *Second Brass Quintet* by the 42-year-old Austrian composer Günther KAHOWEZ, based on folk songs and medieval sequences. *The Tyger* by the 40-year-old Swedish composer Sven-David SANDSTRÖM, inspired by the macroailurophiliac poetry of William Blake. *Palinode No. 4* and *Four Lovesongs by Oswald von Wolkenstein*, two choral works by the 38-year-old composer Hubert STUPPNER. *Cantos del Capitán* for soprano and piano, to words of the great Chilean poet Pablo Neruda, by the 44-year-old Chilean composer Sergio ORTEGA. *The Seasons* for chorus by the 43-year-old Swiss composer and oboe virtuoso Heinz HOLLIGER, after poems by Friedrich Hölderlin. *Ritornella, the Cosmic Wheel* for chorus by the 34-year-old Canadian composer Michel-Georges BRÉGENT, an homage to an ancient selenologist who flourished ca. 2300 B.C.

4 NOVEMBER 1982
On the sixth day of the Fifty-sixth Festival of the International Society for Contemporary Music in Graz, the following electronic works are presented:

Sinfonie Konkret by the 24-year-old Austrian composer Martin SIEREK. *Chaceol-Music for the Early Evening* by the 27-year-old Austrian composer Martin SCHWARZENLANDER. *Minimal Splitting Movements* by the 29-year-old Austrian composer Werner JAUK. *Current Loops* by the 38-year-old German-born composer Helmut DENKER. *Orquideas Primaverales (Spring Orchids)* by the 43-year-old Argentine composer Eduardo KUSNIR. *Austera* by the 46-year-old Argentine composer Oscar BAZÁN. *Natal del Rei (The King's Birthday)* by the 42-year-old Uruguayan composer Conrado SILVA. *La Cuidad (Caution)* by the 27-year-old Bolivian composer Cergio PRUDENCIO. *Ceremonias* by the 39-year-old Argentine composer Lionel FILIPPI.

4 NOVEMBER 1982

The sixth day of the Fifty-sixth Festival of the International Society for Contemporary Music in Graz continues with the following program presented in the evening:

Samba for chamber ensemble by the 47-year-old Dutch composer Bent LORENTZEN, a modernistic transfiguration of the Brazilian folk dance. *Polifonica, Monodia, Ritmica* for chamber orchestra by the 58-year-old Italian composer Luigi NONO, the most prominent practitioner of dodecaphonic realizations of classical forms. *Music for Orchestra No. 6* by the 61-year-old Polish composer Andrzej DOBROWOLSKI, symbolizing the embryonic and fetal formation of unicellular motives. *Alabaster* for three orchestras by the 31-year-old Japanese composer Isao MATSUSHITA, in which the constituent groups represent the three a's in the word alabaster, all bathed in the milky color of the substance in question. *Homenaje a Federico García Lorca* for chamber orchestra by the revolutionary Mexican composer Silvestre REVUELTAS (1899–1940), an homage to the great Spanish poet slain by Franco's fascists. *Nocturnes II* for orchestra by the 63-year-old Polish composer Roman HAUBENSTOCK-RAMATI, a wistful invocation of the fading of the light. *Saudades do Parque Balneario Hotel* for alto saxophone and piano by the 60-year-old Brazilian composer Gilberto MENDES, being a nostalgic tribute to a hotel in a Brazilian spa. *À Varsovie* for orchestra by the 41-year-old Polish composer Bronislaw K. PRZYBYLSKI, a dedication to the long-suffering city of Warsaw. *Concerto* for alto saxophone and twelve players by the 46-year-old Austrian composer Erich URBANNER.

5 NOVEMBER 1982

The Fifty-sixth Festival of the International Society for Contemporary Music in Graz concludes with the following program:

Mutatio Perpetua for chamber ensemble and tape by the 48-year-old Korean composer Sukhi KANG, an experiment in tonalities, dynamics, rhythm and articulation, consisting of seventy-three musical units combining and separating in perpetual mutations. *Giardino religioso (Religious Garden)* for chamber ensemble by the cosmopolitan conductor and composer Bruno MADERNA (1920–1973). *Cantata for Makronissos* by the 35-year-old Greek composer Thanos MIKROUTSIKOS, composed in the concentration camp of Makronissos where the composer was confined by the reactionary military authorities. *Fasce* for orchestra by the 56-year-old Austrian composer Friedrich CERHA. *Entrata/Encore* by the 57-year-old Italian modernist Luciano BERIO. *A Handsome-Smooth-Sweet-Clear Stroke; or else play not at all* for orchestra by the 38-year-old British composer Michael NYMAN, the title being taken from *Musick's Monument* by Thomas Mace, published in London in 1676.

7 NOVEMBER 1982
Double Concerto for piano, cello and orchestra by the 58-year-old American composer Benjamin LEES is performed for the first time in New York.

9 NOVEMBER 1982
Bumberboom: Scherzo diabolique for orchestra by the 48-year-old Canadian composer Sydney HODKINSON is performed for the first time in Montreal.

19 NOVEMBER 1982
The posthumous premiere of the *Fifteenth Symphony* by the romantic Swedish composer Allan PETTERSSON, completed in 1978, is given in Stockholm.

23 NOVEMBER 1982
Tenebrae, concerto for cello and orchestra by the 51-year-old Norwegian composer Arne NORDHEIM, is performed for the first time in Washington, D.C.

28 NOVEMBER 1983
Passio Domini nostri Jesu Christi secundum Joannum for chorus and ensemble by the 47-year-old Estonian composer Arvo PÄRT is performed for the first time in Munich.

15 DECEMBER 1982
Third Symphony by the 50-year-old Soviet composer Sergei SLONIMSKY, in four conjointed movements, *Andante, Allegro, Presto* and *Adagio,* making use of dodecaphonic progressions and microtones, is performed for the first time in Leningrad.

20 DECEMBER 1982
Artur RUBINSTEIN, Polish-born Jewish pianist of titanic powers, an inspired performer of profoundly human music, unexcelled interpreter of Chopin and Schumann, and self-acknowledged lover of many women, dies at the extreme age of ninety-five in his apartment in Geneva, which he shared with his last object of admiration, who helped him to write his candid autobiography.

∾ 1983 ∾

11 JANUARY 1983
Krzysztof PENDERECKI conducts the Berlin Philharmonic Orchestra in the
first performance of his *Second Cello Concerto* with Mstislav Rostropovich as soloist.

18 JANUARY 1983
Concerto for kettledrum, trumpet and orchestra by the 48-year-old
German composer Siegfried MATTHUS is performed for the first time in
East Berlin.

30 JANUARY 1983
Sinfonia Ricercata for organ and violinless and percussionless orchestra
by the 52-year-old Spanish composer Cristóbal HALFFTER is performed for
the first time in Vienna.

3 FEBRUARY 1983
The two-evening spectacle *United States* by the 35-year-old avant-garde
performance artist Laurie ANDERSON, a multimedia epic on the themes
of politics, money and love, opens for its first complete performance at
the Brooklyn Academy of Music in New York.

9 FEBRUARY 1983
Frank ZAPPA, radical rock musician and enthusiastic admirer of ultramodern classical music, presides over a concert in San Francisco commemorating the approximate centennials of the birth of Edgar VARÈSE
and Anton von WEBERN, conducting Varèse's *Ionisation* and *Intégrales*.
The balance of the program included Varèse's *Poème electronique* and
Offrandes, and *Variations for Piano*, op. 27, and vocal works by Anton
von Webern, conducted by Jean-Louis LeRoux.

10 FEBRUARY 1983
Concerto for Orchestra by the 43-year-old British composer and pianist
John McCABE is performed for the first time in London.

12 FEBRUARY 1983
Eubie BLAKE, black American musician, master of piano ragtime who
proudly demonstrated unfailing digital fluency on television well into his
ninety-ninth year, dies in Brooklyn five days after reaching the glorious
mark of one hundred years of age.

17 FEBRUARY 1983

Eleventh Symphony by the industrious Danish composer Vagn HOLMBOE is performed for the first time in Copenhagen.

22 FEBRUARY 1983

Sir Adrian BOULT, English conductor of impeccable classical bent who presented a number of congenial performances of works by modern British composers, dies in Tunbridge Wells at the age of ninety-three.

24 FEBRUARY 1983

Sixteenth Symphony by the Swedish composer Allan PETTERSSON (1911–1980), originally designated *Alto Saxophone Concerto*, written for the American saxophonist Fred Hemke, is performed for the first time, posthumously, with Hemke as soloist, in Stockholm.

7 MARCH 1983

Igor MARKEVITCH, greatly talented Russian composer and conductor who rose to sudden fame in Paris where he became known as "second Igor," (the first being, of course, Stravinsky) and who later devoted himself mainly to conducting, dies in Antibes, France, at the age of seventy.

7 MARCH 1983

Claude VIVIER, 34-year-old Canadian composer, is murdered in his Paris apartment where he was installed on a Canadian government subsidy, stabbed twenty-four times by a chance acquaintance and strangled with pads of paper stuffed in his mouth to stifle his cries for help. (His body was discovered on 12 March 1983.)

8 MARCH 1983

Sir William WALTON, illustrious British composer who began his career as an *enfant terrible* of modern music and who in his maturity created operatic and symphonic masterpieces in the aristocratic British tradition, dies at the island of Ischia in Italy where he lived for many years, three weeks before his eighty-first birthday.

11 MARCH 1983

A Death in the Family, opera by the 57-year-old American composer William MAYER, based on the emotionally moving semiautobiographical 1958 Pulitzer Prize-winning novel by James Agee, is performed for the first time in Minneapolis.

12 MARCH 1983

To the Edge of Dream for guitar and orchestra by the 52-year-old Japanese composer Toru TAKEMITSU is performed for the first time in Liège, France.

18 MARCH 1983
Siddharta, opera by the 50-year-old prime Norwegian composer Per NØRGAARD, is produced in Stockholm.

3 APRIL 1983
Counterbomb Renga, a spectacle by about one hundred poets and musicians protesting against the proliferation of nuclear weapons, conceived and coordinated by the 63-year-old Estonian-born Canadian composer Udo KASEMETS, is relayed by the Canadian Broadcasting Corporation.

5 APRIL 1983
Dialogues for cello and orchestra by the 65-year-old American composer Robert WARD is performed for the first time in Chattanooga, Tennessee.

10 APRIL 1983
Third Piano Concerto by the Soviet composer Tikhon KHRENNIKOV is first performed in Moscow, with the composer as soloist.

14 APRIL 1983
Elisabeth LUTYENS, English composer who wrote music in different genres marked by an effective use of modern techniques while preserving the melodic essence of English folk music, dies in Hampstead at the age of seventy-six.

21 APRIL 1983
Piano Concerto by the 36-year-old American composer Peter LIEBERSON, gifted son of a talented father, Goddard Lieberson, commissioned by the Boston Symphony Orchestra for its centennial, is performed for the first time by Peter Serkin as soloist, Seiji Ozawa conducting the Boston Symphony.

23 APRIL 1983
Triple Duo by Elliott CARTER, scored for flute and clarinet, violin and cello, and piano and percussion, is performed for the first time in Symphony Space in London, by a group called Fires of London.

24 APRIL 1983
The Australian-born pianist Geoffrey Douglas Madge courageously plays the American premiere of Kaikhosru Shapurji SORABJI's formidable four-hour piano work, *Opus Clavicembalisticum*, at the University of Chicago.

27 APRIL 1983
Poem for piano and orchestra by the 59-year-old Serbian composer Vasilije MOKRANJAC, his last large work, set in a lyrical meditative manner, is performed for the first time in Belgrade.

30 APRIL 1983

George BALANCHINE, Russian choreographer extraordinaire (his real name was Balanchivadze, and his country of origin was Georgia, in the Caucasus), who transplanted himself and his art to New York, dies at the age of seventy-nine, crippled by a dreadful neurological illness that reduced his once lithe body to the state of a mindless mass of flesh.

6 MAY 1983

Ra, multimedia work with audience participation by the 49-year-old Canadian composer R. Murray SCHAFER, based on the myth of the Egyptian sun god, is presented in a continuous performance from dawn to dusk in Toronto.

12 MAY 1983

Sounder Rounds for orchestra by the innovative American composer Earle BROWN is performed for the first time in Saarbrücken, Germany.

14 MAY 1983

Second Symphony, subtitled *Summer Music*, by the 48-year-old Welsh composer William MATHIAS is performed for the first time by the Royal Liverpool Philharmonic Society.

17 MAY 1983

Organ Concerto by the masterly 82-year-old Austrian-born American composer Ernst KRENEK is performed for the first time by Martin Haselböck as soloist with the Melbourne Symphony Orchestra under the direction of John Hopkins.

18 MAY 1983

Guitar Concerto by the 40-year-old Swedish composer Sven-David SANDSTRÖM is performed for the first time in Malmö.

19 MAY 1983

Fratres I for string orchestra and percussion by the 47-year-old Estonian composer Arvo PÄRT is performed for the first time in Göteborg, Sweden.

20 MAY 1983

Seventh Symphony, subtitled *Ecliptical Instincts*, by the 52-year-old Danish composer Ib NØRHOLM is performed for the first time in Copenhagen.

31 MAY 1983

Second Sinfonia by the 34-year-old English composer Nigel OSBORNE is performed for the first time by the Leicestershire Schools Symphony Orchestra, Peter Fletcher conducting.

2 JUNE 1983
The English Cat, comic opera by Hans Werner HENZE, is performed for the first time in Schwetzingen, West Germany.

2 JUNE 1983
Afterimages for orchestra by the 42-year-old Italian composer Marc-Antonio CONSOLI, in three movements, *October Lights Refrains, Elegiac Lullaby* and *The Dream at the End of Joy Tract Road* (the name of a country street in the Adirondack mountains, where Consoli spent summers during his American sojourn), is performed for the first time by the New York Philharmonic, conducted by Raymond Leppard.

3 JUNE 1983
Raleigh's Dream, opera by the Scottish composer Iain HAMILTON, is performed for the first time in Durham, North Carolina.

3 JUNE 1983
Foci I for orchestra by the 58-year-old American composer Leonard ROSENMAN, the entire work being derived from the opening chord in the woodwinds forming its first focus, is performed for the first time in its revised version by the New York Philharmonic, Arthur Weisberg conducting. (The original version, for chamber ensemble, was first performed in New York by the Los Angeles Chamber Orchestra, conducted by Gerard Schwarz, on 11 April 1981.)

8 JUNE 1983
Canti del Sole for tenor and orchestra by the English-born American composer Bernard RANDS, winner of the 1984 Pulitzer Prize, which presents a day's progression from dawn to dusk through a continuous setting of poems in several languages about the sun, is performed for the first time by Paul Sperry as soloist with the New York Philharmonic, Zubin Mehta conducting.

17 JUNE 1983
A Quiet Place by Leonard BERNSTEIN, constituting a sequel to his one-act opera *Trouble in Tahiti* produced in 1952, is performed for the first time in Houston, Texas.

17 JUNE 1983
Peter MENNIN, American composer of symphonies in a faultless neo-classical manner touched with Mediterranean songfulness (he was of an Italian family and his real name was Mennini), dies in New York at the age of sixty, a victim of incurable lung cancer.

19 JUNE 1983

Seid nüchtern und wachet . . . (Be wakeful and Watchful . . .), cantata by the 48-year-old Soviet composer of German origin Alfred SCHNITTKE, based on a version of the Faust legend published in 1587 under the title *Historia von Doktor Johann Faustus*, and commissioned by the Vienna Choral Academy for its 125th anniversary, is performed for the first time in Vienna. (Its Moscow premiere took place on 23 October 1983.)

24 JUNE 1983

Second Symphony by the 48-year-old Dutch composer Peter SCHAT is performed for the first time by the Rotterdam Philharmonic Orchestra.

25 JUNE 1983

Alberto GINASTERA, immensely talented Argentine composer who began his career as a fashioner of pulsating Latin American rhythms in song and symphony, but who developed a stern code of advanced atonal, polytonal and dodecaphonic techniques in his later works, dies in his home in Geneva, Switzerland, racked by lung cancer, at the age of sixty-seven.

10 JULY 1983

Werner EGK, significant German composer who allegedly changed his original and undistinguished name Mayer to a seemingly self-complimentary acronym for "ein grosser (or even, ein genialer) Komponist," but who claimed that he did so as a tribute to his wife, Elisabeth Karl (with the middle guttural letter added "for euphony"), whose music was marked by pleasingly acrid harmonies and dense contrapuntal involvement, dies in Inning, near Munich, at the age of eighty-two.

16 JULY 1983

Reflections for orchestra by the 61-year-old Czech-born American composer Karel HUSA is performed for the first time in Greensboro, North Carolina.

17 JULY 1983

Cello Concerto by the 80-year-old English composer Sir Lennox BERKELEY is performed for the first time in Manchester.

23 JULY 1983

Georges AURIC, French composer, member of the legendary group Les Six (the others were Milhaud, Honegger, Poulenc, Durey and Germaine Tailleferre), dies in Paris at the age of eighty-four.

27 JULY 1983

Piano Concerto by the 31-year-old British composer Dominic MULDOWNEY is performed for the first time in London.

17 AUGUST 1983

Ira GERSHWIN, supreme American lyricist who wrote the great libretti for his brother George's musicals in gloriously rhymed verse, dies at his home in Beverly Hills, California, at the age of eighty-six.

23 SEPTEMBER 1983

Akhenaten for chorus and orchestra by the 76-year-old German-born American composer Gene GUTCHË is performed for the first time in St. Louis.

29 SEPTEMBER 1983

Third Symphony by the highly distinguished Polish composer Witold LUTOSLAWSKI, who worked on it for nearly ten years, is finally performed after its successful completion, in Chicago.

30 SEPTEMBER 1983

À l'approche du Feu méditant by the 45-year-old French composer Jean-Claude ELOY, set for the traditional Japanese Gagaku ensemble, with two choirs of Buddist monks and five Bugaku dances, is performed for the first time in Tokyo.

1 OCTOBER 1983

Fourth Symphony by the 51-year-old Soviet composer Sergei SLONIMSKY, dedicated to the memory of his father, the novelist Mikhail Slonimsky, in four movements, *Allegro scherzando, Andante, Allegro marziale* and *Marche funèbre*, is performed for the first time in Kuibishev on the Volga River. (Its first Leningrad performance took place on 23 March 1984.)

4 OCTOBER 1983

The Photographer, theater piece by the ingeniously simplistic American composer Philip GLASS, in three acts of drama, concert music and dance, portraying in vivid colors the extraordinary life of the pioneer motion-analyzing photographer Eadweard Muybridge, who was the first to prove that, like a galloping horse, a trotting horse had at moments all four hooves off the ground, who killed the lover of his wife but won an acquittal in a sensational trial, is performed in a new version, with the subtitle *Far From the Truth*, at the Brooklyn Academy of Music. (The world premiere of the original version took place at the Holland Festival in June 1982.)

7 OCTOBER 1983

Wenn Bach Bienen gezüchtet hätte (If Bach Had Raised Bees), concertino for harpsichord, electric bass guitar, electric tape and ensemble by the 48-year-old Estonian composer Arvo PÄRT, based on the theme B–A–C–H, is performed for the first time in Graz, Austria.

7 OCTOBER 1983
Double Concerto for flute, bassoon and orchestra by the 57-year-old Austrian avant-garde composer Friedrich CERHA is performed for the first time in Graz.

8 OCTOBER 1983
Concerto primaverile (Spring Concerto) for violin and string orchestra by the 51-year-old Soviet composer Sergei SLONIMSKY, in three movements, *Allegro capriccioso, Romanze* and *Vivace ben ritmato*, is performed for the first time in Vilnius, by Sergei Stadler, soloist, and the Lithuanian Chamber Orchestra under the direction of Saulus Sondetskis. (A Leningrad performance was given on 17 October 1983.)

9 OCTOBER 1983
Monodrama for cello and orchestra by the 31-year-old German composer Wolfgang RIHM is performed for the first time in Graz.

19 OCTOBER 1983
Otadžbina (The Fatherland), oratorio by the Serbian prime romantic composer Petar KONJOVIĆ (1883–1970), in three "singing actions" inspired by the epic folksong about the Serbian defeat in the Battle of Kosovo in 1389, is produced in Belgrade.

20 OCTOBER 1983
Double-bass Concerto by Gian Carlo MENOTTI is performed for the first time by James VanDemark as soloist with the New York Philharmonic, Zubin Mehta conducting.

29 OCTOBER 1983
The Fifty-seventh Festival of the International Society for Contemporary Music opens in Aarhus, Denmark, with a performance of *I Ching* for percussion solo by the 51-year-old Danish composer Per NØRGAARD, after the ancient Chinese book of oracles based on sixty-four different states of all living things, in four movements: *Thunder Repeated, the Image of Shock; The Taming Power of the Small; The Gentle, the Penetrating;* and *Towards Completion: Fire Over Water.*

At an afternoon concert, the following program of chamber music by Danish composers is presented:

Aquarelles by 38-year-old Ole BUCK. *Pianissimo Furioso* by 36-year-old Karl Aage RASMUSSEN, an oxymoronic etude in which inner fury is expressed in soft sounds. *Haven med stier der deleg sig (The Garden with Separating Paths),* to text of Jorge Luis Borges, by 52-year-old Ib NØRHOLM, with its seven instruments all following separate metronome beats. *Perceptive Constructions* by 51-year-old Henning CHRISTIANSEN, in four sections, being an essay in aggressive simplicity without falling into psychedelic abecedarianism. *Seadrift* by 51-year-old Per NØRGAARD, in two movements, *Being Together* and *Torn Apart*, inspired by the poetry of Walt Whitman.

29 OCTOBER 1983

The first day of the Fifty-seventh Festival of the International Society for Contemporary Music continues in Aarhus with the following program of symphonic works at an evening concert:

Tre Concerti Piccoli by the 57-year-old German composer Hans Werner HENZE, a set of interludes from his ninth opera, *The English Cat*, which deals with an innocent victim of ailurophobia. *Third Symphony* by the 70-year-old Polish composer Witold LUTOSLAWSKI. *Fifth Symphony* by the Danish classical romanticist Carl NIELSEN.

29 OCTOBER 1983

On the first day of the Fifty-seventh Festival of the International Society for Contemporary Music in Aarhus, a nocturnal concert of chamber music is presented with the following program:

Night Fantasies for solo piano by the 75-year-old American composer Elliott CARTER, suggested by a hypnopompic interlude of nocturnal wakefulness. *Pyonkyong* for piano and percussion by the 38-year-old Korean composer trained in Germany Younghi PAGH-PAAN. *String Quartet* by the 28-year-old French composer Pascal DUSAPIN. *Fourth String Quartet* by the 78-year-old Italian composer Giacinto SCELSI.

30 OCTOBER 1983

On the second day of the Fifty-seventh Festival of the International Society for Contemporary Music in Aarhus, *Mantra* by Karlheinz STOCKHAUSEN for two pianists, tape, ring modulator, woodblocks and antique cymbals, subdivided into thirteen cycles integrated into a mystical invocation of Hindu ritual, is presented at an afternoon concert. At a later concert, the following program entitled "Is Darmstadt Alive?" is presented:

/L for amplified piano, four hands, by the 35-year-old Finnish composer Jukka TIENSUU, an essay in modulated sonorities. *String Quartet* by the 34-year-old British composer Jonathan HARVEY, in one movement based on gradual expansion of melodic ornaments. *Second String Quartet* by the 40-year-old British composer Brian FERNEYHOUGH, a labyrinthine exercise in serialistic melodies and pauses. *Salut für Caudwell* for two guitars by the 48-year-old German composer Helmut LACHENMANN, dedicatory essay to a modern esthetician. *Tetras* for string quartet by the 61-year-old commanding master of teleological structures Iannis XENAKIS, set in a tetradic ensemble.

30 OCTOBER 1983

The second day of the Fifty-seventh Festival of the International Society for Contemporary Music continues in Aarhus, at an evening concert with the following program:

Treppenmusik (Staircase Music) for saxophone quartet, clarinet quartet, string quintet and electronics by the 39-year-old Canadian composer John REA, a musical counterpart of Dutch artist M. C. Escher's heterodimensional ladders. *Epigrams,* to a text by Takis Antoniou, for soprano and chamber orchestra by the 48-year-old Greek composer Theodore ANTONIOU, influenced by Byzantine hymnology. Two parts from *Four Compositions,* "Plain Song" and "Variations" for flute, clarinet, horn, piano and string quintet by the 34-year-old Danish composer Poul RUDERS. *Two Shôgas (Two Solfeges)* for soprano, flute, oboe, percussion, harp, piano and violins by the 76-year-old Japanese composer Yoritsuñe MATSUDAIRA, sonorous exercises in onomatopeia. *Incenters* for trumpet, horn, trombone and chamber group by the 55-year-old American composer Jacob DRUCKMAN, corresponding in geometry to a triangle inscribed in a circle or a pyramid within a sphere, with blocks of brassy sounds set against the equilibrium in the rest of the ensemble.

31 OCTOBER 1983

On the third day of the Fifty-seventh Festival of the International Society for Contemporary Music in Aarhus, a morning concert of electronic mixed media from Scandinavia presents the following program:

Openings by the composer and visual artist team Par and Jörgen LINDGREN, an attempt at a musical utopia in a conflict with electronic and concrete sounds. *In Dagbrott (Daybreak)* by the 32-year-old Swedish composer Rolf ENGSTRÖM, corresponding to the palimpsest or pentimento in painting. *Organ Music 1980* by the 44-year-old Hungarian-born composer Akos RÓZMANN. *Å propos Marcel* by the 47-year-old poet/composer/sonologist Sten HANSON and 47-year-old photographer/artist Nino Monastra, an artistic commentary on the famous modern painter and chessmaster Marcel Duchamp.

31 OCTOBER 1983

On the third day of the Fifty-seventh Festival of the International Society for Contemporary Music in Aarhus, an afternoon concert of minimal music presents the following program:

Music for Mallet Instruments, Voices and Organ by the 47-year-old American composer Steve REICH, based on the technique of the gradual phase displacement and stratification of the parameters of thematic content. *Litanie I* for piano by the 60-year-old Belgian composer Karel GOEYVAERTS, an elaboration of Balinese and African techniques of drumming. *Impho 102/6* for six crotales (miniature cymbal clapper-pairs) by the 40-year-old Hungarian composer Zoltán JENEY, the title being the Telex number of a hotel in Tokyo. *The Knight of Richerenches* for two pianos by the 35-year-old Ukrainian-born Canadian composer Lubomyr MELNYK, invoking the legend of the medieval Knights of the Temple. *Music for Horns, Piano and Cymbals* by the 41-year-old American composer John McGUIRE, consisting of a chain of thirty-six sections of responsorial exchange.

31 OCTOBER 1983

The third day of the Fifty-seventh Festival of the International Society for Contemporary Music continues with the following program at an evening concert in Aarhus:

Bells of Light for four choirs by the 24-year-old Canadian composer James HARLEY, to a text of syllabic phonemes gradually shifting phases to construct a sound sculpture. *Carrousel-Constellations* for two pianos, flute, cello and percussion by the 36-year-old Canadian composer Walter BOUDREAU, a cycle of nine pieces reflecting the topographical aspects of the nine planets of the solar system. *Three Pieces for Two Pianos, Eight Hands* by the 28-year-old Dutch composer Robert NASVELD, based on octotonic and enneatonic scales. *Linea* for two pianos and percussion by the 58-year-old Italian composer Luciano BERIO, involving a constant reshaping of a simple basic melody. *Trio for Violin, Horn and Piano* by the 60-year-old cosmopolitan modernist György LIGETI, in three movements based on heterometric variations on asymmetrical melodies.

31 OCTOBER 1983

On the third day of the Fifty-seventh Festival of the International Society for Contemporary Music in Aarhus, the following program, entitled "From Composition to Improvisation," is presented at a late night concert:

Recitations for voice without accompaniment by the 38-year-old Greek-born French composer Georges APERGHIS, consisting of fourteen fragments of aleatory music, each marked by an expressive command, such as "secretive," "contemptuous," etc. *Japan*, one of the works from *For Times to Come*, which consists of seventeen texts of Intuitive Music by the 55-year-old German master of modernity Karlheinz STOCKHAUSEN. *n* for four uncoordinated instrumental parts by the 37-year-old British composer Michael FINNISSY. *Turba* for double-bass solo by the 29-year-old British composer Oliver KNUSSEN. *Echo III* for trumpet solo and tape by the 40-year-old British composer Roger SMALLEY. *Organic Music* for any number of instruments by the British composer Lyell CRESSWELL, giving improvisatory freedom to the performers.

1 NOVEMBER 1983

On the fourth day of the Fifty-seventh Festival of the International Society for Contemporary Music at Aarhus, the following program is presented at an afternoon concert, under the general heading "Neotonality":

Heavy Metal Two-step for brass quintet by the British composer David SUTTON-ANDERSSON, with the imperious tuba entry establishing a commanding Gestalt.

Fratres for violin and piano by the 48-year-old Estonian composer Arvo PÄRT, in which the meandering violinistic figures and solemn hymnodic harmonies are united in an appeal for the brotherhood of men. *For Renée* for flute, cello, piano and percussion by the 45-year-old Icelandic composer Thorkell SIGURBJÖRNSSON, a birthday salutation in five moments. *C'est la mer melée au soleil* (*It is the Sea Mixed with the Sun*) for guitar solo by the 29-year-old Danish composer Erik HØJSGAARD, to a poem by Arthur Rimbaud. *In Dark Times*, eight songs to texts by Bertolt Brecht by the 31-year-old British composer Dominic MULDOWNEY, scored for soprano, tenor, bass, flute, clarinet, viola, cello and piano.

1 NOVEMBER 1983

The fourth day of the Fifty-seventh Festival of the International Society for Contemporary Music in Aarhus continues with an evening concert of "Theatrical Expressions," featuring the following program:

De profundis for piano four hands by the 34-year-old Belgian composer Paul BEELAERTS, a hymnal lament. *Heiligenlegende* for recorder, eight-part vocal ensemble, speaker and tape by the 42-year-old Austrian composer Dieter KAUFMANN, based on Psalm 129 by Ernesto Cardenal, the Nicaraguan priest imprisoned under dictator Somoza. *Tuba mirum* for tuba player by the 37-year-old British composer Trevor WISHART, representing a prisoner in a mental hospital. *Questions* for thirty-two voices by the 54-year-old Japanese composer Joji YUASA, in six movements depicting both physical and metaphysical inquiries.

At a late night concert wind instrumentalists Morten Carlsen and Jesper Zeuthen present a program of improvisational fusion music, combining folk and art music from the Third World with Western avant-garde jazz.

2 NOVEMBER 1983

On the fifth day of the Fifty-seventh Festival of the International Society for Contemporary Music, *Sinfonie querrière et amoureuse* for organ by the 51-year-old Italian composer Niccolò CASTIGLIONI is performed at a morning concert in the Aarhus Cathedral. At an afternoon concert, the following program, under the general heading "The Social Commitment," is presented by the Dutch orchestra De Volharding (The Perseverance):

Tango for Jet by 37-year-old Diderik WAGENAAR. *Balada do amor militante* to the text of Manuel Alegre by 38-year-old Portuguese-born Dutch composer Amilcar Vásques DIAS. *Blues voor de Volharding* by 29-year-old Huub DE VRIEND. *Workers Union* by 44-year-old Louis ANDRIESSEN. *Järn* (*Iron*) by Klas TORSTENSSON. *Moeilijkheden* (*Difficulties*) by 39-year-old Klaas DE VRIES. *On Jimmy Yancey* by Louis ANDRIESSEN. *Dressoir* by 48-year-old Russian-born Dutch composer Misha MENGELBERG.

2 NOVEMBER 1983

The fifth day of the Fifty-seventh Festival of the International Society for Contemporary Music continues with the Aarhus Symphony Orchestra presenting the following program at an evening concert:

Arc of Life by the 83-year-old great composer Ernst KRENEK, a philosopher of modern music who successfully combines profound truths of life with dodecaphonic artistry. *Gondwana* by the 36-year-old French composer Tristan MURAIL, the title referring to the mythical sunken continent. *Beati pauperi II (Blessed Be the Poor)* with vocal soloists by the 59-year-old Swiss composer Klaus HUBER, a "Kontrafaktur" of two motets by Orlando Lassus. *Symphony, Antiphony* by the 51-year-old Danish composer Pelle GUNDMUNDSEN-HOLMGREEN, a pair of homogeneous and heterogeneous works.

At a night concert the Australian pianist Geoffrey Douglas Madge performs *Opus Clavicembalisticum*, the brobdingnagian masterpiece by the supreme British Parsi individualist Kaikhosru Shapurji SORABJI.

3 NOVEMBER 1983
On the sixth day of the Fifty-seventh Festival of the International Society for Contemporary Music in Aarhus, the following audiovisual works are presented at an early afternoon concert:

Claustraphonie by the 48-year-old Swiss composer Jürg WYTTENBACH, a salad bowl of musical quotations from Schubert to Schoenberg to the Beatles. *Patches of Life*, an opera-oratorio for television by the 40-year-old Swedish composer Daniel BÖRTZ, extolling nature's struggle against man's lust for destruction. *Kasaanin Synty (The Genesis of Kazan)* by the 37-year-old Finnish composer Pekka SIRÉN, based on an old Mordvinian poem telling the story of self-immolation among the pagan population of Kazan on the Volga river.

3 NOVEMBER 1983
The sixth day of the Fifty-seventh Festival of the International Society for Contemporary Music continues in Aarhus with an afternoon concert featuring the following electronic works:

Bouwstenen for bass clarinet and multiple tape delay by the 39-year-old Dutch composer Harry SPARNAAY. *Berceuse* for tape by the 50-year-old Polish composer Eugeniusz RUDNIK. *Violin Control* for violin and synthesizer by the 46-year-old Swiss composer Thomas KESSLER. *Voyage au Centre de la Tête* for tape by the 51-year-old French composer François BAYLE. *Invention V* for percussion and electronics by the 31-year-old Norwegian composer Kjell SAMKOPF.

3 NOVEMBER 1983
On the sixth day of the Fifty-seventh Festival of the International Society for Contemporary Music in Aarhus, the following program of chamber music is presented at an evening concert:

String Quartet by the 29-year-old Hungarian composer Miklós CSEMICZKY. *Sei danze* for violin solo by the 34-year-old Italian composer Fernando MENCHERINI. *Brains and Dancin'* for string quartet by the 33-year-old Swedish composer

Mikael EDLUND, purported to reflect the cerebral and choreographic elements in music. *Oriens III* for three flutes by the 35-year-old Brazilian composer Ronaldo COUTINO DE MIRANDA, in three movements of diversified content. *Looking at Silence* for cello solo by the 43-year-old Israeli composer Joseph DORFMAN, with the cello tuned in scordatura, which determines its atonal character. *Tashi Quartet* for clarinet, violin, cello and piano by the 37-year-old American composer Peter LIEBERSON, son of the renowned recording executive Goddard Lieberson.

4 NOVEMBER 1983

On the seventh day of the Fifty-seventh Festival of the International Society for Contemporary Music in Aarhus, the following program featuring Danish music is presented at an afternoon concert:

Second String Quartet by 31-year-old Hans ABRAHAMSEN. *Fresques*, Part III, for guitar solo by 74-year-old Swiss-born Gunnar BERG. *Mambo* for clarinet, cello and piano by 48-year-old Bent LORENTZEN, inspired by the rhythms of Afro-Cuban music. *A Dream in Violet* for string trio by Poul Rovsing OLSEN (1922–1982), based on an eight-note theme converging on the central middle A in the coda. *String Quartet* by 27-year-old Steen PADE. *Piano Quintet* by 59-year-old Axel BORUP-JØRGENSEN.

4 NOVEMBER 1983

The seventh day of the Fifty-seventh Festival of the International Society for Contemporary Music continues in Aarhus at an evening concert with the Danish Radio Symphony Orchestra performing the following program:

Le Pinceau (The Paint Brush) by the 39-year-old Japanese composer Yoshiyuki DOI, a shimmering palette of superimposed and interwoven timbres. *The Magic Mountain* for piano and orchestra by the 34-year-old British composer John HOPKINS, after the novel by Thomas Mann describing the tragic monotony of a tubercular retreat. *Otto poesie da un soldo (Eight Poems for a Penny)* for tenor and orchestra, inspired by the writings of James Joyce, by the 37-year-old Italian composer Claudio BILUCAGLIA. *Space* for four orchestral groups by the 30-year-old Rumanian-born German resident composer Adriana HÖLSZKY, depicting the vivacious cosmogony of the Maori people of New Zealand.

4 NOVEMBER 1983

The Fifty-seventh Festival of the International Society for Contemporary Music in Aarhus concludes with the following program at a late night concert:

Dressur for trio of wooden percussion instruments by the audacious experimenter who was born in Argentina and took residence in Germany, Mauricio KAGEL, herein purporting to advocate the training of musicians similar to the *dressage* of performing horses. *Invention* for tape by the 45-year-old Venezuelan composer Alfredo DEL MONACO, an electronic study focusing on the relationship between duration and tone color. *Tango* for clarinet, cello, piano and trombone by the 29-year-old Polish composer Tadeusz WIELECKI, in which the participating instruments dance a tango with one another. *Six Songs* for voice and piano by the 40-year-old British composer Mick WILSON, to his own words. *On Shooting Stars*, an homage to the Chilean folksinger/poet/playwright Victor Jara who fell victim of the military clique in Chile, for chamber ensemble by the 33-year-old Australian composer Vincent PLUSH.

7 NOVEMBER 1983
Morephonemena, highly serialized work for twelve unaccompanied voices to a text created from phonemes by the 57-year-old American composer Milton BABBITT, in which every musical feature of the work relates to the number 12 (twenty-four consonants and twelve vowels in the text, twelve minutes in length, written in twelve-tone style, etc.), is given its first performance at the San Francisco Museum of Modern Art by the vocal ensemble Ariel, Christopher Fulkerson conducting.

7 NOVEMBER 1983
Germaine TAILLEFERRE, the last surviving member of Les Six, the French group of early modernists, dies in Paris at the age of ninety-one.

7 NOVEMBER 1983
Gallery 83 for chamber ensemble by the 60-year-old American composer and timpanist William KRAFT, based on paintings by the composer, Claude Monet and Jackson Pollock, receives its first performance at the San Francisco Museum of Modern Art, the composer conducting.

13 NOVEMBER 1983
Viola Concerto by the 31-year-old German composer Wolfgang RIHM is performed for the first time in West Berlin.

19 NOVEMBER 1983
Perfect Lives (Private Parts), video opera by Robert ASHLEY, in seven acts each lasting exactly twenty-five minutes and fifty seconds, with the composer narrating his song in quasi-singing vocal inflections, is televised from New York.

28 NOVEMBER 1983
Saint François d'Assise, first opera by the 74-year-old French composer of devotional and ornithological music Olivier MESSIAEN, to his own libretto suffused with deep religious thought and depicting the immanent aspects of Grace in the soul of Saint Francis, who was himself a devout birdman, its melodious score replete with trills and refrains characteristic of flying creatures, in five sections culminating with an angelic choir vibrant with

the sounds of an Ondes Martenot and a wordless women's chorus, is performed for the first time at the Paris Opéra.

4 DECEMBER 1983
Claudio SANTORO, Brazilian composer of progressive tendencies in music as well as in politics, conducts in Rio de Janeiro the first performance of his *Tenth Symphony*.

❧ *1984* ❧

11 JANUARY 1984
De Snelheid (Velocity), orchestral poem by the modern flying Dutchman Louis ANDRIESSEN, a study in reciprocally counteractive forces reflected in relative velocity of instrumental parts, is performed for the first time as a commissioned work by the San Francisco Symphony Orchestra under the direction of its Dutch conductor Edo de Waart.

14 JANUARY 1984
Paul BEN-HAIM, accomplished Israeli composer who fled his native Germany and established himself in Israel, changing his real name Frankenburger to the Hebrew appellation Ben-Haim (meaning "son of bliss"), who wrote a number of orchestral and vocal works inspired by Biblical themes, dies in Tel Aviv at the age of eighty-four.

24 JANUARY 1984
Ralph SHAPEY conducts the first performance of his *Double Concerto* for violin, cello and orchestra at the Juilliard School of Music in New York.

28 JANUARY 1984
Prismatic Variations by the 57-year-old American composer Donald ERB, scored for orchestra with the participation of three harmonicas, slide whistle, piano, electric piano, electric organ and about eighty young people in the audience, is performed for the first time as a commissioned work by the St. Louis Symphony Orchestra, Leonard Slatkin conducting.

2 FEBRUARY 1984
Bells, an anti-war work by the 62-year-old American composer Pia GILBERT, to texts taken from Bertrand Russell, John Cage, Gertrude Stein, and others, opening with the Sanskrit apostrophe, "We want more cows!" accompanied by a whole campanology of popular demands, is performed for the first time at El Camino College in Torrance, California.

11 FEBRUARY 1984

Howl for three dogs and twenty human voices organized by Kirk NUROCK, founder of the Natural Sound Center, is performed for the first time in New York.

18 FEBRUARY 1984

Western Springs by the American composer Henry BRANT, a spatial assembly for two orchestras, two choruses and two jazz combos, in five sections descriptive of hot springs in five Western states, is performed for the first time in La Jolla, California.

21 FEBRUARY 1984

Dhammapada for soprano, harp and percussion, after the classic Buddhist epic poem, by the 51-year-old Soviet composer Sergei SLONIMSKY, is performed for the first time in Leningrad.

9 MARCH 1984

Concerto for timpani and orchestra by the 60-year-old American composer and percussion virtuoso William KRAFT is performed for the first time by Thomas Akins as soloist with the Indianapolis Symphony Orchestra, John Nelson conducting.

10 MARCH 1984

The Black Theatre of Hermes Trismegistos to text and music by the 50-year-old Canadian composer R. Murray SCHAFER, for actors, singers and instrumentalists, depicting marriage according to the rites of medieval alchemists, is performed for the first time at the Contemporary Music Festival at the California Institute of the Arts in Valencia, California.

14 MARCH 1984

Scritti di Leonardo, the first musical setting of words by Leonardo da Vinci, by the 29-year-old American composer Christopher FULKERSON, for tenor solo, vocal quartet and instrumental ensemble of viola, guitar, harp, flute and bass clarinet and set in a "simultaneous form" arising from the sometimes overlapping, sometimes sequential and sometimes simultaneous placement of its numerous arias, quartets and instrumental pieces, receives its first performance by Patrick Neve as tenor soloist and the vocal ensemble Ariel at the San Francisco Museum of Modern Art, the composer conducting.

17 MARCH 1984

Sendings by Kirk NUROCK, hopefully scored for winds, three guinea pigs and a Siberian husky, with the application of microtonal pulses and circular breathing, is performed for the first time at the Natural Sound Center in New York.

21 MARCH 1984

Violin Concerto by Roy HARRIS, written in 1938 and scheduled for performance by Josef Gingold with the Cleveland Orchestra but rejected by the imperious conductor George Szell after the orchestral parts turned out to be in disarray, is retrieved in 1984 and performed for the first time in Wilmington, North Carolina, by Greg Fulkerson as soloist with the North Carolina Symphony Orchestra, Gerhardt Zimmermann conducting. (Part of the melodic material in the *Concerto* went into the opening of the *Third Symphony* by Harris.)

22 MARCH 1984

First Symphony by the 45-year-old American composer John HARBISON is performed for the first time in Boston.

24 MARCH 1984

Akhenaton, opera by the 48-year-old American composer Philip GLASS, based on the story of the Eighteenth-Dynasty pharaoh who introduced monotheism to Egypt, is performed for the first time at the Württemberg State Theater, Dennis Russell Davies conducting.

27 MARCH 1984

Starlight Express, a musical by the 36-year-old top-notch British melo-rhythmicist Andrew LLOYD WEBBER, the central characters being steam locomotives performed by singing actors on roller skates, is produced in London.

2 APRIL 1984

Study for Contextures II: The Final Beast by William KRAFT, scored for soprano, tenor and two ensembles, one of modern instruments, the second of historical instruments, to texts from a 3,000-year period, including Homer, Psalms, Longfellow, etc., commissioned by the Los Angeles Philharmonic, is performed for the first time by the Los Angeles Philharmonic New Music Group, the composer conducting.

5 APRIL 1984

The Mask of Time for four soloists, large chorus and orchestra by the grand and royally ennobled 79-year-old British composer Sir Michael TIPPETT is performed for the first time by the Boston Symphony Orchestra, Colin Davis conducting.

12 April 1984
Fourth Symphony by the 49-year-old Soviet modernist Alfred Schnittke is performed for the first time in Moscow.

20 April 1984
Cantata No. 6, Flower Songs for mixed chorus and string orchestra by the 68-year-old American composer Vincent Persichetti is performed for the first time in Philadelphia.

23 April 1984
Sunday in the Park with George, musical by the versatile American composer and lyricist Stephen Sondheim, inspired by the painting by Georges Seurat entitled "A Sunday Afternoon on the Island of La Grande Jatte," astutely transmuting Seurat's pointilistic techniques into a colorful panneau of a merry Paris of yore populated by moustachioed, sideburned boulevardiers and visited by stolid American tourists, is produced in New York.

24 April 1984
The Abduction of Figaro, an innocuous mockery in the form of a Mozartean pasticcio in which Don Giovanni is Donald Giovanni and Papageno is Papa Geno, by P.D.Q. Bach, a.k.a. Peter Schickele, the amiable American mountebank of performing arts, is produced in Minneapolis.

26 April 1984
Count Basie, black American bandleader who led his groups from the piano keyboard using grunts and eyelid movements to give specific cues for dynamics, tempo and timbre, and who received the honorific sobriquet Count in appreciation of the nobility of his interpretations (his real name was William), dies in Hollywood, Florida, at the age of seventy-nine.

14 May 1984
Fourth Symphonic Fantasy by the 83-year-old American composer Otto Luening is performed for the first time in New York.

15 May 1984
The Moscow Contemporary Music Festival opens with a concert of symphonic music in the following program:

Overture to the opera *Colas Breugnon* by the 79-year-old doyen of Soviet music Dmitri Kabalevsky. *Double Concerto* for violin, cello and orchestra by the 57-year-old Rumanian composer Anatol Vieru. *Querela pacis (The Dispute of Peace)* for two choirs and orchestra by the 57-year-old Norwegian composer Oddvar S. Kvam, to words after Erasmus. *Self-Portrait*, a set of orchestral variations by the 51-year-old Soviet composer Rodion Shchedrin. *Eighth*

Concerto for Orchestra by the 79-year-old Italian composer Goffredo PETRASSI. *Second Rhapsody* by the Soviet conductor Evgeny SVETLANOV.

Our Spring Music Festival is intended to popularize the music of composers promoting the ideals of humanism and democracy in their compositions, strengthening peace and friendship among peoples. The progressive mission of the Moscow Festival has found its reflection in the motto: "Music for Humanism, for Peace and Friendship among Nations." This motto is especially topical these days—days of concern for the fates of humanity, days when imperialist forces threaten the existence of world civilization. We, however, believe in the power of Reason and Good, in the power of Art uniting people in the name of Life and Beauty. (From the introductory address by Tikhon Khrennikov, Secretary-General of the Union of Soviet Composers.)

16 MAY 1984
On the second day of the Moscow Festival the following program is presented at a noon concert:

The Song of Peace for mixed choir a cappella by the 63-year-old Greek composer Iakovos HALIASSAS. *Song of 3 June 1983*, a cantata on the opening of the Library of Stockholm University by the 46-year-old Swedish composer Eskil HEMBERG. *Podhozarje* (*In the Hills of Khozara*) for chorus by the 51-year-old Yugoslav composer Vojin KOMADINA. *El Jicaro* for chorus by the 67-year-old Nicaraguan composer Juan MORENO. *Second String Quartet* by the 54-year-old Japanese composer Michio MAMIYA. *Piano Pictures* by the 31-year-old composer from Cyprus Nicolas ECONOMU, performed by the composer. *Sixth String Quartet* by the 55-year-old Australian composer Peter SCULTHORPE.

16 MAY 1984
The second day of the Moscow Festival continues with an evening concert featuring the following program of symphonic works:

Western Suite by the 75-year-old American composer Elie SIEGMEISTER. *Cello Concerto* by the 56-year-old Japanese composer Nobuo TERHARA. *Symphonic Prologue* by the 45-year-old Bulgarian composer Georgi MINCHEV. *Flute Concerto* by the 50-year-old East German composer Siegfried MATTHUS. *Piano Concerto*, subtitled *Let Korea Be United*, by the North Korean composer Jun Chun NAM.

17 MAY 1984
On the third day of the Moscow Festival, the following program of chamber music is presented:

Three Pieces for string quartet by the Argentine composer Alicia TERZIAN. *Five Pieces* for piano by the 60-year-old Egyptian composer Gamal ABDEL-RAHIM. *Trio Concertante* for violin, viola and cello by the 38-year-old Czech composer Ladislav KUBIK. *Brass Quintet* by the 54-year-old Hungarian composer Emil PETROVICS. *Synthesen* for string quartet by the 57-year-old East German composer Siegfried KÖHLER. *Sonatina* for flute and piano by the Ecuadoran composer Claudio AIZAGA. Three pieces from *Six humeurs* for cello and piano by the 54-year-old Belgian composer Jacqueline FONTIJN.

17 MAY 1984

The third day of the Moscow Festival continues at an evening concert with the following program of symphonic works:

Simon Bolivar, overture for orchestra by the 54-year-old Mexican composer Enrique SANTOS. *Viola Concerto* by the 78-year-old East German composer Ernst Hermann MEYER. *Festive Prologue* by the 59-year-old Austrian composer Thomas Christian DAVID. *Le Bal des Pendus*, to poems from Rimbaud, by the 85-year-old French composer Emmanuel BONDEVILLE. *Piano Concerto* by the 30-year-old Luxembourg composer Walter CIVITAREALE. *Clarinet Concerto* by the Bulgarian composer Lubomir PIPKOV (1904–1974).

18 MAY 1984

On the fourth day of the Moscow Festival the following program of chamber music is presented at an afternoon concert:

Prelude and Fugue, subtitled *Epitaph to Béla Bartók*, for cello and piano by the 55-year-old Finnish composer Einojuhani RAUTAVAARA. *Movement* for cello and piano by the 66-year-old Hungarian composer András MIHÁLY. *Piece* for cello and piano by the Nigerian composer Akin EUBA. *Serenade* for cello by the 57-year-old German composer Hans Werner HENZE. *Six Japanese Folksongs* for cello and piano by the 54-year-old Japanese composer Michio MAMIYA. *Ritmicas* for wind quintet and piano by the Cuban composer Amadeo ROLDÁN. *Pieces* for guitar by the 42-year-old Mexican composer Miguel ALCAZAR. *Kuema (Wave)* for string quartet by the 54-year-old Finnish composer Usko MERI-LÄINEN. *Pieces* for piano by the 52-year-old Norwegian composer Arne NORD-HEIM.

18 MAY 1984

The fourth day of the Moscow Festival continues with the following program of choral music:

The Will for soloist and mixed choir by the 59-year-old Yugoslav composer Vlastimir NIKOLOVSKI. *Bells Clanging* for reciter, soloists, mixed choir, oboe and percussion, in sixteen movements, by the 44-year-old Soviet composer Valery GAVRILIN. *Three Estonian Songs* for mixed choir, entitled *Windmill, Tying up the Finger* and *Ship*, by the 54-year-old Estonian composer Veljo TORMIS. *The Pushkin Wreath*, concerto for choir by the 68-year-old Soviet composer Georgy SVIRIDOV.

18 MAY 1984

On the fourth day of the Moscow Festival the following program of symphonic works is presented at an evening concert:

Unfinished March by the 59-year-old Tunisian composer Salah EL-MAHDI. *Double-bass Concerto* by the 81-year-old Italian composer Virgilio MORTARI.

Third Symphony by the 77-year-old Soviet composer Andrei BALANCHIVADZE. *Invincible Revolution,* hymn of Soviet-Afghan Friendship by the 54-year-old Afghani composer Salim SARMAST. *Cello Concerto* by the 63-year-old Soviet composer Karen KHACHATURIAN. *Metamorphosen über ein Fragment von Mozart* for flute, oboe, string quartet and orchestra by the 67-year-old Austrian composer Helmut EDER.

19 MAY 1984
On the fifth day of the Moscow Festival the following program of chamber music is presented at a noon concert:

First String Quartet by the 50-year-old Hungarian composer Zsolt DURKÓ. *Legend of the Raven* for piano by the Canadian composer Alex PAUK. *Musica Viva* for percussion by the 43-year-old Cuban composer José LOYOLA. *Duets for Two Violins* by the 51-year-old Czech composer Ilja ZELJENKA. *Third String Quartet* by the 68-year-old Norwegian composer Knut NYSTEDT.

19 MAY 1984
The fifth day of the Moscow Festival continues with the following program of chamber music at an afternoon concert:

Nocturne for tenor, seven obbligato instruments and strings by the British composer Benjamin BRITTEN (1913–1976). *Guitar Concerto* by the Brazilian composer Heitor VILLA-LOBOS (1887–1959). *Frescoes of Saint Sophia in Kiev,* symphony-concerto for harp and chamber orchestra by the 43-year-old Soviet composer Valery KIKTA. *Concierto Barroco* for piano, violin and chamber orchestra by the 58-year-old Colombian composer Luis Antonio ESCOBAR. *Eighth Symphony* for chamber orchestra by the 40-year-old Soviet composer Mirsadyk TADJIEV.

19 MAY 1984
On the fifth day of the Moscow Festival the following program of symphonic works is presented at an evening concert:

Orpheus in Hiroshima, concert version of the opera for soloists, mixed choir and orchestra by the 58-year-old Japanese composer Yasushi AKUTAGAWA. *Concerto for Orchestra* by the 62-year-old Bulgarian composer Alexander RAICHEV. *Violin Concerto* by the 82-year-old Spanish composer Joaquín RODRIGO. *Memory* by the 71-year-old Czech composer Ján CIKKER.

20 MAY 1984
On the sixth day of the Moscow Festival the following program of chamber and choral music is presented at an afternoon concert:

Funeral Music, dedicated to the memory of Ché Guevara, for chamber orchestra by the 56-year-old Spanish composer Ramón BARCE. *Sonata for* piano, wind quintet, strings and timpani by the Czech composer Václav DOBIÁŠ (1909–

1978). *Divertimento* for flute, strings and celesta by the 81-year-old Soviet composer Andrei SHTOGARENKO. *Romancero of Love and Death* to the text by Federico García Lorca for mixed choir, two electric guitars, piano and percussion by the 54-year-old Soviet composer Nicolai SIDELNIKOV.

20 MAY 1984
On the sixth day of the Moscow Festival the following program of symphonic works is presented at an early afternoon concert:

Fragments from the ballet *Yerma* by the 43-year-old Filipino composer Francisco FELICIANO. *Violin Concerto* by the 66-year-old Filipina composer Lucrecia KASILAG. Suite from the ballet *Kni* by the 56-year-old Vietnamese composer Van KY. Suite from the comic opera *King Pomádé's New Clothes* by the 76-year-old Hungarian composer György RÁNKI. *Piano Concerto* by the 69-year-old Turkish composer Bülent TARÇAN. *Chorali* for thirty-two winds, percussion, harp and celesta by the 49-year-old Finnish composer Aulis SALLINEN.

20 MAY 1984
On the sixth day of the Moscow Festival the following program of symphonic works is presented at an evening concert:

Intrada by the 59-year-old Austrian composer Fritz LEITERMEYER. *Second Symphony*, subtitled *The Age of Anxiety*, for piano and orchestra by the 65-year-old American composer Leonard BERNSTEIN. *Festivity* by the 38-year-old Soviet composer Tolib-khon SHAKHIDI. *Second Piano Concerto* by the 79-year-old Soviet composer Dmitri KABALEVSKY.

21 MAY 1984
The American premiere of *The Trials of Peter the Hebrew*, chamber opera by the 54-year-old French composer Henri POUSSEUR, drawing from an incident in the life of Arnold Schoenberg when at the age of seventy he was denied a grant from the Guggenheim Foundation, in three acts divided into twenty-one sections, each of which represents a conflict between an individual (Schoenberg, Moses, Abraham, Noah) and a social group (population, generation, class), is produced in Los Angeles. (The original version was premiered in Berlin in 1974 under the title *Die Erprobung des Petrus Hebraicus*.)

21 MAY 1984
On the seventh day of the Moscow Festival the following program of chamber music is presented at a noon concert:

Concerto for Strings by the Argentine composer Alberto GINASTERA (1916–1983). *Concerto for String Orchestra* by the 70-year-old Rumanian composer Ion DUMITRESCU. *Clarinet Concerto* by the 83-year-old American composer Aaron COPLAND. *Music for String Orchestra* by the 62-year-old Finnish composer Joonas KOKKONEN. *Four Love Sonnets* to the words of Shakespeare for baritone, strings and harpsichord by the Polish composer Tadeusz BAIRD (1928–1981). *Adagio* for strings and vibraphone by the 33-year-old Mongolian composer Tsogzolyn NATSAGDORDG.

21 MAY 1984
The seventh day of the Moscow Festival continues at an afternoon concert with the following program of works for wind orchestra:

March on Russian Folk Themes by the Soviet composer Nicolai IVANOV-RADKEVICH (1904–1962). *Heroic Prelude* by the 60-year-old East German composer Heinz ARENZ. *Concertino* for piano, wind instruments, percussion and harp by the 55-year-old Hungarian composer Kamilló LENDVAY. *English Rhapsody* for brass band by the 53-year-old Norwegian composer Trevor FORD. *Spanish Metamorphoses* for two wind orchestras by the 45-year-old Czech composer Eugene ZÁMEČNIK. Finale from *Sakarska Suite* by the Bulgarian composer Filip KUTEV (1903–1982). *Poème du Feu* by the 51-year-old French composer Ida GOTKOVSKY. *Concerto* for saxophone and wind orchestra by the Soviet composer Mikhael GOTLIB (1907–1978). *Variations on a Japanese Folk Song Theme* by the 56-year-old Dutch composer Henk VAN LIJNSCHOOTEN. *Olympic Overture* by the 43-year-old Czech composer Ivana LOUDOVÁ. *Circus Suite* by the Swedish composer Julius JACOBSEN. *Overture Ritmica* by the 52-year-old East German composer Klaus-Peter BRUCHMANN. *March for Spartakiad* by Sergei PROKOFIEV.

21 MAY 1984
On the seventh day of the Moscow Festival the following program of symphonic works is presented at an evening concert:

Women—Heroines of the Native South by the Vietnamese composer Nguyen Thi NHUNG. *Tout un monde lointain . . .* to the text by Baudelaire for cello and orchestra by the 68-year-old French composer Henri DUTILLEUX. *A Heavy Harvest in the Fields of Chkhonsan* by the North Korean composer Kim Ok SON. *Memory* by the Moroccan composer Mustapha BENNIS. *Oboe Concerto* by the 59-year-old Soviet composer Andrei ESHPAI. *Sixth Symphony* by the 62-year-old Italian composer Mario ZAFRED.

22 MAY 1984
On the eighth day of the Moscow Festival the following program of chamber music is presented at a noon concert:

Ancient Voices of Children for soprano, child's voice and instrumental ensemble by the 54-year-old American composer George CRUMB. *Folk Songs* for soprano and seven instruments by the 58-year-old Italian composer Luciano BERIO. *Three Madrigals* for soprano and five instruments by the 49-year-old Soviet composer Alfred SCHNITTKE. *About Love and Nostalgia* for chamber orchestra by the 50-year-old Argentine composer Bruno D'ASTOLI.

22 May 1984

On the eighth day of the Moscow Festival the following program of symphonic works is presented at an evening concert:

Violin Concerto by the 53-year-old Soviet composer Andrei PETROV. *Fifth Symphony* by the 57-year-old German composer Hans Werner HENZE. *Requiem* for five soloists, mixed chorus and orchestra by the 77-year-old Portuguese composer Fernando LOPES-GRAÇA.

23 May 1984

On the ninth day of the Moscow Festival the following program of chamber music is presented at an afternoon concert:

Adagio for Strings by the American composer Samuel BARBER (1910–1981). *Variations on a Theme of Haydn* for cello and orchestra by the 55-year-old Soviet composer Edison DENISOV. *Concerto Funebre* for violin and string orchestra by the German composer Karl Amadeus HARTMANN (1905–1963). *Concerto* for two string orchestras by the 79-year-old British composer Sir Michael TIPPETT.

23 May 1984

On the ninth day of the Moscow Festival the following program of symphonic works is presented at an evening concert:

Music in Memory of Leonid Kogan, subtitled *Missa pro defunctis*, for soloists, mixed chorus and orchestra by the 60-year-old Italian composer Franco MANNINO. *Theme and Eight Variations* by the 58-year-old Soviet composer Boris TCHAIKOVSKY. *Second Cello Concerto* by the 50-year-old Polish composer Krzysztof PENDERECKI. *Symphonic Metamorphoses on Gesualdo* by the 65-year-old German composer Jürg BAUR.

24 May 1984

The Moscow Festival of Contemporary Music concludes with the following program of symphonic works:

Seventh Symphony, subtitled *Spring*, for soloists, chorus and orchestra by the 58-year-old Greek composer Mikis THEODORAKIS. *Third Piano Concerto* by the 70-year-old Soviet composer Tikhon KHRENNIKOV, with himself as soloist.

4 June 1984

Bamboula Squared for orchestra by the 46-year-old American composer Charles WUORINEN is performed for the first time in New York.

7 June 1984

A Haunted Landscape by the 54-year-old American composer George CRUMB, scored for orchestra, amplified piano and a set of exotic instruments including Caribbean steel drums, Cambodian angklungs, Japanese Kabuki blocks, the Brazilian cuica and the Appalachian hammered dulcimer, the title reflecting the mystery of certain places on the planet Earth, with a unifying factor provided by a low B-flat, is performed for the first time in New York, Arthur Weisberg conducting.

16 JUNE 1984
Bran(d)t aan de Amstel by Henry BRANT, the nonpareil American artificer of unearthly sounds in a terrestial environment, scored for ten dozen flutes, choirs and bands, carilloneur, four Dutch hand organs and sundry sonorifers, is presented for the first time in Amsterdam, Holland, in a procession on boats and barges plying the canals of Amsterdam.

20 JUNE 1984
The Double Life of Amphibians, electronic tone poem by the 51-year-old American composer Morton SUBOTNICK, featuring fourteen performers interacting with a computer, in three parts, *Ascent into Air* (written especially for IRCAM's computer system in Paris and premiered there on 18 January 1982), *The Burghers of Calais* and *The Fluttering of Wings* for string quartet and computer, is performed for the first time in its entirety at the Los Angeles Olympic Arts Festival.

1 JULY 1984
The King Goes Forth to France, opera by the 49-year-old Finnish composer Aulis SALLINEN, is produced in Helsinki.

9 JULY 1984
Randall THOMPSON, American composer who took pride in writing music in a euphonious traditional manner without being seduced by modern innovations, whose choral work *The Testament of Freedom* to words by Thomas Jefferson became a national classic, and who for many years taught composition at Harvard University, dies in Boston at the age of eighty-five.

14 JULY 1984
Sweeney, opera by the Broadway composer Stephen SONDHEIM, ingeniously arranged from his successful musical *Sweeney Todd* (which was originally produced in New York on 1 March 1979 and which ran for 557 performances) after a grisly tale, *The String of Pearls, or the Fiend of Fleet Street*, published serially in a London newspaper in 1846, dealing with a mad barber who cuts the throats of his unsuspecting customers for his even madder landlady who uses the throats and other meaty parts for her culinary concoctions ("Man eats man," Sweeney sings), is produced in Houston, Texas. (The first New York performance was given by the New York City Opera on 11 October 1984.)

17 July 1984

La Prison, cantata for soprano, cello and orchestra by Marcel LANDOWSKI, with cellist Mstislav Rostropovitch, his wife, Galina Vishnevskaya, as soprano soloist, Jean-Claude Casadesus conducting the Orchestre National de Lille, is performed for the first time anywhere at Aix-en-Provence.

20 July 1984

Gail KUBIK, inventive American composer who wrote symphonies and other works of merit but made a popular hit with his idiomatic setting of the animated cartoon *Gerald McBoing-Boing,* dies in Covina, California, at the age of sixty-nine, a victim of a deadly tropical disease, kala-azar, which he contracted during one of his trips to Africa.

29 July 1984

American Sing for orchestra by the 70-year-old American composer Morton GOULD, commissioned for the opening concert of the Los Angeles Olympic Games, is performed for the first time at the Hollywood Bowl.

31 July 1984

Paul LE FLEM, doyen of French music criticism, who was also a composer (he continued to write music until the age of ninety-five when he lost his sight almost totally), dies at the incredible age of one hundred and three years, four months, and thirteen days at his summer retreat in Trégastel (Côtes-du-Nord), France.

2 August 1984

Love of Don Perlimplín, one-act opera by the American composer Conrad SUSA, after the eponymous play by Federico García Lorca, who described it as an "erotic lace-paper valentine," is produced at State University of New York at Purchase.

12 August 1984

Un Re in ascolto (A King Listening), "musical action" in two parts by Luciano BERIO, is performed for the first time in Salzburg, Lorin Maazel conducting.

14 August 1984

John COUSINS, 40-year-old member of the faculty at Canterbury University in Christchurch, New Zealand, presents the first British demonstration of his Urinal Technique of Composition, inspired by the sound of dripping water in a New Zealand canyon, by urinating on a set of glass tubes covered with rubber membranes and producing an untempered scale of melodious tones.

11 SEPTEMBER 1984

Fourth Violin Concerto by the 49-year-old Soviet composer Alfred SCHNITTKE is performed for the first time in West Berlin.

12 SEPTEMBER 1984

Organ Concerto by the 49-year-old English composer William MATHIAS is performed for the first time by Gillian Weir as soloist with the BBC Welsh Symphony Orchestra under the direction of Erich Bergel in London.

23 SEPTEMBER 1984

The Fifty-eighth Festival of the International Society for Contemporary Music opens in Toronto, Canada, with an afternoon concert of mostly choral music, in the following program:

Two pieces by the 51-year-old experimental Canadian composer R. Murray SCHAFER, *Sun* to plural words for sun in multiple tongues, and *Epitaph for Moonlight,* being an ear-training exercise for school children. *Carnatus* by the enterprising Norwegian composer Cecile ORE to texts of Latin names for butterflies and moths. *Choralis* by 36-year-old Nigel OSBORNE of Great Britain in a pluralistic hemidemisemioriental manner (only the first and third sections of the work were performed). *L'Infinito* by 51-year-old Arno MELLNÄS of Sweden, to words by Giacomo Leopardi. *Monodie* by the 45-year-old Canadian composer Robert AITKEN for flute and voices with the composer himself piping up. *Car nos vignes sont en fleur* by the 58-year-old Dutch composer Ton DE LEEUW, to words from the biblical *Song of Songs.*

24 SEPTEMBER 1984

Concerto for bassoon, cello and orchestra by the 55-year-old Soviet composer Edison DENISOV is performed for the first time in Venice.

24 SEPTEMBER 1984

On the second day of the Fifty-eighth Festival of the International Society for Contemporary Music in Toronto, an afternoon concert of works for solo piano and solo flute is presented with the following program:

Pieces of Piano by the 26-year-old American composer Scott LINDROTH, which require adjustments of piano strings to make them sound like an Oriental gamelan. *Distancias* for piano by the 41-year-old Argentine composer Mariano ETKIN, the distances of the title referring to the antagonistic employment of distant registers of the keyboard. *En ré* for piano by the 61-year-old Uruguayan composer Hector TOSAR, centered on the thematic tone of D, modified harmonically, rhythmically, dynamically and timbrally, with application of direct action on the strings. *Rivers* for piano by the 47-year-old Canadian composer Ann SOUTHAM, a Chopinesque piece in which fundamental and incidental motives appear in polytonal superimposition. *Flute Sonata* by the 56-year-old Rumanian composer Tiberiu OLAH, set in three sections separated by deep silences and interspersed with slap-tonguing doubled by the performer's natural voice lapsing into the non-tempered zones of sound. *Yta I* for flute solo by the 26-year-old Finnish composer Esa-Pekka SALONEN, set in a fast, "sempre nervoso" tempo. *Traits suspendus* for amplified double-bass flute by the 47-year-old Iraqi-born French composer Paul MÉFANO, using antiflutational sounds like the tongue-ram, slap-tones and circular respiration, producing sounds by inhaling as well as exhaling. *Man-Pa (Huge Stream)* for solo flute accompanied by a triskaidecaphiliac coven of multifarious flutes in all sonic registers by the 50-year-old Korean composer Sukhi KANG, purporting to represent stormy winds blowing through a bamboo thicket. *Conspiracies* for solo flute accompanied by a whole sanhedrin of flutes by the 37-year-old American composer Martin BRESNICK, the title meaning breathing together, rather than plotting. *Ryoanji II* by the fearless American disestablishmentarian guru John CAGE, with some flute glissandi the notation of which was inspired by the pattern of stones bounding the famous rock-and-sand garden at the Zen Buddhist temple in Kyoto.

24 SEPTEMBER 1984
On the second day of the Fifty-eighth Festival of the International Society for Contemporary Music in Toronto, an evening concert is presented in a program of the following symphonic works:

Canti del Sole for tenor and orchestra by the 50-year-old spiritually modernistic British-born American composer Bernard RANDS, to texts by a number of romantic European poets all glorifying the circadian and seasonal cycles of the sun. *Miroirs célestes* by the 41-year-old Rumanian-born French composer Costin MIEREANU, conceived as a narrative reflection of celestial mirrors with multiple images in a sort of musical palimpsest. *Exú* for violin and orchestra by the 31-year-old Australian composer Gerard BROPHY, the title being one of the many ingenious names of the devil, with a reference to the demonic nature of Paganini, whose virtuosity was attributed to Satan. *Divertimento No. 7* for French horn and string orchestra by the 71-year-old Canadian composer John WEINZWEIG, in nine interconnected sections linked by horn solos.

25 SEPTEMBER 1984
On the third day of the Fifty-eighth Festival of the International Society for Contemporary Music in Toronto, an afternoon piano recital is given by Ivar Mikhashoff, featuring the following program:

For Cornelius by the American composer Alvin CURRAN, a memorial to the British creator of Scratch Music, Cornelius Cardew, who was killed by an errant automobile in 1981. A selection of piano waltzes by Philip GLASS, Lou HARRISON, Milton BABBITT, Robert MORAN, John CAGE and Virgil THOMSON. *Mort de Phèdre* by the 52-year-old Italian composer Sylvano BUSSOTI. *Tangos* from the *International Tango Collection* by John CAGE, Marlos NOBRE, Betsy JOLAS, Zoltan JENEY, William DUCKWORTH, Conlon NANCARROW, Anthony GENGE and others. *Achilles and the Tortoise* by the 52-year-old Danish composer Per NØRGAARD, illustrating the famous paradox of the Greek philosopher Zeno on the infinite divisibility of a given distance. *Piano Piece No. 4* by the 46-year-old American composer Frederic RZEWSKI, based on a Chilean folksong.

25 September 1984

The third day of the Fifty-eighth Festival of the International Society for Contemporary Music in Toronto continues with an evening concert of chamber music featuring the following program:

Tesserae III for solo viola by the 47-year-old American composer Brian FENNELLY, the title referring to the mosaic construction of the music, with each motive representing a four-cornered unit. *Trio* op. 21 for clarinet, cello and piano by the 28-year-old Finnish composer Jouni KAIPAINEN. *For Marimba and Tape* by the 39-year-old Australian composer Martin WESLEY-SMITH. *Dzei (Voices of Fire)* for chamber ensemble by the 52-year-old Canadian composer Gilles TREMBLAY, ostensibly depicting the transmutation of elements by the spirit of fire as conceived by the Greek philosopher Heraclitus.

25 September 1984

Gespenstersonate, opera by the 48-year-old German composer Aribert REIMANN, after Strindberg's play *The Ghost Sonata*, is produced in Berlin.

26 September 1984

On the fourth day of the Fifty-eighth Festival of the International Society for Contemporary Music in Toronto, an afternoon concert of chamber music presents the following program:

Six Melodies for Violin and Keyboard by the 72-year-old guru of new American music John CAGE, composed in 1950, reflecting his penetrating study of Oriental homophony. *Breakfast Rhythms I & II* for clarinet, piano, percussion, cello, violin and flute by the 45-year-old American composer Joan TOWER, a domestic celebration of matutinal prandium set in enjoyable visceral modalities. *Synchronisms No. 6* for piano and electronic tape by the 50-year-old Argentine composer Mario DAVIDOVSKY. *Three for Six* in three movements for six instruments by the 63-year-old American composer Ralph SHAPEY, written in the technique of massive collage. *First String Quartet* by James DILLON. *Ancora* for string quartet by the 44-year-old Swedish composer Jan MORTHENSON.

26 September 1984

On the fourth day of the Fifty-eighth Festival of the International Society for Contemporary Music in Toronto, the following program of orchestral works is presented at an evening concert:

Vanishing Points by the 40-year-old Canadian composer John REA, the title alluding to the half-tints in art creating a vanishing point in infinite perspective. *Ritratto (Portrait)* for eighteen players by the 26-year-old Finnish composer Magnus LINDBERG, in four sections: diagonals, polarities, linearities and verticals. *Into the Distant Stillness . . .* by the 42-year-old Canadian composer Brian CHERNEY, written as part of a triptych of stillnesses for various instrumental combinations. *Alchemies* by the 33-year-old Canadian composer John BURKE, in which a central chord is transmuted into heterogeneous elements in varying tonal colors. *Mirage* by the 51-year-old Canadian composer Alex PAUK, purporting to reflect the phantasmagoria of aural intangibilities, optical refractions, topographical distortions and retinal illusions.

27 SEPTEMBER 1984
In the course of the Fifty-eighth Festival of the International Society for Contemporary Music in Toronto, *Chaconne* for viola and orchestra by the 52-year-old American composer Michael COLGRASS, inspired by the famous *Chaconne* of Bach, is performed for the first time.

27 SEPTEMBER 1984
On the fifth day of the Fifty-eighth Festival of the International Society for Contemporary Music in Toronto, an afternoon concert of chamber music is presented with the following program:

Musica for five instruments by the Argentine composer Marcello KOC; *Ambivalencia* by the Mexican composer Manuel ENRIQUEZ. *Feedback* by the Chilean composer Juan Amenabar RUIZ; *Tableaux* by the Italian-born Australian composer Riccardo FORMOSA. *Three Monograms* by the Argentine composer Salvador RANIERI. *Estrias* by the Brazilian composer Raul DO VALLE. *Rhapsody on a Gagaku Theme* by the 77-year-old Japanese composer Yoritsuné MATSUDAIRA.

27 SEPTEMBER 1984
On the fifth day of the Fifty-eighth Festival of the International Society for Contemporary Music in Toronto, the following program of electronic works is presented at an evening concert:

Rubrics for bassoon and electronics by the 36-year-old American composer David GRIMES. *Love in the Asylum* by the 32-year-old American composer Michael McNABBY, a computerized tribute to modified insanity. *Sticherarion* by the 41-year-old American composer Larry LAKE, an electronic version of a Byzantine collection of stylized psalm melodies making a joyful noise unto God. *Clim of the Clough* by the 37-year-old American composer David JAEGER, a submissive celebation of the famed Canadian bandit. *Klang* by the 32-year-old British composer Jony HARRISON, a sonorific clang of exuberant onomatopoeic motives. *Wildfire* by the 41-year-old American composer James MONTGOMERY, a sequentially structured work in which the traditional string trio textures are transfigured into electronic equivalents.

28 SEPTEMBER 1984
On the sixth day of the Fifty-eighth Festival of the International Society for Contemporary Music, the following program is presented in Montreal:

Sonata by the 30-year-old Polish composer Pawel SZYMANSKI. *Concertante in moto perpetuo* for oboe solo and chamber ensemble by the 32-year-old British composer Simon BAINBRIDGE. *Turns* for violin and koto by the 53-year-old Japanese composer Makoto SHINOHARA. *East* for orchestra by the 51-year-old Canadian composer R. Murray SCHAFER, a musical meditation of an Oriental nature. *Lonely Child* for soprano and chamber orchestra by the Canadian composer Claude Vivier (1948–1983). *Plages* by the 55-year-old Canadian composer Serge Garant, an orchestral suite of entities of time and of color with the basic material formed of five notes.

29 September 1984
On the seventh day of the Fifty-eighth Festival of the International Society for Contemporary Music in Montreal, an afternoon concert of chamber music is presented with the following program:

Pearls by the 34-year-old Canadian composer Alexina Louie, a group of pieces of diminutive structures suggesting a string of pearls. *Arpeggio* by the 37-year-old American composer John Celona, based on a heptatonic series of notes worked in a combinatorial process generated by a digital synthesizer. *Tellus* by the 72-year-old Canadian composer Barbara Pentland, the title meaning earth, herein regarded as a living planet, the music being worked out by aleatory processes involving the vision of a roll of surf on a sandy beach. *Escalator* by the 30-year-old Canadian composer Owen Underhill, a series of successive escalations rich in hidden transmutations of an elementary design. *Hesitation* by the 33-year-old American composer Stephen Chatman, a vanishing dialogue between the violin and celesta, dissolving into a sonic nirvana. *Elegy* by the 45-year-old Canadian composer Bruce Mather, a lyrical memorial to an artistic friend.

30 September 1984
On the eighth day of the Fifty-eighth Festival of the International Society for Contemporary Music in Montreal, the following program for chamber ensemble is presented at an evening concert:

Gestalten (Forms) by the 23-year-old South Korean composer Unsuk Chin, a musical evocation of three paintings by Paul Klee. *Five Epigrams* by the 45-year-old Cuban guitarist and composer Leo Brower. *Cantos del amor y la eternidad* by the 58-year-old Argentine composer Rodolfo Arizaga. *Shantini-ketan* by the Argentine composer Alicia Terzian. *Tres impresoes cançone-irigenas* by the Brazilian composer Jorge Antunes. *Quintet* by the Argentine composer Guillermo Graetzer.

1 October 1984
On the ninth day of the Fifty-eighth Festival of the International Society for Contemporary Music in Montreal, an afternoon concert of percussion music is presented with the following program:

Circuit I for six percussionists by the 55-year-old Canadian composer Serge Garant. *Kétiak* for six percussionists by the 31-year-old Japanese composer Akira Nishimura, based on Balinese dance motives. *États* for violin and six percussionists by the 58-year-old American-born Parisian composer Betsy

Jolas. *Vertiges* by the 31-year-old Canadian composer Pierre Trochu, the vertiginous elements in the work being symbolized by the prestidigitation of the marimba player. *Pulau Dewata* by the Canadian composer Claude Vivier, for any combination of percussion instruments, thematically based on Balinese modalities.

An evening concert by the Montreal Symphony is conducted by Charles Dutoit in a program that includes *Exemplum in memoriam Kwangju* by the 67-year-old politically active South Korean composer Isang Yun, dedicated to the victims of the massacre in Kwangju, perpetrated by the brutal Korean police on 28 May 1980.

1 October 1984

On the ninth day of the Fifty-eighth Festival of the International Society for Contemporary Music in Montreal, a late evening concert by the Arditti String Quartet presents the following chamber works:

Quartet op. 1 by the 58-year-old Hungarian composer György Kurtág. *Adagissimo* by the 41-year-old British composer Brian Ferneyhough. *Ricercate* by the 31-year-old American composer Susan Blaustein. *Fifth Quartet* by the 32-year-old German composer Wolfgang Rihm. *Solos and Shadows* by the 36-year-old Danish composer Karl Rasmussen. *String Quartet* by the 41-year-old British composer Roger Smalley.

1 October 1984

Fifth Symphony by the 52-year-old Soviet composer Sergei Slonimsky (incidentally a nephew of the American musicologist Nicolas Slonimsky), in three movements: *Presto* unified by a dominant rhythmic pulse; *Andante* related in its melodic content to the freely flowing folk tunes of the "mother river" of eternal Russia, the Volga; *Vivace*, an energetic apotheosis of motoric gaiety in bell-like sonorities, is performed for the first time in the Volga town of Kuibishev and dedicated to the quadricentennial of the city, originally named Samara.

2 October 1984

On the tenth day of the Fifty-eighth Festival of the International Society for Contemporary Music in Montreal, an afternoon concert of electronic works is presented with the following program:

Points de fuite (*Vanishing Points*) by the 58-year-old French-born Canadian composer Francis Dhomont. *Chronaxie ou Ce désert acharnement de couleurs* for percussion and tape by the 30-year-old Canadian composer Serge Arcuri. *Conte-à-Nino* by the 38-year-old French composer Philippe Ménard, an electronic fairy tale realized on the digital synthesizer. *Petite musique sentimentale* for piano and tape by the 38-year-old Canadian composer Yves Daoust. *Manu*

Militari for tuba and tape by the 29-year-old Canadian composer André Luc DESJARDINS. *Étude à la quatre-vingt-dix-neuvième nuit* by the 29-year-old Canadian composer Claude FRENETTE. *Vortex* by the 38-year-old New Zealand composer Denis SMALLEY. *Rite of Passage* by the 30-year-old Swedish composer Anders HILLBORG.

2 OCTOBER 1984

On the tenth day of the Fifty-eighth Festival of the International Society for Contemporary Music in Montreal, the Society of Contemporary Music of Quebec Ensemble performs the following program at an evening concert:

Planetary Folklore II by the 29-year-old Japanese composer Mamoru FUJIEDA, making use of canonic processes from Bach's *Musical Offering*. *Tangente* by the 31-year-old Canadian composer Pierre TROCHU, wherein disjointed events seek their tangential focus. *Écrits sur toiles* (*Written on Canvases*) by the 48-year-old French composer Gilbert AMY, an essay in form of variations based on letters by R. M. Rilke. *Pohjatuuli* by the 38-year-old Canadian composer Michel LONGTIN, the title being the Finnish word for North Wind, drawing inspiration from Sibelius.

3 OCTOBER 1984

The Fifty-eighth Festival of the International Society for Contemporary Music concludes in Montreal with a performance by the group Les Événements du Neuf, featuring the following program at an afternoon concert:

Oleada for bass soloist and instrumental ensemble by the 56-year-old Spanish composer Ramon BARCE, to a text inspired by Apollonius of Rhodes, in four scenes depicting the legends of the Argonauts, Orpheus, Theseus and the conquest of the Golden Fleece, with the voice in Sprechgesang. *Plastiques Faber* for four recorder players by the 31-year-old French composer Daniel TOSI, written for the Faber Quartet (faber meaning artisan in Latin), the specification "plastique" referring to a graphic notation employed herein. *Observations on Weather Forecast* by the 55-year-old Japanese composer Joli YUASA, a meteorological fantasy for a vocal duo. *Voix intimes* for two sopranos, clarinet quartet and percussion by the 33-year-old Canadian composer Denis GOUGEON.

In the evening, the musical theater piece *Transit* by the 46-year-old Canadian composer Micheline Coulombe SAINT-MARCOUX, depicting the anxiety of a woman waiting in an airport, is produced.

3 OCTOBER 1984

Creations, two scenes from *Genesis* for narrator and chamber orchestra by the 46-year-old American composer John CORIGLIANO, is performed for the first time in Milwaukee, Wisconsin.

3 OCTOBER 1984
Cosmic Cycle for orchestra by the 89-year-old American composer, painter and mystical philosopher Dane RUDHYAR is performed for the first time in Milwaukee, Lukas Foss conducting.

12 OCTOBER 1984
Sinfonia by the 47-year-old American composer Olly WILSON is performed for the first time by the Boston Symphony Orchestra, Seiji Ozawa conducting.

12 OCTOBER 1984
Celebration for Orchestra, festive piece by the 45-year-old American composer Ellen Taaffe ZWILICH, is performed for the first time in Indianapolis, John Nelson conducting.

24 OCTOBER 1984
Minette Fontaine, opera by the black American composer William Grant STILL (1895–1978), completed in 1958, depicting the life of the French opera diva in New Orleans in the 1880's, is given its posthumous world premiere in Baton Rouge, Louisiana.

25 OCTOBER 1984
The American premiere of *Desert Music* for orchestra by Steve REICH, to a text of poems by William Carlos Williams, is performed by Steve Reich and Musicians, with chorus and members of the Brooklyn Philharmonic Orchestra, Michael Tilson Thomas conducting, in New York. (The absolute first performance took place in Cologne, Germany, in March 1984.)

29 OCTOBER 1984
Forgiving and forgetting the émigré status of the great Russian basso Fyodor CHALIAPIN, the Soviet authorities arrange to transfer his remains from Paris, where he died in 1938, to the Novodevichy Cemetery in Moscow, alongside the graves of Scriabin, Prokofiev and Shostakovich.

Without Russia Chaliapin found life tedious and abhorrent. Now he is returned to his motherland, and we bow deeply to him for all he did for the culture of his country and his people. Let the native earth be light on him. (From a graveside eulogy by the Russian bass singer Evgenyi Nesterenko.)

31 OCTOBER 1984
Hora eius, work for three sopranos in eight movements by the 53-year-old Hungarian composer László KALMAR, to a Latin text depicting Christ's disciples on the night of the crucifixion calling to one another on the

Mount of Olives, receives its first complete performance in San Francisco by the vocal ensemble Ariel, conducted by Christopher Fulkerson.

3 November 1984

Sixth Symphony by the 75-year-old American composer Elie SIEGMEISTER, characterized by him as a "search for intensity of expression" and using a vast armamentarium of melodic, harmonic, rhythmic and timbral means, in three movements reflecting the dialectically dramatic, hedonistically exuberant and solipsistically meditative moods, all this enlivened by diversified percussion battery, is performed for the first time by the Sacramento Symphony Orchestra, Carter Nice conducting.

23 November 1984

Concerto Quaternio for violin, flute, oboe, trumpet and orchestra with tape-recorded human voice by the 59-year-old American composer Gunter SCHULLER is performed for the first time by the New York Philharmonic, Zubin Mehta conducting.

1 December 1984

The Bride Stripped Bare by Her Bachelors, Even for solo singers, orchestra and chorus by the 49-year-old American composer and critic Charles SHERE, to a surrealistic text based on Marcel Duchamps' painting *The Large Glass* as well as his numerous verbal and literary utterances, is produced for the first time at Mills College in Oakland, California.

1 December 1984

Seventh Symphony by the 58-year-old German modernist Hans Werner HENZE is performed for the first time in Berlin. (The United States premiere took place on 18 April 1985, the composer conducting the Cleveland Orchestra.)

13 December 1984

Oboe Concerto by the 66-year-old American composer George ROCHBERG, in four distinct sections, set in an enhanced tonal style without any attempts at surreal virtuosity, is performed for the first time by the New York Philharmonic as a commissioned work, with Joseph Robinson as oboe soloist and Zubin Mehta conducting.

14 December 1984

Bernard RANDS conducts the San Diego Symphony Orchestra in the first performance of his orchestral suite *Le Tambourin*.

15 December 1984

Anthony DAVIS conducts the San Francisco Symphony in the first performance of his work *Wayang V* for piano and orchestra.

22 DECEMBER 1984

Les Fourberies de Scapin, opéra-bouffe in three acts by the 48-year-old Soviet composer Yuri FALIK, after Molière's comedy dealing with an audacious valet, modeled after the rascal servant Scapino in the Italian commedia dell'arte, is performed for the first time in Tartu, Estonia.

ℒ 1985 ℒ

1 JANUARY 1985

Montségur, opera by the 69-year-old French composer Marcel LANDOWSKI, is produced in Toulouse.

9 JANUARY 1985

Sir Robert MAYER, German-born British philanthropist and erstwhile piano wunderkind, who with his first wife, a concert singer, started in London a series of youth concerts, dies in London at the incredible age of one hundred and five, five years after marrying, as a nuptially hopeful centenarian, a lady of an uncertain but definitely postnubile age named Jacqueline Noble.

10 JANUARY 1985

The last known song written by Richard STRAUSS, dated 23 November 1948, consisting of seventy-two bars in the key of E-flat major, set for soprano and piano, entitled *Malven* (mallow flowers) dedicated to his favorite singer, Maria Jeritza (it is inscribed "my last rose"), and depicts an "odorless flower resembling a tear-stained and pallid face, washed by the golden, heavenly light," is performed for the first time anywhere in New York as an encore to the New York Philharmonic program by Kiri Te Kanawa, with piano accompaniment. (The original manuscript was purchased in 1984 by a New York philanthropist from the estate of Maria Jeritza, for an incredible sum of $60,500.00.)

10 JANUARY 1985

Riverrun for piano and orchestra by the 54-year-old avant-garde composer Toru TAKEMITSU, inspired by the famous first word of Joyce's *Finnegans Wake*, which begins in the middle of a sentence and ends in the middle of the same sentence, the river being Dublin's Liffey, is performed for the first time by the American proponent of modern music Peter Serkin, son of the romantic pianist Rudolf Serkin, and the Los Angeles Philharmonic.

11 JANUARY 1985

Jacob's Room, monodrama in two parts based on Virginia Woolf's novel of that name and *Eleni* by Nicholas Gage, by the 51-year-old American composer Morton SUBOTNICK, scored for string quartet and voice and set in an agonizingly permutated quasi-tonal idiom, is performed for the first time in San Francisco by the Kronos String Quartet and Subotnick's wife, soprano Joan La Barbara. (Later, a third part was added, to the text of Elie Weisel, portraying the horrors of Nazi transportation of Jews to their final destination, death.)

16 JANUARY 1985

Rhapsody for violin and orchestra by the 46-year-old American composer Charles WUORINEN (completed on 5 December 1983), thematically based on one of Stravinsky's unfinished sketches (G, E, F, D-flat, C, A) with the total time span of 19 minutes and 31 seconds, is performed for the first time by Daniel Kobialka and the San Francisco Symphony, Edo de Waart conducting.

23 JANUARY 1985

The United States Government issues a twenty-two-cent stamp with a double picture of Jerome KERN, the celebrated composer of popular music, to mark (four days early) the centennial of his birth. (Kern himself was a noted philatelist.)

24 JANUARY 1985

Requiem for soloists, chorus and orchestra by the scholarly 63-year-old American composer Andrew IMBRIE, written in mournful memory of his intellectually endowed young son, who died suddenly, to texts from the traditional Latin Requiem, Kyrie, Dies Irae, Offertorium and Benedictus, interspersed with devotional poems by Willim Blake, George Herbert and John Donne, suffused with darksomely lucent tense, dense, contrapuntally saturated sonic masses in mutually conciliated dissonances, is performed for the first time by the San Francisco Symphony Orchestra and Chorus, conducted by Edo de Waart.

13 FEBRUARY 1985

Forty years after an apocalyptic assault by vengeful British and American air fleets upon the defenseless, porcelainlike, lovely town of Dresden, setting its fragile habitations on hellish fire, incinerating 35,000 living people, Dresden's legendary Opera House, where Weber and Wagner once led their works, is restored to its former glory with punctilious attention to artistic detail, and opens its first postwar season with a performance of Weber's opera *Der Freischütz*, symbolically proclaiming unceasing struggle against brutality, oppression and autocracy.

228

14 February 1985

Winds of Nagual—A Musical Fable for Wind Ensemble on the Writings of Carlos Castaneda by the 52-year-old American composer Michael COLGRASS is performed for the first time at the New England Conservatory of Music in Boston.

17 February 1985

Music for Twelve for chamber ensemble by the 66-year-old American composer Leon KIRCHNER is performed for the first time by the Chamber Players of the Boston Symphony Orchestra at the New England Conservatory of Music, the composer conducting.

19 February 1985

Third Symphony by the British composer Peter Maxwell Davies is performed for the first time in Manchester, England.

23 February 1985

Three centuries have elapsed since the birth in the Saxon town of Halle of Georg Friedrich HÄNDEL, creator of operas, oratorios and instrumental music of incomparable magnificence, who emigrated to England where he changed the spelling of his name to George Frideric Handel, a close contemporary of Bach who was born not far from him on the plains of Saxony but whom he never met. (The tombstone of Handel in Westminster Abbey bears the date of his birth as 23 February 1684, a discrepancy owing to the calendar of the time in which the years began in March.)

1 March 1985

Harriet, the Woman Called Moses, opera by Thea MUSGRAVE, Scottish composer dwelling in America, to the story of the valiant abolitionist Harriet Tubman who smuggled Negro slaves to freedom in Canada before the Civil War, is performed for the first time by the Virginia Opera in Norfolk, conducted by the composer's husband, Peter Mark.

12 March 1985

Eugene ORMANDY, the ultra-professional Hungarian conductor who as successor to the aureole-laureled Leopold Stokowski perfected the "Philadelphia sound" of the great Philadelphia Orchestra and who held the podium for a record forty-four years before yielding it to his Italian successor, Riccardo Muti, in 1980, dies of a prosaic pulmonary ailment in Philadelphia, at the age of eighty-five.

15 March 1985

Contrabassoon Concerto by the 58-year-old American composer Donald ERB, a rare opus for this unwieldy instrument, is performed for the first time by Greg Henegar as soloist with the Houston Symphony Orchestra, Sergiu Comissiona conducting.

16 MARCH 1985

Roger SESSIONS, great American composer of densely contrapuntal, harmonically complex and yet poetic and lyrical eight symphonies, two operas, technically demanding concertos, tersely crafted chamber pieces, intransigently unyielding to the public tastes ("my music was born difficult," he once explained), who earned the devotion of his many students and colleagues, and whose intellectual equipment included profound knowledge of philosophy, philology and history (he spoke four languages besides English), dies as a result of a cerebral hemorrhage in Princeton, at the age of eighty-eight.

21 MARCH 1985

Harmonielehre for orchestra by the 38-year-old American composer John ADAMS, an ostensibly didactic composition but in substance an essay in human learning, set in an asymmetric pulse in three parts, the second titled *The Anfortas Wound* with an allusion to *Parsifal*, and the third *Meister Eckhardt and Quackie*, is performed for the first time by the San Francisco Symphony, Edo DE WAART conducting.

21 MARCH 1985

Three hundred years have passed since the birth in the Saxon town of Eisenach of Johann Sebastian BACH, the great lawgiver of music whose importance is comparable to that of Aristotle in philosophy and Leonardo da Vinci in art, and whose scientific precision of technique in counterpoint, fugue, harmony, and sonorous structures of instrumentation became an instructive model for untold generations of composers.

12 APRIL 1985

Casanova's Homecoming, opera by the 57-year-old American composer Dominick ARGENTO, is performed for the first time in St. Paul, Minnesota.

18 APRIL 1985

Flute Concerto by the multifaceted American composer Morton GOULD is performed for the first time by the Chicago Symphony Orchestra, Georg Solti conducting.

19 APRIL 1985

Behold the Sun, an opera by the 52-year-old English composer Alexander GOEHR, is produced in Duisberg in a German version as *Die Wiedertäufer*.

25 APRIL 1985

Concerto for orchestra by the 63-year-old Czech-American composer Karel HUSA is performed for the first time by the New York Philharmonic, Zubin Mehta conducting.

13 JUNE 1985

March to Tonality for orchestra by the 48-year-old American composer David DEL TREDICI is performed for the first time by the Chicago Symphony Orchestra under the direction of Michael Tilson Thomas, for whom the work was written.

13 JULY 1985

"Live Aid," the first global rock concert, a telethon to raise money for famine victims in Africa, opens simultaneously in Philadelphia and London, televized to about 150 countries and watched by something like 1,500,000,000 people, expected to raise something like $70,000,000, with the Philadelphia portion utilizing about 90,000 nails driven into the 23,744-square-foot plywood stage and 75 miles of cable connecting 16 tons of lighting equipment with 2 million watts of power, and involving 37 acts and 30 equipment changes, with hundreds of spectacular celebrities gracing the stage with their uninhibited crooning and howling presence, and hundreds of humble roadies donating their essential labor.

Additions,
Amplifications,
Corrections

Where corrections occur, the original entries (or relevant portions thereof) are included in small type as an aid to comprehensibility. The additional entries for 1969 carry the chronological compilation forward from the initial selenic step of humankind achieved with the lunar landing of 20 July 1969, at which point the parent volume terminates its chronicle.

⚛ 1900-1909 ⚛

1 JANUARY 1900
Chris and the Wonderful Lamp, opera by the American March King John
Philip SOUSA, based on the epic tales of the *Arabian Nights*, is performed
for the first time in New York.

10 MARCH 1900
Ballet music from the opera *Azara* by James Knowles PAINE, learned
Bostonian composer and first chairman of the music department at
Harvard University, to his own scenario after the medieval French tale
Aucassin et Nicolette (in this version Nicolette is Azara, a daughter of
a Saracen chieftain), is performed for the first time by the Boston Symphony Orchestra. (A concert performance of the entire opera, with
considerable cuts, was given at Symphony Hall in Boston on 9 April
1907, almost a year after Paine's death.)

22 MARCH 1900
Samuel COLERIDGE-TAYLOR, Afro-British composer, conducts at the Royal
Choral Society in London the first performance of *Hiawatha's Departure*,
his choral work with orchestra, the third of his trilogy on the life of the
legendary Indian.

6 APRIL 1900
Piano Concerto by the 32-year-old American composer Mrs. H.H.A. BEACH
is performed for the first time by the Boston Symphony Orchestra with
the composer as soloist.

24 NOVEMBER 1900

First Symphony in E minor by Alexander SCRIABIN, couched in a Russianized
Wagnerian idiom presaging the proclamatory style of his later music, is performed, without its sixth choral movement, at the Russian Symphony Concerts in St. Petersburg, under the direction of Anatoli Liadov. (A complete
performance, including the last choral movement, entitled *Hymn to Art*, was
given in Moscow on 29 March 1901.)

Scriabin's *First Symphony* is in E major (not E minor).

23 MARCH 1901
Herzog Wildfang, opera in three acts by the industrious son of a great
father, Siegfried WAGNER, to his own libretto, is performed for the first
time in Munich.

1 November 1901

Priscilla; or, the Maid of Plymouth by Francesco Rogers FANCIULLI, based on Longfellow's *The Courtship of Miles Standish*, is produced in Norfolk, Virginia.

10 March 1902

Gustav MAHLER, forty-one years old, marries Alma Maria Schindler, twenty-three, ten weeks after the premarital consummation of their union. (Alma Schindler wrote on 4 January 1902: "Wonne über Wonne!")

Mahler's marriage was notarized on 9 March (not 10 March) 1902, according to the signed entry in the marriage registry.

18 April 1902

The Celestial Country, cantata by Charles IVES, scored for chorus, string quartet, trumpet, euphonium, timpani and organ, in seven sections, is performed for the first time at Central Presbyterian Church in New York, where Ives served as organist.

25 May 1902

Consuelo, prologue in three acts by the 49-year-old Italian composer Alfonso RENDANO, to a libretto after a novel of the same name by George Sand, depicting the life of an opera singer resembling the career of Pauline Viardot (1821–1910), is produced in Turin.

6 January 1903

Boris BLACHER, composer of abstract chamber operas and concrete instrumental music, who was to identify himself with the cause of German modernism, is born in Newchwang, China, of Russian-bred ethnically Estonian-German parents.

This date of Blacher's birth is given in old style calendar; it should be 19 January 1903, according to the Gregorian calendar.

16 February 1903

Tapu, opera by the New Zealand composer Alfred HILL, to his own libretto having to do with rituals of the Maori Indians, is performed for the first time in Wellington, New Zealand, with the composer conducting.

9 September 1903

The Afro-British composer Samuel COLERIDGE-TAYLOR conducts at the Hereford Festival the first performance of his cantata *The Atonement*.

30 November 1903

Le Roi Arthurs, opera by Ernest Chausson, to his own libretto based on the life of the legendary King Arthur, is performed posthumously for the first time in Brussels.

20 December 1903

Zlatorog (Russian word for *Goat with Golden Horns*), fairy-tale opera in five acts by the 59-year-old German composer Georg Rauchenecker, is produced in Elberfeld.

16 March 1904

Edward Elgar conducts the Hallé Orchestra of Manchester, England, in the first performance of his orchestral work *In the South*.

10 May 1904

Hugo Alfvén, 32-year-old Swedish composer of romantically suffused music, conducts in Stockholm the first performance of his symphonic work, *Midsommarvaka (Midsummer Vigil)*, subtitled *Swedish Rhapsody No. 1*, thematically derived from Swedish folk tunes with the addition of two sub-Scandinavian melodies from Schleswig-Holstein, representing a rustic revelry during the summer solstice festival of St. John's Eve. (The score was choreographed by the Ballet Suedois and produced under the French title *Le Nuit de Saint-Jean* in Paris on 25 October 1920.)

27 May 1904

Der Bundschuh, opera by the 37-year-old German composer Waldemar von Bausznern, based on an episode in the peasant rebellion in southern Germany in 1525, led by a revolutionary group named Der Bundschuh (The Council Boot), is performed for the first time in Frankfurt.

2 December 1904

Le réveil de Bouddha, a Hindu mystery by the 46-year-old English composer Isadore de Lara (whose real name was Isadore Cohen), is performed for the first time, to a French libretto, in Ghent, Belgium.

15 April 1905

Fischer und Kalif, opera by Felix Draeseke, is produced in Prague.

The absolute premiere of the opera *Fischer und Kalif* was on 12 March (not 15 April) 1905.

27 April 1905

On his eleventh birthday Sol Mysnik stages, in the recreation hall of High School No. 11 in St. Petersburg, in which he is a student, the world première of his politico-revolutionary opera in eleven scenes, *The X-Ray Vindicator*, scored for three countertenors, basso profundo, piano, balalaika, toy pistol and a static electricity generator, the action dealing with a young scientist confined in the dreaded Peter-and-Paul Fortress for advocating the extermination of the Tsar and the termination of the Russo-Japanese war, who escapes by directing a stream of Röntgen rays at himself from a hidden cathode tube as a Secret Police officer enters his cell to question him, putting him to flight in superstitious horror by appearing as a skeleton, and then calmly walking through the open gate to resume his terroristic propaganda, with petty-bourgeoisie characterized by insipid arpeggios on the balalaika and the playing of the waltz *On the Dunes of Manchuria* on the phonograph, revolutionary fervor by the songs "The Sun Goes Up, the Sun Goes Down, I Wish the Tsar Would Lose his Crown" and "We Fell as Martyrs to Our Cause Because We Scorned the Tsarist Laws," the X-rays by chromatically advancing sequences of diminished seventh-chords, and Freedom through Terror by blazingly incandescent C major.

Sol Mysnik is an obvious anagram of the last name of the author of the present volume, who indeed turned eleven on that date. *The X-Ray Vindicator* is a fantasy generated in the corpus callosum, medulla oblongata or some other part of his inchoate cerebellum long after his eleventh birthday. No such opera ever existed on paper, on the piano keyboard or on the balalaika. And it is basso profondo, not profundo.

16 December 1905

Lucullus, opera-burlesque in three acts by the 44-year-old Russian-born ethnically German composer Erik Meyer-Helmund, to his own libretto depicting the extravagant orgies of a Roman epicurean of that name who flourished in the first century before the Christian era, is produced, in German, in Riga.

8 November 1906

Hermes, opera in three acts by the 32-year-old Italian composer Attilio Parelli, to a mythological libretto about the messenger of the Olympian gods, is performed for the first time in Genoa.

10 November 1906

The world première is given at the Leipzig Opera of a German version of the three-act opera *The Wreckers*, composed by the mannish English suffragette Ethel Smyth, after the original French drama *Les Naufrageurs* by Henry Brewster, wherein a youth and a maid who light fires to warn off mariners on stormy nights in a Cornish seacoast village are left to die in a cave at high tide by looters of wrecked ships, with a score full of Wagnerian sound and fury.

The German title of the opera *The Wreckers* is *Strandrecht*, which means "salvage rights."

19 MARCH 1907

Edward ELGAR, the Edwardian English composer of marvelously outspoken and hearty symphonic and choral music, makes his first American appearance conducting the Oratorio Society of New York City in a performance of his reverentially reverberant oratorio *The Apostles.*

This was not Elgar's first American appearance, but his third; previous appearances were in 1905 and 1906.

27 APRIL 1907

First Symphony by Igor STRAVINSKY, dedicated "to my dear teacher Nicolai Andreyevich Rimsky-Korsakov," in E-flat major . . . is performed for the first time in St. Petersburg, at a private concert of the orchestra of the Imperial Chapel. (The first public performance was given by the same orchestra on 22 January 1908.)

The first public performance of Stravinsky's *First Symphony* was given on 5 February 1907 according to the Gregorian calendar (not 22 January 1908 as given in the last line of this entry.)

10 MAY 1907

Stará práva (Ancient Rights), opera by the Czech composer František SPILKA, is produced in Prague.

Stará Práva was produced in Prague on 10 May 1917 (not 10 May 1907.)

29 OCTOBER 1907
Shafras, lyric drama by the Argentine composer Constantino GAITO to an Italian libretto, the central character Shafras being a heroic Gypsy during the repression of the tribe in the Ottoman Empire, is produced in Buenos Aires.

7 NOVEMBER 1907
Piano Quintet by Anton von WEBERN is performed for the first time in Vienna at a concert of works by students of Arnold Schoenberg.

2 January 1908

At the aristocratic Paris salon of Armande de Polignac, patroness of arts and herself a composer of songs, the avant-garde pianist Blanche SELVA plays for the first time the three pieces of the third book from the piano suite *Iberia* by Isaac ALBÉNIZ, *El Albaicín*, *El Polo* and *Lavapiés*.

Armande de Polignac was not a musician. She was an American heiress—daughter of the sewing machine magnate Isaac Merritt Singer—who married Prince de Polignac.

4 November 1908

Anton von WEBERN conducts the Tonkünstlerverein Orchester in Vienna in the first performance of his *Passacaglia for Orchestra*, marked op. 1, scored for woodwinds, four horns, three trombones, bass tuba, timpani, percussion, harp and strings, in which the subject in D minor, in duple meter, undergoes twenty-three variations. *See* 10 June 1921.

30 January 1909

Vampuka, African Bride, Exemplary in all Respects, one-act opera-parody with text and music by V. ERENBERG, ridiculing the preposterous type of exotic operatic libretti, is performed for the first time at the cabaret "Crooked Mirror" in St. Petersburg.

6 February 1909

Scherzo fantastique by Igor STRAVINSKY, scored for a luxuriant orchestra including three harps and a celesta, suggesting by its entomologically buzzing chromatics the intense activity of a beehive, the nuptial flight of the queen bee in the soaring piccolos, the death of her discarded mate in sonorously Wagnerian augmented triads and the return of the cycle of life and death in tremulous diminished-seventh-chord harmonies, is performed for the first time in St. Petersburg, Alexander Siloti conducting.

The composer recounted of this work:

I had for quite some time an idea to write a symphonic Scherzo, but I had no program for it. But now I happened to read *La Vie des Abeilles* by Maeterlinck, a partly philosophical, partly literary work, which completely captivated me. I had thought of selecting quotations from the book as a programmatic element of the music. However, I realized that it was impractical because the scientific language in it is linked too closely with the literary passages. So I decided to follow a definite programmatic plan without actual quotations, and to entile my score simply *Bees* (after Maeterlinck), *a fantastic scherzo.* (From Stravinsky's letter to Rimsky-Korsakov, dated 1 July 1907.)

Some bad literature about bees was published on the flyleaf of my *Scherzo*, to satisfy my publisher who thought it would help to sell the music. (*Conversations with Igor Stravinsky* by Robert Craft, New York, 1959.)

5 May 1909

Robins Ende, first opera, in two acts, by the German composer Eduard KÜNNECKE, is produced in Mannheim.

The correct spelling of the composer's name is KÜNNEKE (not Kunnecke).

♫ *1910-1919* ♫

8 February 1910

Fünf Sätze für Streichquartett, op. 5, by Anton von WEBERN, is performed for the first time in Vienna.

21 April 1910

Daniel Hjort, opera in five acts by the 32-year-old Finnish composer Selim PALMGREN, dealing with a patriotic son of the slain leader of the peasant rebellion against the feudal power of the Catholic church in Sweden in 1599, who sides with the victorious future King Charles IX, is produced in Turku, to a libretto in Swedish. (A production in a Finnish translation took place in Helsinki on 20 February 1929; a second redaction, again in Finnish, was produced in Helsinki on 27 February 1938.)

5 May 1910

Alba eroica, opera by Domenico MONLEONE, to a libretto by his brother Giovanni Monleone dealing with the heroic struggle against Austrian rule led by the brothers Attilio and Emilio Bandiera who were captured and executed in 1844, is performed for the first time in Genoa, in commemoration of half a century of the sailing from Genoa of Garibaldi's liberating force.

12 June 1910

Bamboula Rhapsodic Dance by the Afro-British composer Samuel COLERIDGE-TAYLOR, based on Indian folk songs, is performed for the first time in Litchfield, Connecticut.

2 October 1910

Kleider machen Leute (Clothes Make the Man [lit., people]), comic opera in three acts by the greatly significant 38-year-old Viennese composer Alexander von ZEMLINSKY, deriding the moral hypocrisy of the bourgeoisie who judge people by the clothes they wear, is produced in Vienna.

4 October 1910

Der Schneemann, pantomime by the prodigiously precocious musically mature adolescent Erich Wolfgang KORNGOLD, written by him in piano score at the age of eleven and orchestrated by his teacher Alexander Zemlinsky . . . , is produced at the Vienna Opera, with Zemlinsky himself conducting.

Korngold's *Der Schneemann* was conducted by Franz Schalk, not by Zemlinsky.

10 December 1910

Leif Erickson, three-act opera set in Vineland (America) and Greenland in 1001 B.C. by Gerard TONNING, with a Norwegian text by C. M. Thuland, is produced for the first time, in its original language, in Seattle, Washington.

4 January 1911

Pocahontas, opera by the 57-year-old American composer Willard PATTON, relating the story of the Indian princess, daughter of a powerful inter-tribal leader, who according to legend saved the life of the founder of the Jamestown Colony, Capt. John Smith, was converted to Christianity and died of smallpox in 1617, is performed for the first time in concert form in Minneapolis.

24 April 1911

String Quartet, op. 3, by Alban BERG is performed for the first time in Vienna.

30 April 1911

Monsieur Bonaparte, opera-farce by the 52-year-old Silesian composer Bogmil ZEPLER, to a libretto dealing with a fashionable Paris tailor who looks like Napoleon, is produced in Leipzig.

3 July 1911

Madeline SCHILLER, London-born American pianist of German extraction, once so fresh of flesh and comely of countenance, who made musicological history by playing the world premiere of Tchaikovsky's *Second Piano Concerto* with the New York Philharmonic on 12 November 1881, six months before its Russian performance, and whose artistic appearances spanned all English-speaking countries, dies of a piteously unesthetic uterine cancer at the wrinkled age of sixty-five.

12 November 1911

La Vendetta, opera by the 36-year-old French composer Jean NOUGUÈS, melodramatically portraying vengeful mores among the Mediterranean coast villagers, is performed for the first time in Marseilles.

7 FEBRUARY 1912

Jaufré Rudel, one-act opera by the 23-year-old Italian composer Pasquale SAYA, dealing with a legendary trouvère of Provence who sang of his eternal love for a distant fair lady, is produced in Messina.

12 MARCH 1912

On the day after his fifteenth birthday Henry COWELL presents at the San Francisco Music Club the first demonstration of his "tone-clusters," pandiatonic and panpentatonic, played on the white or on the black keys of the piano keyboard with fists or forearms. (In a remarkable synchronization of invention, the Russian composer Vladimir REBIKOV published in 1912 a *Hymn to the Sun* for piano, in special columnar notation, indicating that the conglomeration of keys are to be encompassed with the edge of the palm of the hand.)

This is a premature date. The Cowell performance of tone clusters took place at the San Francisco Music Club on 5 March 1914; the pieces he banged on the piano keyboard with fists and forearms constituted excerpts from his incidental music to *Creation Dawn,* which was first performed in Carmel on 16 August 1913.

25 OCTOBER 1912

Radda, one-act opera by the 47-year-old Italian composer Giacomo OREFICE, to a libretto based on Maxim Gorky's tale *Makar Chudra,* dealing with a proudly beauteous Ukrainian maiden Radda who is stabbed to death by a passion-inflamed Gypsy fiddler who is in turn fatally knifed by Radda's father, is produced in Milan.

17 NOVEMBER 1912

Der Schneider von Malta, comic opera by the 39-year-old German composer Waldemar WENDLAND, dealing with a Maltese tailor who became involved in a conspiracy against the governor of Malta in 1850, is performed for the first time in Leipzig.

15 JANUARY 1913

Gala plácida, lyric drama by the Catalan composer Jaime PAHISSA, dealing with a heterogenetic passion of a patrician Roman matron for a chieftain of the barbarian Goths, symbolizing the conflict between Mediterranean and Teutonic cultures, with a musical setting in a sumptuous modernistic idiom, is produced in Barcelona.

The title of Pahissa's opera is *Gala Placidia* (not *Gala plácida*), named for a Roman matron captured by the Visigoths in A.D. 410 during the sack of Rome. After being carried to Catalonia, she ignites the passions in the Teutonic heart of King Ataulfo, marries him and, upon his assassination, returns to Italy, marries a future Roman emperor and, upon his death, becomes regent for their son.

10 FEBRUARY 1913

The Days of Our Life, opera by the 37-year-old Russian composer Alexei GLUKHOVTZEV, after a play of that title by the famous Russian writer Leonid Andreyev, inspired by the popular Russian student song "The Days of Our Life (flow fast, like ocean waves)" and focused on the life of a student whose family name is coincidentally the same as that of the composer, is produced in Kiev.

20 FEBRUARY 1913

The Sun Dance, Indian opera in five acts by the 25-year-old American composer William HANSON, who spent his youth among the Sioux Indians where he became known under the nickname Ampa-o-Luta, meaning "the first light at the red dawn," or more intimately as "Big Elm," is first performed in Vernal, Utah.

3 DECEMBER 1913

Victory Over the Sun, futuristic extravaganza to a text in surrealistic language made up from unwieldy Russian vocables by the poet Kruchenykh, with a prologue by another lingual surrealist Khlebnikov, and stage and costume designs by the chief of the Suprematist school of abstract painting Kazimir Malevich, set to a rude and crude musical score by Mikhail MATIUSHIN, is performed for the first time at the Luna Park Theater in St. Petersburg.

9 JANUARY 1914

The King of the Jews, mystery play by the Russian Grand Duke Konstantin Romanov, with incidental music by Alexander GLAZUNOV, is performed for the first time by the Imperial Russian Court Orchestra, Hugo Warlich conducting, at the Hermitage at St. Petersburg.

26 JANUARY 1914

Postolar od Delfta (The Cobbler of Delft), fantastic opera by the 40-year-old Serbo-Croatian composer Blagoje BERSA, to a libretto in the Serbo-Croatian language translated from the original German text *Der Schuster von Delft,* from a story derived from the fairy tale *Lykkens kalosker (Lucky Galoshes)* by Hans Christian Andersen, is performed for the first time in Zagreb. (The German version was given for the first time in Vienna on 7 November 1918.)

28 OCTOBER 1914

Richard HEUBERGER, Austrian composer of numerous respectable musical works in the manner of Brahms (whose worshipful friend he was), who achieved his more or less durable fame mainly with an operetta *Das Opernball*, dies in Vienna at the age of sixty-four.

Richard Heuberger died on 27 October (not 28 October) 1914.

1 DECEMBER 1914

Hunold der Spielmann (Hunold the Player), folk opera by the 58-year-old German composer Hermann GENSS, to his own libretto, is produced in German in San Francisco.

12 DECEMBER 1914

Three Poems from the Japanese by Igor STRAVINSKY, scored for soprano, 2 flutes, 2 clarinets, piano and string quartet are performed for the first time in Petrograd.

The world premiere of Stravinsky's *Three Poems from the Japanese* took place in Paris on 14 January (not in Petrograd on 12 December) 1914.

21 JULY 1915

Four centuries have elapsed since the birth of St. Philip NERI, whose Christian piety was so intense that during one of his penitential implorations his heart became supernaturally dilated and broke two ribs in his thoracic cavity, whose place in music history was secured because he was the spiritual father of the Oratorio, so named after the place of religious meetings accompanied by singing which Neri organized in 1558 in a chapel (*oratorio*, prayer room).

1 SEPTEMBER 1915

Igor STRAVINSKY composes a militantly anti-German piano piece, *Souvenir d'une Marche Boche*, as a protest against the "unheard-of barbarism of the German hordes," for *The Book of the Homeless*, published in London in 1916 for the benefit of Belgian war orphans.

28 DECEMBER 1915

Everyman, an ancient morality play set to a blandly homophonic score by the British singer Liza LEHMANN, in which a pious Everyman is advised by a bevy of personified abstractions such as Good Deeds, Knowledge, Discretion, Strength and Riches to reconcile himself to Death, and is ultimately led by a chorus of his sinless cousins to a sanctified grave, is produced in London.

15 JANUARY 1916

The Lover's Knot, opera with action taking place in postbellum Norfolk, Virginia, by the Russian-born American composer Simon BUCHAROFF, is produced by the Chicago Opera.

17 JANUARY 1916

Ferruccio BUSONI appears as soloist in Zürich in the first performance of his *Indianische Fantasie* for piano and orchestra, written in three sections (*Fantasy*, *Canzona* and *Finale*) in an expansively rhapsodic vein with extensive cadenzas covering the entire range of the piano keyboard, and making use of authentically pentatonic American Indian melodies in opulently harmonic dressing.

Busoni first performed his *Indianische Fantasie* in Berlin on 12 March 1914. The Zürich performance of the work on 17 January 1916 was a local premiere.

1 APRIL 1916

Die drei Schneider von Schönau (Three Tailors of Schönau), comic opera in three acts by the 47-year-old Dutch composer Jan BRANDTS-BUYS, is produced in Dresden.

15 OCTOBER 1916

Das Höllisch Gold, a "German Singspiel" in one act by the Austrian composer Julius BITTNER, his most successful opera, to his own libretto after a medieval fairy tale of Hans Sachs, centered on a simple-minded devilkin sent from the nether regions to the surface of the earth with a mission to corrupt a virtuous couple by gold, but becoming converted himself by their purity of soul, written in the manner of a folk play with simple illustrative motives forming its thematic substance, is performed for the first time in Darmstadt.

The correct title of Bittner's singspiel is *Das höllische Gold*. Its Austrian premiere was given in Vienna on 17 April 1917.

24 NOVEMBER 1916

Klara Militch, opera in four acts by the 60-year-old Russian composer Alexander KASTALSKY, to his own libretto after a novel of that name by Turgenev, inspired by the fate of Russian singer Eulalia Kadmina who committed suicide at the age of twenty-eight in 1881, is produced in Moscow.

10 DECEMBER 1916

A concert of music by Sergei PROKOFIEV is given in St. Petersburg, featuring the first performance of his narrative ballad for voice and piano *The Ugly Duckling.* . . .

The Ugly Duckling, singing narrative for voice and piano by the 24-year-old Russian composer Sergei PROKOFIEV, after Hans Christian Andersen, telling the story of a beautiful white cygnet hatched accidentally by a duck from a swan egg and scorned by his anatine siblings as an "ugly duckling," is performed for the first time in Petrograd on 12 February, 1915. (Maxim Gorky, hearing the piece, said, "Prokofiev described himself in this tale!")

29 DECEMBER 1916
Concerto for Two Pianos and Orchestra by the 78-year-old German composer Max BRUCH is performed, in a drastically revised version, for the first time by the sibling American piano team Ottilie and Rose Sutro with the Philadelphia Orchestra under the direction of Leopold Stokowski. (In 1971 the authentic version was discovered in Berlin. It was given its first performance by Nathan Twining and Mer Berkofsky with the London Symphony, Antal Dorati conducting, on 6 May 1974.)

20 JANUARY 1917

Third Symphony by Karol SZYMANOWSKI, subtitled *Song of the Night*, in three connected movements for orchestra, chorus and tenor solo, to the words of the mystical *divan* by the Persian poet Jalal al-Din Rumi (1207–1273) . . . is performed for the first time in Petrograd, conducted by Alexander Siloti.

Szymanowski's *Third Symphony* was indeed announced for performance on this date, but was cancelled because of the revolutionary rumblings at the time. It was not performed until 26 November 1921 in London, conducted by Albert Coates, but at the performance the chorus was replaced by the organ, and the tenor solo by cello. The first completely authentic performance, with chorus, took place in Lwów in 1928.

1 APRIL 1917
Scott JOPLIN, creator of throbbing ragtime pieces such as *The Maple Leaf Rag*, dies in New York at the age of forty-eight, of a stroke aggravated by tertiary syphilis.

19 JUNE 1917
Gergana, opera by the 36-year-old Bulgarian composer Georgi ATANASOV, dealing with the trials and tribulations of the Bulgarian girl Gergana nicknamed "white-legged" in consideration of the incandescent immaculacy of her habitually naked nether limbs, is produced in Sofia. (A revised version was first performed in Stara Zagora on 1 July 1925.)

7 DECEMBER 1917
Alois MINKUS, Austrian composer of ballets who went to Russia in 1853 as leader of the unique serf orchestras organized by Prince Yusupov and

later wrote music for a number of ballets for the Imperial Theaters in Moscow and St. Petersburg, of which *Don Quixote* and *La Bayadère* suited the popular Russian tastes by their unsophisticated tunes and cosmopolitan dance rhythms so well that they became perennial favorites of Russian audiences through both the Czarist and Bolshevik regimes, dies in his native Vienna whither he returned in 1891, at the venerable but totally oblivious age of ninety-one.

14 JANUARY 1918
Der Eroberer (The Conqueror), comic opera in two acts by the 49-year-old Dutch composer Jan BRANDTS-BUYS, is produced in Dresden.

5 DECEMBER 1918
Malvolio, opera in three acts by the 44-year-old British composer Fritz HART, after Shakespeare's comedy *Twelfth Night*, is performed for the first time in Melbourne by local conservatory students.

5 APRIL 1919
Das Dorf ohne Gloke (The Village Without a Bell), singspiel by the German operetta composer Eduard KÜNNEKE, is performed for the first time in Berlin.

30 APRIL 1919
Anti-Symphonie, subtitled *Musikalische Kreisguillotine*, by the Ukrainian emigrant composer Jef GOLYSCHEFF, an early exponent of serial tonal techniques, in several sections surrealistically entitled "Provocational Injections," "Chaotic Oral Cavity, or Submarine Aircraft" and "Clapping in Hyper F-sharp Major," is performed for the first time at a Dada exhibition in Berlin.

9 AUGUST 1919

Ruggero LEONCAVALLO, pioneer of Italian Verismo, who cultivated dramatic verisimilitude in operatic libretti and musical characterization, and who as a young man wrote an immortal opera, *Pagliacci*, but could never duplicate this success in his many subsequent theatrical works, dies at Montecatini at the age of sixty-one.

Leoncavallo died at the age of sixty-two, not sixty-one. (According to the official birth certificate of the city of Naples, he was born at 4:00 in the afternoon of 23 April 1857, not on 8 March 1858.)

☙ *1920-1929* ☙

30 JANUARY 1920

First Symphony by the American composer Frederick S. CONVERSE, set in an academically solid cosmopolitan romantic style, is performed for the first time by the Boston Symphony Orchestra.

Converse's *Second Symphony* (not his *First*) was first performed on this date.

27 APRIL 1920

Ragtime for eleven instruments, including cimbalom, by Igor STRAVINSKY is performed for the first time in London.

4 NOVEMBER 1920

L'Aviatore Dro, "futurist opera" by the Italian composer Francesco Balilla PRATELLA, to his own libretto in which the aviator Dro abandons his beauteous mistress to be alone with his beloved biplane, and flies aloft to merge with the universe, with a motorcycle engine included in the score to illustrate the revving up of an airplane, is performed for the first time in the composer's native town of Lugo.

The premiere of *L'Aviatore Dro* took place in Lugo on 4 September (not 4 November) 1920.

11 FEBRUARY 1921

Fanfulla, tragicomedy in three acts by the 46-year-old Italian composer Attilio PARELLI, to a libretto dealing with the heroic sixteenth-century Italian warrior Giovanni Bartolomeo Fanfulla, is performed for the first time in Trieste.

15 APRIL 1921

Der Vetter aus Dingsda (The Cousin from Dingsda), light opera by Eduard KÜNNEKE, is performed for the first time in Berlin.

27 MAY 1921

The Society for Private Musical Performances presents in Vienna a special concert of waltzes by Johann STRAUSS, arranged for string quartet, piano and harmonium in a program including, among others, *Wine, Women and Song* arranged by Alban BERG and *Treasure Waltz* from

The Gypsy Baron arranged by Arnold SCHOENBERG, the performers being Schoenberg and Rudolf Kolisch as violinists, Anton von Webern as cellist, Alban Berg at the harmonium and Eduard Steuermann at the piano.

10 JUNE 1921

Passacaglia for orchestra, op. 1, by Anton VON WEBERN, written in 1908 in a firmly tonal idiom in the explicitly indicated key of D minor, but already containing the foretaste of the atonal principle of nonrepetition of thematic notes in the subject (D, C-sharp, B-flat, A-flat, F, E, A, D), is performed for the first time at Bochum, Germany, at a concert of modern Austrian music.

This was not the world premiere of Webern's *Passacaglia*, but only the first German performance. The absolute premiere took place in Vienna under Webern's direction on 4 November 1908.

31 JULY 1921

The first Festival for Promotion of Contemporary Music opens in Donaueschingen, Germany, with the following programs: (1) Morning concert: first performance of *String Quartet No. 4* by the Czech pioneer of fractional music Alois HÁBA, making use of quarter-tones and multiples of quarter-tones (3/4, 1¼ tones and resulting icositetraphonic complexes). . . .

Hába's *String Quartet No. 4* was not a quarter-tone quartet; it was his *String Quartet No. 1*, performed on 31 July 1921, that was written in quarter tones.

5 FEBRUARY 1922

Romantisches Klavierkonzert in E major by the Viennese composer Joseph MARX, in three movements exuding the aroma of tardigrade romanticism, is performed for the first time in Vienna, Felix Weingartner conducting.

The work by Joseph Marx performed at this concert was not his piano concerto but his *Herbstsymphonie*.

8 APRIL 1922

Glauco, opera in three acts by the 61-year-old Italian composer Alberto FRANCHETTI, wherein Glauco, the protective god of sailors and fishermen, falls in love with the nymph Scylla, arousing the murderous jealousy of the proprietary temptress Circe, who transforms Scylla into a hexacephalous monster and assigns her to guard the Strait of Messina opposite another monster, Charybdis, is performed for the first time in Naples.

21 April 1922

Second Symphony by the American composer Frederick S. Converse, written in a consolidated Brahmsogenic idiom, in three competent movements expressive of "suffering, resolute defiance and solace in hope," is performed for the first time by the Boston Symphony Orchestra.

This was the premiere of Frederick S. Converse's *Third Symphony* (not his *Second*).

6 May 1922

Leila, opera by the 31-year-old Georgian composer Victor Dolidze, dealing with a girl of the Lezgin tribe, is produced in Tbilisi in the Georgian language.

19 May 1922

Dr. Eisenbart, comic opera in three acts by the 52-year-old Viennese composer Rolf Rueff, dealing with the devious career of a settecentesco trumpeter and medical quack, Quirin (who actually existed), nicknamed Eisenbart (literally, Iron Beard), is performed for the first time in Kiel. Two days later another opera on the same subject, *Doktor Eisenbart*, by Hermann Zilcher was premiered in two cities, Leipzig and Mannheim.

21 November 1922

Zingareska, orchestral suite by the 22-year-old American composer George Antheil, is performed for the first time in Berlin.

3 February 1923

Ballade for piano and orchestra by the only female member of Les Six, Germaine Tailleferre (the other five were Georges Auric, Louis Durey, Arthur Honegger, Darius Milhaud and Francis Poulenc), is performed for the first time by Ricardo Viñes at the Concerts Pasdeloup in Paris.

18 February 1923

Germelshausen, fantastic opera by the 37-year-old German composer Hans Grimm, recounting the tale of the village of Germelshausen, obliterated from the face of the earth by a vengeful deity for its unspeakable sins, with a merciful amendment allowing it to revive in its pristine hypostasis for twenty-four hours once in a hundred years, is produced in Augsburg.

31 March 1923

Zapustialata Vodenitza (Abandoned Watermill), opera in two acts by the 41-year-old Bulgarian composer Georgi Atanasov, is produced in Sofia.

26 APRIL 1923

The White Buffalo Maiden, "a Western music-play" in one act by the 34-year-old American composer Eugene FARMER, dealing with the life of Sioux Indians, is produced for the first time in Boise, Idaho.

25 JUNE 1923

Raquela, one-act opera by the 39-year-old Argentine composer Felipe BOERO, is produced in Buenos Aires.

19 OCTOBER 1923

Der Hochzeiter (The Bridegroom), comic opera in two acts by the 43-year-old German composer Karl BLEYLE, to his own libretto derived from the novella *Aus dem Regen in die Traufe (Out of the Rain into the Gutter),* is performed for the first time in this version, the original being titled *Hannele und Sannele,* in Rostock.

16 DECEMBER 1923

Der Schmied von Marienburg, opera in three acts by Siegfried WAGNER, glorifying the exploits of Teutonic German knights fighting the Poles at one of the many medieval encounters at Marienburg during which a brave local smith excels in love and war, the actions depicted in resonant fanfares of loyally filial Wagneromantic colors, is produced in Rostock.

29 DECEMBER 1923

Epiphanie for cello and orchestra in three movements, *Cortège, Prière de Melchior, Danse des petits nègres,* by the French conductor and master orchestrator André CAPLET, who had helped Debussy in putting together his ballet scores and who himself was impressionistically inclined in his symphonic inspirations, is performed for the first time at the Concerts Colonne in Paris, Maurice Maréchal soloist, Gabriel Pierné conducting.

13 JANUARY 1924

Octandre (meaning a flower having eight stamens) by Edgar VARÈSE, scored for flute, clarinet, oboe, bassoon, horn, trumpet, trombone and double-bass, constructed in a typical Varèsian manner and moving in harmonic blocks supported by deep sonorous layers, is performed for the first time in New York.

28 JANUARY 1924

Das verfemte Lachen (The Forbidden Laughter), comic opera by the 45-year-old German composer Fritz CORTOLEZIS, based on a historical episode in the life of the Danish crown prince who became King Christian VI of Denmark and Norway and who issued an order in 1722 forbidding laughter in or around his hunting lodge, is produced in Rostock.

29 MAY 1924

Alexandre GRETCHANINOFF conducts in Kiev the first performance of his *Symphony in E major*, op. 100, written in a broad Russian manner, with epic, lyric and dramatic episodes neatly balanced and effectively orchestrated.

Gretchaninoff's *Symphony in E major* was his *Third Symphony*.

19 JULY 1924

Six Bagatelles for string quartet, op. 9, by Anton von WEBERN, is performed for the first time at the Donaueschingen Festival of New Music, lasting only two minutes in all.

22 SEPTEMBER 1924

Piano Concerto for left hand alone in one movement by Erich Wolfgang KORNGOLD, written in an engagingly romantic manner but bristling with technical formidabilities that would challenge even a two-armed soloist, is performed for the first time in Vienna by Paul WITTGENSTEIN, the Austrian pianist who lost his right arm on the preposterous Russian front in World War I and who made a career by commissioning famous composers to write left-handed concertos. (Korngold himself conducted the orchestral accompaniment.)

9 OCTOBER 1924

Anton von WEBERN conducts the first performance in Vienna of his *Five Sacred Songs* for soprano, flute, clarinet, bass clarinet, trumpet, harp, violin and viola.

13 OCTOBER 1924

Fire Flies, comedy of masks in one act by the 59-year-old English composer Philip Napier MILES, is produced in Clifton, near Bristol, on the same program with his dramatic sketch *Markheim*, after a novella by Stevenson.

11 NOVEMBER 1924

Ilseino Srdce (*Else's Heart*), lyric comedy in three acts by the Czech composer Rudolf KAREL, is produced in Prague.

Ilsenio Srdce was first performed on 11 October (not 11 November) 1924.

13 NOVEMBER 1924

Irish Symphony by Sir Hamilton HARTY is performed in Manchester for the first time in its final version, after several revisions.

The absolute premiere of the original version of Harty's *Irish Symphony* took place in Dublin on 18 May 1904.

16 NOVEMBER 1924

Příhody Lišky Bystroušky (*Cunning Little Vixen*), comic opera in three acts by Leoš JANÁČEK to his own libretto in the form of an animal parable . . . is produced for the first time in Brno.

Příhody Lišky Bystroušky was first produced on 6 November (not 16 November) 1924.

16 NOVEMBER 1924

Die Bürger von Krähwinkel, comic opera in three acts by the 38-year-old German composer Kuno STIERLIN, after a comedy *Die deutschen Klein-städter* by Kotzebue ridiculing the provincial mores of the inhabitants of a mythical little German town named Krähwinkel (literally, crow corner), is performed for the first time in Osnabrück.

2 DECEMBER 1924

Drei kleine Stücke for cello and piano, op. 11, by Anton von WEBERN, is performed for the first time in Mainz.

31 JANUARY 1925

Alladina a Palomid, opera by the 31-year-old Czech composer Osvald CHLUBNA, after Maeterlinck's drama dealing with a passionate encounter of the fiancé of a royal princess and her Greek slave maid servant, is produced in Brno in the Czech translation, on the same evening with the ballet *Kdo je na světě naimocnější?* (*Who Is the Most Powerful Person in the World?*) by Bohuslav MARTINŮ.

13 FEBRUARY 1925

Leo ORNSTEIN, 32-year-old Russian-born modernistically minded composer, experimenter in meta-pianistic sonorities, plays the first performance with the Philadelphia Orchestra, Leopold Stokowski conducting, of his *Second Piano Concerto,* arranged from his earlier sonata for two pianos of 1921, its modernity expressed by the absence of key signature and the abundance of metrical shifts, the finale pursuing its course in rapid 5/8 time.

Leo Ornstein performed his *First Piano Concerto* (not his *Second*) at this concert of the Philadelphia Orchestra.

26 FEBRUARY 1925

Violin Concerto in E minor by the 64-year-old romantic Austrian composer Emil Nikolaus von REZNIČEK, in three movements, patently patterned after Mendelssohn's famous concerto in the same minor key and containing further borrowing from Cherubini's melodious legacy, is performed for the first time in Berlin.

1 MARCH 1925
Intégrales by Edgar VARÈSE, a captivating piece of "organized sound," scored for eleven winds and seventeen percussion instruments integrated in a magnificent tonal symmetry with a germinal motive in the center of ever-expanding spiral melody, is performed for the first time in New York.

If it be music to . . . make sounds like an injured dog's cry of pain or a cat's yell of midnight rage . . . then this is the real thing. (W. J. Henderson, *New York Sun*, 2 March 1925.)

Varèse's *Intégrales* sounded a good deal like a combination of early morning in the Mott Haven freight yard, feeding time at the zoo and a Sixth Avenue trolley rounding a curve, with an intoxicated woodpecker thrown in for good measure. (Ernest Newman, *New York Evening Post*, 2 March 1925.)

3 MARCH 1925
Joseph the Beautiful, ballet with music by Sergei VASILENKO, based on the biblical story of the aborted seduction of the beautiful Jewish lad Joseph by the lecherous queen of Egypt, is performed for the first time at the Experimental Theater in Moscow.

11 MARCH 1925

No No Nanette, musical comedy by Vincent YOUMANS . . . is produced for the first time in London, England, before its New York opening on 16 September 1925. (A brief tryout of *No No Nanette* took place in Chicago in 1924.)

The absolute positive world premiere of the musical comedy *No, No, Nanette* took place in Detroit on 21 April 1924; it was next staged in Chicago on 5 May 1924, and after nearly a year was produced in London on 11 March 1925, finally reaching Broadway on 16 September 1925.

28 NOVEMBER 1925

Music for the Theatre, suite for small orchestra with piano by the 25-year-old American composer Aaron COPLAND, in five imaginative movements (*Prologue, Dance, Interlude, Burlesque, Epilogue*) . . . is performed for the first time at a concert of the League of Composers in New York, conducted by Serge Koussevitzky to whom the score is dedicated.

This was not the first performance of Copland's *Music for the Theatre*. Its absolute premiere took place on 20 November 1925, given in Boston, Serge Koussevitzky conducting the Boston Symphony Orchestra.

255

26 December 1925

A Light From St. Agnes, "lyric tragedy" in one act by the 38-year-old American composer William Franke HARLING, to a libretto dealing with sacrilegious desecration of a church in Louisiana, theft of a crucifix and murder, set to a score making use of saxophones and banjos for local color, is produced in Chicago.

25 February 1926

Die zehn Küsse (Ten Kisses), "merry opera" in four acts by the 53-year-old German composer Bernhard SEKLES, after Hans Christian Andersen's tale *Svinedrengen (Swineherd)*, is produced in Frankfurt.

10 April 1926

Die Opferung des Gefangenen (The Sacrifice of the Captive), sectarian drama from Aztec life for voices and dance in one act by the learned Austrian composer Egon WELLESZ, is produced in Cologne.

20 May 1926

Leonora Christina, opera in four acts to a Danish libretto by the 41-year-old Danish composer of German-Jewish origin Siegfried SALOMON, dealing with the tragic seventeenth-century Danish princess who spent twenty-two years in the Blue Tower of the Copenhagen Prison as wife of the traitor Count Ulfelt, is produced in Copenhagen.

23 May 1926

Hypatia, opera in three acts by the 54-year-old Italian composer Roffredo CAETANI, dealing with the death on the Ides of March in A.D. 415 of the philosopher and astronomer Hypatia (370–415), who was torn limb from limb by a mob of Christian fanatics instigated by Bishop Cyril of Alexandria, is performed for the first time, in a German translation of the original Italian libretto, in Weimar.

11 November 1926

Winona, three-act opera by the 44-year-old Italian-born American composer Alberto BIMBONI, dealing with the dramatic peripeteia of an Indian girl named Winona (which means first-born) who, thwarted by the stern chief Red Hat in her love for a brave youth from another tribe, in despair jumps from a cliff into a lake below, the score replete with genuine Indian motifs, is produced in Portland, Oregon, the composer conducting.

8 January 1927

The first performance is given in Vienna by the Kolisch String Quartet of *Lyrische Suite* by Alban BERG, written in a distinctive individual style, wherein the Schoenbergian method of twelve-tone composition is applied in alternation with nondodecaphonic, tonal and even triadic procedures, melodically and harmonically anchored on additive intervalic complexes of fourths and tritones summing up to major sevenths, and fifths and tritones summing up to minor ninths, in six movements: (1) *Allegretto giovale,* (2) *Andante amoroso,* (3) *Allegro misterioso,* (4) *Adagio appassionato,* (5) *Presto delirando,* (6) *Largo desolato.*

Alban Berg's *Lyric Suite* contains a germinal four-note motive H, F, A, B (German notation for B, F, A, B♭), the initials of Hanna Fuchs-Robettin (Berg's secret love), with metronome markings and bar numbers throughout the score being multiples of 23 (Alban Berg's mystic number, embodied in a Vienna publication entitled *23*) and 10, Hanna's astrological numeral.

2 APRIL 1927

Concerto for flute, cello and string orchestra by Vincent D'INDY, is performed for the first time in Paris.

The complete scoring of Vincent d'Indy's *Concerto* is for piano, flute, cello and string orchestra.

11 AUGUST 1927

Study in Sonority for ten violins, an atonal essay in polyphonic writing by the scholarly American composer Wallingford RIEGGER, written as a school exercise, is performed for the first time by the student orchestra of Ithaca Conservatory, New York, where Riegger served as a member of the faculty. (Leopold Stokowski quadrupled the number of violins and performed the work with the Philadelphia Orchestra on 30 March 1929.)

22 DECEMBER 1927

Willem PIJPER, 33-year-old Dutch modernist, plays the piano solo with the Concertgebouw Orchestra in Amsterdam, Pierre Monteux conducting, in the first performance of his *Second Piano Concerto* (completed on 26 August 1927), consisting of four symphonic pieces with piano obbligato separated by three unaccompanied piano solo sections.

This was originally Pijper's *Second Piano Concerto;* the *Orkeststuk* for piano and orchestra, first performed by Pijper in Utrecht on 11 December 1915, was *Piano Concerto No. 1,* but the numeral was subsequently removed and the erstwhile *Second* was redesignated simply *Piano Concerto.*

18 March 1928

Žena a Bůh (A Woman and God), one-act opera by the 37-year-old Czech composer Karel Boleslav Jirák, centered on a neo-Pythagorean philosopher of the first century A.D. named Apollo of Tyan, who was reputed to be a miracle worker, is performed for the first time in Brno.

3 May 1928

Tam-Man-Nacup, opera based on Indian spring chants by the 40-year-old American composer William F. Hanson, is produced for the first time in Provo, Utah.

12 May 1928

Il Patto dei tre, comic opera in three acts by the 53-year-old Italian composer Domenico Monleone, dealing with three friends who formed a pact of eternal faith symbolized by a rock in the form of a large bell, is produced in the Genoese dialect in Genoa.

5 August 1928

Aphrodite, grand opera by the Italian-born Argentine composer Arturo Luzzatti, with a French libretto based on the aphrodisiac novel by Pierre Louys, is produced at the Teatro Colón in Buenos Aires.

8 September 1928

Vikerlased (The Vikings), national opera in three acts by the 28-year-old Estonian composer Evald Aav, dealing with the Estonian resistance to the invading Scandinavians in the twelfth century, and focusing on the love of an Estonian youth for a patriotic Estonian maiden who is lustfully coveted by an overweening Swede, to a musical score thoroughly marinated in Wagneromantic fluids, is produced in the Estonian language in Tallinn.

2 October 1928

Concerto for clarinet and orchestra by the Danish grandmaster Carl Nielsen (completed on 15 August 1928), in one compact movement, set in a quasi-modernistic idiom, stressing the dichotomy of the polar tonalities at a tritone's distance, while thematic melorhythms remain well within the traditional forms, is performed for the first time in Copenhagen.

Carl Nielsen's *Clarinet Concerto* was first performed in Humlebaeck (not Copenhagen) on 14 September (not 2 October) 1928. It is in four sections rather than in one compact movement: *Allegretto un poco, Poco Adagio, Allegro non troppo* and *Allegro vivace.*

14 OCTOBER 1928

Wakuta, opera in four acts by the 53-year-old American composer E. Bruce KNOWLTON to the composer's own libretto on an Indian subject, is produced in Portland, Oregon.

14 OCTOBER 1928

Tyll, opera in three acts by the 26-year-old German composer Mark LOTHAR, detailing the adventures of the legendary character Ulenspiegel, is produced in Weimar.

1 DECEMBER 1928

Moschopulos, opera in three tableaux by the 25-year-old German composer Rudolf WAGNER-RÉGENY, to his own libretto dealing with a malevolent Oriental magician, is produced in Gera, on the same program with his opera after Hans Christian Andersen's tale *Der nackte König (The Emperor's New Clothes)*.

4 APRIL 1929

The Woodsman, opera in three acts by the 53-year-old American composer Bruce KNOWLTON to his libretto dealing with love, infidelity, bastardy and murder among frontier woodsmen, is produced by the composer's own Bruce Knowlton Opera Company, in Portland, Oregon.

6 APRIL 1929

Edison DENISOV, Soviet composer of avant-garde leanings whose works compass a large spectrum of modernistic devices, from neomedieval homophony to postimpressionistic colorism and coruscating sonorism, whose first name was given to him by his electrical engineer father in homage to the great American inventor Edison, and which incidentally formed a 6/7 anagram of his last name, is born in Tomsk, Siberia.

25 SEPTEMBER 1929

The Woman Who Laughed at Faery, fantastic opera in one act by the 55-year-old English composer Fritz HART, is produced in Melbourne, Australia.

3 DECEMBER 1929

Lara, "musical fresco" in three acts by the 52-year-old Belgian composer Armand MARSICK, to a Flemish libretto after Byron's poem by that name dealing with the leader of rebellious peasants, is produced in Antwerp.

◇ *1930-1939* ◇

26 JANUARY 1930

Galatea, Greek opera in one act by the 47-year-old German composer Walter BRAUNFELS, to his own libretto after Ovid, in which Galatea, a water nymph, loves a shepherd who is slain out of jealousy by the cyclops Polyphemus, but who joins her beloved in her natural element when his blood becomes a river, is performed for the first time in Cologne. (The story in the basic volume of *Music Since 1900*, in which Galatea is a statue with which her sculptor is infatuated, is incorrect. The tale of sculptural adoration is that of Pygmalion, king of Cyprus; however, in some versions of his story the statuary object of his passion after being brought to life is called Galatea, in utter disregard of the niceties of mythological consistency.)

7 MAY 1930

Die Richterin (The Woman Judge), opera in three acts by the 44-year-old Austrian composer Hermann GRABNER, is produced in Wuppertal.

16 OCTOBER 1930

Nikolai LOPATNIKOFF plays in Düsseldorf the piano part in the first performance of his *Second Piano Concerto*, in three movements, a propulsive *Allegro energico*, an angularly lyrical *Andantino* and a neo-Baroque *Allegro molto*.

Nikolai Lopatnikoff did not play the piano part in the first performance of his *Second Piano Concerto*; Walter Frey was the soloist.

11 NOVEMBER 1930

Lord Spleen, comic opera by the 28-year-old German composer Mark LOTHAR, freely adapted from Ben Jonson's play *Epicine, or the Silent Woman*, wherein the main character, whose family name is Morose, is nicknamed Lord Spleen, is produced in Dresden, on the same bill with the premiere of Emil Nikolaus von REZNIČEK's one-act opera *Spiel oder Ernst? (In Play or in Earnest?)*.

10 JANUARY 1931

The absolute world première is given in New York by Nicolas Slonimsky, conducting his Chamber Orchestra of Boston, of *Three Places in New England* by the prophetic genius of American music Charles E. IVES, limning three tonal images of historic American sites, landscapes and monuments . . . (1) *Colonel Shaw and His Colored Regiment*, evoked by the famous basrelief on Boston

Common . . . (2) *Putnam's Camp*, suggested by martial relics of the American Revolution . . . (3) *The Housatonic at Stockbridge*, painting the majestic flow of the great New England river in polymetric designs of great complexity, mathematically precise as to rhythmic values and yet spacious and free in its poetic progress, with the main motto formed by ZENNER's *Missionary Chant* and the "Fate motive" of Beethoven's Fifth Symphony, annexing in its course a number of old American tunes, expanding into a fantastic panoply of simultaneous melodies and polytriadic harmonies, and after a thunderous climax ending suddenly in a residual hymnal chorale, a unique effect of colorful sonority.

The correct name of the composer of the *Missionary Chant* is Charles ZEUNER, not Zenner. He was a German organist who emigrated to America in 1830, and killed himself for unknown reasons in 1857.

1 MARCH 1931

Igor MARKEVITCH, 18-year-old Russian-born pianist, composer and conductor, plays the solo part with the Orchestre Symphonique de Paris, Pierre Monteux conducting, in the first performance of his *Piano Concerto* in three vivaciously lyric movements, written in a Gallic neo-Baroque manner.

An earlier performance of Markevitch's *Piano Concerto* was given in London on 15 July 1929. *The Times* of London in its review characterized the music as "Bach gone wrong."

19 APRIL 1931

Das Ziel (The Goal), opera in four tableaux by Otto KLEMPERER, to his own libretto, is performed for the first time in a concert version, conducted by Klemperer himself, in Berlin.

3 SEPTEMBER 1931

Washington's Birthday by Charles IVES, an orchestral potpourri of a popular gathering on Washington's birthday, is performed for the first time in San Francisco.

10 SEPTEMBER 1931

Los Rubios, opera depicting in abecedarian harmonies the early history of Los Angeles by the 58-year-old American composer Mary Carr MOORE, is produced in Los Angeles.

11 FEBRUARY 1932

Krieg über Sonja, "musical stage poem" in three acts by the 47-year-old German composer Horst PLATEN, to a libretto dealing with the conflicting loves of two German soldiers for a Russian girl named Sonia during the First World War, is produced in Hamburg.

12 FEBRUARY 1932

Rip van Winkle, opera by the 57-year-old American composer Edward MANNING to a libretto prepared by the composer, after the famous tale by Washington Irving dealing with the predicament of a man who slept for many years to awake in an entirely different society, is produced in New York.

22 MAY 1932

The Marriage of Aude, one-act opera by the American composer Bernard ROGERS, is produced in Rochester, New York.

The Marriage of Aude was produced on 22 May 1931 (not 1932).

5 SEPTEMBER 1932

Concerto for two pianos and orchestra by Francis POULENC, written in a sybaritically hedonistic manner, in three movements, *Allegro ma non troppo, Larghetto* and *Finale,* the stylistic pendulum swinging nonchalantly from mandatory urbanity to pseudosophisticated sentimentality with a fashionable admixture of acrid polytonalities, is performed for the first time at the Venice Festival, with the composer and Jacques Février as dual soloists.

29 OCTOBER 1932

Der Schmied von Gent, fairy opera in three acts by Franz SCHREKER, to his own libretto dealing with a Ghent blacksmith who sells his soul to the devil to save himself from political persecution by the Spanish authorities of the Netherlands in the late Middle Ages, but refuses to carry out his bargain and instead opens a restaurant at the heavenly gates, ingratiating himself by his culinary art with St. Peter and the Holy Family, until he is finally granted admission to Heaven, is produced in Berlin.

The libretto of *Der Schmied von Gent* was based on a story by the Belgian writer Charles de Coster, *Smeetse Smee,* from his anthology of *Les légendes flamandes.*

19 NOVEMBER 1932

Lázaro, lyric drama in one act by the Argentine composer Constantino GAITO, the first opera to incorporate a tango, is produced at the Teatro Colón in Buenos Aires.

16 DECEMBER 1932

TRITON, Paris society dedicated to the propagation of modern chamber music presents . . . *String Quartet* by Albert ROUSSEL. . . .

This was the first Paris performance of Roussel's *String Quartet*; the world premiere of the work was given in Brussels a week earlier.

23 JANUARY 1933

Béla BARTÓK plays in Frankfurt the solo part in the first performance of his *Second Piano Concerto*, in three classically molded movements: (1) *Allegro* (for piano, wind instruments and percussion); (2) *Adagio*, opening with a chorale-like prelude, suddenly bursting out in *Presto*, and then returning to a pacific *Adagio*; and (3) *Allegro molto*, exploding with untamed energy, with the piano and the kettledrums engaged in a percussive antiphony.

6 FEBRUARY 1933

Angels and Devils by the American composer Henry BRANT, scored for seventy-six flutes, alternatively angelic (represented by avian tunes in bucolic diatonic fashion) and demonic (depicted by double and triple tonguing in jazzy syncopation), is performed for the first time in New York, directed by the supreme French panpipist Georges Barrère.

11 MARCH 1933

Carl EBERT, director of the Berlin Municipal Opera, and Fritz STIEDRY, its conductor, are summarily removed from their posts by the Ministry of Propaganda of the Nazi Government as non-Aryans.

Carl Ebert had in fact pure Aryan blood flowing in his Teutonic veins and arteries; he was dismissed from his post as director of the Berlin Municipal Opera for having polluted his racial and cultural purity by an association with avowed and even possibly Jewish modernists abominated by the stolid Nazi establishment; he left Germany voluntarily.

13 NOVEMBER 1933

Corsaresca (Lady Pirate), "tragic spectacle" *(visione tragica)* by the 53-year-old Italian composer Pasquale LA ROTELLA, is produced in Rome. (It was first performed as an oratorio in Milan on 24 September 1933.)

22 NOVEMBER 1933

Three Dance Movements by the 28-year-old American composer William RUSSELL, scored for expanded and ameliorated piano, with tone clusters and piano strings activated by a fork, a cymbal played by drawing the teeth of a saw across its edge, and a bottle to be broken at the climax, is performed for the first time in New York.

2 DECEMBER 1933

La giornata di Marcellina (Marcellina's Day), "merry opera" in two acts by the 59-year-old Italian composer Attilio PARELLI, is performed for the first time on the Turin Radio. (A stage performance took place in San Remo on 24 February 1940.)

5 JANUARY 1934
First Symphony by Ernst BACON is performed for the first time by the San Francisco Symphony Orchestra, Issay Dobrowen conducting.

2 APRIL 1934
Little Women, two-act opera by Eleanor Everest FREER, based on Louisa May Alcott's novel of the same name, is performed for the first time in Chicago.

3 MAY 1934
Popieliny, opera in two acts by the 31-year-old Russian-born Polish composer Michal KONDRACKI, freely arranged after the Polish medieval mysterium *Marcholt gruby a sprośny (Fat and Obscene Marcholt)*, is performed for the first time in Warsaw.

10 AUGUST 1934
Rock and Roll, with a score by Richard WHITTING and lyrics by Sidney CLARE, the first musical composition bearing a title that was to generate the most powerful form of American popular music, originally designed for use in the motion picture *Transatlantic Merry-Go-Round*, with the key words indicating the rolling and rocking movement of an ocean liner, is copyrighted in Washington, D.C. (It was published on 8 October 1934 by the Irving Berlin Corporation.)

7 NOVEMBER 1934

Serge RACHMANINOFF plays at a concert of the Philadelphia Orchestra in Baltimore, conducted by Leopold Stokowski, the piano part in the first performance anywhere of his *Rhapsody on a Theme by Paganini*, composed between 3 July and 24 August 1934, in A minor, consisting of twenty-four variations on Paganini's *Caprice No. 24* (the same that Brahms used for his piano variations), written in a superlative virtuoso manner, covering the entire range of the keyboard, with the eighteenth variation presenting an ingenious inversion of the subject, so that the ascending minor phrase becomes the descending major motive, curiously resulting in a Slavic-flavored ballad-like melody, the whole work culminating in a grandiose invocation of the thematically related medieval hymn *Dies Irae* (which had already been introduced in the piano part of the 7th variation).

The theme of the eighteenth variation of Rachmaninoff's *Rhapsody on a Theme by Paganini* is the precise reproduction of a passage from William Byrd's *Credo* in the Mass for three voices with the words "non erit finis," which Rachmaninoff happened to have heard in March 1934.

264

25 November 1934

Short Symphony by the prime American composer Aaron COPLAND, a magnetic piece of pulsing rhythms and lyric invocations, opulent in thematic intercommunications, and reaching its climax in a jazzified celebration of the American spirit, is performed for the first time in Mexico City, conducted by Carlos Chávez. (A chamber music version of the *Short Symphony* was made by Copland in 1937 in the form of a sextet for string quartet, clarinet and piano.)

6 December 1934

Almos, opera by the pioneer Hungarian composer Mihály MOSONYI, composed in 1862, is performed for the first time in Budapest, sixty-four years after Mosonyi's death.

15 December 1934

Hester Prynne, three-act opera by Avery CLAFLIN based on Nathaniel Hawthorne's *The Scarlet Letter*, is produced in an abridged version in Hartford, Connecticut.

26 December 1934

Klein Dorrit, singspiel by the 49-year-old German operetta composer Eduard KÜNNEKE, making use of story material of *Little Dorrit* by Dickens, is produced in Oberhausen.

24 January 1935

Eroii de la Rovine, grand opera by the 47-year-old Rumanian composer Nicolae BRETAN, to his own libretto glorifying the heroic victory of the Walachian warriors against the invading Ottoman Turks at the battle of Rovine in 1394, is performed for the first time in Cluj.

23 February 1935

Prologue to the operatic cycle in four acts *Hri o Marii (Deeds of Mary)* by the prime Czech composer Bohuslav MARTINŮ, based on medieval sacred dramas, in the Czech text by Martinů, is performed for the first time in Brno. (The four parts of the cycle, unperformed, are *Wise and Unwise Maidens, Mariken of Neumegen, Nativity* and *Sister Pascalina*.)

23 March 1935

Music for a Scene from Shelley for orchestra by the 25-year-old American composer Samuel BARBER, written in a poetic neo-Romantic idiom, is performed for the first time by the New York Philharmonic.

Barber's *Music for a Scene from Shelley* was first performed by the New York Philharmonic on 24 March 1933 (not 23 March 1935).

24 MARCH 1935
Das kalte Herz, radio opera by the 32-year-old German composer Mark LOTHAR, after a fairy tale dealing with a greedy miser who trades his own warm heart for a magician's cold heart, is produced in Berlin.

17 APRIL 1935

Brothers Karamazov, opera in five acts, after Dostoyevsky's famous novel, by the Czech composer Otakar JEREMIÁŠ, is produced in Prague.

The true premiere of *Brothers Karamazov* by Otakar Jeremiáš took place on 8 October 1928 (not 17 April 1935).

25 OCTOBER 1935
Constantin Brăvcoveanu, opera by the 41-year-old Rumanian composer Sabin DRĂGOI, to a libretto in Rumanian dealing with the ruler of Valachia (1654–1714) of that name, is produced in Bucharest.

28 OCTOBER 1935
Two one-act operas by the 62-year-old English-born South African composer William Henry BELL, *The Pillow of Kantan*, inspired by the Japanese Noh theater, and *The Wandering Scholar*, are produced in Capetown.

14 NOVEMBER 1935
Gwalia, a Welsh Rhapsody for orchestra by the 45-year-old American composer Philip JAMES is performed for the first time in New York.

25 DECEMBER 1935

A triple opera, in three acts, *Das almächtige Gold*, *Harla* and *Dame in Traum*, by Franz SALMHOFER, is produced in Vienna.

Salmhofer's opera *Dame im Traum* was first performed on 26 December (not 25 December) 1935; the other two operas, *Das almächtige Gold* and *Harba* (not *Harla*), were never produced.

9 FEBRUARY 1936
Genoveva, opera by the 32-year-old German composer Alexander ECKLEBE, dealing with the virtuous Genevieve of Brabant, unjustly accused of infidelity by her suspicious husband, the margrave of Trier, is produced in a radio broadcast in Berlin. (The first stage performance took place at Hagen, Westphalia, on 22 April 1937.)

266

25 FEBRUARY 1936
Bakhtrioni, opera by the 33-year-old Georgian composer Grigori KILADZI, in the Georgian language, based on the legendary defense of the ancient castle Bakhtrioni in the Caucasian mountain country against invaders, is produced in Tbilisi (Tiflis).

26 FEBRUARY 1936
Farhad and Shirin, first national Uzbek operatic drama, notated and organized from genuine native motives for a choral ensemble singing chants in unison and orchestrated for indigenous instruments by the Russian composer and ethnomusicologist Victor USPENSKY, to a libretto dealing with the exotic love match of the Chinese prince Farhad and Armenian maiden Shirin, is produced in Tashkent.

19 APRIL 1936
Meredith WILLSON conducts in San Francisco the first performance of his *First Symphony* on the thirtieth anniversary of the San Francisco earthquake.

24 NOVEMBER 1936

The Astrology of Personality by Dane RUDHYAR, French-born American composer who changed his original name Daniel Chennevière to a more theosophic cognomen, Rudhyar, which means, in sanskrit, "dynamic action," is published in New York, the first book on astrology ever written by a professional musician.

The Astrology of Personality is said to be the future of astrology what Ptolemy's *Tetrabiblos* has been for astrology of the past. It reveals a new philosophy of Creative Time, of an Algebra of Life. (Rudhyar's self-appraisal made shortly after the publication of the book.)

The quotation equating in significance Rudhyar's book on astrology to Ptolemy's *Tetrabiblios* is not his own (which would be egomaniac), but his publisher's.

7 APRIL 1937
The Bleeding Heart of Timpanogos, Indian opera by the 50-year-old American composer William HANSON, to a libretto based on a legend that a stalactite in the shape of a human heart in a cave in Mount Timpanogos melts away in bloody tears at tragic moments in the lives of a local Indian tribe, is produced at Brigham Young University in Provo, Utah.

20 MAY 1937
Third Symphony by the unappreciated but significant American composer John BECKER, subtitled *Symphonia Brevis*, is performed for the first time in Minneapolis.

16 June 1937

Tá Mar, opera by the Portuguese composer Ruy Coelho, is produced in Lisbon.

The title *Tá Mar* is a dialect expression used by Portuguese fishermen in Estremadura for "o mare esta bravo" (the sea is rising).

26 September 1937

Refused admission to a white hospital after being gravely injured in an automobile accident, Bessie Smith, the greatest of Blues singers, dies in Memphis, Tennessee, before the arrival of a properly segregated Negritudinal ambulance.

Bessie Smith died in Clarksville, Mississippi (not Memphis, Tennessee).

12 November 1937
Das Opfer (The Sacrifice), opera in three acts by the 32-year-old German composer Winfried Zillig, depicting the tragic Antarctic expedition of 1912, is produced in Hamburg.

27 November 1937
Vikings by the 53-year-old Belgian composer Arthur Meulemans, to a libretto in the Flemish language, is performed for the first time in Antwerp.

19 December 1937
Second Symphony by the 42-year-old American composer William Grant Still is performed for the first time by the Philadelphia Symphony Orchestra under the direction of Leopold Stokowski.

28 December 1937

Maurice Ravel, great French composer, supreme artificer of tonal art whose masterly precision in handling exquisitely molded melodies and fine-textured impressionistic harmonies has created a magic world of translucently oscillating rhythmic images suffused with the prismatic light of instrumental coloration, described in the citation of the honorary degree of Doctor of Music conferred upon him by Oxford University as "Musarum interpretes modorum daedalus Mauritius Ravellus," dies in Paris at the age of sixty-two, nine days after brain surgery made necessary by an acute state of apraxia and dysphasia.

An additional tribute includes the following:

France loses in Ravel one of its great musicians whose prestige is recognized in the entire world. History will assure for him the glorious place in the domain of music which he has earned with such great courage and such firm conviction. (Igor Stravinsky in *Instransigeant*, Paris, 29 December 1937.)

16 JANUARY 1938

Béla BARTÓK and his wife Ditta play in Basel, Switzerland, the solo parts in the first performance of his *Sonata for Two Pianos and Percussion*, in three movements: (1) *Assai lento—Allegro molto* (2) *Lento ma non troppo* (3) *Allegro non troppo.* . . . (Bartók made an orchestral arrangement of his sonata in 1940, and renamed it *Concerto for Two Pianos, Percussion and Orchestra.* The first performance of this version took place in London on 14 October 1942, with the Royal Philharmonic Orchestra, Sir Adrian Boult conducting; the pianists were Louis Kentner and Llona Kabos. The first American performance of the *Concerto* was given by the New York Philharmonic, Fritz Reiner conducting, on 21 January 1943, with Béla Bartók and his wife as soloists; it is erroneously listed as the *Uraufführung* in the authoritative edition, *Béla Bartók, Weg und Werk, Schriften und Briefe* by Bence Szabolcsi, published in Budapest in 1957.)

The first performance of Bartók's *Concerto for Two Pianos, Percussion and Orchestra* took place on 14 November (not 14 October) 1942, with the London (not the Royal) Philharmonic Orchestra.

28 FEBRUARY 1938

Ramona, opera in three acts by the German-American composer Gustave STRUBE, is produced in Baltimore.

The opera *Ramona* by Gustave Strube was renamed *The Captive.*

8 APRIL 1938
Fourth Symphony by the 38-year-old American composer Harl McDONALD is performed for the first time by the Philadelphia Orchestra under the direction of Eugene Ormandy.

2 MAY 1938
Second Symphony for strings by the 41-year-old French composer Jean RIVIER is performed for the first time in Paris.

12 MAY 1938
Schneider Wibbel, comic opera in four acts by the 35-year-old German composer Mark LOTHAR, is produced in Berlin.

28 MAY 1938

Mathis der Maler, opera in seven scenes by Paul HINDEMITH . . . is produced in Basel, Switzerland, after Hindemith had been declared persona non grata in

Nazi Germany. (Symphony *Mathis der Maler*, incorporating the interludes from the opera, was first performed in Berlin on 12 March 1934.)

Hindemith's opera *Mathis der Maler* was first produced in Zürich (not Basel).

24 JUNE 1938

Zadig, musical comedy by the 52-year-old Swiss composer Jean DUPÉRIER, after Voltaire's Oriental tale *Zadig, ou la destinée*, with the central character being a youth named Zadig, is produced in Paris.

2 DECEMBER 1938

First Piano Concerto by Darius MILHAUD, composed in 1933, in three contrasting movements, marked *Très Vif*, *Mouvement de Barcarolle* and *Final*, is performed for the first time by the Minneapolis Symphony Orchestra, with Dimitri Mitropoulos acting in the dual capacity as piano soloist and conductor.

This was not the first performance of Milhaud's *First Piano Concerto*; the absolute premiere took place on 23 November 1934, in Paris.

10 DECEMBER 1938

Alfred, "heroic opera" by Antonin DVOŘÁK glorifying the reign of Anglo-Saxon King Alfred the Great, translated from the original German libretto used by Dvořák in 1870 when he wrote the opera, is produced in a Czech translation for the first time in Olomouc, thirty-four years after Dvořák's death.

15 DECEMBER 1938

Sensemayá, "indigenous incantation to kill a snake" for voice and orchestra by the great Mexican composer Silvestre REVUELTAS, to the text of the Afro-Cuban poet Nicolas Guillen, full of voodoo words (Mayombé, Bembé, Mayombé!), with a bumbling bass tuba giving the main theme, is performed for the first time in Mexico City.

11 MARCH 1939

Die Komödie der Irrungen, opera in two acts after Shakespeare's play *The Comedy of Errors*, by the German composer Carl LORENZ, is produced in Stettin sixteen years after Lorenz's death.

5 APRIL 1939

Fifth Symphony by the 74-year-old Russian composer Alexandre GRETCHANINOV is performed for the first time by the Philadelphia Symphony Orchestra, Leopold Stokowski conducting.

23 APRIL 1939

Violin Concerto by Béla BARTÓK, completed by him on 31 December 1938, is performed for the first time by Zoltán Székely in Amsterdam, with Willem Mengelberg conducting the Concertgebouw Orchestra.

Bartók's *Second Violin Concerto* was first performed on 23 March (not 23 April) 1939.

20 JUNE 1939

Las vírgenes del Sol, grand opera by the Argentine composer Alfredo SCHIUMA to the story of a sacrifice to the Inca Sun God of a verified genuine virgin, is performed for the first time at the Teatro Colón in Buenos Aires.

30 OCTOBER 1939

San Juan Capistrano, two nocturnes for orchestra by the 40-year-old American composer Harl McDONALD, subtitled *The Mission* and *The Fiesta*, is performed for the first time by the Boston Symphony Orchestra, Serge Koussevitzky conducting.

22 NOVEMBER 1939

Blennerhassett, radio opera by the 36-year-old American composer Vittorio GIANNINI, written in a flowingly melodious and ingratiatingly harmonious idiom, dealing with the seditious ruminations of the imperial-minded Vice President of the United States Aaron Burr on the island of Blennerhassett on the Ohio River, is performed for the first time by the Columbia Broadcasting Company in New York.

Giannini's radio opera was first performed on 2 November (not 22 November) 1939.

16 DECEMBER 1939

Fascinated by the rhythmically scanned injunction on a cautionary paper sign in a Harvard University men's room, "Do Not Throw Paper Towels in Toilets," Igor STRAVINSKY rips it off and jots down a fitting melody in duple time marked *Andante* 2/4: efD, ddd, (cd), e, d C (capital letters represent quarter notes; small letters represent eighth notes; run-together letters represent sixteenth notes; letters in parentheses are to be sung on a single syllable).

❧ 1940-1949 ❧

11 JANUARY 1940

The Great American Goof, ballet by the 26-year-old American composer Henry BRANT, is performed for the first time in New York.

5 FEBRUARY 1940

Second Symphony by Ernst BACON is performed for the first time in Chicago.

24 NOVEMBER 1940

Toktogul, opera in four acts by the 41-year-old Soviet composer Aleksander VEPRIK, to a libretto in the Kirgiz language glorifying a pioneer of national Kirgiz arts named Toktogul Satylganov (1864–1933), is performed for the first time in Frunze, capital of the Kirgiz Soviet Socialist Republic.

30 DECEMBER 1940

Mergen, opera in five acts by the 65-year-old Soviet ethnomusicologist Anton EICHENWALD, to a libretto in the Bashkir language depicting the great national deed of an ethnically conscious patriot by the name of Mergen, is produced in Ufa, capital of the Bashkir Autonomous Soviet Socialist Republic.

20 MAY 1941

In the course of the Eighteenth Festival of the International Society for Contemporary Music, at Columbia University, Bernard WAGENAAR, Dutch-born American composer of neo-Baroque music, conducts a broadcast performance of his *Triple Concerto* for flute, cello, harp and orchestra.

The absolute first performance of Wagenaar's *Triple Concerto* took place in Philadelphia on 18 March 1938, with Georges Barrère, Carlos Salzedo and Horace Britt as soloists. The New York premiere followed four days later, on 22 March 1938.

23 OCTOBER 1941

Scenario, tone poem by Jerome KERN based on the thematic material of his great song "Ol' Man River" from his musical *Show Boat,* is performed for the first time by the Cleveland Orchestra, Artur Rodzinski conducting.

7 NOVEMBER 1941

Second Symphony, subtitled *Kormtchaya* (stochastic, goal-directed, teleological, leading), by the 49-year-old Russian composer Arthur LOURIÉ, consisting of ten variations without a theme and couched in an austerely modal manner, is performed for the first time by the Boston Symphony Orchestra under the direction of Serge Koussevitzky.

9 APRIL 1942
Fourth Symphony by Alexandre GRETCHANINOV, Russian composer of deeply felt national roots now dwelling in New York, dedicated to the memory of Tchaikovsky, in four movements each containing quotations from Tchaikovsky's works, is performed for the first time by the New York Philharmonic, John Barbirolli conducting.

1 MAY 1942
Gold and the Señor Commandante, ballet by the 21-year-old American composer William BERGSMA, is performed for the first time in Rochester, New York.

13 APRIL 1943

The Testament of Freedom by Randall THOMPSON, for men's voices and orchestra, written for the 200th anniversary of the University of Virginia at Charlottesville, to a text from the writings of Thomas Jefferson, the University's founder, with a musical score conceived in the spirit of simplicity, leaving not a discord untamed in its prevalent C major, is presented for the first time by the Virginia Glee Club, with the composer at the piano.

The Testament of Freedom was written to commemorate the 200th anniversary of Thomas Jefferson's birth (not the 200th anniversary of the University of Virginia, which was founded in 1819).

5 SEPTEMBER 1943
The Automatic Pistol, chorus by Ellis KOHS, to text from the U.S. Army Weapons Manual, is performed for the first time by the Army Music Chorus in Washington, D.C., William Strickland conducting.

18 OCTOBER 1943
Symphony by the 30-year-old American composer Jerome MOROSS, in four movements, the third being based on the hobo song "Midnight Special," is performed for the first time by the Seattle Symphony under the direction of Thomas Beecham.

24 NOVEMBER 1943
Symphonie de danses by André JOLIVET is performed for the first time in Paris.

5 December 1943
Das Werbekleid, "merry opera in three acts" by the 46-year-old Viennese composer Franz SALMHOFER, to his own libretto wherein an ambitious Tyrolean villager spurns a hefty local milkmaid for a slender-legged city damsel, a happy ending vouchsafed when the abandoned maiden dons a "Werbekleid," a lucky ancestral attire which had helped many of its previous wearers to win back a fickle lover, the whole thing set to music in an engagingly waltzing manner, is produced in Salzburg.

18 April 1944

Cécile CHAMINADE, French composeress of ingratiatingly harmonious piano pieces adorned with endearingly sentimental titles, possessing a perennial appeal to frustrated spinsters and emotional piano teachers, dies in war-darkened Monte Carlo at the hopeless age of eighty-six.

Chaminade died on 13 April (not 18 April) 1944.

24 October 1944

A Stopwatch and an Ordnance Map, a realistic piece of wartime music by Samuel BARBER, scored for men's chorus and kettledrums, is performed for the first time in Columbus, Ohio.

The absolute premiere of Barber's *A Stopwatch and an Ordnance Map* took place in Philadelphia on 23 April 1940 (not in Columbus on 24 October 1944).

31 October 1944
Sebastian, ballet by the 33-year-old Italian-born composer Gian Carlo MENOTTI, is produced for the first time in New York.

5 December 1944
Cinq danses rituelles, orchestral suite by André JOLIVET, which received the Prix de l'État in 1942, is performed for the first time in a Paris, now cleansed of Nazi infestation.

20 December 1944
Il Giuoco del Barone, opera by the Italian composer Valentino BUCCHI, is performed for the first time in Florence.

22 March 1945
First Symphony, subtitled *Sinfonia pastorale,* by the Swedish composer Hilding HALLNÄS, is performed for the first time in Göteborg.

8 April 1945

At the approach of the final hour of Nazidämmerung, the Austrian conductor Leopold REICHSWEIN, one of the few musicians who was lured by the opportunities for individual and racial aggrandizement offered by the Nazi doctrine, kills himself in Vienna.

The name of the Austrian conductor is Leopold REICHWEIN (not Reichswein).

17 August 1945

Gino MARINUZZI, 63-year-old Italian conductor and composer of Wagneromorphic operas and of a jubilee piece on the occasion of Hitler's meeting with Mussolini, is murdered in the streets of the disoriented and turbulent city of Milan by Italian resistance fighters on the justified suspicion of being a militant Fascist.

Gino Marinuzzi was not murdered; he died of hepatitis.

15 September 1945

Anton VON WEBERN, 61-year-old Austrian composer of music so subtle and succinct that not only notes, but intervals, dynamic marks and durations assume thematic significance, philosopher-musician and pioneer of integral serialism as an expansion of the dodecaphonic concept formulated by his master Arnold Schoenberg, is accidentally shot and killed by an American soldier of the army of occupation in Mittersill, near Salzburg, in the house of his son-in-law suspected of black market speculation. (Webern's son-in-law was subsequently sentenced to one year's imprisonment; the unwitting killer of Anton von Webern, though cleared of blame, died in 1950 of acute alcoholism induced by remorse.)

The name of the American who shot Webern was Raymond Bell, a cook in the U.S. Army. Bell died on 3 September 1955 (not in 1950), as a result of alcoholism aggravated by remorse over his murderous deed.

10 November 1945
First Symphony by the English composer Sir Michael TIPPETT, written in an extremely self-contained contrapuntal idiom, with a double fugue in the finale concluding on a chord of the eleventh which dissolves into a unison on E, is performed for the first time in Liverpool.

27 November 1945
Second Symphony by the 22-year-old American composer Peter MENNIN (his real surname was Mennini; he was of Italian parentage) is performed for the first time at the Eastman School of Music in Rochester, New York.

23 MARCH 1946

Airborne, oratorio for narrator, singers and orchestra, by the American composer Marc BLITZSTEIN, depicting in twelve vivid musical tableaux the history of human flight from Icarus to the fighting airmen of World War II, with brassy detonations punctuating the terse declarative prose of the narration, is performed for the first time by the New York City Symphony Orchestra, Leonard Bernstein conducting.

Airborne by Marc Blitzstein is a symphony (not an oratorio).

20 APRIL 1946

Deirdre of the Sorrows, first Canadian grand opera, dealing with a Celtic love triangle in Ulster in A.D. 1, composed by Healey WILLAN, himself an Ulster Celt, is performed for the first time, in concert form, by the Canadian Broadcasting Corporation in Toronto.

The true title of Willan's opera is simply *Deirdre*.

2 MAY 1946

Equinox, opera by Marjan KOZINA, 38-year-old Slovenian composer, to a libretto dealing with a love contest in 1860 at a Dalmatian port town between a native youth and an American visitor, both infatuated with the same Slovenian girl, is produced in Ljubljana.

5 MAY 1946

From These States by Ernst BACON, a "cycle of people's songs" presented as a symphonic reflection of geographic, demographic and psychological aspects of America, is performed for the first time in New York.

21 MAY 1946

Central Park in the Dark by Charles IVES, written in 1906, is performed for the first time at Columbia University, New York. It is in three-part form, with strings maintaining the dreamy shimmering of the dark, in intervallic columns, first in major thirds (forming whole-tone harmonies), then in quartal structures, then in tritones overlapped by fifths, then in pure quintal harmonies, while the middle section erupts in shrill sounds of the youthful revelry contrasted with the still continuing lyric reverie. (A forgotten performance of the piece was given about 1907. Ives wrote in a hasty note: "*Central Park* was played between the acts in a downtown theater in New York, in 1906 or 1907. The players had a hard time with it—the piano player got mad, stopped in the middle, and kicked in the bass drum. However it would be hardly fair to those old fellers who stood up for a dangerous job to say this was the first performance. The present 1946 performance was the first." An alternative title was *A Con-*

templation of Nothing Serious, or *Central Park in the Dark in the Good Old Summer Time.*)

17 JANUARY 1947

First Symphony by the 30-year-old Finnish composer Einar ENGLUND is performed for the first time by the Helsinki Philharmonic, Leo Funtek conducting.

28 JANUARY 1947

Reynaldo HAHN, Venezuelan-born Parisian composer of urbane theater music, mundane entertainment pieces, and daintily cadenced, lavender-scented chansons, who was the slender model of the delicately perfumed, sensitively capricious character of Vinteul in Proust's *A la recherche du temps passé,* dies in Paris at the age of seventy-one.

Reynaldo Hahn died at the age of seventy-two (not seventy-one).

19 MARCH 1947

The Minotaur, ballet by the 38-year-old American composer Elliott CARTER, depicting in somberly dramatic tones the classical horrors of the gluttonously carnivorous Cretan bull, with Ariadne unwinding her quaquaversally labyrinthine thread to lead the heroic but ungentlemanly tauricide Theseus out to safety, is performed for the first time by the New York Ballet Society.

The date of the first performance of *The Minotaur* was 26 March 1947. The performance was originally scheduled for 19 March, but was postponed because of technical difficulties. The corrected date is confirmed by a notice in the *New York Times* of 23 March 1947 and in a review published on 6 April 1947.

19 MARCH 1947

Willem PIJPER, Dutch composer of atmospheric symphonies, coloristic chamber music and impressionistic chansons, whose persistent use of the scale of alternating whole tones and semitones caused it to be known in Holland as the "Pijper scale" (Rimsky-Korsakov had a long established priority on it, and in Russia it is known as "Rimsky-Korsakov scale"), dies at Leidschendam at the age of fifty-two.

Willem Pijper died on 18 March (not 19 March) 1947.

26 MARCH 1947

Tic-Tac, operetta by the Swiss composer Willy BURKHARD, is performed for the first time in Zürich.

Tic-Tac is an operetta by Paul BURKHARD (not by Willy Burkhard, who never wrote operettas).

21 DECEMBER 1947

Saul, opera in five scenes by the German composer Hermann REUTTER, to the biblical story of a tortured superstitious king of the Hebrews, punctuated by Handelian trumpet calls and tinctured by modern Angst, expressed by tumid dissonances and corrosive orientalistic chromatics, is produced by the Hamburg State Opera.

The Hamburg performance of the opera *Saul* was that of its third version; the original work, in one act, was first performed in Baden-Baden on 15 July 1928; the second version was produced in Düsseldorf on 18 November 1928.

29 FEBRUARY 1948

Die Nachtschwalbe, "dramatic nocturne" in one act by the 45-year-old Manchurian-born German-Estonian composer Boris BLACHER, to a libretto centered on a company of pimply pimps and putative putains in a small German town, during which the head of the vice squad finds out that one of the "night swallows" is his orphaned daughter, set to music in poignant dissonant harmonies and asymmetrically angular rhythms, is produced in Leipzig.

Die Nachtschwalbe was first performed on 22 February (not 29 February) 1948.

4 MARCH 1948
Second Symphony, subtitled *Sinfonia notturna*, by the Swedish composer Hilding HALLNÄS, is performed for the first time in Göteborg.

26 MARCH 1948

Hanns EISLER, German composer of atonal symphonies and optimistically triadic proletarian songs, who came to the United States in 1942, leaves America as a "voluntary deportee," after the House of Representatives Committee on Un-American Activities, in its campaign directed mainly against Eleanor Roosevelt and other liberals who helped to save Eisler's life by obtaining an American visa for him, uncovers the fact of his brief membership in the German Communist Party in 1926, and thunders that "he has perjured his way in and out of the United States at will, going to Soviet Russia and other countries when he pleased."

I recall reading in a French newspaper in 1933 that Hitler put a price on my head. I was not surprised. But I never dreamed that I would experience the same sort of thing in the United States, a country that I love. (Eisler's state-

278

ment in Los Angeles upon posting $1,000 bail for himself and $500 for his wife pending a hearing with the Commissioner of Immigration to answer charges of perjury.)

Hanns Eisler came to the United States in 1933 (not 1942).

9 APRIL 1948
Saga of the Mississippi, tone poem by the 48-year-old American composer Harl McDONALD, in two parts, *Prehistoric Mississippi* and *Father of Waters*, is performed for the first time by the Philadelphia Orchestra, Eugene Ormandy conducting.

3 OCTOBER 1948
Third Symphony, subtitled *Little Symphony*, by the Swedish composer Hilding HALLNÄS, is performed for the first time in Göteborg.

13 NOVEMBER 1948

Arnold SCHOENBERG addresses an indignant letter to the editors of the *Saturday Review of Literature* protesting against the unlicensed use of his method of composition with twelve tones related only to one another, in Thomas Mann's musicosophical novel *Doctor Faustus* featuring a mythical German composer of 12-tone music, Adrian Leverkühn (1885–1943), who wrote dissonances to express hope and gladness and used consonant triadic harmonies to portray deep anguish.

The dates for the mythical composer Adrian Leverkühn in Thomas Mann's novel *Doktor Faustus* are 1885–1940 (not 1885–1943). (For another Mann-related contretemps, involving Gustav MAHLER, see Part One, 16 June 1973, above.)

18 MARCH 1949
Fourth Symphony, subtitled *The Cycle*, for chorus and orchestra by the 25-year-old American composer Peter MENNIN, is performed for the first time in New York.

3 APRIL 1949
First Symphony, subtitled *Jean de la Peur*, by the 34-year-old French composer Marcel LANDOWSKI, in three movements of deep mystical content descriptive of the pious individual Jean's struggle against fear in his soul, is performed for the first time in Paris.

17 OCTOBER 1949

On the centenary of CHOPIN's death, Paulina CZERNICKA, a middle-aged Polish lady pathologically obsessed with the image of Chopin, who manufactured and circulated a number of letters purportedly written by Chopin to Delfina Potocka, which represented him as a pornographic sensualist using anachronistic verbal vulgarity (some obscene Polish slang found in the letters was of World War I vintage), shoots herself to death in Warsaw. (In October 1961 the Chopin Institute in Warsaw officially declared the correspondence to be a forgery.)

Paulina Czernicka killed herself not by shooting but by taking an overdose of sleeping pills, after a violent quarrel with her son, and died in the early morning of 2 September (not 17 October) 1949.

❧ *1950-1959* ❧

18 JANUARY 1950
The Barrier, two-act opera on the subject of race relations in Georgia by Jan MEYEROWITZ, to a libretto by Langston Hughes based on his *Mulatto* and *Father and Son*, is produced for the first time at Columbia University in New York.

19 FEBRUARY 1950
Concerto for flute and string orchestra by André JOLIVET, in four contrasting movements, is performed for the first time in Paris under the composer's direction, with Jean Pierre Rampal as soloist.

2 APRIL 1950
Fifth Symphony by the 26-year-old American composer Peter MENNIN is performed for the first time by the Dallas Symphony Orchestra, Walter Hendl conducting.

18 MAY 1950

The Jumping Frog of Calaveras County, opera in two scenes by the 27-year-old Berlin-born American composer Lukas Foss, after Mark Twain's famous story of a frog race, is performed for the first time at the University of Indiana in Bloomington, during the week in May when actual jumping frog contests are held annually in Calaveras County, California.

Foss's *The Jumping Frog of Calaveras County* was produced at Indiana University (not the University of Indiana) in Bloomington.

9 AUGUST 1950

Nicolai MIASKOVSKY, Russian composer of twenty-seven symphonies, the greatest number written by anyone since Haydn, and teacher of a generation of Soviet composers, dies in Moscow of an inoperable intestinal cancer, at the age of sixty-nine.

Nicolai Miaskovsky died on 8 August (not 9 August) 1950.

22 JANUARY 1951

Ernst VON DOHNÁNYI appears as soloist in the first performance anywhere with the Florida State Symphony Orchestra in Tallahassee (where he made his home in 1949 as professor of music at Florida State College) of his *Second Piano Concerto* in B minor, written in Austria in 1947.

Dohnányi's *Second Piano Concerto* was first performed on 3 December 1947 in Sheffield, England; the Tallahassee performance was the first in America.

18 MARCH 1951
Fourth Symphony, subtitled *Autochthonous*, by William Grant STILL, in four movements, representing the optimistic, the pensive, the humorous and the humanistic aspects of the American character, is performed for the first time by the Oklahoma City Symphony Orchestra, Victor Alessandro conducting.

22 MARCH 1951

Willem MENGELBERG, German conductor, who excelled in performances of Beethoven, Mahler and Strauss (the score of *Ein Heldenleben* is dedicated to him), dies in Chur, Switzerland, an exile from his native Holland, where he was barred from conducting for his cultural collaboration with the Nazis during the Hitlerian occupation.

Willem Mengelberg was Dutch (not German); he died on 21 March (not 22 March) 1951.

10 APRIL 1951
Violin Concerto by the 44-year-old American composer David VAN VACTOR is performed for the first time in Knoxville, Tennessee.

12 MAY 1951
Krešimir BARANOVIĆ, eminent Croatian composer, conducts the first performance of his comic opera *Nevjesta od Cedtingrada (The Bride from Cedtingrad)* in Belgrade.

19 JUNE 1951

André JOLIVET plays in Strasbourg the piano part in the first performance of his *Piano Concerto*, subtitled *Equatoriales*, evoking in its three movements the statically placid, humidly erotic and pacifically contemplative geographical regions lying on the equator, Central Africa, the East Indies and Polynesia, making colorful use of drums, bells, shakers, vibrators and other indigenous percussion instruments.

André Jolivet did not play but conducted the first performance of his *Piano Concerto*; Lucette Descaves was piano soloist.

8 NOVEMBER 1951
Theme and Variations for orchestra by the 37-year-old American composer Charles MILLS is performed for the first time by the New York Philharmonic Orchestra, Dimitri Mitropoulus conducting.

27 NOVEMBER 1951

Henri COLLET, French music critic who coined the title "Les Six Français," dies in Paris at the age of sixty-six.

Henri Collet died on 23 November (not 27 November) 1951.

27 JANUARY 1952
The Pulitzer Prize–winning *Symphonie concertante* for piano, viola, trumpet and orchestra by the 37-year-old American composer Gail KUBIK is performed for the first time in New York.

13 FEBRUARY 1952

Alfred EINSTEIN, eminent German music scholar and lexicographer, first cousin of Albert Einstein, dies in his California retreat at El Cerrito, at the age of seventy-one.

Alfred and Albert Einstein were friends and came from the same part of Germany. Although they themselves believed that they were related, a thorough search through birth and death registers for many generations failed to discover a common ancestor.

3 APRIL 1952
Third Symphony by the American composer Roger GOEB is performed for the first time by the CBS Symphony under the direction of Leopold Stokowski.

6 APRIL 1952
First Concerto for String Orchestra by the 40-year-old Swedish composer Allan PETTERSSON is performed for the first time on the Swedish Radio in Stockholm.

17 APRIL 1952

Fourth Symphony, subtitled *Metamorfose Sinfonische*, by the Swedish composer Hilding HALLNÄS, is performed for the first time in Göteborg.

3 MAY 1952

Fifth Symphony by the 56-year-old Austrian composer Johann Nepomuk DAVID is performed for the first time in Stuttgart.

17 JULY 1952

A Provincial Episode; or, Gay Little World, chamber opera in one act and one scene by Max WALD, to a libretto by the composer, is produced for the first time, with two-piano accompaniment, at Ohio University in Athens, Ohio.

12 OCTOBER 1952

Concerto for harp and chamber orchestra by André JOLIVET in three cyclic movements is performed for the first time at the Donaueschingen Festival.

28 OCTOBER 1952

The first public concert of tape recorder music in the United States takes place at the Museum of Modern Art in New York, featuring *Sonic Contours* by the 40-year-old American composer Vladimir USSACHEVSKY, and three pieces by the 52-year-old American composer Otto LUENING: *Low Speed* and *Invention* for tape, and *Fantasy in Space* for flute solo and tape on which Luening himself was recorded, by a sound-on-sound method, playing four different flute parts, and which in turns accompanies Luening as live soloist.

20 NOVEMBER 1952

Francis POULENC plays the solo piano part in the first performance of his *Aubade*, "concerto choréographique," at the Opéra-Comique in Paris.

Poulenc's *Aubade* was first performed on 18 June 1929 (not 20 November 1952).

29 NOVEMBER 1952

Concerto for piano four hands by the 37-year-old American composer Vincent PERSICHETTI is performed for the first time in Pittsburgh.

2 JUNE 1953

Homage to the Queen, ballet by the 31-year-old British composer Malcolm ARNOLD, is performed for the first time at Covent Garden in London, in honor of the coronation of Queen Elizabeth II.

22 July 1953

Endymion, opera by the 49-year-old Australian composer John Henry ANTILL, is performed for the first time in Sydney.

8 November 1953

The Magic Apple Tree, ballet by the 23-year-old Russian composer Andrei PETROV, is performed for the first time in Leningrad.

20 November 1953

The Taking of T'ung Khan, tone poem by the 34-year-old Chinese-born American composer Jacob AVSHALOMOV, with an orientally flavored orchestral score, is performed for the first time by the Detroit Symphony Orchestra, Leopold Stokowski conducting.

7 December 1953

First Symphony by the 25-year-old German-born American composer Samuel ADLER is performed for the first time in Dallas, Texas.

15 December 1953

Fables by Ernst BACON for narrator and orchestra, partly to his own texts, is performed for the first time in New York.

17 January 1954

Sixth Symphony by the industrious English symphonist Edmund RUBBRA, written in a rhapsodically neo-romantic idiom charged with dissonant counterpoint, but strongly anchored in tonal centers, is performed for the first time in London.

Edmund Rubbra's *Sixth Symphony* was first performed on 17 November (not 17 January) 1954.

4 March 1954

First Symphony by the Czech composer Karel HUSA is performed for the first time by the Belgian Radio Orchestra in Brussels.

15 March 1954

The University Greys, opera in two acts and nine scenes by the 47-year-old American composer Arthur KREUTZ, to a libretto based on Maud Morrow Brown's novel of the same name in which a young man leaves his university studies to go to war, returning to die in the arms of his sweetheart whom he had married during his first leave, is produced for the first time by the University of Mississippi. (The work was commissioned by the University in 1953 and revived in 1961 to commemorate the centennial of the Eleventh Mississippi Regiment's departure to war. The Greys constituted a regiment drawn from men at the University, none of whom survived the war.)

20 MARCH 1954
Rhapsodic Variations for orchestra and electronic tape by Otto LUENING and Vladimir USSACHEVSKY, the first score ever composed that combined electronic sounds with human musicians, is performed for the first time by the Louisville Orchestra in New York.

14 APRIL 1954
Twenty-five Pages, an "open form" work for piano solo by the 27-year-old American composer Earle BROWN, a paradigm of a musical "mobile" in which some fragments, and indeed whole pages, can be freely permutated, is played for the first time in New York by the prime votary of the musical avant-garde, David Tudor.

18 APRIL 1954
Profile for Orchestra by the 30-year-old American composer Benjamin LEES is performed for the first time in New York.

9 MAY 1954
Second Symphony in a single long movement by the turbulently melancholic Swedish composer Allan PETTERSSON, thematically set in a series of widely dispersed unstable intervals, ending in a deeply sunk moribund organ point on C, is performed for the first time on Swedish Radio in Stockholm.

24 MAY 1954
The first National Macedonian opera, *Goce*, by the 29-year-old composer Kiril MAKEDONSKI to his own libretto depicting the uprising, under the leadership of Goce Delčev, of the people of Macedonia against Ottoman rule in 1903, is produced in Skopje.

27 MAY 1954
Hello, Out There, opera by the American composer Jack BEESON, is produced for the first time in New York.

17 JUNE 1954
Violin Concerto by the South African-born English composer John JOUBERT is performed for the first time at the York Festival in England.

14 SEPTEMBER 1954

Ivesiana, a ballet score put together from several short works by Charles IVES, *In the Inn, In the Night, Central Park in the Dark* and *The Unanswered Question,* is performed for the first time in this collage, choreographed by George Balanchine in New York.

28 SEPTEMBER 1954

Concerto des oracles for baritone, piano and orchestra by Germaine TAILLEFERRE, the sole female member of Les Six, is performed for the first time in Hilversum, Holland, with the 62-year-old composer playing the piano part.

26 OCTOBER 1954

Franco ALFANO, Italian composer of effective melodramatic operas, dies in San Remo at the age of seventy-eight.

Franco Alfano died on 27 October (not 26 October) 1954.

20 NOVEMBER 1954

The Cask of Amontillado, opera after Edgar Allan Poe by the 30-year-old black American composer Julia PERRY, is performed for the first time at Columbia University in New York.

30 NOVEMBER 1954

Concerto for bassoon, string orchestra, harp and piano by André JOLIVET in four varied movements, *Recitativo, Allegro giovale, Largo cantabile* and *Fugato,* is performed for the first time in Paris.

2 DECEMBER 1954

Déserts, symphonic poem by Edgar VARÈSE, scored for wind instruments, percussion and electronic sounds, the first work ever composed for orchestral instruments combined with a pre-recorded magnetic tape and conceived in an athematic idiom of agglutinated melorhythmic molecules, according to Varèse's doctrine of "organized sound," is performed for the first time in Paris. (*Poem in Cycles and Bels* for tape recorder and orchestra by Otto LUENING and Vladimir USSACHEVSKY was composed later than *Déserts,* but had its first performance two weeks earlier than Varèse's work.)

An even earlier work for live instruments combined with electronic sounds by Luening and Ussachevsky was their *Rhapsodic Variations,* first performed by the Louisville Orchestra in New York on 20 March 1954.

12 MARCH 1955
Charlie PARKER, nicknamed "Bird" (his real forenames were Charles
Christopher), black American jazz saxophone player, a pioneer archpriest
of bebop, dies at the unfulfilled age of thirty-four in a state of physical
exhaustion caused by alcoholism and drug addiction, in the luxurious
New York apartment of his ardent admirer Baroness Pannonica de
Konigswarter.

12 MARCH 1955
First Symphony, in four movements, by the 34-year-old Soviet Armenian
composer Karen KHACHATURIAN, nephew of Aram Khachaturian, is performed for the first time in Moscow.

21 APRIL 1955
Il Cappello di paglia di Firenze (The Little Straw Hat of Florence), comic
opera by Nino ROTA, is performed for the first time at the Teatro Massimo
in Palermo.

30 APRIL 1955
Kineska priča (Chinese Tale), ballet by the 60-year-old Croatian composer
Krešimir BARANOVIĆ, is performed for the first time in Belgrade.

11 JUNE 1955
Trumpet Concerto by the 25-year-old Russian composer Alexandra
PAKHMUTOVA is performed for the first time in Moscow.

22 JUNE 1955
Sixth Symphony by Johann Nepomuk DAVID is performed for the first time
in Wiesbaden.

12 JULY 1955
The Hollow Men for chorus, clarinet, three trombones and piano by the
26-year-old American composer Donald KEATS, to words by T. S. Eliot, is
performed for the first time in Hamburg, Germany.

14 NOVEMBER 1955
Sixth Symphony by Henry COWELL is performed for the first time in
Houston, Texas.

3 FEBRUARY 1956
Clarinet Concerto by Elie SIEGMEISTER, written in a vesuviatingly jazzy
manner with nostalgic remissions in the blues tempo, is performed for the
first time by the Oklahoma City Symphony, Guy Fraser Harrison conducting, with Earl Thomas as soloist.

15 FEBRUARY 1956

The Wife of Martin Guerre, opera by the 34-year-old American composer William BERGSMA, is produced in New York.

15 FEBRUARY 1956

Declamations for string orchestra and piano by Benjamin LEES is performed for the first time in Oklahoma City.

19 FEBRUARY 1956

Cello Concerto by the 32-year-old American composer Peter MENNIN is performed for the first time by Leonard Rose and the Juilliard School of Music Orchestra under the direction of Jean Morel, in New York.

24 FEBRUARY 1956

The first performance is given in New York of the *Fifth Symphony* by Walter PISTON, commissioned by the Juilliard School of Music to commemorate the fiftieth anniversary of its foundation, written in a characteristic Pistonian Bostonian style and idiom, abstaining from using tonally explicit key signatures, but observing a sense of tonality, set in three symmetrically converging movements: (1) *Lento*, in rolling, barca-rolling meter as an introduction to a propulsive, impulsive *Allegro con Spirito* soon initiating a deep, steep descent into an initial relented *Lento*; (2) *Adagio*, a dirge surging from the lower depths, embroidered with microrhythmic melismas, finally returning to the tenebrous caverns of the bass register; and (3) *Allegro lieto*, in prancing, dancing time in a mood of secular laetification in a clearly implied white key of perlucent C major. (Piston's *Sixth Symphony* received its first performance three months before, in Boston, on 25 November 1955.)

12 APRIL 1956

First Symphony by the South African-born English composer John JOUBERT is performed for the first time in Hull, England.

26 APRIL 1956

First Piano Concerto by Benjamin LEES is performed for the first time in Vienna.

4 JUNE 1956

At the second concert of the Thirtieth Festival of the International Society for Contemporary Music in Stockholm the following program of chamber music is presented: . . . *Violin Sonata* in three movements by the 21-year-old Icelandic composer LEIFUR. . . .

288

The name of the Icelandic composer is Leifur THÓRARINSSON (not simply Leifur).

27 JUNE 1956

Pane Lesna Rusalim, opera in three acts by the 47-year-old Rumanian composer Paul CONSTANTINESCU, dealing with an early 19th-century peasant girl participant in a Rumanian rebellion against the Turkish overlords, is performed for the first time in Bucharest.

The title is *Pană Lesnea Rusalim* (not *Pane Lesna Rusalim*).

18 AUGUST 1956
On the Nature of Things, a spatial work by the 42-year-old American composer Henry BRANT, scored for string orchestra, wind instruments and glockenspiel, is performed for the first time in Bennington, Vermont.

28 AUGUST 1956
Frescoes of Piero della Francesca, a symphonic suite in three movements by Bohuslav MARTINŮ, reflecting the deep veneration for the austere Italian Renaissance painter, is performed for the first time in Salzburg.

10 OCTOBER 1956

The First "Warsaw Autumn" International Festival of Contemporary Music opens in Warsaw, inaugurating a series of concerts concluding on 21 October 1956, presenting works by [among twenty-five established composers] . . . Jean-Louis MARTINOT . . . Henri BARRAUD . . . and a number of contemporary Polish composers [including] . . . Teodor ROGALSKI. . . .

Correct spellings: Jean-Louis MARTINET (not Martinot); Henry (not Henri) BARRAUD; Theodor (not Teodor) ROGALSKI, who was Rumanian, not Polish.

14 OCTOBER 1956
Third Symphony by Alan HOVHANESS is performed for the first time by the Symphony of the Air in New York, Leopold Stokowski conducting.

30 OCTOBER 1956
Piano Concerto by the 51-year-old British composer Sir Michael TIPPETT is performed for the first time in Birmingham.

21 NOVEMBER 1956
Third Symphony by the Swedish composer Allan PETTERSSON is performed for the first time in Göteborg.

1 DECEMBER 1956

Candide, musical comedy by Leonard BERNSTEIN based on Voltaire's novella retailing the extraordinary adventures of an unregenerate idealist who retains his optimism through all the tortuous peripeteia during his forced peregrinations, set to music with a sense of hedonistic persiflage, and incorporating parodies on classical dance music, as well as the first detected twelve-tone row in any musical comedy (in the introduction to the second act), is produced in New York.

A new redaction of Leonard Bernstein's *Candide*, as an "opera house version," with considerable changes in the libretto, was produced by the New York City Opera on 13 October 1982.

14 DECEMBER 1956
The Open Window, opera by the 35-year-old British composer Malcolm ARNOLD, is produced in London.

6 MAY 1957
The Boor, one-act opera by the 29-year-old American composer Dominick ARGENTO, to a libretto based on a play by Chekhov dealing with an ill-tempered young man who is about to propose to the lady of his heart but ruins his chances by starting a boorish argument about an inconsequential matter, set to music in a modernistically rambunctious vein, is performed for the first time in Rochester, New York.

22 JUNE 1957
First Symphony in five movements by Karl Amadeus HARTMANN, subtitled *Versuch eines Requiem*, for contralto solo and orchestra, composed in 1936 and revised several times, is performed in a final version in Vienna with words from Walt Whitman's *Leaves of Grass* in the solo voice.

31 JULY 1957

Sem DRESDEN, prime Dutch composer, author of romantic songs and instrumental pieces, dies at The Hague, at the age of seventy-six.

Sem Dresden died on 30 July (not 31 July) 1957.

1 SEPTEMBER 1957

Dennis BRAIN, 36-year-old British virtuoso horn player, scion of a family of horn players, is killed in an automobile accident after hitting a tree on a winding road in Hatfield, Hertfordshire, while driving at night at high speed from Birmingham to London.

Dennis Brain was returning from a performance in Edinburgh (not Birmingham) when he was killed in an automobile crash.

2 DECEMBER 1957
Third Symphony by the 36-year-old British composer Malcolm ARNOLD is performed for the first time in London.

4 DECEMBER 1957
Pierre BOULEZ conducts the first performance in Cologne of his work *Le Visage nuptial* for soprano, contralto, chorus and orchestra.

19 DECEMBER 1957
The Music Man, musical play by the 55-year-old American composer Meredith WILLSON, to his own lyrics dealing with the satirical yet somehow patriotic subject of a traveling salesman of band uniforms and musical instruments who sold them to hicktown suckers, opens on Broadway in New York.

15 JANUARY 1958
Second Symphony by the 57-year-old American composer Colin McPHEE, utilizing pentatonic scale forms and other melodic material collected by him during his sojourn in Bali, is performed for the first time by the Louisville Orchestra under the direction of Robert Whitney.

10 FEBRUARY 1958
Mythical Beasts by the American composer Henry BRANT, scored for soprano and sixteen instruments, is performed for the first time in New York.

12 FEBRUARY 1958
Second Symphony by the 29-year-old German-born American composer Samuel ADLER is performed for the first time in Dallas, Texas.

27 FEBRUARY 1958
Love in Transit, opera by the 40-year-old British composer Richard ARNELL, is performed for the first time in London.

10 MARCH 1958
Pan by the 63-year-old Croatian composer Krešimir BARANOVIĆ, scored for narrator, voices and orchestra, is performed for the first time in Belgrade.

14 MARCH 1958
Third Concerto for String Orchestra by the innovative, but determinedly romantic Swedish composer Allan PETTERSSON is performed for the first time on the Swedish Radio in Stockholm.

2 APRIL 1958
Ninth Symphony in E minor by Ralph Vaughn WILLIAMS, his last, written at the age of 85 . . . is performed for the first time, a few months before the composer's death, by the London Philharmonic Orchestra, Sir Adrian Boult conducting.

The first performance of Williams' *Ninth Symphony* was conducted by Malcolm Sargent (not by Sir Adrian Boult).

18 APRIL 1958

First Symphony by the 24-year-old American composer Easley BLACKWOOD (completed by him on 9 December 1952, at the age of 19) . . . is performed for the first time by the Boston Symphony Orchestra, Charles Munch conducting.

Blackwood's *First Symphony* was written between November 1954 and December 1955 (not in 1952). He did not complete it at the age of nineteen, but at the age of twenty-two.

30 MAY 1958

First Violin Concerto by Béla BARTÓK (composed between 1 July 1907 and 5 February 1908) in two contrasting movements, *Andante Sostenuto* (later incorporated into the first section of *Two Portraits* for orchestra), representing an Ideal and based on a "personal" leitmotiv, D—F-sharp—A—C-sharp, of the Hungarian violinist Geyer Steffy for whom the Concerto was written, and who was in possession of the unpublished and unperformed manuscript until her death in 1957, and *Allegro giocoso*, a hedonistic rondo, is performed for the first time in Basel.

The name of the violinist is Steffi Geyer (not Geyer Steffy, which would be a Hungarian inversion); she died in 1956 (not 1957).

28 NOVEMBER 1958
Fourth Symphony, subtitled *Crazy Horse Symphony* as a tribute to the legendary Sioux Indian Chief, by the 44-year-old American composer Charles MILLS, is performed for the first time in Cincinnati.

8 FEBRUARY 1959
Third Symphony by Elie SIEGMEISTER is performed for the first time in Oklahoma City.

17 FEBRUARY 1959

Percussion Concerto by André JOLIVET in four movements, *Robuste, Dolent, Rapidement* and *Allègrement,* is performed for the first time in Paris.

24 MARCH 1959

Gruppen, spatial work by the 30-year-old German apostle of the avant-garde Karlheinz STOCKHAUSEN, for three chamber orchestras, each governed by individual serial parameters determining meter, rhythm, intervallic structure, dynamics, instrumentation and differentiated noises, with three synchronized conductors beating time in three different tempi ($M_1 = 70$, $M_2 = 113.5$, $M_3 = 94$), is performed for the first time at Cologne.

The date of the first performance of *Gruppen* was 24 March 1958 (not 1959).

19 APRIL 1959

Third Symphony by the 35-year-old American composer Ned ROREM, in five classically designed movements, opening with a Passacaglia, and couched in a euphonious idiom with an invigorating injection of non-toxic dissonances, is performed for the first time in New York.

Rorem's *Third Symphony* was first performed on 16 April (not 19 April) 1959. On the same program was *Second Symphony,* subtitled *Titans,* by the 30-year-old American composer William Joseph RUSSO.

27 APRIL 1959

The Hunted, opera by the 26-year-old American composer Martin MAILMAN, is performed for the first time in Rochester, New York.

15 AUGUST 1959

Alexandra, opera by the Israeli composer Menahem AVIDOM, dealing with the martyrdom of Alexandra, the last ruler of the Hasnonean dynasty, is produced in Tel Aviv.

12 OCTOBER 1959

Frigate Victory, opera by the Russian composer Boris ARAPOV, after Pushkin's novella *The Moor of Peter the Great,* is given its radio premiere in Leningrad.

15 NOVEMBER 1959

Third Symphony by Ned ROREM is performed for the first time by the Denver Symphony.

This was not the first performance of Rorem's *Third Symphony*; its first performance took place in New York on 16 April 1959.

19 NOVEMBER 1959

La Notte di un Nevrastenico, opera buffa by the 47-year-old Italian composer Nino ROTA, dealing with sexual frustrations of a neurasthenic youth bedeviled by the amorous groans made by a heterosexual couple occupying an adjacent room in his hotel, is performed for the first time in concert form in Turin.

La Notte di un Nevrastenico was first performed (in concert form) on 9 July (not 19 November) 1959.

᧞ *1960-1969* ᧞

13 FEBRUARY 1960

Sixth Symphony by Jean RIVIER, in four contrasting movements, embanked within the bounds of traditional symphonic forms, is performed for the first time in Warsaw.

The first performance of Rivier's *Sixth Symphony* took place on 11 December 1958 (not 13 February 1960).

26 FEBRUARY 1960

Il Dottore di vetro, radiophonic opera by the 40-year-old Rumanian-born Italian composer Roman VLAD, dealing with a senescent Spanish doctor dissuaded by a scheming barbering surgeon from marrying a nubile damsel who diagnoses the gout from which he suffers as a case of incipient vitrification resulting from unbridled sexual fantasies, is produced in Rome.

Il Dottore di vetro was first performed in Turin on 23 February 1959 (not in Rome on 26 February 1960).

18 MARCH 1960

Antal DORATI, 53-year-old Hungarian conductor, conducts the Minneapolis Symphony Orchestra, of which he is musical director, in the first performance of his *Fifth Symphony*, in five movements, designated by formal content: Sonata (*Vivace con brio*), Variazioni (*Andante*), Scherzo (*Presto*), Adagio (*Notturno*), and Rondo Finale (*Allegro robusto*), without key signatures but converging centripetally on a focal A, with thematic elements derived from chromatic permutation and containing spacious pentatonic melodies of millennial antiquity redolent of the primeval modes of the Szekels and Magyars in immemorial Pannonia, culminating in a terse and curt finale.

This symphony was Dorati's *First* (not his *Fifth*).

31 MARCH 1960

Joseph HAAS, whose liturgic works written in a grand Germanic manner (*Deutsche Singmesse, Deutsche Kindermesse, Deutsche Gloria*) with their emphasis on the hypostatic Germanism of God, seem to justify the appellation "Der Spielmann Gottes" bestowed on him by his admirers, dies in Munich 12 days after his 81st birthday.

Joseph Haas died on 30 March (not 31 March) 1960.

27 APRIL 1960

Constellations for chamber orchestra by the 35-year-old Croatian avant-gardist Milko KELEMEN, in which melodic, rhythmic and dynamic groups continually return in varying combinations, is performed for the first time in Zagreb.

8 MAY 1960

Second Symphony by the 53-year-old American composer Ross Lee FINNEY is performed for the first time by the Philadelphia Orchestra at the Sixty-seventh Annual May Festival at Ann Arbor, Michigan.

This was not the first performance of Finney's *Second Symphony*; the actual world premiere took place in Philadelphia on 13 November 1959.

10 MAY 1960

Stari mladić (The Old Bachelor), opera by the 58-year-old Yugoslav composer Tihomil VIDOŠIĆ, using folk melos of Istria for local color, is produced in Rijeka (Fiume).

11 MAY 1960

Una notte in Paradiso, opera by the 43-year-old Italian composer Valentino BUCCHI, is performed for the first time in Florence.

14 JULY 1960

Sea Symphony for bass-baritone and orchestra by the 70-year-old American composer Philip JAMES is performed for the first time in Frankfurt, Germany.

10 OCTOBER 1960

The Philharmonic Orchestra of Israel opens its international tour in Paris under the direction of Carlo-Maria Giulini in a program containing a *Psalm* by the 25-year-old Israeli composer Noam SHERI.

The correct spelling is Noam SHERIFF (not Sheri).

12 DECEMBER 1960
Eleventh Symphony in C by Darius MILHAUD, pointedly subtitled *Romantique*, with its typically melodian Milhaudean three movements, *Intense, Méditatif, Emporté,* is performed for the first time by the Dallas Symphony Orchestra, as a specially commissioned work, Paul Kletzki conducting.

22 DECEMBER 1960
Die Natali, "chorale preludes for orchestra" by Samuel BARBER, glorifying Christmastide in its Latin title, which means "on the day of the Nativity," and including adroit variations of several Christmas songs, is performed for the first time at Lincoln Center in New York by the Boston Symphony Orchestra under the direction of Charles Munch.

27 JANUARY 1961
Fourth Symphony by the Swedish composer Allan PETTERSSON is performed for the first time in Stockholm.

20 FEBRUARY 1961

Percy GRAINGER, romantic Australian-born pianist and composer whose first steps in music were tenderly fostered by Grieg . . . who wrote folksy pieces with homely English titles . . . and whose own life as a wandering artist was full of heartache . . . romance . . . virtue . . . and eccentricity . . . dies in White Plains, New York, at the age of seventy-eight.

Percy Grainger's Last Will and Testament directed in part:

. . . that my flesh be removed from my bones and the flesh destroyed. I give and bequest my skeleton to the University of Melbourne, Australia, for preservation and possible display in the Grainger Museum.

3 MARCH 1961
Sabbatai Zevi, le faux Messie, "fresque lyrique" in four acts with a prologue, by Alexandre TANSMAN, to a libertto dealing with a seventeenth-century Jewish Kabbalist who inflames his Zionist followers with faith in him as a Messiah destined to assume the throne of Zion in the fatidic year 1666, but is arrested by the Sultan as he tries to enter the

Holy Land, then part of the Ottoman Empire, and embraces the Islamic faith to save himself, is produced in Paris.

17 APRIL 1961
William Arundel ORCHARD, Nestor of Australian composers, conductors and pedagogues, dies six days short of his ninety-fourth birthday, at sea on board *Dominion Monarch*, at Latitude 23°49′ South and Longitude 09°33′ East, off Sydney, Australia.

30 APRIL 1961
Violin Concerto with Lights by the 47-year-old American composer Henry BRANT, wherein kaleidescopically activated beams of light are manipulated by five musicians manning/womanning five push buttons, is performed for the first time in New York.

6 MAY 1961
The Scarlet Letter, first opera written in the United States by Walter KAUFMANN, in three acts to a libretto by the composer based on Hawthorne's novel of the same name set in Salem, Massachusetts, in the seventeenth century, is produced for the first time at Indiana University in Bloomington.

10 MAY 1961
Le Héros et son miroir, surrealist ballet by the 37-year-old avant-garde Croatian composer Milko KELEMEN, a dodecaphonic portrayal of a former hero who contemplates his own image in a retrospective mirror and suffers agonies at recalling his once glorious past, is produced in Paris.

29 MAY 1961
Ninth Symphony, subtitled *Aerosymfonien*, by the 41-year-old Danish composer Niels Viggo BENTZON, is performed for the first time in Odense.

12 JUNE 1961
Hello, Kansas!, a musical play in observance of the hundredth anniversary of the statehood of Kansas by the American composer John POZDRO, is performed for the first time in Lawrence, Kansas.

7 AUGUST 1961
Early Dawn, opera in three acts by the 55-year-old American composer Norman LOCKWOOD to a libretto by Russell Porter dealing with the emotional unrest of two brothers torn between love and patriotism on the eve of the outbreak of the Civil War and making use of homespun folk materials cast in memorable melodies, is produced for the first time at the University of Denver, Thomas Scherman conducting.

2 December 1961

Son of Science, cantata for the machine age for boys' voices, chorus, tenor, piano, percussion and strings by the 31-year-old British composer Philip CANNON, is performed for the first time in Aylesbury.

6 December 1961

The Padrone, two-act opera by George Whitefield CHADWICK, in which the figure of the padrone, in the period of Italian and Irish immigration in the late nineteenth century, symbolizes human corruption in the exploitation of poor immigrants, musically based "on the union of Wagner's symphonic recitative and Italian lyricism," with its four principal characters singing in Italian and all others in English, is produced in an abridged concert version in Carnegie Hall.

9 January 1962

Symphony for Strings by André JOLIVET, in three movements, *Farouche*, *Flottant* and *Trépidant*, is performed for the first time in Paris.

16 March 1962

Die Glücksfischer (Fishermen for Luck), opera in two acts by the 59-year-old German composer Mark LOTHAR, is produced in Nürnberg.

17 May 1962

Concert for Eight, an octet for flute, clarinet, guitar, mandolin, double-bass, accordion, piano and percussion, by the foremost Spanish avant-gardist making his home in London, Roberto GERHARD, is performed for the first time in London.

21 May 1962

Momente, for soprano, singing, speaking and screaming choruses, instruments and percussion by the guru of the international avant-garde Karlheinz STOCKHAUSEN, is performed for the first time in Cologne.

30 May 1962

Journey into Jazz for narrator, jazz quartet and orchestra by the multi-faceted 36-year-old American composer and jazzologist Gunther SCHULLER is performed for the first time in Washington, D.C.

8 June 1962

The Outcasts of Poker Flat, one-act opera by the German-born American composer Samuel ADLER, after a story by Bret Harte, is performed for the first time in Denton, Texas.

28 June 1962

Two Peruvian Preludes for orchestra by the 45-year-old American musician and scholar of formidable capacities in ubiquitous fields Robert STEVENSON, is performed for the first time in Philadelphia, Leopold Stokowski conducting. (A revised version, titled *Tres Preludios peruanos*, was premiered in Mexico City on 20 July 1963, Luis Herrera de la Fuente conducting.)

9 July 1962

Heterophonie, a compound of five successive and/or simultaneous heterophonic symphonic variations on a theme by the Argentinian-born German composer Mauricio KAGEL, is performed for the first time in its third version at the International Summer Festival in Darmstadt. (The world première of the combined versions I/II was given over Cologne Radio on 22 May 1962.)

In Kagel's *Heterophonie* there are five sections, optionally played or unplayed, with the tuning given by the oboe mischievously playing A-sharp, instead of customary A.

12 August 1962

Don Perlimplín, radio opera by the 42-year-old Italian conductor and composer Bruno MADERNA, after a text by Federico García Lorca, is broadcast for the first time over RAI Radio in Rome.

28 September 1962

At the Philharmonic Hall in Lincoln Center for the Performing Arts in New York, the Juilliard School Orchestra presents the first performances of two commissioned works: *Toccata for the Sixth Day* by William BERGSMA, dean of the Juilliard School of Music, and *Song of Orpheus* for cello and orchestra by William SCHUMAN, President of Lincoln Center.

A *Song of Orpheus*, written in a modernistically atonal manner, suggesting that Orpheus charmed men, animals and plants by the power of expressionistic angst, by William Schuman was first performed in Indianapolis (not in New York), on 17 February 1962 (not on 28 September 1962), with Leonard Rose as soloist, Izler Solomon, conductor; the work was commissioned by the Ford Foundation (not by Lincoln Center).

20 November 1962

First Cello Concerto by André JOLIVET, in three expressive movements, *Méditatif*, *Hiératique* and *Cursif*, is performed for the first time in Paris.

16 DECEMBER 1962
The Departure, opera in three acts by the 55-year-old English composer Elizabeth MACONCHY, is produced in London.

24 JANUARY 1963
Fifth Symphony, subtitled *Sinfonia aforistica*, by the Swedish composer Hilding HALLNÄS, is performed for the first time in Göteborg.

2 FEBRUARY 1963
Concerto for Orchestra by the 27-year-old Georgian Soviet composer Giya KANCHELI is performed for the first time in Tbilisi.

7 FEBRUARY 1963
Violin Concerto by the 66-year-old Slovenian composer Matija BRAVNIĆAR, making use of the quasi-oriental Istrianic scale, is performed for the first time in Ljubljana.

5 MARCH 1963
Tenebrae for orchestra by the 42-year-old American composer Louis MENNINI is performed for the first time in New Orleans.

8 APRIL 1963
Concerto for Violin, Viola and Orchestra by the 42-year-old Slovenian composer Primož RAMOVŠ, in four connected movements for an orchestra without the violin and viola sections, and set in a free dodecaphonic technique, is performed for the first time in Ljubljana.

10 MAY 1963
Still Are New Worlds for narrator, tape, choir and orchestra by the 56-year-old American composer Ross Lee FINNEY is performed for the first time in Ann Arbor, Michigan.

23 MAY 1963
Hymnody for wind instruments, percussion and two pianos by the dean of the Spanish musical avant-garde, Roberto GERHARD, who went to England after the Falangist victory in Spain, is performed for the first time in London.

31 MAY 1963
Christopher Sly, comic opera by the 35-year-old American composer Dominick ARGENTO, based on a scene from Shakespeare's play *The Taming of the Shrew*, is produced in Minneapolis for the first time.

23 June 1963

Die Errettung Thebens, opera in three acts by the Swiss composer Rudolf KELTENBORN, to his own libretto drawn freely from Aeschylus, in which seven princes from Argos assail the seven gates of Thebes, is produced in Zürich.

The name of the composer is Rudolf KELTERBORN (not Keltenborn).

2 July 1963

Our Man in Havana, opera in three acts by the 31-year-old composer Malcolm WILLIAMSON of New Zealand, after the melodramatic novel by Graham Greene, with spies and counterspies matching wits in wry atonalities over ostentatious pseudo-Cuban rhythms, is produced in London.

Malcolm Williamson is from Australia (not New Zealand).

21 September 1963

The newly erected Place des Arts opens in Montreal, Canada, with a concert by the Montreal Symphony Orchestra, featuring the world première of *Miroir* by the Canadian composer Jean-Papineau COUTURE. . . .

The Canadian composer's name should read Jean PAPINEAU-COUTURE (not Jean-Papineau Couture).

28 October 1963

Juha, romantic opera by the Finnish composer Aarre MERIKANTO, composed in 1922, in which an elderly Finn named Juha kills himself after his chronologically and genetically more youthful bride lets herself be imprudently impregnated by a transient philanderer, set to music in somber tones vested in dramatically romantic Germanic harmonies in which the musical images of Sibelius and Richard Strauss coalesce, is performed for the first time on the stage in the small Finnish locality of Lahti, five years after Merikanto's death. (A radio premiere of *Juha* was first performed in Helsinki on 3 December 1958, also posthumously, within nine weeks of the composer's death.)

8 November 1963

Fifth Symphony in one long movement, by the individualistic, innovative, unfailingly romantic Swedish composer Allan PETTERSSON, is performed for the first time on the Swedish Radio.

29 November 1963

First Symphony by the 41-year-old American composer Irwin BAZELON is performed for the first time in Kansas City, Missouri.

6 DECEMBER 1963

Genghis Khan, symphonic poem by the 56-year-old Berlin-born American composer Gene GUTCHË (whose real name was Romeo Gutsche), expressionistically portraying the murderous character of the great Mongolian khan, is performed for the first time in Minneapolis.

12 DECEMBER 1963

Symphony in One Movement by the 54-year-old Scottish composer Robin ORR, a dramatically introspective soundpiece marked by periodic outbursts of massive sonorities alternating with austerely pentatonic Caledonian progressions, and concluding with a series of immaculate open fifths, is performed for the first time in London.

10 JANUARY 1964

Pierre BOULEZ conducts in Basel the first performance of a fragment of his *Figures, Doubles, Prismes. . . .*

Boulez conducted his *Figures, Doubles, Prismes* in Strasbourg (not in Basel).

30 JANUARY 1964

Night Music I for soprano, piano and percussion by the 34-year-old American composer George CRUMB, to verses by Federico García Lorca, is performed for the first time in Paris.

9 FEBRUARY 1964

The Liverpudlian vocal quartet that assumed the name THE BEATLES (derived from the beat rather than the insect) is revealed to an expectant American public on the Ed Sullivan television show, instantly winning the hearts, eyes, ears, minds and viscera of millions of cisatlantic enthusiasts. (The Beatles presented a public concert in Washington, D.C., on 11 February 1964, as their first living contact with the subjugated American masses.)

6 MARCH 1964

The Swedish pianist Karl-Erik Welin wounds himself in the knee with a power saw during the Stockholm performance of an enhanced piano piece by Knut WIGGEN requiring the explosion of a pyrotechnical device purporting to be a charge of dynamite and sawing off the legs of the piano preliminary to working over the keyboard with the intention of demolishing it, too. (Welin's knee injury was not grave, and the prognosis excellent. Because of his failure to operate the power saw properly, the Swedish music critic Sten Broman suggested the incorporation of classes in power saw handling at the Stockholm High School of Music.)

22 MARCH 1964

Royal Invitation, orchestral suite subtitled *Homage to the Queen of Tonga* by the 36-year-old American composer Dominick ARGENTO, is performed for the first time by the St. Paul Philharmonic in Minneapolis.

4 APRIL 1964

Sir Gawain and the Green Knight, opera by the 33-year-old American composer Richard FELICIANO, is produced in San Francisco.

24 APRIL 1964

The Swiss Exposition of Industry opens in Lausanne, architecturally reflecting the modern world in its wall-less Pavillon Échange, with the world première of *Les Échanges* by Rolf LIEBERMANN, scored for fifty-two machines, including teletypes, cash registers, staplers and copying devices, timed by an electronic computer to last exactly 195 seconds.

The actual title of Liebermann's work is *Concert des Échanges* (not *Les Échanges*). It is scored for 156 machines (not fifty-two).

26 MAY 1964

Aaron COPLAND conducts the London Symphony Orchestra in the first performance of his *Music for a Great City* (commissioned by that orchestra on the occasion of its fiftieth anniversary), a symphonic cyclorama of sights and sounds of New York City, intensely realistic in its illustrative effects, in four tableaux, *Skyline, Night Thoughts, Subway Jam* and *Towards the Bridge.*

The Copland work was commissioned for the London Symphony's sixtieth (not fiftieth) anniversary.

30 MAY 1964

At the third concert of the Thirty-eighth Festival of the International Society for Contemporary Music in Copenhagen, the following program of chamber music by Danish composers is given: *Passacaglie* for flute, violin, cello and piano by the 41-year-old Poul Rovsing LOSEN, in five movements, each based on a different rhythmic mode. . . .

The composer's name is Poul Rovsing OLSEN (not Losen).

30 MAY 1964

In the course of the Eighteenth Festival at Ojai, California, a program of international avant-garde and electronic music is given: *Samstirni* by the Icelandic composer Magus Blondal JOHANNSSON. . . .

The correct spelling of the composer's name is Magnus (not Magus) Blöndal (not Blondal) Jóhannsson.

12 June 1964

Paučina (The Weaving), opera by the 32-year-old Macedonian composer Toma Prošev, a sociopsychological drama portraying the lives of Slavic emigrants in America, is produced in Rijeka (Fiume).

12 June 1964

First Symphony by the 20-year-old Polish composer Krzysztof Meyer is performed for the first time in Cracow.

25 June 1964

Le Chant du dépossédé (The Song of the Dispossessed), after Mallarmé, for narrator, baritone and orchestra by the 40-year-old French composer Serge Nigg, is performed for the first time in Strasbourg.

3 July 1964

The Lady from Colorado, third opera by the 46-year-old American composer Robert Ward, based on the fanciful biography of a woman of the pioneer days in the silver-mining country, is performed for the first time in Central City, Colorado.

7 August 1964

André Jolivet conducts in Mexico City the first performance of his *Third Symphony*, in four contrasting movements marked *Obstiné, Fulgural, Lyrique* and *Véhément*.

12 August 1964

I Hear an Army for soprano and string quartet by the 27-year-old American composer David Del Tredici, based on a poem by James Joyce, is performed for the first time in Tanglewood, Massachusetts.

12 August 1964

Sinfonia Sacra by Andrzej Panufnik, 50-year-old expatriate Polish composer, based on medieval plainchant of the Polish church, opening with three "visions" and concluding with a hymn based on "Bogurodzica," a legendary Polish hymn of immense political and religious content, scored for four quadraphonically spaced trumpets, strings, percussion and orchestra, is performed for the first time in Monte Carlo, after receiving first prize in the Prix de Composition Musicale Prince Ranier III de Monaco.

27 AUGUST 1964

Non-Stop for piano by the innovative master of Polish musical modernism Boguslaw SCHAEFFER is performed for the first time by a relay team of two pianists at the first Polish Happening in Cracow, with a total duration of eight hours.

6 SEPTEMBER 1964

Hyperion, a "lyric spectacle" by the 44-year-old Italian conductor and composer Bruno MADERNA, is performed for the first time at the Venice Festival.

20 SEPTEMBER 1964

Le nouveau locataire (The New Lodger), opera in one act by the 40-year-old avant-garde Croatian composer Milko KELEMEN, after a whimsical play by Ionesco, is produced in Münster, Germany.

22 SEPTEMBER 1964

Fiddler on the Roof, nostalgic musical depicting the life of intermittently pogromized Jews in Czarist Russia with music by Jerry BOCK and choreography by Jerome Robbins, opens in New York, destined to become one of the most durable popular musical spectacles in Broadway history.

17 OCTOBER 1964

Couleurs de la Cité céleste, an apocalyptic suite by Olivier MESSIAEN, scored for a large orchestra with a resonant assortment of tinkling, banging and tintinnabulating percussion instruments, superadded upon ornithological chirping, twitting and crackling sounds of two birds from New Zealand and one from Brazil, is performed for the first time at the Donaueschingen Festival, under the direction of Pierre Boulez.

31 OCTOBER 1964

Oblaci (The Clouds) by the 70-year-old Croatian composer Krešimir BARANOVIĆ, scored for mezzo-soprano and orchestra, is performed for the first time in Belgrade.

4 NOVEMBER 1964

Napuštene (The Abandoned Ones, also known under the title *Las Apasionadas),* ballet by the 40-year-old modernistic Croatian composer Milko KELEMEN, after a text by Federico García Lorca, is produced in Lübeck.

19 JANUARY 1965

Third Symphony for string quartet and orchestra by Benjamin LEES, 41-year-old Manchurian-born American composer of Russian parentage, is performed for the first time in Kansas City, Missouri.

The work performed was Lees' *Concerto for String Quartet and Orchestra* (not his *Third Symphony*).

3 FEBRUARY 1965
Night Music II, four *Nocturnes* for violin and piano by the 35-year-old American composer George CRUMB, is performed for the first time in Buffalo, New York.

8 FEBRUARY 1965

Appassionato for orchestra by the German-born American composer Lothar KLEIN is performed for the first time in Dallas, Texas.

The first performance of Klein's *Appassionata* (not *Appassionato*) took place on 19 April 1964 (not on 8 February 1965).

15 FEBRUARY 1965
Die Soldaten, "pluralistic opera" by the 46-year-old German composer Bernd Alois ZIMMERMANN, based on an eighteenth-century play dealing with a naïve provincial girl whose unquenchable ambition to meet influential people leads her to yield to the psychological needs of every officer of the local garrison, is produced in Cologne. It is written in a highly original serial idiom, making use of multifarious techniques of the modern theater, from cinema to collage, incorporating in the score fragments of Bach's chorales and vesuviating epiphanies of polyrhythmic jazz, with dramatic pluralism emphasized by the subdivision of the stage into simultaneous but separate compartments.

2 APRIL 1965
The Shape of Time for two antiphonal percussion and double-bass groups by the 38-year-old American composer Robert WYKES is performed for the first time in St. Louis, Missouri.

6 APRIL 1965
Das Lächeln am Füsse der Leiter, opera by the 43-year-old Italian composer Antonio BIBALO, after Henry Miller's story *The Smile at the Foot of the Ladder,* is produced at the Hamburg State Opera with a German libretto translated from the original Italian version, *Sorrisi ai piedi d'una scala.*

11 APRIL 1965
Second Symphony by the 32-year-old Soviet composer Rodion SHCHEDRIN, in four movements, the third being a precisely notated process of tuning the orchestra, is performed for the first time in Moscow.

2 May 1965

The Seattle Symphony Orchestra, Milton Katims conductor, presents a Contemporary Festival Concert under a grant from the Rockefeller Foundation and under the auspices of the University of Washington School of Music, in the following program of first performances by American composers: *Oracles* by William Bolcom; *Elegiac Symphony* by Donald Keats; *Graffiti* by Roger Reynolds; and *Symphony of Overtures* by Donald Erb.

Donald Erb's *Symphony of Overtures* was first performed on 11 February (not 2 May) 1965 at Indiana University in Bloomington (not the University of Washington).

5 May 1965

Music for Solo Performer by the 34-year-old American composer Alvin Lucier, in which encephalographic waves produced by a human brain activate percussion instruments, is performed for the first time in Waltham, Massachusetts.

21 May 1965

In C, an orchestral piece by the 29-year-old American composer Terry Riley, obdurately sticking to the key of C, with an intrusive F sharp occasionally making its appearance as a fleeting *trompe l'oreille* effect, is performed for the first time in San Francisco.

22 May 1965

The Happy Prince, opera by the 33-year-old New Zealand composer Malcolm Williamson, after Oscar Wilde, scored for 8 soloists, chorus, semi-chorus, piano duet and percussion, is performed for the first time at the Farnham Festival in England.

Malcolm Williamson is an Australian (not a New Zealander).

16 June 1965

In the course of the Holland Music Festival two operas by Dutch composers are presented for the first time in Amsterdam: *De Droom* (*The Dream*) by Ton de Leeuw . . . and *Jean Léveck* by Guillaume Landré, to Guy de Maupassant's story *Le Retour*, wherein a vagabond returning to his abandoned and long remarried wife, agrees to disappear again so as not to disturb her new happiness, set in a euphoniously dissonant idiom.

The correct spelling of Guillaume Landré's opera is *Jean Lévecq* (not *Léveck*).

20 June 1965

L'Hymne aux Morts by Olivier MESSIAEN, commemorating the dead of the two world wars, is presented for the first time at the Cathedral of Chartres, on the occasion of the visit there of President Charles de Gaulle.

L'Hymne aux Morts, a suite in five movements to texts from the Vulgate, scored for a large orchestra with cow bells, chimes, gongs and tam-tams, was first performed under the title *Et expecto resurrectionem mortuorum* at Sainte-Chapelle, Paris, on 7 May (not 20 June) 1965.

7 July 1965

Fibonacci-Mobile for string quartet, two pianos and a coordinator, by the modern magus of profoundly calculated yet humanly experienced music Ernst KRENEK, based on a Fibonacci series in which each successive number is the sum of the two preceding numbers, is performed for the first time at a festival of contemporary music in Hanover, New Hampshire.

10 August 1965

The government of Ecuador issues a memorial stamp for the composer of the Ecuadorian national anthem, the Corsican-born ethnically German musician Antonio NEUMANN (1818–1871).

21 August 1965

Nun's Priest's Tale, after Chaucer, scored for folk singer, electric guitar and small orchestra by the 58-year-old American composer Ross Lee FINNEY, is performed for the first time at Dartmouth College in Hanover, New Hampshire.

23 September 1965

The Toronto Symphony presents at the Commonwealth Arts Festival in Glasgow, Scotland, a program of orchestral music, including the first performance of *Suite* for harp and chamber orchestra by Harry SOMERS of Canada.

Harry SOMERS's *Suite* was first performed in Toronto (not Glasgow) on 11 December 1952 (not 23 September 1965).

15 November 1965

Musique for eleven wind instruments and timpani by the 36-year-old Soviet composer Edison DENISOV is performed for the first time in Leningrad.

31 January 1966

Twelfth Symphony, subtitled *Tunis*, by the Danish composer Niels Viggo BENTZON is performed for the first time in Aarhus.

11 FEBRUARY 1966

Mirror Twenty-five for chorus and orchestra by the 26-year-old Swedish composer Johnny GRADERT, in which the score includes a machine gun, and the chorus is invited to belch at some points, is performed for the first time in Stockholm.

18 FEBRUARY 1966

Madrigals, Book I, for soprano, double-bass and the vibraphone by the 36-year-old American composer George CRUMB, to the text by Federico García Lorca, is performed for the first time in Philadelphia.

4 MARCH 1966

David DEL TREDICI conducts in San Francisco the first performance of his *Night Conjure-Verse,* scored for soprano, mezzo-soprano, woodwind septet and string quartet, to a text by James Joyce.

10 MARCH 1966

Concerto for four percussion soloists and orchestra by the 42-year-old American composer and percussion virtuoso William KRAFT is performed for the first time in Los Angeles.

11 MARCH 1966

Madrigals, Book II, for soprano, flute and percussion by the 36-year-old American composer George CRUMB, to text by Federico García Lorca, is performed for the first time in Washington, D.C.

18 MARCH 1966

The Judgment of St. Francis, one-act opera by the 38-year-old American composer Nicolas FLAGELLO, is produced in New York.

16 MAY 1966

Koshare, ballet by the American Indian composer Louis BALLARD, evoking the creation of the world as seen through the eyes of the Hopi Indians, is performed for the first time in Barcelona, Spain.

12 JUNE 1966

Herman SCHERCHEN, intellectual German conductor and an ardent champion of modern music, dies in Florence, whither he fled to escape the dark Nazi apocalypse, a day after his seventy-fifth birthday.

23 JUNE 1966

First Symphony by the Welsh composer William MATHIAS, in four movements with the overall tonal center of C and dedicated to his wife, is performed for the first time in Birmingham.

3 JULY 1966

The White Gods, opera in three acts depicting the fearful Aztec view of the conquistadors by the 49-year-old American composer Robert KELLY, is performed for the first time in Urbana, Illinois.

7 JULY 1966

Purgatory, one-act opera by the 28-year-old British composer Gordon CROSSE, to a libretto after Yeats dealing with posthumous retribution, wherein a remorseful old man kills his son to end his family's crime-ridden history (he killed his father to avenge his brutal treatment of his mother, who died during his childbirth) and to secure the entrance to Purgatory for all of them, is produced at the Cheltenham Festival.

1 AUGUST 1966

Mesa, electronic musical event for cybersonic bandoneon devised by Gordon MUMMA and David TUDOR, is performed for the first time by its creators at an electronic laboratory in St. Paul de Vence, France.

3 SEPTEMBER 1966

Belisa, opera after Federico García Lorca by the 43-year-old Danish composer and ethnomusicologist Poul Rovsing OLSEN, is performed for the first time in Copenhagen.

10 SEPTEMBER 1966

Klimentu (To Kliment), oratorio by the 41-year-old Macedonian composer Vlastimir NIKOLOVSKI, an homage to an early Christian cleric set in Byzantine modalities, is performed for the first time in Skopje.

25 OCTOBER 1966

Dr. Atom, surrealistic ballet by the 60-year-old Croatian composer Boris PAPANDOPULO, is produced in Rijeka (Fiume).

31 OCTOBER 1966

Sinfonia II, subtitled *Susudil*, by the 43-year-old Danish composer and ethnomusicologist Poul Rovsing OLSEN, based on Arabic and Turkish modes, is performed for the first time in Copenhagen.

17 DECEMBER 1966

Apocalypse for narrator, chorus and instruments by the 26-year-old Polish composer Edward BOGUSLAWSKI, written in an expansive grandiloquent manner, with allusions to ecclesiastical chants providing an eschatological ambience, is performed for the first time in Warsaw.

The correct date of the first performance of *Apocalypse* is 17 December 1965 (not 1966).

6 JANUARY 1967

André JOLIVET conducts in Moscow the first performance of his *Second Concerto* for cello and orchestra, with Mstislav Rostropovich as soloist.

22 JANUARY 1967

Sixth Symphony by Ernst TOCH, in three movements, *Allegro comodo, Molto grazioso e leggiero* and *Allegro energico*, set in an endearing neo-romantic mood, is performed posthumously for the first time by the Zürich Radio Orchestra.

29 JANUARY 1967

Die Doppelgängerin, opera in three acts by the Czech-American composer Jan MEYEROWITZ, based on Gerhardt Hauptmann's play *Winterballad*, to a libretto of murderous violence and preternatural revenge by an alter ego of the victim (hence the title) in sixteenth-century Sweden, set to music in neo-medieval modalities, is performed for the first time in Hannover, Germany.

Jan Meyerowitz is a German-born American (not Czech-American) composer.

13 FEBRUARY 1967

Sinfonietta for string orchestra by Ernst TOCH, in three cyclic movements, is performed posthumously for the first time in Philadelphia.

23 MARCH 1967

A memorial stamp is issued by the Malagasy Republic (Madagascar) in honor of the native composer Norbert RAHARISOA (1914–1963), a graduate of the Lyon Conservatory in France, who in 1959 wrote the national hymn of Madagascar.

20 APRIL 1967

Carmen Suite, ballet arranged from Bizet's famous opera *Carmen* by Rodion SHCHEDRIN for strings and drums, with the music deromanticized by blunt percussive rhythms, is performed for the first time in Moscow, with Shchedrin's wife, Maya Plisetskaya, as prima ballerina.

27 APRIL 1967

Phorion for orchestra, electronic organ, harpsichord and guitar by the 44-year-old ultra-modern American composer Lukas Foss, a metamorphosis of Bach's violin *Partita in E* (*phorion* means stolen goods in Greek, and the idea came to

Foss in a dream when he heard, and observed on paper, "torrents of Baroque sixteenth notes washed ashore by ocean waves and sucked in again"), with the thematic materials transmogrified by aleatory permutations, acrobatic inversions, congenial perversions and melorhythmic singultations, is performed for the first time by the New York Philharmonic, under the direction of Leonard Bernstein.

The orchestration of *Phorion* by Lukas Foss includes electric guitar and electric piano (not harpsichord). *Phorion* was later incorporated into *Baroque Variations*, with thematic material derived not only from Bach's *Partita*, but also from Handel's Suite in E major and Scarlatti's Sonata in E major.

1 MAY 1967
Diastasis, As in Beer (that is, a mixture of ingredients of malt from which beer is made), for two cybersonic guitars by Gordon MUMMA, is performed by its creator and Christian Wolff at Harvard University in Cambridge, Massachusetts.

16 MAY 1967
Voie for three choirs and orchestra by the 32-year-old avant-garde Slovenian-born composer and trombonist Vinko GLOBOKAR, to a text by Mayakovsky sung in Russian by a men's choir, in French by a women's choir, and in Slovenian by a mixed choir, is performed for the first time in Zagreb.

26 MAY 1967
Echoes of Time and the River: Processionals for Orchestra by the 37-year-old American composer George CRUMB is performed for the first time in Chicago and receives the Pulitzer Prize.

1 JUNE 1967
Seventh Symphony by Ernst TOCH, his last, in four cyclic movements, *Molto lento, Allegro moderato, Allegro giocoso* and *Allegro risoluto*, is performed posthumously for the first time in Munich.

3 JULY 1967
Fourth Symphony, subtitled *Das Siegeslied*, by the nonagenarian English polysymphonist Havergal BRIAN, to the text of Psalm 68 in the Lutheran German version and scored for soprano, double chorus and orchestra, comes to its belated first performance in London, thirty-four years after its composition.

17 JULY 1967
John COLTRANE, remarkable American jazz musician and a virtuoso on the tenor saxophone who initiated an enlightened type of composition

and performing practice that led to the formation of sophisticated black primitivism, dies in Huntington, Long Island, New York, at the age of forty.

9 AUGUST 1967

Concert Piece for Syn-Ket and Orchestra by the 32-year-old American composer John EATON, the first of its genre, set for a portable electronic synthesizer invented by the Russian engineer Paul Ketoff (hence, Syn-Ket), is performed for the first time at the Berkshire Music Festival at Tanglewood, Massachusetts.

24 OCTOBER 1967

Il Pozzo e il Pendolo (The Pit and the Pendulum), opera by the Italian composer Bruno BETTINELLI, after Edgar Allan Poe, is performed for the first time in Bergamo.

6 NOVEMBER 1967

Tovarishch Andrei, opera-oratorio in ten scenes, with a prologue and an epilogue, by the 56-year-old Soviet composer Boris GIBALIN, a series of musical tableaux illustrating the revolutionary life of Jacob Sverdlov, known in the Tsarist underground as "Tovarishch Andrei," is performed for the first time in Sverdlovsk, the Ural city, formerly Ekaterinburg, renamed Sverdlovsk after Sverdlov was assassinated by an anti-Bolshevistically inspired Russian Charlotte Corday in 1918.

Jacob Sverdlov was not assassinated. He died in 1919 of natural causes.

7 NOVEMBER 1967

Sixth Symphony, subtitled *Musica Intima*, by the Swedish composer Hilding HALLNÄS, is performed for the first time in Malmö.

13 NOVEMBER 1967

"Cross Talk No. 1," a concert of ultramodern music, is presented in Tokyo, featuring works by Charles IVES, and by three Japanese composers: *Chromamorphe 1* for seven instruments by Yuji TAKAHASHI; *Provisional Color* for piano by Shuko MIZUNO; and *Icon* for magnetic tape by Joji YUASA.

20 NOVEMBER 1967

Smell Piece for Mills College for frying pans and foods by the intransigently radical 30-year-old American avant-garde composer Robert MORAN, originally intended to produce a conflagration sufficiently thermal to burn down the college, is performed for the first time at Mills College in Oakland, California.

12 December 1967
Mooga Pook, a tetraphallic action for dancers by the 22-year-old American composer Charles AMIRKHANIAN, notated on graph paper with anatomical precision, is performed for the first time in San Francisco.

5 January 1968

Piano Concerto by the Canadian composer Jean PAPINEAU-COUTURE is performed for the first time in Quebec.

Papineau-Couture's *Piano Concerto* was first performed in Toronto on 6 February 1966 (not in Quebec on 5 January 1968).

18 January 1968
Anachronie I for orchestra by the 28-year-old Dutch composer Louis ANDRIESSEN, dedicated to the memory of Charles Ives, is performed for the first time in Rotterdam.

20 January 1968
Ode in Memory of Ché Guevara for clarinet, piano and percussion by the 38-year-old Soviet composer Edison DENISOV is performed for the first time in Moscow.

21 January 1968
Sixth Symphony, in a single very long movement, by the neo-romantic Swedish composer Allan PETTERSSON, culminating in a pessimistic conclusion in the melancholy key of B-flat minor, is performed for the first time on the Swedish Radio in Stockholm.

3 February 1968
Concert Piece for orchestra by the 38-year-old American composer Donald KEATS is performed for the first time in Columbus, Ohio.

20 February 1968
The Bride Comes to Yellow Sky, opera by the 46-year-old Amecian composer Roger NIXON, from a story by Stephen Crane, written in a songful quasiatonal manner, descriptive of the purchase of a mail-order wife by an hombre in the Western frontier town called Yellow Sky, is produced at Eastern Illinois University. (The opera was revised and performed in San Francisco in a new version on 22 March 1969.)

20 February 1968
Fünf Geschichten vom Herrn Keuner for tenor and seven instruments by the 38-year-old Soviet composer Edison DENISOV, to original German texts by Bertolt Brecht, is performed for the first time in Berlin.

5 March 1968
Reunion, a synthetic electronic work, formally determined by the movements of chessmen in a game between John Cage and the famous painter Marcel Duchamp on an electronic chess board built by Lowell Cross, takes place at a special session at the Polytechnical Institute in Toronto, Canada. (Duchamp gave Cage a handicap of a knight and still beat him handily.)

26 March 1968
Blackboard Piece with Girls and Loops for two girls and two pitch-producing blackboards by the 31-year-old American avant-garde composer Jon Hassell is performed for the first time in New York.

28 March 1968
Fourth Symphony by the 61-year-old Norwegian composer Klaus Egge, based on the initials of Bach and Egge himself, subtitled *Sinfonia sopra B.A.C.H.—E.G.G.E.*, is performed for the first time in Detroit, Michigan.

29 March 1968
Forte e Piano for two pianos and orchestra by the 46-year-old Polish composer Kazimierz Serocki is performed for the first time in Cologne.

4 April 1968
Contextures: Riots—Decade '60 for orchestra by the 44-year-old American composer William Kraft is performed for the first time in Los Angeles.

7 April 1968

Piano Concerto by the American composer John Corigliano is performed for the first time by the San Antonio Symphony, conducted by Victor Alessandro.

Corigliano's *Piano Concerto* was first performed on 5 April (not 7 April) 1968, with Hilde Somer as soloist.

12 April 1968
Hétéromorphie for orchestra by the 40-year-old Rumanian composer Stefan Niculescu is performed for the first time in Bucharest.

21 April 1968
Rainforest, a musical event designed by David Tudor and Gordon Mumma with the Merce Cunningham Dance Company, is created for the first time by the Public Broadcast Laboratory Television Production in New York.

21 APRIL 1968

Concerto for Synket and Orchestra in three movements by Jerome ROSEN, the
first of its genre, with a portable electronic instrument, invented by the Russian
acoustician in Rome named Paul Ketoff, is performed for the first time on the
campus of the University of Washington in Seattle.

This was not the first work of its genre; see 9 August 1967, above.

25 APRIL 1968

Rain, opera by the 62-year-old Russian composer Boris ARAPOV, based on
Somerset Maugham's short story, is produced in Leningrad.

12 MAY 1968

First Symphony by the 32-year-old Georgian Soviet composer Giya
KANCHELI, in two movements, *Allegro con fuoco* and *Largo*, is performed
for the first time in Tbilisi.

5 JUNE 1968

Two stage works by the 61-year-old British composer Elizabeth
MACONCHY, *The Three Strangers*, opera after Thomas Hardy, and *The
Birds*, operatic extravaganza after Aristophanes, are produced in London.

8 JUNE 1968

Punch and Judy, a heterogeneous stage fable in which elements of a
children's play combine with a ritualistic horror story set to a raucously
lyrical score by the British avant-garde composer Harrison BIRTWISTLE,
is performed for the first time at the Aldeburgh Festival.

28 JUNE 1968

Malcolm ARNOLD conducts the BBC Northern Symphony in the first performance in Sheffield, England, of his *Sixth Symphony*, which draws its
inspiration from the jazzy muse of the American saxophonist Charlie
Parker, popularly known as the "Bird."

6 JULY 1968

Syzygy by the 31-year-old American composer David DEL TREDICI,
scored for soprano, horn, bells, drums and chamber orchestra, to the text
by James Joyce, symbolizing the precision of leptokurtic equilibration of
two mutually related celestial bodies when they achieve straight-line
alignment with a third body, is performed for the first time in New York.

30 JULY 1968

Jon LEIFS, foremost composer of Iceland who succeeded in embodying
the stark Arctic modalities of his native island in universal musical terms

within the framework of romantic, largely Germanic harmonies, dies in Reykjavik at the age of sixty-eight.

2 AUGUST 1968
Sayings for Our Time for chorus and orchestra by the 37-year-old American composer Roger HANNAY, to a text from "current news media," is performed for the first time in Winston-Salem, North Carolina.

4 AUGUST 1968
Second Symphony by the 35-year-old American composer Alan STOUT, in three movements, *Prologue, Processional* and *Recitative*, each subdivided into allusively baroque sections such as antiphons, trio ostinato, fanfares and apogaeum, filled with ostentatiously displayed polyphonic devices, is performed for the first time in Highland Park, Illinois, by the Chicago Symphony Orchestra, Seiji Ozawa conducting.

11 AUGUST 1968
Musique pour Nouvelle Orléans by Darius MILHAUD, in the characteristically melodious Milhaudean three movements, *Large, Très lent et tendre* and *Vigoureux*, originally commissioned for the 250th anniversary of New Orleans in 1966 but rejected by the anniversary committee as spiritually, melodically, harmonically and orchestrally unfit, is performed for the first time, still under its original title, by the Aspen Festival Orchestra in Aspen, Colorado, conducted by the composer.

26 AUGUST 1968
Étude pour folklore II for orchestra by the 34-year-old French-born Slovenian composer Vinko GLOBOKAR, using such native instruments as gusle, tapan, double whistle and darabukka, in six sections subject to aleatory permutations, is performed for the first time in Frankfurt.

7 SEPTEMBER 1968
Traumdeutung (Meaning of Dreams), psychodrama for four choruses and four instruments (celesta, harp, vibraphone and guitar) by the 34-year-old French-born Slovenian composer Vinko GLOBOKAR, representing a Freudian psycho-analysis of four persons relating four dreams about an identical experience, is performed for the first time in Rotterdam.

23 SEPTEMBER 1968
The first "Styrian Autumn" festival of contemporary music opens in Graz with the following program:

Lux Aeterna for an a cappella chorus of sixteen voices by the 45-year-old Hungarian-born Austrian composer György LIGETI. The European premiere of

317

Aegrotavit Ezechias, a motet for two female soloists and female chorus by Ernst KRENEK. The world premiere of *Mass* for chorus a capella by the 66-year-old Austrian composer Erich MARCKHL. *Hiob (Job),* a "sacra rappresentazione" for speaker, soloists, chorus and chamber ensemble by Luigi DALLAPICCOLA.

25 SEPTEMBER 1968
The first "Styrian Autumn" festival of contemporary music in Graz continues with the following program:

The world premiere of *Concerto* for guitar and string orchestra by the 42-year-old composer Thomas Christian DAVID. *Ode an die Musik* for alto and chamber orchestra by the England-domiciled master of ancient and new music Egon WELLESZ. *Concerto* for viola da gamba, string orchestra and percussion by the 41-year-old Austrian composer Paul ANGERER. *Nil admirari* by the 51-year-old composer Helmut EDER.

26 SEPTEMBER 1968
The first "Styrian Autumn" festival of contemporary music in Graz continues with the following program featuring works by Yugoslav composers:

Tâches (Spots) for piano and chamber orchestra by the 38-year-old composer Stanko HORVAT. *Sequenzen* for chamber orchestra by the 30-year-old composer Igor KULJERIĆ. *Komposition* for Ondes Martenot and chamber orchestra by the 37-year-old composer Ruben RADICA. *Verklärungen (Transfigurations)* for baritone and chamber orchestra by the 38-year-old composer Krešimir ŠIPUŠ. *Formen und Flächen (Forms and Surfaces)* for chamber orchestra by the 31-year-old composer Dubravko DETONI.

26 SEPTEMBER 1968
Crystals by Jacob GILBOA, *Continuum* by Kazimierz SEROCKI and *Cantata* by Zbyněk VOSTŘÁK, originally scheduled for performance on this date at the Warsaw Autumn Festival, were not performed "for reasons of force majeure" (see full scheduled program in *Music Since 1900*). They were performed instead at the 1969 Festival in Hamburg: *Crystals* and *Cantata* on 22 June 1969, *Continuum* on 24 June 1969.

3 OCTOBER 1968
Anna LOCKWOOD, 39-year-old New Zealand-born pioneer in aural, oral, visual, tactile, gustatory and olfactory techniques of composition, holds in London a musico-spiritualistic séance, at which a total combustion of an upright piano is achieved, crowned by the epiphany of the spirit of Beethoven who metapsychically records on magnetic tape some of his posthumous music in an astonishingly modern idiom. (Instructions for burning the piano read as follows: "Overtune the strings as high as possible so as to get maximum sound when they snap with the heat. Cover microphones with asbestos and fasten inside the piano. To start fire, splash

small amount of kerosene at the back of the piano, in one corner, so that the fire spreads slowly.")

6 OCTOBER 1968
Quadi for jazz quartet and orchestra by the 42-year-old black American composer and jazz clarinetist William O. SMITH is performed for the first time in New York with the Modern Jazz Quartet as soloists.

10 OCTOBER 1968
Heracles, opera by the 33-year-old American composer John EATON, is performed for the first time in Turin, Italy.

10 OCTOBER 1968

Luciano BERIO, 42-year-old Italian avant-garde composer, conducts the New York Philharmonic and Swingle Singers in the first performance of his *Sinfonia,* surrealist musicorama in four parts . . . the last, a sonic collage beginning with a whispering of atomized vocables and concluding with a panacoustical coagulation of aleatory matrices.

In 1970 Luciano Berio remodeled the *Sinfonia* by rewriting the finale for greater tension and percussive punctuation; the revised score was first performed by the New York Philharmonic on 8 October 1970, Leonard Bernstein conducting.

13 OCTOBER 1968
Seventh Symphony by the remarkable Swedish composer Allan PETTERSSON, the most popular of all his symphonic works, and like most of his symphonies set in a single protracted movement diversified by clearly demarcated divisions in varying tempos, is performed for the first time by the Stockholm Philharmonic, conducted by Antal Dorati.

27 OCTOBER 1968
Symphony '68, identified simply by year of composition (1968), by the 47-year-old Slovenian composer Primož RAMOVŠ, in two movements set in a radically modernistic sonic language, is performed for the first time in Opatija, Yugoslavia.

27 OCTOBER 1968
Third Symphony, subtitled *Mikrosimfonija,* by the 41-year-old Serbian composer Aleksandar OBRADOVIĆ is performed for the first time in Opatija.

28 OCTOBER 1968
Bílá nemoc (The White Sickness), opera by the 51-year-old Czech composer Tibor ANDRAŠOVAN, is performed for the first time in Bratislava.

5 November 1968

King Samuel, opera by the 43-year-old Macedonian composer Kiril MAKEDONSKI, to his own libretto depicting turbulent events in Macedonia in the tenth century, is produced in Skopje.

8 November 1968

Changeant for cello and orchestra by the 44-year-old Croatian modernist Milko KELEMEN, suggesting the constant changes in musical continuity, is performed for the first time in Cologne.

17 November 1968

Epitaph for the Victims of Katyn, symphonic elegy by the 54-year-old Polish composer resident in England Andrzej PANUFNIK, dedicated to the memory of hundreds of Polish officers and soldiers slain in Katyn, Lithuania, in 1941, during the rapid advance of the Nazi armies into Russia, is performed for the first time in New York by the American Symphony, Leopold Stokowski conducting.

The original Polish title of Panufnik's symphonic elegy is *Katyń Epitaph*.

18 November 1968

Concerto for Two Pianos and Orchestra by Paul CRESTON is performed for the first time in Montavallo, Alabama, by the New Orleans Philharmonic Symphony, Werner Torkanowsky conducting.

The correct spelling of the town in Alabama is Montevallo (not Montavallo).

27 November 1968

Second Symphony by the 48-year-old Soviet Armenian composer Karen KHACHATURIAN, in two movements, is performed for the first time in Moscow.

1 December 1968

Second Concerto for string orchestra, composed in 1956 by the foremost Swedish composer Allan PETTERSSON, is performed for the first time on Swedish Radio, ten years after the performance of his *Third Concerto* for string orchestra.

9 December 1968

Stimmung (Tuning) by Karlheinz STOCKHAUSEN, scored for six shoeless singers sitting cross-legged in a circle with musical material selected from a matrix of fifty-one pitch patterns and occasionally intoning "magic names," is performed for the first time in Paris.

12 DECEMBER 1968

Yes Speak Out Yes, cantata by the 38-year-old Spanish composer Cristóbal HALFFTER, to the text by Norman Corwin, in honor of the twentieth anniversary of the United Nations Declaration of Human Rights, is performed for the first time in New York.

17 DECEMBER 1968

Spider-Song, a comic book and event by the 31-year-old American avant-gardist Stanley LUNETTA, in collaboration with Larry AUSTIN, is demonstrated for the first time in New York.

17 DECEMBER 1968

Les Pleurs, vocal cycle by the 39-year-old Russian composer Edison DENISOV, for a passionately tearful soprano accompanied by an anguished piano (with application of painful fingernail pizzicato and glissando on the grand piano strings) and three groups of exotic percussion instruments, to texts from age-long fitfully repetitious crying spells of Russian funeral folklore, portraying with soul-wrenching realism the nailing of the coffin's cover by strokes of claves, is performed for the first time in Brussels.

7 JANUARY 1969

Six Studies of Francis Bacon for orchestra by the 44-year-old British composer Gerard SCHURMANN, comprised of *Figures in a Landscape, Popes, Isabel, Crucifixion, George and the Bicycle* and *Self-Portrait*, is performed for the first time in Dublin.

31 JANUARY 1969

Music for Prague for band by the 47-year-old Prague-born Americanized composer Karel HUSA, in four diversified movements, with the third movement, *Interlure*, scored for percussion instruments only, and with the last section including a series of improvisations, the total effect being an integral representation of the historic, social, and cultural aspects of the great city, is performed for the first time in Washington, D.C. (A revised version of the score, for full orchestra, was performed for the first time in Munich on 31 January 1970.)

5 FEBRUARY 1969

Clarinet Concerto by the 40-year-old Scottish composer Thea MUSGRAVE, representing a set of variations on a diatonic tune, with the clarinet soloist instructed to ambulate among members of the audience, is performed for the first time in London.

13 FEBRUARY 1969

Hommage à Charles Ives for string orchestra by the 27-year-old Swedish composer Ulf GRAHN is performed for the first time in Trondheim, Norway.

15 FEBRUARY 1969

Second Symphony, subtitled *Epitaphium Stanislaw Wiechowicz in memoriam,* with mixed chorus by the 25-year-old Polish composer Krzysztof MEYER, is performed for the first time in Katowice.

18 FEBRUARY 1969

Enantiodromia (Opposed Pathways) for orchestra by the 43-year-old Greek composer Jani CHRISTOU is performed for the first time in Oakland, California.

19 FEBRUARY 1969

Photoptosis, symphonic movement by the 50-year-old German composer Bernd Alois ZIMMERMANN (the title denotes the drooping of the upper eyelid, due to the imperfect function of the levator palpebrae superioris under the influence of light), containing a montage of particles from Beethoven's *Ninth Symphony,* Scriabin's *Poem of Ecstasy,* Wagner's *Parsifal,* Bach's First Brandenburg Concerto and Tchaikovsky's *La danse de la fée dragée* from the *Nutcracker Suite,* is performed for the first time in Gelsenkirchen.

3 MARCH 1969

Ocean, opera by the 67-year-old Yugoslav composer Danilo ŠVARA, after the drama by Leonid Andreyev, written in an expressionist manner including the use of dodecaphony, is produced in Ljubljana.

29 MARCH 1969

Songs, Drones and Refrains of Death by the 39-year-old American composer George CRUMB, scored for baritone, electric guitar, electric double-bass, amplified piano and two percussionists, to the text by Federico García Lorca, is performed for the first time in Iowa City, Iowa.

2 APRIL 1969

String Figures Disentangled by a Flute for flute and string orchestra by the 37-year-old American composer Joyce MAKEEL is performed for the first time in Boston.

5 APRIL 1969

The Seventh Trumpet for orchestra by the 42-year-old American composer Donald ERB is performed for the first time by the Dallas Symphony.

19 APRIL 1969

Let's Build a Nut House, opera in memory of Paul Hindemith by the 32-year-old American avant-gardist Robert MORAN, a wistfully perverse homage to the modern German creator of Gebrauchsmusik who wrote a children's opera, *Wir bauen eine Stadt (Let's Build a City)*, is produced in San Jose, California.

24 APRIL 1969

Don Juan, ou l'Amour de la Géometrie, surrealist opera by Ivan SEMENOFF (1917–1972), is produced in Saint-Denis, near Paris.

6 MAY 1969

Charles FUSSEL conducts the first performance of his *Second Symphony*, scored for soprano and orchestra, at the Eastman School of Music in Rochester, New York.

9 MAY 1969

Fifth Symphony by the 46-year-old American composer Irwin BAZELON is performed for the first time in Indianapolis.

9 MAY 1969

Igra riječi (Word Game) for two speakers, chorus, eight instruments and tape by the 54-year-old Croatian composer Natko DEVČIĆ, in which the sonic elements of the Serbo-Croatian language are represented in musical terms, is performed for the first time in Zagreb.

15 MAY 1969

Das Märchen von der schönen Lilie, opera in two acts after Goethe's gentle tale of pastoral love, by the 43-year-old German composer Giselher KLEBE, is performed for the first time in Düsseldorf.

16 MAY 1969

HPSCHD (Harpsichord, in vowelless computer language) by John CAGE, scored for seven amplified harpsichords, fifty-two film projectors, 340-foot circular screen, suspended sheets measuring 40 × 100 feet each and fifty-two channels of sound for magnetic tapes, is performed for the first time on the Urbana Campus of the University of Illinois.

16 MAY 1969

Musique romantique, unromantic piece for oboe, harp and string trio by the innovative Soviet composer Edison DENISOV, is performed for the first time in Zagreb.

19 May 1969
Children's Crusade, cantata by the British composer Benjamin BRITTEN, evoking a historical event when many children perished at sea, is performed for the first time at St. Paul's Cathedral in London.

7 June 1969
La Transfiguration de Notre Seigneur Jesus-Christ for chorus and orchestra by the 61-year-old French composer Olivier MESSIAEN, in fourteen sections, covering all states of transfiguration, is performed for the first time in Lisbon.

20 June 1969
Violin Concerto in C by the 93-year-old English composer Havergal BRIAN, composed in 1934–1935, receives a belated first performance in London.

22 June 1969

At the 43rd Festival of the International Society for Contemporary Music in Hamburg, two programs are given, one in the afternoon and one in the evening. Afternoon program . . . *Cantata* for mixed choir, wind instruments and percussion by the 49-year-old Czech composer Zbyněk VOSTŘÁK, to the words by Franz Kafka in Czech translation of the original German text, expressing the surrealistic anguish of quotidian reality in acute dissonant counterpoint.

This was not the first performance of the *Cantata* by Vostřák; it was first performed in Prague on 12 March 1968.

24 June 1969

At the 43rd Festival of the International Society for Contemporary Music in Hamburg the following concert of choral and orchestral music is presented . . . *AMB* by the 39-year-old German composer Dieter SCHÖNBACH, for 7 groups of speaking vocalists, to the text of a liturgy (AMB is the vowelless Hebrew spelling of Amen). . . .

The name of the composer of *AMN* (not *AMB*) is Dieter SCHNEBEL (not Schönbach).

27 June 1969
Richard MAXFIELD, American composer, realizer of the tussive symphonic piece entitled *Cough Music*, first performed in New York on 13 January 1961, commits suicide at the age of forty-two by self-defenestration from a hotel room in Los Angeles.

29 June 1969

Reconstruction, a brobdingnagian anti-imperialist pasquinade with a musical score by Louis ANDRIESSEN, Reinbert DE LEEUW, Peter SCHAT, Misha MENGELBURG and Jan VAN VLIJMEN, denouncing Yankee incursions into bucolically vulnerable Latin American countries (Cuba is represented as a naked young bride exposed to the libidinous insults of an American Don Juan, who is eventually hurled all the way down to hell by a forty-foot statue of Ché Guevara), is produced at the Holland Festival in Amsterdam.

1 July 1969

Eryri for mixed chorus and orchestra by the 39-year-old Welsh composer Alun HODDINOTT is performed for the first time at the Investiture of the Prince of Wales in Cardiff.

3 July 1969

Bravo, Mozart, a playful homage by the 41-year-old American composer Dominick ARGENTO for chamber orchestra of Mozartean dimension, is performed for the first time in Minneapolis.

9 July 1969

Third Symphony by the British composer Lennox BERKELEY is performed for the first time at the Cheltenham Festival.

16 July 1969

A Celtic Requiem, dramatic cantata for soloists, children's chorus, chorus and orchestra by the 25-year-old British composer John TAVENER, is performed for the first time in London.

21 July 1969

La Comédie, "anti-opera" by the 49-year-old Polish composer Roman HAUBENSTOCK-RAMATI, scored for one male and two female speech-singers and three percussionists, to a text by Samuel Beckett, is performed for the first time in St. Paul de Vence in Alpes-Maritimes, France.

25 July 1969

Douglas MOORE, American composer whose erudite symphonic and chamber music reflected the cultural trends of American cosmopolitanism, and who recreated in his "folk opera" *Ballad of Baby Doe* a historical moment of genuine Americana, dies in Greenport, Long Island, New York, at the age of seventy-five.

30 July 1969

How Much Better if Plymouth Rock Had Landed on the Pilgrims, a historic wish-fulfillment for acoustic and electronic instruments, devised by the 21-year-old American composer David ROSENBLOOM, begins its continuous performance with a projected duration of about seventy-two hours at the Electric Ear Series of the Electric Circus in New York.

1 AUGUST 1969

Hra o láske a smrti (Play of Love and Death), opera by the 58-year-old Slovak composer Ján CIKKER, after a novella by Romain Rolland, is performed for the first time in Munich.

10 AUGUST 1969

Chuench'i, cycle of seven songs from the Chinese for voice and orchestra by the 45-year-old British composer Gerard SCHURMANN, is performed for the first time in Harrogate. .

15, 16, 17 AUGUST 1969

The Woodstock Music and Arts Fair is held on the alfalfa field in Bethel, fifty miles south of Woodstock, New York, attended by nearly half a million celebrants and enthusiasts of rock 'n' roll, marijuana and angel dust, a three-day festival that crystallized the emotions of a generation of flower children and social rebels, evoking comparison with Mecca and Gettysburg as sites of historic events.

20 AUGUST 1969

Thirty-nine Minutes for Thirty-nine Autos by the 32-year-old American avant-garde composer Robert MORAN, "environmental work for thirty skyscrapers, thirty-nine auto horns, Moog synthesizer and human performers, employing 100,000 persons," directed from atop Twin Peaks in San Francisco and making use of autos, airplanes, searchlights and local radio and television stations, is revealed to the populace of San Francisco and the world for the first time.

24 AUGUST 1969

Aloys MOOSER, learned Swiss musicologist who sojourned early in the century in Russia and took lessons with Rimsky-Korsakov, author of exemplary volumes on Russian eighteenth-century music, dies in his native Geneva at the age of ninety-two.

23 SEPTEMBER 1969

Sixth Symphony by the Swiss composer Robert BLUM is performed for the first time in Zürich.

24 SEPTEMBER 1969

Erasmi Monumentum for organ and orchestra by the distinguished Swiss composer Frank MARTIN, a musical homage to the great skeptical philosopher Erasmus who wrote *In Praise of Folly*, is performed for the first time in Rotterdam.

25 SEPTEMBER 1969
200,000 Taler, opera by the Manchurian-born composer Boris BLACHER after a tale by Sholom Aleichem, is performed for the first time in Berlin.

27 SEPTEMBER 1969
Fifth Symphony, subtitled *Sinfonia dolce quasi passacaglia*, by the 63-year-old Norwegian composer Klaus EGGE, is performed for the first time in Oslo.

29 SEPTEMBER 1969
Fourteenth Symphony by Dmitri SHOSTAKOVICH, scored for soprano, bass and chamber orchestra, in eleven sections with texts by Federico García Lorca, Apollinaire, Rilke and the Russian poet Wilhelm Küchelbecker, a friend of Pushkin, each poem of a quasi-thanatological coloration, with the musical score revealing a tremendous inner tension within the threshold of tonality, is performed for the first time in Leningrad.

9 OCTOBER 1969
Fulgar (Lightning) for band, percussion, two harps, piano, celesta and tubular chimes by the 45-year-old French composer Serge NIGG is performed for the first time in Paris.

19 OCTOBER 1969
. . . pianissimo . . . for orchestra by the 34-year-old Soviet avant-gardist Alfred SCHNITTKE is performed for the first time at the Donaueschingen Festival of Contemporary Music.

22 OCTOBER 1969
Concerto for timpani and orchestra by the 63-year-old Croatian composer Boris PAPANDOPULO is performed for the first time in Zagreb.

23 OCTOBER 1969
Lovely Thing for piano by the American avant-garde composer Harold BUDD, with directions to the player: "Select a chord—if in doubt call me (in lieu of performance) at 213-662-7819 for spiritual advice," is performed for the first time in Memphis, Tennessee.

25 OCTOBER 1969
Continuum, subtitled *Trauerminuten für Dana Kosanova*, for chamber orchestra by the 34-year-old Bulgarian composer Bojidar DIMOV, commemorating a 15-year-old Czech girl student killed in the course of the

Soviet invasion of Czechoslovakia in 1968, is performed for the first time in Graz.

25 OCTOBER 1969
The Strange Story of Arthur Rowe, opera by the 40-year-old Czech composer Ivan JIRKO, after Graham Greene's novel *Ministry of Fear*, is produced in Liberec.

29 OCTOBER 1969
Superball for four players with hand-held magnetic tape heads by the 32-year-old American avant-gardist Jon HASSELL is performed for the first time in Ithaca, New York.

11 NOVEMBER 1969
Jed z Elsinoru (Poison from Elsinore) by the Czech composer Karel HORKÝ, after the radio play *Urhamlet*, inspired by the conviction that the assassination of President Kennedy, like the murder of Hamlet's father in Shakespeare's tragedy, was the result of a struggle for power guided by a wily American Polonius who urges the reactionary government to conceal the truth, with a somber chorus voicing the conscience of America, is produced in Brno.

11 NOVEMBER 1969
Catharsis: Open Style for Two Improvisation Ensembles, Tapes and Conductors by the American composer Larry AUSTIN, exemplifying his concept of coordinated improvisation with optional beginnings and endings of individual sections, is performed for the first time in Oakland, California.

13 NOVEMBER 1969
Epimetheus USA, symphonic poem by the 62-year-old Berlin-born American composer Gene GUTCHË, conjuring up an American counterpart of the brother of the igniferous Prometheus and mundiferous Atlas and husband of the vitigerous Pandora, is performed for the first time in Detroit.

13 NOVEMBER 1969
Maria Triptychon for soprano, violin and orchestra by the 79-year-old Swiss composer Frank MARTIN, consisting of three separate works, *Ave Maria, Magnificat* and *Stabat Mater*, is performed for the first time in Rotterdam.

14 NOVEMBER 1969
The Lobster Quadrille by the 32-year-old American composer David DEL TREDICI, scored for soprano, folk group, mandolin, banjo, accordion and orchestra, inspired by the writings of Lewis Carroll, is performed for the first time in London, Aaron Copland conducting.

23 NOVEMBER 1969

La Voz del Silencio, one-act opera by the 33-year-old Argentine composer Mario PERUSSO, to a symbolistic libretto, with indeterminate characters described only by sex or age (a woman, a man, a youth, a visitor) colliding and rotating on the stage in aleatory motion, set to an appropriately atonal score, is produced for the first time at the Teatro Colón in Buenos Aires.

27 NOVEMBER 1969

Marriage of the Whale, symphonic chorus for three voices, chorus and orchestra by the 59-year-old Japanese composer Kozaburo HIRAI, is performed for the first time in Tokyo.

6 DECEMBER 1969

Lukas Foss conducts in Hamburg the first performance of his *Geod,* a "musical action for orchestra, without development, without rhetoric," suggestive of the power of geodesic constructions, and scored for full orchestra.

9 DECEMBER 1969

Vesalii Icones by the 35-year-old English modernist Peter Maxwell DAVIES, scored for cello solo, small instrumental group and dancers, in fourteen sections, corresponding to fourteen anatomical drawings by the famous Renaissance anatomist Vesalius but audaciously paralleling successive postures of musculatures and skeletal figures with the stages of Christ's passions, the music varying eclectically from excruciating atonality expressing Christ's agony to ostentatious piano pounding in the manner of the Victorian music-hall to represent the Roman soldiery, is performed for the first time in London.

11 DECEMBER 1969

Fifth Symphony for baritone solo and orchestra, subtitled *Wine of Summer,* by the English polysymphonist Havergal BRIAN, comes to its belated first performance in London, thirty-two years after its completion.

15 DECEMBER 1969

Sixth Symphony by the 61-year-old Serbian composer Milan RISTIĆ, written in a neoclassical manner, is performed for the first time in Belgrade.

25 DECEMBER 1969

The First Christmas, opera by the 65-year-old Australian composer John Henry ANTILL, is presented for the first time by the Australian Broadcasting Corporation.

Documents

Introduction

In my search of documentary evidence connecting musical practices with political events, I came upon the mention of a "laboratory" within the United States Department of the Army that investigated the ways and means of influencing the policies of the Soviet Union by broadcasting Western music of a humanistic nature. The purely musical purpose of such broadcasts was to counteract the prevalence of marching tunes and patriotic songs typical of Soviet music. I wrote the Department of the Army for a copy of the declaration of aims of this musical laboratory. To my surprise, the Department of the Army replied that no such laboratory existed. Yet references to its work appeared in reputable sources. I wrote to my friend William Lichtenwanger, then head of the Reference Department of the Music Division of the Library of Congress, asking him to make further inquiries on the subject. Accordingly, he addressed an inquiry to the Department of the Army, but received a reply that such documents were classified information. He then repeated his request under the recently promulgated Freedom of Information Act. This time he received a copy of the document, marked "Unclassified." The present text represents the most important parts of this remarkable document.

The following excerpts from official Chinese publications represent the period of the extreme anti-Western and isolationist trend in the People's Republic of China, usually associated with the so-called "Cultural Revolution." They are here reproduced as documentary evidence of irrationality that strikes otherwise intelligent people and forces them to embrace the most fantastic notions of history and civilization.

COMMUNIST VULNERABILITIES TO THE USE OF MUSIC IN PSYCHOLOGICAL WARFARE

by

James S. Young

Approved:

CARLETON F. SCOFIELD
Director of Research
Psychological Warfare Division

MEREDITH P. CRAWFORD
Director
Human Resources Research Office

The George Washington University
HUMAN RESOURCES RESEARCH OFFICE
operating under contract with
THE DEPARTMENT OF THE ARMY

Technical Report 4
March 1954

Copy_____of
Log No.   A-2

OBJECTIVES

1. The original research requirement for this study came from the Operations and Training Branch, Propaganda Division, Office of the Chief of Psychological Warfare. This requirement called for lists of musical selections appropriate for use in propaganda broadcasts by Army operational units to certain specified target audiences. For this reason, initial attention in the research was concentrated upon problems of an operational nature. As the project progressed, however, it acquired the broader aspect of vulnerability research—the vulnerabilities of the Soviet Union and selected European Communist countries to the use of music in psychological warfare. Inquiry was directed toward:

(a) Finding the major areas of vulnerability to the use of music in psychological warfare, through a study of the recent music practices of target countries.

(b) Selecting compositions judged most appropriate for exploiting these vulnerabilities.

2. The operational objectives of the research were:

(a) To facilitate procurement of music recordings by the Department of the Army for use in psychological warfare programs.

(b) To guide Army psychological warfare operators in exploiting the propaganda possibilities in music broadcasts to audiences in the Soviet Union, Czechoslovakia, Hungary, Poland, Rumania, Yugoslavia, Bulgaria, and Albania.

3. It was considered appropriate to these objectives to present the research findings in three parts:

(a) A textual report which analyzes the music situation in the target countries, estimates the vulnerabilities resulting from that situation and from the nature of music as a medium of communication, and suggests ways in which those vulnerabilities may be exploited through psychological warfare. This report may be found on pages 3–18 of this volume. A brief discussion of the ways in which music performers recently escaped from Communist countries may be used as additional sources of information for psychological warfare units and as a reservoir of talent for broadcasts employing music is presented in Appendix A, pages 21–25 of this volume.

(b) A brief handbook-type summary for each target country studied, containing a calendar of its national holidays and festivals, an analysis of its recent musical diet, a list of its important music performers and ensembles, and a selected list of sources where further music information pertinent to the target country can be obtained. These summaries are attached as Appendices B through I of the textual report, and may be found on pages 27–84 of this volume.

(c) A catalogue which provides an individual listing for music recordings judged most suitable for use by psychological warfare operators, together with facts about the recordings which may be useful for procurement and propaganda purposes. This catalogue is separate from the present volume. Its contents are briefly described in Appendix J, pages 85–86 of this volume.

REGRADED UNCLASSIFIED ORDER
SEC ARMY BY TAG PER
7 5 0 2 4 4

1. Music is currently regulated in the Soviet Union, Czechoslovakia, Hungary, Poland, Rumania, Bulgaria, and Albania in accordance with a policy formulated in the Soviet Union by the late Andrei A. Zhdanov in 1948.

2. In certain aspects, the policy reflects the musical tastes of the people, tending to approve music which the majority of the people likes and to disapprove that which the majority does not like. Current policy demands simple, melodic music, using traditional harmonies and rhythms, prefers songs over instrumental music, favors the more popular pre-Communist composers over contemporary composers (both Western and indigenous), and prohibits the playing of modern Western jazz and art music. Folk music is in the highest favor, and music showing contemporary Western influences is disapproved.

3. In other aspects, current policy is designed to further the political and propaganda goals of the Communist regimes. It provides an opportunity to control "subversive" cliques of musical artists, enlists popular support for the regime in terms of the emotional responses induced by officially approved music, provides an opportunity for propaganda through the music, serves to "popularize" the intellectual accomplishments of the music world, and provides an additional opportunity to condemn Western culture.

4. The chief vulnerabilities in the countries studied (with the exception of Yugoslavia) to the use of music in psychological warfare would seem to be these:

(a) The official policies on music illustrate the regimes' distrust of all free and individual expression, and reveal how the desire of the regimes to preserve their own power conflicts with the desires of the people.

(b) The failure of the Communist-approved musical diet wholly to satisfy certain target groups disposes them favorably toward United States programs offering music they like but cannot hear over their own Communist-controlled media of communication.

(c) The nature of music itself makes it valuable for inducing desired moods, creating a certain emotional atmosphere for broadcasts, and suggesting certain ideas.

CAUTIONS

1. The findings of this research cannot supplant area knowledge. They may serve to guide the psychological warfare operator who is not acquainted with the music practices of the target countries and to provide a convenient reference for area specialists.

2. The findings of this research are not based on first-hand testing or interviewing of escaped target nationals to ascertain actual music preferences in the target countries. Sources used include publications, interviews with music and area specialists, and monitoring reports of music broadcast by selected radio stations in the target countries.

3. Alienation of target audiences may result from (a) broadcasting music unattractive to the audience, (b) overemphasizing a single type of music, a single technique of presentation, or musical as against verbal programs.

4. The psychological warfare operator who uses music for propaganda purposes

will be competing with the Communists' well-formulated and systematic programs of indoctrination through music. Failure to display equal skill may not only reduce the effectiveness of music as a United States propaganda weapon, but may even generate negative attitudes toward United States propaganda efforts employing other techniques.

OPERATIONAL SUGGESTIONS

Note: Inasmuch as the Army research requirement which necessitated this study presented problems of an operational nature, certain suggestions for the guidance of personnel conducting psychological warfare operations have been made on the basis of the research accomplished. These suggestions, listed below, are offered with the understanding that broader policy objectives and the immediate operational situation may limit their usefulness.

1. The diverse content of musical expression and the various emotional responses elicited by music listening suggest that music can be adapted for the following purposes in psychological warfare:
    (a) To express certain United Nations and United States values
    (b) To popularize the expression of antagonism toward the Communist regime
    (c) To popularize the expression of favorable attitudes toward the United States
    (d) To increase nationalistic sentiments
    (e) To illustrate propaganda themes
    (f) To promote themes of internationalism
    (g) To increase the audience appeal of fables or legends which have political overtones
    (h) To attract attention, to induce certain moods, and to impute connotations to verbal matter
    (i) To induce the defection of target artists
2. The use of contemporary indigenous music having pro-Communist connotations as well as compositions frequently broadcast by the Communist radio should for the most part be avoided in United States broadcasts.
3. Modern Western music of the dissonant or "radical" type—among both jazz and art music repertories—should not be used in United States broadcasts.
4. Both the Communist music policies and the music preferences of target groups (with respect to performers as well as compositions) can change rapidly and unpredictably. Psychological warfare operators intending to use music for propaganda purposes should, therefore, supplement the information contained in this report with intelligence on the *current* musical diet and preferences of the audience to be reached. Current intelligence, for instance, might void both suggestions 2. and 3. in the case of certain target audiences.

FOREWORD

The following text begins with an analysis of the official Soviet music policy promulgated in 1948 by the late Andrei Zhdanov. Although many factors contributed to this policy, the specific directives laid down in the policy represent what, at that time, seemed to Communist officials the most expedient way of making musical expression serve the propaganda and political objectives of their regime. As indicated in the text, it is likely that the Zhdanov policy will be changed or even supplanted altogether, and, since the writing of this report, there have been indications that the Malenkov regime is attempting to erase Zhdanov's influence. Even if the directives of the Zhdanov policy change, however, it is unlikely that the basic aims of this policy will be abandoned. For these aims are rooted in a fundamental tenet of Communism: that all artistic expression must embody, portray, and teach Communist values, and perform a function useful to Communist society. Thus, because music is regarded under Communism as a political and propaganda resource, the desire of the Communist propaganda machine to make use of it will not easily be thwarted. The techniques of employing this resource (the Zhdanov policy, for example) may vary from time to time, but any policy changes will be limited by those basic Communist values which require the subordination of cultural activity to the interests of the regime.

In order to preserve the strategic and tactical value of this report against revisions of the Zhdanov policy, the discussion has not been limited to a description of that policy. Instead, the Zhdanov policy is used as a starting point for discussing the more enduring goals which the policy was designed to serve. This approach, it is hoped, will enable propaganda specialists to make a meaningful appraisal not only of the Zhdanov policy, but also of the policies which may succeed it. It is hoped particularly that the information provided will enable the reader to recognize, where it exists, the underlying continuity and consistency in what may appear to be drastic changes in the Zhdanov policy.

It should be emphasized that this report discusses vulnerabilities other than those stemming from Communist political control over music. The text, together with the appendices, is designed as background material to guide propaganda specialists in using the catalogue of music recordings supplied by this research.

339

In commemoration of the thirtieth anniversary of the Russian Revolution in December 1947, a new opera entitled *The Great Fellowship*, by the Georgian composer Vano Muradeli, was performed at the Bolshoi Theater in Moscow. It was a "closed" performance, given for about 500 high-ranking Soviet officials, one of whom presumably was Stalin himself. At the end of the performance, such an intense dispute developed about the music that the director of the theater suffered a heart attack and died on the spot.

Immediately thereafter, music compositions by modern Soviet composers were expurgated from concert repertories in the Soviet Union. Rumors personally critical of certain outstanding Russian composers began to circulate, as did speculation about the possibility of a "purge" in the music world.

All doubt vanished in the middle of January, 1948. Russian composers, music teachers, and critics were summoned to a meeting by the Central Committee of the Communist Party to hear a blistering attack on contemporary Soviet music and musicians delivered by the late Andrei A. Zhdanov, Party Chief of Leningrad during the German siege, and cultural spokesman for the Party.

Following the musicians' meeting, the Party published a decree denouncing by name the six idols of Soviet music—Shostakovich, Prokofiev, Khachaturian, Shebalin, Popov, and Miaskovsky. They were accused of disregarding the "social role of music," of catering to the "degenerate tastes of a handful of estheticising individualists," of indulging in "decadent bourgeois formalism," and of manifesting "anti-People" tendencies.

Immediately after publication of the decree, Shostakovich and Miaskovsky were expelled from their teaching posts at the Moscow Conservatory, and Shebalin was dismissed as its director. Khachaturian was removed from his position as Secretary-General of the Union of Soviet Composers and from the chairmanship of its Organizing Committee, which, in conjunction with the Committee on Arts of the Ministry of Education, decides what music works will be published and recommends those to be performed. Other familiar figures in the music world were arrested. Several months later a Party member suggested that composers infected with bourgeois tendencies "could very profitably move out of Moscow to the periphery of the vast Soviet land and get their inspiration from a close contact with the life of the people in the provinces, in collective farms and factories."

The new music policy begun in the Soviet Union in 1948 was later exported to the satellite countries. Eight months after the January meeting in Moscow, the first Working Congress of Czechoslovak Composers and Musical Scholars published directions for musicians that were strictly in accordance with the Soviet decree. In 1949, Polish composers were summoned to a meeting at Logow which turned out to be strikingly similar to the Moscow convention presided over by Zhdanov. The outcome of the Logow meeting was a demand for "breaking down the formalistic influence of the West" and "applying the methods of socialist realism . . . either by creating new musical forms . . . or by an increasingly stronger accentuation of the essentially ideological content" in music. Soon thereafter, official attention was directed to the schooling of singers' collective groups. Rumanian musicians suffered a purge in 1952. As in the Soviet Union, the theme of the purge was formalism, and its result the development of a militant, combative, and partisan music, reflecting the "realities" of working class life, according to Party orders. After the purge, courses in Marxism and Leninism were conducted for musicians by the Rumanian Federation of Composers. Thus far, Hungary, Bulgaria, and Albania seem to have escaped purges, although in all of these countries, the radio music diet is generally restricted to compositions which currently enjoy the approval of the Soviet Communist Party.

Since 1948, many of the composers attacked in the Soviet decree have produced works designed to restore them to the Party's graces, but their acceptance by the Party has been only partial. A considerable amount of their music is still banned in the Communist world, and the Party has officially reported that "some formalist elements" still persist in their works and their "transformation [is] proceeding rather slowly."

The purpose and effect of the new policy has been to cramp musical expression into a role utilitarian to the Communist state. This "utility" music is fostered by the use of two techniques: prescribing musical standards for composers, and educating musicians in Communist doctrine. Traditionally accepted music likewise is manipulated to make it politically useful by such techniques as symbolizing its content in political terms or associating the music with political, economic, or military events. The same end is served by lending the prestige of the official media of communication to favored works, denying a hearing for works with adverse connotations, slanting with pro-Communist language the texts of familiar songs, and "capturing" the names of great composers of the past and imputing Communist ideas to their works.

The cultural offensive inside the Soviet Union has by no means been limited to music; music was merely the last victim. Similar attacks against literature and philosophy (also launched by Zhdanov), the graphic arts, drama, and cinema preceded the attack on music. But of these victims, music suffered the most radical and violent assault. That this should be the case is surprising, especially since the composers singled out for denunciation by the 1948 decree had long been the ones most highly revered in Soviet music. With the music-loving public, theirs were household names; they were idolized by the government and showered with numerous Stalin prizes for their compositions. Only once previously, in 1936, had any of the musicians named in the 1949 decree been criticized by the Party. This offender was Shostakovich, who was reprimanded by *Pravda* for "formalistic tendencies" in his opera *Lady Macbeth of Ttensk*. Shostakovich had returned to Party grace by 1948, however. Less than a year before the 1948 attack, the leading Russian music historian and critic Asafiev wrote of Shostakovich that he could not have created subsequent to the reprimand in 1936 "those immensely human symphonies which are the admiration of the whole world" had it not been for the prior "fatherly directness and care" shown by the Party in 1936.

The 1948 policy was a reversal of the official attitude not only toward the leading composers themselves, but also on the merit of various music forms developed under Soviet rule. Before 1948, the symphonic form was in highest favor; according to Asafiev, "The great revolutionary struggle of our people, the building of Socialism in our country, the gigantic upsurge in all fields of human activity, the mighty growth of artistic and scientific thought in our country . . . is reflected in our music; and all that was best and most important in this respect we find in the music of our *symphonists*" (emphasis added). However, less than a year after Asafiev had made this statement, symphonic music was singled out by Zhandov for particularly strong criticism. The principal complaints were that composers had devoted more attention to symphonic than to operatic music and that—what the Party now views as one of the cardinal musical sins—"as a result of the underestimation of folk music by our symphonic composers," they had allowed symphonic music to become divorced from native folk music expression.

Why, then, did the Party take such a sweeping interest in music? Part of the answer lies in the fact that a political unit of totalitarian pretensions, by the logic of its own assumptions, is committed to an extension of its authority into even those areas of behavior which are least critical for the maintenance of political control and ideological solidarity. Specific applications of political authority to such areas of behavior are further encouraged when, as in the case of Russian Communism, the totalitarian ideology calls for reforming the very substance of culture itself. Likewise, extremist measures are resorted to when the regime becomes insecure, and tends to fear every uncontrolled or truly spontaneous activity as a potential source of disaffection.

Another significant factor in the 1948 attack is the fact that new music, like other art forms embodying novel and original concepts, is almost never readily accepted by the larger public, and in fact frequently provokes strongly hostile reactions. Thus it becomes possible for a dictatorial policy, under the guise of expressing the affirmative desires of a majority of the people, to condemn vast segments of contemporary repertories and approve the more familiar and traditional styles without risking protest from the listening public.

Another partial explanation for the Party's sudden and disruptive attack on music may have been that a musical clique professionally jealous of the denounced musicians was trying to gain favor. Competition within the Party, in which Zhdanov and Georgi Malenkov were then rivals, may also have been a factor; Zhdanov, having been entrusted with responsibility for cultural matters in the Party, may have used this opportunity to gain the favor of Stalin, whose artistic tastes, like Zhdanov's, were plebeian.

In this general context, however, other factors contributed more directly to the Soviet music policy. These factors, and the vulnerabilities they indicate, can best be understood by evaluating, first, the content of that policy and, second, the ways in which the Communist state benefits by it. Such an analysis may also provide a basis for evaluating future changes in Soviet music policy.

MUSIC APPROVED BY THE PARTY

What is currently regarded by the Communist Party as the music most suitable for the ears of the populations it controls?

(1) *Music that is not "formalistic."* "Formalism" in musical expression may be described as overemphasis on external form as against content. It implies an elaborate structure of motifs or themes not unified by an underlying principle, a concern with craftsmanship rather than thought content, and, in its extreme form, reliance on established forms at the expense of originality. As described by one of Zhdanov's followers, it occurs "whenever the composer shows an insufficient creative will to follow [the] road of life's fundamentals to the utmost limit of his consciousness. If he is creatively lazy, he will stop at the beginning of the road, and the thread that leads him to the final goal snaps. His musical images, as a result, become vague, incomplete, and distorted."

This question of form and content is one of the central problems of the artist, a problem inherent in artistic endeavor itself. How to be original in thought and at the same time to express it musically in a form that is understandable in comparison with existing, familiar forms cannot be settled for the artist by political guidance. Nevertheless, because the problem is ever present for the practicing artist, it renders him extremely vulnerable to criticism for failure to solve it.

The simple fact that extreme formalism tends to produce inferior music imparts a certain validity to the use of formalism as a standard for music criticism. However, when applied with political reference, it ceases to have a definable meaning. For example, the Communist Party characterizes most Western music as formalistic, while Russian music, with the exception of the genre criticized in the 1948 decree, is called non-formalistic. Although it is generally true that Russian composers have demonstrated less skill in the matter of musical organization, they nevertheless have relied largely upon the music forms developed in the West, and not a few of them could be classified as formalists. One such musician is the pre-Communist Russian composer, Scriabin. Yet he is currently favored by Communist music policy makers. When, for example, in the midst of the 1948 controversy, he was characterized by a writer in the Communist magazine *Soviet Literature* as a degenerate formalist of the worst sort, the music policy makers behind the Iron Curtain rose to his defense and denounced the writer of the article. Ironically enough, however, the best examples of formalism—defined by the Party as resulting from a failure of creative energy—are to be found in contemporary Soviet compositions which were written in conformity with the very policy which denounces it. For the policy set forth in 1948 has had the effect of inducing composers to imitate the music forms approved by the Party (especially folk music) and to avoid expressing original ideas for fear of not conforming to the officially approved stereotypes.

The concept of formalism that is applied by the Party in criticism of contemporary Soviet and Western music is derived only superficially, therefore, from musical principles. This concept is dictated chiefly by political considerations and expediency, for the formalistic music which Party usage considers unworthy of Communist-controlled audiences turns out to be compositions that either are associated with the West or are not of the type that engenders widespread interest among the masses of the population. That the basis of the whole policy is political in nature becomes apparent from the aspects of the policy which are discussed in the following sections.

(2) *Simple and melodic music.* It follows from the Party's desire to have composers put more "content" into musical expression that its interest goes further in specifying what content is acceptable.

With respect to musical material itself, atonal or strongly dissonant music, as well as music which is overly "naturalistic" (that is, involves excessive use of drums, cymbals, and the like), is regarded as "false, vulgar, and pathological . . . filled with idealistic emotion, alien to the broad masses of the people, and addressed to the few . . . to the elite." In contrast, "singable" melodies are desired.

With respect to musical ideas, "program music" is preferred to "absolute music." The reason is transparent: because program music conveys an impression of a definite series of images, scenes, or events, it is easier to understand and is better adapted as a vehicle of propaganda than absolute music, which is nonrepresentational in nature.

This attitude is in line with the broader outlines of the policy stated by Zhdanov to the effect that the "intrinsic function" of music is to "give pleasure." Hence, any music which the people "cannot understand" is bad. It is under this criterion of "understandability" that the present policy favors long-established music over modern music. For the longer an art work survives in history, the more familiar, and in this sense the more understandable, it becomes. The radical, "disharmonious" type of modern music is considered particularly undesirable, even though its content is apparently pro-Communist; not only is it unpopular and not "useful to society," but it also "affects the correct psycho-physiological functioning of man." If a composer produces disharmonious or atonal works for the sake of sheer novelty, the musical worth of his compositions is certain to be inferior. But a mere reading of Zhdanov's language shows that his criticism reflects more a suspicion of novel and unfamiliar expression than refined musical judgment. The official attitude may be summed up in the phrase: "It's what we don't understand that's dangerous." Or, as the Russian satirist Saltykov said, during the Czarist regime: "What I don't understand is undoubtedly dangerous to the security of the state." In this aspect, too, Communist music policy reflects the necessity of the totalitarian state to suspect everything which, due to lack of knowledge or other reasons, it cannot fully control.

(3) *Music using subjects from Communist doctrine and Soviet life.* Of all the standards demanded of new music, this is the most obviously political in nature. Examples of music fitting this requirement are Beli's "In Defense of Peace," and Prokofiev's "Story of a Real Man" which deals with the heroism of a Soviet fighter pilot who learned how to fly again after having lost both legs.

It is in this connection that the recurrent conflict arises between the internationalist orientation of Communism and the nationalist orientation of Russian politics. Zhdanov dismissed this problem by pronouncing that "one cannot be an internationalist in music, or in any other realm, without being at the same time a genuine patriot of one's own country . . . internationalism arises from the very flowering of national art." To indulge in the "contraband" music forms imported from the West is, for the Russian musician, to become a "homeless cosmopolitan."

(4) *Vocal and operatic music.* The Communist Party favors songs over purely instrumental music, particularly songs that call for large choruses. For this requirement, too, the motivation is obviously political, for vocal music has certain propagandistic values above instrumental music—namely, that it allows for mass participation, is better adapted to convey specific political ideas, and is usually simpler and more understandable than instrumental music, not only because it must have words, but also because its melodies must conform to the limitations in range of the human voice.

(5) *Folk music.* The epitome of the Communist Party's musical standards is folk music. It is constantly eulogized by Party spokesmen: "Just as the lily, in its glorious

and chaste beauty, eclipses the brilliance of brocades and precious stones, so folk music, thanks to its very childlike simplicity, is a thousand times richer and stronger than all the artifices of the learning taught by pedants in the conservatories and musical academies." This fulsome comparison is probably indicative of the real Communist attitude toward art music, an antagonism that is tantamount to denying the validity of this form of music altogether, except as it incorporates folk themes. In contrast, folk music enjoys such high favor because it is a communal, rather than an individualistic art; it is naturally adapted for group participation and more often than not is sung; it uses native subjects; and, simple in melody, harmony, and form, it is readily understood by proletarian and peasant alike.

What the policy amounts to, then, is an espousal by the Communist Party of certain esthetic values, none of them novel in themselves: "realism," comprehensibility, simplicity and tunefulness, beauty, and a preference for popular and folk ideas and for music that is sung. While these values may have an integrity of their own, they cannot be judged solely on their merits because they have been adapted to serve not esthetic, but political ends. So aptly do these values serve the regimes' conquest of power as to suggest that they have been expropriated by the Party chiefly for that reason. An examination of the ways in which Communist music policy benefits the state makes this conclusion even more convincing.

POLITICAL ADVANTAGES IN CONTROLLING MUSICAL EXPRESSION

(1) One of the most important benefits to the Communist state is the opportunity that control provides for maintaining surveillance over composers, music theorists, and critics. Traditionally—in Russia, at least—criticism of the prevailing regime, having been denied an effective political outlet, was expressed through the medium of art, particularly literary art. Thus, with some justification in Russian history, artistic groups are regarded as traditional sources of disaffection and political criticism.

But there is a deeper reason for official control over artists in a totalitarian society. One of the historic attributes of artistic activity is the high value placed upon individuality. The artist insists on the privilege of thinking "freely" and of perceiving without being restricted to the usual patterns. Russian artists in the past have particularly stressed the need for individuality and freedom in order to be truly creative. Illustrative of their thinking on this matter are the statements of the late Nicolas Berdyaev, an exiled member of the Russian intelligentsia: "It is only in the creative act that man prevails over the oppression and enslavement of extraneous influences . . . [creative activity] is individual and indeed rebellious in nature, involving conflict between man and his environment . . . the basic characteristic of a creative act consists in not being wholly determined by its medium, and [in] that it comprises something new, something which cannot be derived from the external world in which it is embodied, or indeed from some fixed repository of ideal forms which press upon the creator's imagination."

Zhdanov himself did not overlook the possible anarchistic implications in this type of thinking; one of the criticisms he made most vehemently was of music that was "rampantly individualistic." It does not appear at all surprising, then, that not one of the arts has escaped state control in the Soviet Union.

Thus, artists in general, and musicians in particular, should be especially susceptible targets for psychological warfare which plays upon this theme and encourages them to defect. The defection of an important artist from the Soviet Union would have an extremely high propaganda value.

(2) By allying itself with longer-established, more familiar, and better-liked music, the regime cultivates the support of the larger public and can receive credit for recognizing "good music." Furthermore, the pleasurable and inspirational emotions that are a part of the musical experience can be associated with, and turned to the advantage of, the regime.

(3) The Communist state also benefits from the way in which control permits the manipulation of music for purposes of conveying verbal propaganda. In this connection, it should be remembered that current policy favors songs, which are particularly

adapted for this purpose. Propaganda that is put into musical form is less overt and, because it is cloaked in a pleasing melody, is less likely to evoke the defenses that an individual may put up against spoken propaganda.

(4) Control over music also serves to further the Communist goal of "popularizing" intellectual accomplishment and activity. One of the concerns of the pre-Communist Russian intelligentsia was justifying the divorce from the life of the people that intellectual activity entails. In the past, various segments in the Russian intelligentsia have resolved this problem by foregoing specialized intellectual life altogether and "returning to the soil"—to the people. While elements of this solution are apparent in the Communist answer, the current solution is more nearly that of bringing culture—used here in the lay sense—to the people, rather than the people to culture. Thus, to justify intellectual accomplishments, such as art music compositions, they must be simplified in order that they may be comprehensible to the masses. This fact is abundantly clear in Zhdanov's requirement that music be "understandable."

(5) Controlling the music diet of the people also provides an additional opportunity to condemn Western culture, to forestall any Western influence that may penetrate the Iron Curtain through music, and to impress the people with the superiority of Russian or native culture.

In summation, the current Communist music policy is based upon considerations of politics and expediency, and is guided by two frequently conflicting goals: first, and more important, to further the propaganda and political goals of the Party; second, to avoid violating the music tastes of the majority. Consequently, sudden and unpredictable shifts may be made in the specific directives laid down in the policy without altering the basic political goals which the policy was designed to serve. Evidence of strong public approval or disapproval of certain composers or compositions, personal jealousies within the music profession, the personal conduct of a musician or his expression of an unpopular viewpoint—all these things, and not solely the music principles stated in the official pronouncements, affect the Party's stand on individual cases. The psychological warfare operator should always attempt, therefore, to ascertain the *current* music situation prior to choosing his propaganda themes.

MAJOR AREAS OF COMMUNIST VULNERABILITY TO MUSIC

The nature and implications of Communist music policy have been discussed here at length because it is the *fact* of control—the existence of a music policy as such—which gives rise to the major vulnerabilities of Communist countries to the use of music in psychological warfare.

(1) Control over musicians is one example of Communist tyranny. It is an especially revealing example because it illustrates specifically the higher value placed by Communism upon the interest of the "community" or "collective life" than upon the dignity of individual men, and because it shows how this "community interest" is being used by the Party as a disguise for its own self-interest. This situation provides a valuable opportunity for exploitation in psychological warfare, and the example of Communist music policy is all the more effective for this purpose because music is so obviously a field virtually unrelated to political interests, and thus least justifiably subject to political control. For this reason, it should be possible, by emphasizing the controls placed on music artists, to convey to target audiences the idea not only that the Party is dedicated chiefly to its own interest, but that, in serving itself, the Party threatens in a concrete way the freedom of activity and expression of those who still enjoy it. It is true, of course, that religious-like devotion to the task of unifying a community can excuse, in the eyes of the faithful, even the most extreme customs of human liberty. Certainly, unless attention is called to the fact, the devotees of such a cause can overlook the deprivations of a small group such as musicians. Their zeal should not be underestimated.

However, even with no exploitation whatever by the West, the music policy initiated by the Soviet Union has been itself sufficient to become a source of major embarrassment to Communists outside Russia. The Communist policy toward music in particular, and art in general, "has caused Russia more harm abroad, among Left-wing, and predominantly pro-Soviet intelligentsia, than anything else. . . . The most powerful Communist Party in the West, that in France, has the strongest mental reservations about Soviet art policy. . . . In Poland and Czechoslovakia, the whole Communist and Left-wing intelligentsia are perturbed and embarrassed by what has happened in Russia in the field of culture." This embarrassment has not been limited to intellectuals abroad; many of the Soviet musicians themselves have become in varying degrees disillusioned as a result of the policy. It is this group that should be particularly susceptible targets for psychological warfare. However, just as music is only one of many forms of expression which have been suppressed by Communist regimes, likewise the potential target in the exploitation of current Communist music policy is by no means limited to musicians. The policy can be used to illustrate the regime's attitude toward free expression in general.

Whether or not it exists in a situation of "thought control," music stands as a symbol of freedom and individuality of expression. It lends itself, therefore, to a psychological warfare theme developed along the following lines:

By dictating musical standards to composers and by banning all compositions that are individualistic or imaginative, or in some other way do not conform to these standards, the regime has denied the freedom of the artist to create and of the listener to hear music of his own choosing. Why won't the regime let people hear certain music? Why is it afraid of music? By playing its own, and not the people's music, it has betrayed the true values of the (Russian) people.

This vulnerability can be exploited not only verbally but also through music. One of the simpler techniques is to broadcast familiar and well-liked music composed by target nationals which has been officially or unofficially banned. In this way, target audiences may be reminded of the deprivations caused by the regime. It is important to recognize, however, that banning is seldom done overtly. The fact that Party organs condemn a certain composer or composition does not necessarily mean that he or his work will be formally banned. The more usual technique is simply the silent removal of the offender from radio and concert repertories: thus he or his work is consigned to oblivion.

(2) A second vulnerability lies in the fact that the Communist policy of reforming music is bound to encounter ingrained popular preferences for music which the Party does not approve, or popular resistance to compositions which the Party does approve. This puts our own psychological warfare operators in the advantageous position of being able to give Communist-controlled audiences a music fare more to their liking than the one they now receive.

The present policy shows that Communist policy-makers have realized that the music tastes of the people cannot be changed overnight, and they have in most instances selected for approval those compositions which are most popular and disapproved those which are not well-liked. There are situations in which popular preferences seem not to have been satisfied, however. In Hungary, for example, there is evidence of resistance to the disproportionate amount of Russian music performed, as compared with Hungarian selections. Hungarian Communist officials feel that they cannot safely foster any substantial amount of Hungarian music because it is for the most part nationalistic in character. Before the Communist coup, Czechoslovakia had developed a distinct liking for Western swing, and to a lesser extent for jazz. In 1949, the charge of "decadence" hurled at Bing Crosby by one of the Party's cultural spokesmen precipitated a riot in Prague. In Russia itself, it appears that Western swing (not "hot" jazz), which is now totally banned, would have a considerable audience. Rumanian urban and upper-class audiences now hear very little of the French music for which they had, during the 1930's, developed a considerable liking —particularly songs of the Charles Trenet and Maurice Chevalier type. In the satellite countries generally, the well-liked, easygoing music in the coffee house and cabaret style of the 1930's is no longer heard. With only a few exceptions, too, religious music is not heard on radios in the Communist world; yet it is improbable that all Communist-controlled peoples have exchanged completely the orthodoxy of the Roman, Greek, or Russian Church for the orthodoxy of Communism.

Furthermore, there is a distinct monotony to the music issuing from the Communist radio. Much of it is pure propaganda, only thinly disguised in music. The "swing" music imitates the Western type, but it would not be considered of even mediocre quality in this country. Folk music is broadcast in great quantity, accompanied by the usual themes of proletarianism. Since the 1948 decree, the "non-art" music of Communist-ruled peoples has tended to become stereotyped, in harmony, melody, and rhythm. After years of this sort of music diet the audiences, especially in the satellites, might welcome a change.

(3) There are other vulnerabilities less directly related to current Communist policy and more directly stemming from the nature of music itself. At first appearance the propaganda value in music alone may seem slight, but in the various target countries considered in this research music is important in the cultural life of the people as a common form of group participation. Because of its unique tonal, rhythmic, and harmonic combinations, music constitutes a means of ready access to people's minds. For this reason, when propaganda content is injected, music still has the advantage of seeming less weighted with the political overtones which so often stigmatize speech as "mere propaganda." Thus, although music is less effective than speech in communicating specific ideas (unless used in conjunction with verbal matter), it frequently becomes *more* effective than speech as a means of suggestion or connotation. This is especially true where direct expression is likely to be inaccurate, suspect, repetitious, or too naive or sophisticated to engender respect. Certainly the Communist Party itself recognizes such possibilities in music, as is evidenced by the attention it has devoted to manipulating the musical idiom and to influencing the output of composers.

With skillful presentation of music compositions in psychological warfare operations, it should not be difficult to establish in the minds of the listeners an association between the American sources and the pleasurable, inspirational, or nostalgic feelings that are a part of the musical experience provided by the American radio.

EXPLOITATION OF VULNERABILITIES THROUGH MUSIC

Some examples of the uses to which music can lend itself for psychological warfare to the Communist countries considered in this research are as follows:

(1) *To express United Nations and United States values.* A great deal of music can be used, with a minimum of verbal explanation, to reveal our more admired national characteristics, our cultural diversity, our freedom, and our knowledge of and respect for the characteristics of target populations and United Nations peoples. Folk music such as our Western melodies may be of great value for this type of presentation, because it may serve to generate interest and curiosity in our broadcasts and, through them, in other aspects of democratic life as well; folk music from other United Nations countries will serve the same purpose. Since the music of nonbelligerent nations (especially South America) has a minimum of political overtones, it can be used in the more subtle type of propaganda designed to suggest the values in nonpartisanship, apathy toward war, and preoccupation with private or domestic concerns.

(2) *To popularize the expression of antagonism toward the regime or of favorable attitudes toward the United States.* In song, music acts as a medium for verbal communication. Although the words of songs may express subversive thoughts, songs may nevertheless achieve wide circulation due to their melodic appeal. This has often been the case with revolutionary songs. It may be profitable to broadcast versions of songs widely known in the target countries, therefore, in which the familiar words have been subtly twisted or replaced with ridiculous or pro-Western verse. In this way, the familiar songs of target peoples may be rendered useless for Communist purposes, and may also provide a way of venting antagonism toward the regime that is less risky than conversation or publication. Just as the German song "Lili Marlene" was adapted by the Allies in World War II, a catchy American tune may be adopted by the target people and serve to attract attention to our broadcasts. In using native songs, operators should be cautioned that Communists frequently change the words

of familiar songs to include pro-Communist matter. An attempt to ascertain whether this has occurred should be made before using such songs.

(3) *To increase nationalistic sentiments.* One of the techniques Russia uses to control satellite countries is the neutralization of any nationalistic sentiments which may obstruct the ultimate "Russification" of the satellite's culture. The broadcasting of music that is peculiar to the target satellite—especially banned anthems and other music having nationalistic connotations—can aid in impeding "Russification" by keeping nationalistic sentiments alive: it can also reveal United States sympathy with the principle of national self-determination for target peoples.

(4) *To illustrate propaganda themes.* The plots of some music compositions, especially operas, and the experiences of some composers may provide vivid illustrations for propaganda themes. For example, a dramatization of Shostakovich's life, with appropriate musical illustrations, to show the inconsistency of his treatment by the Party, may focus public attention on the composer and may make target audiences more aware of certain oppressive aspects of Communist rule. Similarly, propaganda use can be made of the tragic opera "Boris Godunov," by the 19th century Russian composer Moussorgsky. This story of a usurper who betrayed the people and became czar provides an opportunity for drawing parallels with the present Communist leadership.

(5) *To promote themes of internationalism.* There exists a substantial repertory of selections based upon musical themes or legends from countries other than the native country of the composer, which may be used as a medium for propaganda seeking to emphasize the community of interest between the peoples of target countries and the free world. Compositions of this type by target nationals which have been banned because of their "cosmopolitanism" or because they were written in a Western country may be especially useful. They can serve to promote an understanding that the ideas of brotherhood and internationalism originally espoused by the Communist movement have since been betrayed by the regime for the sake of its own entrenchment in power. This may be a particularly potent theme in view of the fact that current Communist music policy prohibits the use of Western ideas by native composers. The late Sergei Prokofiev's "Overture on Hebrew Themes" is an example of banned music valuable for the purpose of pointing up this betrayal of ideals. The banning of such a work illustrates the consequences in Communist-controlled countries of attempting to utilize freely the cultural heritage of all lands.

(6) *To heighten the audience appeal of fables or legends which have political overtones.* Because of their allegorical content and the simplicity of their form, fables and legends may assume effective political overtones when used in a propaganda context. They are particularly suited, too, for audiences with many diverse interests and capabilities, and should stimulate the interest of larger audiences than can be reached through the broadcasting of absolute, or nonrepresentational, music. Some fables and legends have already been adapted to music. Two examples are Prokofiev's "Peter and the Wolf" and "A Walk in the Forest" by the American composer, Herbert Haufrecht. The audience appeal of other fables and legends which have not been adapted to music may be greatly increased if musical illustrations are used in conjunction with their narration. Fables and legends lending themselves to musical illustration can undoubtedly be found in the folklore of target peoples.

(7) *To attract attention, to induce certain moods, and to impute connotations to verbal matter.* Some musical compositions, phrases, and instruments have highly distinctive and easily identifiable rhythmic, tonal, or "mood" qualities which lend themselves readily to symbolic interpretation. Others may have been associated with historical events and former ways of living. These compositions, phrases, or instruments may be used to identify particular persons, broadcasts, transmitters, or situations, or may be interpolated in verbal programs to connote such things as humor, ridicule, disgust, sarcasm, strength, defiance, impending doom, sadness, and nostalgia. Thus the opening three short and one long notes of Beethoven's Fifth Symphony were commonly used as a victory symbol in World War II. At the present time, Radio Free Europe is featuring in its Hungarian broadcasts an old and rare

Hungarian instrument called the tarogato, which has been banned by the Communist government because of its nationalistic associations.

The selection of music compositions which will exploit the possibilities listed above is not an easy task. Guidance could be offered more confidently if opportunity were provided for conducting tests upon and interviewing escaped target nationals in order to ascertain actual music preferences in the target countries, especially for music which has not recently been heard by their populations, jazz in particular.

As a general principle, indigenous contemporary music having pro-Communist connotations and other music broadcast frequently by the Communist radio should not be used in United States broadcasts. The repetition in United States broadcasts of music with Communist connotations might reinforce these connotations, and the repetition of music frequently heard over the Communist radio would not be likely to stimulate audience interest in United States broadcasts. The latter is especially true in those Communist countries where individuals are punished for listening to United States broadcasts.

Modern Western music of the dissonant or radical type—among both jazz and art music repertories—is liable to evoke a confused or adverse response. Unless current intelligence indicates a preference for such music on the part of the target audience, therefore, this type of music also should not be used in United States psychological warfare.

In selecting music that is attractive to the target audience, the operator should be guided primarily by current intelligence on the music preferences in the target countries. In many cases, the Communist Party, for purposes of expediency, has adopted the music most popular with the populations it controls and has stamped it with pro-Communist connotations. Of this music, only those compositions having a definite value for United States psychological warfare broadcasts should be used, and special care should be taken to dissociate these compositions from Communist values. In some instances, the Communist-sponsored music diet has failed fully to satisfy the music preferences of the people. Advantage should be taken of all such situations, and use made of those compositions which the target audiences like but cannot hear over their own officially controlled media of communication.

One final warning is in order. Failure to employ a high degree of skill in using music for psychological warfare purposes may produce an effect that is not merely negative, but severely detrimental to psychological warfare objectives—detrimental because what the Party has told the target audience about Western music and music appreciation may be confirmed, and because the adverse responses induced by an unintelligent use of music may be transferred to non-musical programs. It is highly desirable, therefore, for the psychological warfare operator conducting music broadcasts to have the benefit of some knowledge, either his own or that of advisers, of the music history of the target area. Most important, however, is that the operator supplement the findings and suggestions of this report with current intelligence on the music diet and preferences of the *particular* audience he is attempting to reach.

Musicians who have escaped from Communist countries can be valuable sources of information for psychological warfare units and can provide an effective reservoir of talent for broadcasts using music. A discussion of their potential usefulness is presented in this separate appendix because of its special importance for psychological warfare operations.

Recently escaped musicians have an intimate and fresh knowledge about many aspects of music in target countries, especially the style and types of music which are currently popular and recent changes in the officially controlled music diet of the people. This kind of information was largely inaccessible to research, and hence is dealt with only briefly in the foregoing report. Musicians coming through the Iron Curtain would be the best possible sources of information for checking and supplementing the findings presented in this report. In addition, they would have information which could suggest new psychological warfare themes involving the use of music. Psychological warfare operators without current information of the kind known to such musicians run the risk of broadcasting music which is no longer popular with the audiences they are attempting to reach or music which has recently been sponsored by the Communist Party or in other ways converted to Communist use.

Escaped music performers can be used in several ways to improve the effectiveness of music broadcasts. They can supply operators with compositions valuable for psychological warfare which are not available on records, or, if available, are of inferior broadcast quality. Many compositions of value for psychological warfare (especially folk music and music by native composers of the target country) have never been put on discs. Such hindrances as these could be overcome by having escaped performers tape-record or live-broadcast some of these compositions. Live broadcasts are considerably better than canned programs, being more dramatic and having more of an aura of immediacy and reality than the usual recorded presentation.

Singers can be used to translate the words and change the style of certain American songs in a way that would be understandable and attractive to target audiences. During World War II, the Office of Strategic Services commissioned Marlene Dietrich to record certain American songs in the German style and language in order to attract listeners to U.S. propaganda broadcasts to Germany. This technique may greatly increase the effectiveness of native American songs. In addition, such singers would be able to substitute pro-U.S. verse for the words of Communists songs, or subtly to twist the words of Communist songs to make them appear ridiculous or anti-regime.

Performances by escaped musicians—especially singers—would help to attract listeners to U.S. broadcasts. Such musicians know the style and type of music preferred by their fellow citizens and can "speak" to them in their own language. Many recordings of native music which are commercially available in the United States are performed by Americans who have little knowledge of, or feeling for, the style familiar to target audiences. Others, performed by native artists but recorded in the United States, have been Americanized in some way—as in style, words, or instrumentation. Both types are less useful for psychological warfare purposes than performances by artists who have the immediate feel of their native land. Broadcast performances by escaped performers could be supplemented with their comments about the compositions (adding a personal quality to the broadcast) and also, perhaps, accounts of their escape from behind the Iron Curtain.

The fact that creative artists flee Communist countries is in itself a potent propaganda weapon. Many musicians have emigrated from these countries because of the difficulty of carrying on their professional activities under surveillance by the Communist Party. However, one of the chief hindrances to the emigration of target musicians is their fear of being unable to attain some degree of recognition and to have an opportunity for exercising their skills. To induce defection, therefore, it might be appropriate to offer them an opportunity to perform over the radio and to make a few tape recordings. These recordings could, in turn, be a valuable contribution to the U.S. psychological warfare effort. For the more important musicians of the target countries, it may be fruitful to suggest the professional rewards and satisfactions they would receive should they come to the United States, without exaggerating the hospitality that would be extended to them by music circles in this country.

Although escaped musicians have occasionally in the past been used in various U.S. wartime broadcasting operations, no systematic effort to contact such people and utilize their talents appears to have been made. Undertaking an effort of this kind would add to the usefulness of the research reported in the foregoing text. It would provide a continuing and useful flow of intelligence for operators in the field. It might vastly improve the effectiveness of psychological warfare programs using music. For these reasons, the potential usefulness of such persons has been briefly outlined here to provide a basis for further exploration by psychological warfare planning and operations personnel. A partial list of musicians known to have emigrated recently from Communist countries, and a sample radio script illustrating the use of escaped musicians in broadcasts are given below as an aid to future planning.

PARTIAL LIST OF ESCAPED MUSICIANS

Andre, Lydia — Estonian singer (last heard of in Hamburg, Germany, where she recorded Estonian folk songs for the International Refugee Organization)

Andrejew, Galina — Russian singer (last heard of in Munich, Germany, working as waitress in a cafe)

Black Sea Cossacks — Russian choir (last heard of in Nurnberg, Germany)

Christova, Liliana — Bulgarian pianist (last known address: 220 Katernberger-strasse, Wuppertal-Elberfeld, Germany)

Darzins, G. — Latvian organist and music teacher (last known address: Spokane Conservatory, Spokane, Washington, where he was teaching music)

Ese-Seps, Ludmila — Latvian singer (last heard of in Hamburg, Germany, where she recorded Latvian songs for the United Nations Relief and Rehabilitation Administration)

Estonian Men's Choir — (last heard at Geislingen IRO camp near Stuttgart, Germany)

Joachim (sthal), Walter — German cellist (last heard of in Hamburg, Germany, working as entertainer at the Cafe Faum Betrieb)

Kalnins, A. — Latvian composer (recently emigrated to Canada)

Karolyi, Julian — Hungarian pianist (last known address: Hollywood, Calif.)

Lesta-Miller, Lydia — Estonian pianist (last heard of in Hamburg, Germany, where she recorded Estonian keyboard music for UNRRA)

Medins, J. — Latvian composer (last heard of in Sweden)

Nahruns, Ingus — Latvian cellist (recently emigrated to New York City)

Nemerov, Boris — Russian singer (last heard of in Munich, Germany, working in a night club)

Russian Men's Choir — (last heard of in a Displaced Persons camp near Stuttgart, Germany)

Toi, Roman — Estonian composer and choral director (last heard of in Toronto, Canada, where he was directing an Estonian men's choir)

Tubin, Eduard — Estonian composer (last heard of in Hamburg, Germany)

Zsigmondy, Denes — Hungarian violinist (last known address: 13b Ammerland, Stronbergersee, Bavaria, Germany)

SAMPLE RADIO SCRIPT

(NOTE: The radio script reproduced below was prepared by the
Mutual Network for broadcast on Good Friday, 1951. The broadcast
was designed for consumption by U.S. audiences, and illustrates
the kind of recognition which has been given to escaped music
performers. However, the script should be read with a consideration
of the propaganda possibilities in beaming similar programs to
Communist audiences.)

MUSIC: *Theme. Establish, then under*

PRYOR: In cooperation with the United Nation's International Refugee Organization,
the Mutual Network brings you a special half hour program of music for
Good Friday, as sung by refugees in the IRO's Displaced Persons camps in
Western Germany. We begin with an old Russian version of the Lord's
Prayer, sung by a Russian men's choir, and recorded by Rein Narma and
Ralph Scott in a refugee camp near Munich. This is Don Pryor at IRO
headquarters in Geneva, Switzerland.

MUSIC: *Theme up to close*

PRYOR: Like all DPs under the care of the International Refugee Organization, these
Russian singers are still waiting for a chance to emigrate to some new, free
country. Meanwhile, they sing and pray for a new life. Now, a choir of Black
Sea Cossacks in Nurnberg, Germany, sings a musical prayer in the ancient
Slaviansky language of the Orthodox church. Slaviansky is to the Russian
language approximately what Latin is to our Western languages, and is said
to have originated around the time of Ghengis Khan.

MUSIC: *Cossack Liturgical*

PRYOR: The feeling of desolation and despair is expressed by Roman Toi, a former
Estonian refugee, in this original composition, sung for the first time by an
Estonian Men's Choir of Geislingen, near Stuttgart. The composer has since
been transported by IRO to Canada, where he is now making a new life.
His song—"My Life is a Deserted Heath."

MUSIC: *"My Life is a Deserted Heath"*

PRYOR: Next, a Polish Men's Choir of refugees in DP camp at Wildflecken—a
former SS training center—singing "Kyrie Eleison" in Latin.

MUSIC: *Kyrie Eleison*

PRYOR: In the next number, you may notice that the melody is strangely similar to
the Pilgrim's song, from "Tannhaüser." Actually, it's another version of "The
Lord's Prayer," sung by a mixed choir of Latvian refugees, during a church
service in Nurnberg, Germany.

MUSIC: *Latvian Lord's Prayer*

PRYOR: Now, an old Cossack folk song of the season, sung by the Black Sea Cossacks
in a DP camp near Nurnberg.

MUSIC: *Cossack folk song*

PRYOR: Next, another seasonal folk song, this time from Estonia—sung by an Estonian choir of 27 voices in one of the IRO's Displaced Persons camps at Geislingen, Germany.

MUSIC: *Estonian Nocturne*

PRYOR: Let's return now to the Black Sea Cossacks at Nurnberg, singing another liturgical number from the Orthodox service.

MUSIC: *Cossack Liturgical*

            Pause 3 seconds, then up theme for 12 seconds and under

PRYOR: Now, with our Russian Men's Choir singing "The Lord's Prayer" we bring to an end this special Good Friday program of music by the Displaced, recorded in DP camps operated by the International Refugee Organization, and transcribed at the Organization's headquarters in Geneva, Switzerland.

REGRADED UNCLASSIFIED ORDER
SEC ARMY BY TAG PER
750244

Has Absolute Music No Class Character?

By Chao Hua of the Arts Department of the Central
Institute for Nationalities

[*Peking Review*, No. 9, 1 March 1974]

With the deepening of the movement to criticize Lin Piao and rectify the style of work and new victories being continually won in the struggle-criticism-transformation in the realm of the superstructure, an excellent situation prevails in the country. But the class struggle and the two-line struggle on the art and literary front remain very sharp and complex. The recent weird contention that so-called absolute music has no social content but simply expresses contrasting and changing moods is a sign of a return to the revisionist line in art and literature.

Should the reactionary nature of this erroneous view be exposed or not? This is a cardinal issue of right and wrong and we cannot treat it casually. It involves the question of whether or not the Marxist-Leninist theory of class struggle should be recognized as a universally applicable truth, whether or not the proletarian dictatorship should be exercised in the ideological realm, and whether the Marxist critical attitude should be adopted towards the bourgeois arts or whether they should be "taken over wholesale" as the revisionist fallacies of Chou Yang and his like advocated; it involves the question of whether the proletarian revolution in art and literature can be carried through to the end.

Absolute music in general refers to instrumental music without a descriptive title as to theme or content and it usually is designated by its musical form or tempo. For example, "Symphony in F Major," "Concerto in C Minor," "Largo," "Allegro" and so on.

Bourgeois theorists have long spouted that absolute music is a form of "pure music," devoid of social content and class nature. They fallaciously contend that music is "simply fantasy, not reality" and that "music is music, and nothing else." The modern revisionists, while paying lip-service to music's ties with social life, actually blur the class distinction between proletarian and bourgeois music by describing absolute music as "of the people," "realistic" and so forth. Why should both the bourgeoisie and the revisionists concoct all sorts of arguments to obscure the class character of art? It is because bourgeois ideology, including bourgeois art and literature, serves to prop up the capitalist system. They dare not openly acknowledge the exploiting class character of their art and literature. Instead, to disguise the essential substance of capitalist exploitation, they pose as representatives of the whole people in order to deceive the labouring masses.

Marxist-Leninists hold that all works of music, both absolute and programme music, as a form of ideology "are products of the reflection in the human brain of the life of a given society." Music without titles descriptive of their theme or content is by no means merely "a form of the flow of sounds." Not giving their works a descriptive title is only a means by which composers cover up the class content of their works. In fact, a composer clearly has in mind what he wants to praise or oppose and what content and mood he means to convey, when he is composing absolute music.

When the German bourgeois composer Beethoven (1770–1827) was asked the meaning of his *Sonata No. 17*, a composition without a descriptive title, he replied: "Please read Shakespeare's *The Tempest*." That play, we know, preaches the bourgeois theory of human nature. Of course, the means of expression of music are different from those of literature. Music uses melody, rhythm and harmony to evoke scenes, tell a story or convey emotion, thereby expressing quite plainly or relatively subtly and deviously the composer's world outlook, ideas and feelings. But in any case, the social and class content, thoughts and feelings so expressed can never be abstract, unintelligible "fantasy," for they can be grasped by applying the Marxist theory of knowledge and method of class analysis.

Take for instance the representative work *Symphony in B Minor* (the *Unfinished Symphony*) by Schubert (1797–1828), an Austrian bourgeois composer of the romantic school. The class feelings and social content it expresses are quite clear, although it has no descriptive title. This symphony was composed in 1822 when Austria was a reactionary feudal bastion within the German Confederation and the reactionary Austrian authorities not only ruthlessly exploited and oppressed the workers and peasants, but also persecuted and put under surveillance intellectuals with any bourgeois democratic ideas. Petty-bourgeois intellectuals like Schubert saw no way out of the political and economic impasse, and lacking the courage to resist they gave way to melancholy, vacillation, pessimism and despair, evading reality and dreaming of freedom. This work of Schubert's expressed these class feelings and social content. The opening phrase is sombre and gloomy. The whole symphony continues and expands on this emotion, filling it with petty-bourgeois despair, pessimism and solitary distress. At times the dreaming of freedom does come through but this, too, is escapist and negative.

Absolute music composed in Europe in the 18th and 19th centuries are products of the European capitalist society, upholding the interests of the bourgeoisie and serving the capitalist system. The content and the ideas and feelings with which they are saturated have an unmistakably bourgeois class nature. Marx pointed out: "Capital comes [into the world] dripping from head to foot, from every pore, with blood and dirt." And it is this blood and dirt that bourgeois music extols. Although certain compositions were to some extent progressive in the sense of being anti-feudal, they failed to mirror proletarian thoughts and feelings of their time; and they are, of course, still more incompatible with our socialist system today under the dictatorship of the proletariat. Then why dismiss their class content and extol them? Yet even today there are some who would feed our young people on these musical works uncritically and intact. Where would this lead our young people?

Some devotees of bourgeois absolute music often try to cover up its class nature by holding forth in empty terms on the contrasting, changing moods it presents. This is a reactionary viewpoint of the bourgeois theory of a common human nature transcending classes. For these moods are none other than those of delight and anger, joy and sorrow which vary, as do all men's ideas and feelings, according to the times and society people live in and the class they belong to. Lu Hsun mercilessly repudiated this bourgeois trash that all men share common emotions and feelings. He said: "Of course, it is human nature to know delight and anger, joy and sorrow but the poor are never worried about losing money on the stock exchange, an oil magnate cannot know the trials of an old woman collecting cinders in Peking, and victims of famine will hardly grow orchids like rich old gentlemen. . . ." Are there any feelings that are not stamped with the brand of a class?

"Joy" can be presented in sharply contrasted ways. Thus the music for the despotic landlord's birthday celebrations in the third scene of the modern revolutionary dance-drama *Red Detachment of Women* uses frivolous melody and erratic rhythm to expose the landlord's wanton extravagance and profligacy built on the suffering of the working people. In contrast, the magnificent stirring music of the dance by soldiers and civilians in the next scene presents the brilliant sunshine and jubilation in the revolutionary base. Did these two musical passages project the same emotions?

Again, take the subject of "sorrow." The grief of a feudal monarch after his overthrow is expressed in the verses written by Li Yu, the last king of the Southern Tang kingdom in the 10th century, as he hankered in captivity after his former decadent life in the palace.

> Carved balustrades, jade flagstones still remain,
> But those rosy cheeks are gone.
> How great my lord's grief?
> Endless as the spring river flowing to the east!

But the proletarian fighter Lu Hsun portrayed sorrow of a very different kind when he wrote:

A host of dark, gaunt faces in the brambles,
Yet who dare shake the earth with lamentation?
I brood over our whole far-stretching land
And in this silence hear the peal of thunder.

This indignant denunciation of the savage oppression of the people by the Japanese invaders and Kuomintang reactionaries conveys the class hatred and national enmity of millions of working people. This militant lamentation has nothing at all in common with the grief of a feudal monarch over the loss of his kingdom. To claim that one melody could be used to express these two diametrically opposed feelings would be sheer charlatanry.

As for empty talk about "bright," "healthy" melodies, devoid of class content, this is the metaphysical approach which the revisionists usually resort to when peddling their bourgeois wares. Chou Yang once brayed that the American bourgeoisie whom Walt Whitman extolled was "the new man," "healthy, broad of mind, with high ideals, a pair of working hands, and eternally optimistic" and that that "shiny example" was "worthy of emulating and copying." But we are aware if the proletariat really were to "emulate" and "copy" the bourgeoisie, then what awaits us is not "bright skies" but the darkness of the dungeon.

The bourgeoisie may well believe that the works of the 18th-century Austrian bourgeois composer Mozart embody "bright" and "healthy" sentiments. But we working people know clearly that these sentiments cannot compare with the exuberant and impassioned feelings expressed by the chorus *The Sun Rises* in the seventh scene of *The White-Haired Girl*. Brimming over with jubilation, this chorus extols Chairman Mao, the red sun in the hearts of the Chinese people, as well as the Communist Party, and evokes the soul-stirring scene "of the land of hibiscus glowing in the morning sun" and the emancipation of the downtrodden peasants. No bourgeois music can even remotely compare with this unrestrained healthy burst of joy evoked by this chorus.

Chou Yang and company also raved that "music is a universal language," in order to concoct a theoretical basis for their attempt to peddle the wholesale Westernization of music. In fact, every class speaks its own language and there is no such thing as a so-called universal language transcending classes. *The Internationale* which rings throughout the world is the common language of the proletariat only. The bourgeoisie trembles at the sound of this melody. Lenin aptly said: "In whatever country a class-conscious worker finds himself, wherever fate may cast him, however much he may feel himself a stranger, without language, without friends, far from his native country —he can find himself comrades and friends by the familiar refrain of the *Internationale*."

For over eighty years this stirring song has inspired workers of all countries to unite to smash the old world and fight for the realization of communism. All reactionaries, however, regard this battle-song of the proletariat as a fearful menace and do all in their power to prevent *The Internationale* from circulating among the people. Hence, do the reactionaries share a common language with the proletariat?

Liu Shao-chi, Lin Piao, Chou Yang and their gang, however, shared a common language with the bourgeoisie and all reactionaries at home and abroad, for these renegades, like all imperialists, revisionists and reactionaries, opposed proletarian revolution and proletarian dictatorship and vainly tried to restore capitalism in China. This was like the futile efforts of Confucius, the mouthpiece and defender of ancient China's slave-owning class, who, grieving that "the rites were lost and music was ruined," tried desperately to propagate reactionary music aimed at benumbing and enslaving the people while frantically attacking the new rising folk music in order to preserve the collapsing slave system.

Like the other forms of art, music has always been an instrument of class struggle, and on the art and literary front the class struggle and the two-line struggle have always been extremely acute. In the course of the Great Proletarian Cultural Revolution and the movement to criticize Lin Piao and rectify the style of work, great victories have been won on this front and intellectuals have made much progress, but the pernicious influence of revisionist wares peddled by Liu Shao-chi, Lin Piao, Chou Yang and company for a long time, such as "art and literature of the whole people" and "art and literature to nourish people," is deep-seated and still far from being eliminated. Some people talk about bourgeois classical music with great relish, are mesmerized by it and prostrate themselves before it, showing their slavish mentality for all things foreign. They are nihilists with regard to national art. Their reverence for foreign things is actually reverence for the bourgeoisie. If this erroneous thinking of extolling foreign things and belittling Chinese things is not criticized and repudiated, then proletarian art and literature will not be able to develop and Chairman Mao's revolutionary line in art and literature cannot be implemented.

We do not exclude foreign things indiscriminately. We should conscientiously study the revolutionary theory developed by Marx, Engels, Lenin and Stalin. We should learn from the revolutionary experience of the working class and revolutionary people of all countries and learn from and acquire advanced sciences and technology. We should critically assimilate certain techniques from classical bourgeois music, but we must not uncritically swallow anything and everything. And we must never throw ourselves at the feet of bourgeois artists. As Engels said: "The characterization of the ancients no longer suffices today." We must adhere to the principle of "making the past serve the present and foreign things serve China," learn from the experience in creating the model revolutionary theatrical works and turn out proletarian music and art worthy of our time.

Comrade Chou En-lai pointed out in the political report of the Tenth National Congress of the Communist Party of China that "we should attach importance to the class struggle in the superstructure, including all spheres of culture" and that "we should continue to carry out well the revolution in literature and art." The historical experience of the class struggle on the art and literary front shows that the ideology of the bourgeoisie and all other exploiting classes cannot be buried and done away with by a criticism or two. We must conscientiously study the documents of the Tenth Party Congress, implement the spirit of the Tenth Party Congress, take the Party's basic line as the key link, further deepen the movement to criticize Lin Piao and rectify the style of work and link them to reality in criticizing revisionism and bourgeois world outlook; we must continue to advance along the revolutionary path pointed out by Chairman Mao, and we must never go backwards. We must be on guard and resist a return of the revisionist line in art and literature. We must resolutely defend and develop the fruits of the Great Proletarian Cultural Revolution and carry the proletarian revolution in art and literature through to the end!

(Translation of an article published in "Renmin Ribao," January 14, 1974)

Criticize the Revisionist Viewpoint in Music

By Chu Lan

[*Peking Review*, No. 9, 1 March 1974]

Following is the translation of a commentary entitled "Grasp the Essence, Deepen the Criticism" by Chu Lan which appeared in "Renmin Ribao" recently.—Ed.

The mass struggle to criticize Lin Piao and Confucius is now developing in depth. The discussion on programme and absolute music and the criticism of the revisionist viewpoint which professes that bourgeois classical music has "no profound social content" are also being carried out in a more and more deep-going way. This is a sharp struggle in the field of art and literature between the proletariat and the bourgeoisie and between Marxism and revisionism. The practice of struggle proves that it is most necessary to criticize this erroneous view. We must make this criticism a part of the struggle to criticize Lin Piao and Confucius and carry it through to the end!

In order to carry out criticism more profoundly, we must take class struggle and the two-line struggle as the key link and see through superficial appearances to grasp the essence of the revisionist viewpoint. Only in this way can we completely demolish the revisionist viewpoint and make it abhorrent.

Marxism teaches us that in examining a problem we should look at its essence. The essence of our problem is not whether musical works have titles or not. The main thing is the political content of the class they express and the political line of the class they serve. All bourgeois music, programme and absolute, are weapons to shape opinion to serve the bourgeoisie for seizing and consolidating political power. Numerous facts in the history of music show that absolute music, or music without titles, is merely a means by which bourgeois composers conceal the class content of their works. For certain political aims and to meet the needs of struggle, composers sometimes give descriptive titles to their works and sometimes not. But even if given a descriptive title, this can be disregarded and the work played in a manner far from what the title implies.

Are not impressionist and modernist musical work, often designated with such titles as "pines," "fountains" and "moonlight"? Br. analysis of them from a class viewpoint can clearly reveal the decadent, chaotic life and depraved sentiments of the bourgeoisie the weird cacophony represents. The music of the modern revisionists in particular, frequently under the guise of "revolutionary" titles, slanders and distorts in an unbridled way the revolutionary struggles of the people and heroic images of the working people, and vilely attacks the dictatorship of the proletariat and the socialist system. It can thus be seen that whether a musical work has a descriptive title or not does not in the least change the political content and class essence it expresses, nor the objective social function it performs. Hence, the basic problem lies in the stand, viewpoint and method we adopt towards bourgeois works of music, including programme and absolute music. The crux of the contention is whether one takes the stand of the proletariat, upholds the Marxist class viewpoint and method of class analysis and, taking into account the historical development of class struggle of a specific period, critically analyses the class content of bourgeois music, or whether one takes the stand of the bourgeoisie and replaces concrete class analysis with empty talk about abstract concepts such as "contrasting and changing moods," "healthy" and "bright," which actually is publicizing the bourgeois "theory of human nature" and covering up the class essence of musical works to hoodwink and beguile the broad masses.

We must never abandon class analysis and engage in empty talk as to whether a piece of music has or has not any "profound social content." In class society, all works of art have their concrete social content of a specific class. There is absolutely no such thing as social content that is abstract or above classes and neither is there such a thing as abstract "profundity." The real aim in publicizing bourgeois musical works as having "no profound social content" is to cover up the class content reflected in the music of the bourgeoisie. This can lead only to the revolutionary people lowering their vigilance against corruption by bourgeois ideology and facilitate bourgeois cultural penetration and provide a cover for the bourgeoisie to seize positions from the proletariat in the field of art and literature.

The appearance of the revisionist viewpoint denying the class character of musical works is no isolated, individual, accidental phenomenon. It is the concentrated expression of a tendency in society and in music circles today to make a fetish of foreign things and restore the old order of things. This tendency is reflected in the question of whether or not there is any social content in bourgeois music, both absolute and programme; it is also reflected in composing music, performing music and teaching music. And not only in music, but also in other fields of art. They differ in form only.

A reflection in music of the theory of "the dying out of class struggle" is the publicizing of the bourgeois theory of human nature, denying that music has a class character. We must thoroughly expose this and carry out serious criticisms against it.

The essence of the revisionist viewpoint in this question of absolute and programme music is the landlord-bourgeois theory of human nature. This theory of human nature which denies the class character of music is brought over from the European bourgeoisie and can also be traced back to the doctrine of Confucius, the ideological representative of the decadent slave-owning class of China. We must further criticize this revisionist viewpoint in the course of the struggle to criticize Lin Piao and Confucius.

Chairman Mao has pointed out: "The class struggle between the proletariat and the bourgeoise, the class struggle between the different political forces, and the class struggle in the ideological field between the proletariat and the bourgeoisie will continue to be long and tortuous and at times will even become very acute." We must fully understand the protractedness of the struggle in this field. In our struggle to criticize Lin Piao and Confucius, we must combine it with the actual class struggle in the realm of ideology, particularly in art and literature (including music), carry out sustained revolutionary criticism of all revisionist views and ideological trends which are unfavourable to the development of socialist art and literature and, in the course of tempestuous struggles, further consolidate and develop the socialist positions in the field of art and literature.

Index

364